DOS 5
THE BASICS

193

Ken W. Christopher, Jr.
Barry A. Feigenbaum
Shon O. Saliga

John Wiley & Sons, Inc.

Publisher: Therese A. Zak
Managing Editor: Nana D. Prior
Editing, Design, and Production: G&H Soho, Ltd.

This publication is designed to provide accurate and authoritative information in regard to the subject matter covered. It is sold with the understanding that the publisher is not engaged in rendering legal, accounting or other professional service. If legal advice or other expert assistance is required, the services of a competent professional person should be sought. FROM A DECLARATION OF PRINCIPLES JOINTLY ADOPTED BY A COMMITTEE OF THE AMERICAN BAR ASSOCIATION AND A COMMITTEE OF PUBLISHERS.

Library of Congress Cataloging-in-Publication Data
Christopher, Ken W.
    DOS 5, the basics / Ken W. Christopher, Barry A. Feigenbaum, Shon
O. Saliga.
      p. cm.
    Includes index.
    ISBN 0–471–54211–3
    1. PC DOS (Computer operating system)   I. Feigenbaum, Barry A.
II. Saliga, Shon O.   III. Title.
QA76.76.063C4885   1991
005.4'469 – dc20   91–13563

Printed in the United States of America
10 9 8 7 6 5 4 3 2 1

*To Milena, Martha, and Cindy
for putting up with us
throughout the writing
of this book.*

Trademarks

Foreword

Now in its fifth major revision, the Disk Operating System continues to be a major platform that IBM and others will offer as a base for customer solutions. The introduction of the latest DOS version, 5.0, clearly demonstrates our continued market driven support for this popular product. With its improvements in usability and function along with its reduced memory requirement, DOS 5.0 will set new standards for quality and user satisfaction.

DOS continues its strategic importance as the low end operating system for personal systems. It complements the other industry standard operating systems: Operating System/2™ and UNIX™. The improved DOS user shell conforms to the IBM Common User Access subset of Systems Application Architecture, allowing for easy transfer of knowledge from DOS to these other operating systems.

The authors of this book, by drawing on their extensive DOS development experience, have provided, in a single book, a clear and easy-to-use introduction to DOS versions 3.3, 4.0, and 5.0. They complement and extend the documentation included with DOS. I am sure you will find this book, with its extensive tutorials, plain explanations, and insightful tips, a valuable learning and reference guide.

James Cannavino
IBM Vice President and General Manager
Personal Systems Line of Business

Preface

This book is intended to help you learn how to use DOS and to master its many functions. Using short discussions, examples, and short tutorial lessons, we cover the features and functions provided by DOS. We approach DOS from both introductory and in-depth perspectives. Information is also provided about special DOS features not available in other publications. Here we cover the three currently available DOS versions: DOS 3.3, DOS 4.0, and DOS 5.0.

The topics covered in this book include, among many others:

- Basic DOS concepts, such as directories, files, and programs

- The DOS Shell — an easy-to-use interface to DOS and how to use it

- The DOS commands and utilities and how to use them

- How to performance tune DOS

- How to protect your data

DOS 5: The Basics is organized into several self-contained sections that allow you to read at your own pace and still take advantage of the features of DOS as you learn them. Each section builds on the previous one and thus provides a gradual, easy way of mastering each feature of DOS. Many features of DOS are discussed several times, because each discussion brings out new aspects of the feature. We do this to ensure that you are not overloaded with details when you are just becoming familiar with a concept. This approach allows you to digest DOS in stages. As you are ready for more information, it is available.

We have organized the book into 13 chapters, with each broken down into small sections or lessons. Following is a summary of the chapters.

Chapter 1   Introduces DOS. It briefly describes DOS and the differences between DOS 3.3, DOS 4.0, and DOS 5.0.

Chapter 2   Introduces basic DOS concepts. It describes fixed disks and diskettes. It introduces you to DOS files, directories, and applications. Finally, it introduces you to the DOS Shell and the use of the DOS Command Line.

This book does not necessarily reflect the views or opinions of the IBM Corporation. Although it was authored by IBM employees, IBM was not a party to its creation and is not responsible for its content.

Acknowledgments

We thank our managers, Bob Bulkley and Laura Weber, for their support and patience during the period in which we developed this book. We also thank the DOS Product Manager, DeeAnne Safford, and the Boca Programming Center Director, Tom Steele, for their support in this endeavor. For help in understanding the changes in DOS 5.0, we are grateful to the entire DOS development team and especially Doug Love and Bob Maddaloni.

Finally, we would like to express our appreciation for all the hard work and creative energy expended by developers in both Boca Raton and Redmond in producing three excellent revisions of the DOS product.

Contents

Introduction

This book is intended to help you learn how to use DOS. It is geared to beginning DOS users or those users who have been uncomfortable using DOS in the past. It is also intended to be used as both a learning aid and a reference guide for those users upgrading to a more recent version of DOS. As you use DOS more and more, your understanding of how it works will increase. Above all, we want you to have fun reading and using this book. After a while, you may want to have a reference guide that explains all about DOS and its commands and utilities in great detail. A separate book entitled *DOS 5 Command Reference* provides a quick "how to" reference summary of the ideas presented in this book. If you are interested in more technical information about DOS, we recommend the book *Developing Applications Using DOS*. These two books are also written by us and published by John Wiley & Sons, Inc.

It is assumed that you have access to a personal computer and a copy of DOS 3.3, DOS 4.0, or DOS 5.0. Many of the lessons provided in this book are best understood by actually following along on a computer. This book covers most of the features and functions provided by DOS versions 3.3, 4.0 (also 4.01), and the newest version, DOS 5.0, by using short discussions, examples, and lessons.

Some extremely detailed aspects of DOS are not covered in this book. We encourage you to use it first as an introduction. Then use the books included with your copy of DOS for more information. If you have used DOS in the past, you will find that the books that come with versions 4.0 and 5.0 are much improved and are easier to use.

Although specific computer references in this book are to the IBM Personal System/2™ family of computers, this book can help anyone using any IBM-compatible personal computer. Most computer manufacturers provide features similar to those available on the IBM Personal System/2 family of computers. If you want an introduction to computers in general, and the

IBM Personal System/2 family of computers in particular, we recommend you read *IBM Personal System/2™: A Business Perspective,* Second Edition, by Jim Hoskins, also published by John Wiley & Sons, Inc.

You do not have to read this book all at once. It has been divided into sections that you can use as the need arises. Near the beginning of this book are chapters that introduce the most commonly used features of DOS with lessons that help you learn how to use those features. At the end of this book are chapters that cover the more advanced topics of DOS. You can use DOS without ever reading these last chapters, but we recommend that you do read them. We describe many features there that will make using DOS both more convenient and less time-consuming.

There are several chapters designed to help you learn to use DOS with particular emphasis on the DOS Shell. As you will see, the DOS Shell offers a simple way to use the services provided by DOS.

WHAT'S IN A NAME?

The name DOS stands for Disk Operating System. With "Disk" as such an important part of DOS's name, you can appreciate that a large part of what DOS does is related to supporting disks. There are two kinds of disks: *diskettes* and *fixed disks.* The term *disk* can refer to either a diskette or fixed disk. In many ways diskettes and fixed disks can be treated as the same thing. We will talk more about diskettes and fixed disks later.

You might well ask what Operating System means. An operating system is a special program that "operates," or controls, your computer. It is a type of master program that helps both you and your application programs use the computer efficiently. The term *system* is used because DOS consists of many different parts that work together as a whole to get the job done.

DOS provides many different services. As you shall see, the vast majority of services relate to disks. Other services support your computer's keyboard, display, printer (or printers), mouse, and memory. Still other services are used only by your application programs. We discuss each of these services in detail later in this book.

Microsoft® calls its version of DOS *MS-DOS,* whereas IBM calls its version of DOS *IBM-DOS.* Other manufacturers typically use MS-DOS, but they may also change the name of DOS. To avoid confusion, we will use the generic name *DOS* throughout this book when we discuss common DOS features or functions. When we use *MS-DOS,* we mean that the feature or function is specific to the Microsoft version. If we use *IBM-DOS,* then we mean that the feature or function is specific to the IBM version.

A LITTLE HISTORY

Since the introduction of the first IBM Personal Computer in August 1981, personal computers have advanced in function and capacity at a very rapid pace. To keep up with these advances, the operating system also needed to be enhanced in both function and capacity. With the introduction of DOS 5.0 there have been five major revisions of DOS and numerous minor revisions. The 3.3, 4.0/4.01, and now the 5.0 versions of DOS are widely used today. The older versions are now considered out of date.

The major differences between these version of DOS can be grouped into the following areas:

1. **Hardware Support.** Each DOS version has added support for the the rapidly increasing memory and disk capacities of personal computers. Support for new classes of devices, such as mice, have also been added.

2. **Ease-of-use Improvements.** The DOS Shell, introduced in DOS 4.0, is the most significant improvement in DOS usability. Prior to the DOS Shell, the only method to use DOS was through a command line approach that required you to remember many minute details about how DOS works. The Shell's menu-driven approach provided an alternative method to use DOS that requires much less memorization and is thus much easier to use for most people. DOS 5.0 also provides a new and improved editor program to ease the creation of text files.

Also introduced in DOS 4.0, and improved in DOS 5.0, is a new, menu-driven, installation process that assists users in installing DOS. This is one of the most difficult tasks for new DOS users. The installation aids in the new version greatly simplify the process of installing or upgrading DOS.

New commands and utilities have been added to every new version of DOS, and existing commands and utilities have been improved, making these commands and utilities more functional and easier to use. For example, DOS 5.0 has added a command line help feature.

As new features are added to DOS, more of your computer's memory is used. For instance, the many enhancements of DOS 4.0 make it take up significantly more space than DOS 3.3 does. Many computer applications require as much computer memory as possible. A significant portion of the changes made to DOS 5.0 take advantage of the recent trend towards universal use of the Intel® 80286, 80386, or 80486 microprocessor instead of the less powerful 8086 microprocessor. These new processors allow DOS to increase the amount of memory available to your application programs so that they can have more memory for their own use.

DOS 5.0 also provides an enhanced BASIC interpreter, called *QBASIC*. QBASIC augments the BASICA interpreter provided by DOS 3.3 and DOS 4.0, adds more language features, and adds an online help and reference facility.

This book covers the three most recent versions of DOS. As we discuss the features and functions, it will be clear which versions apply. Thus, you will always know what features are or are not provided in *your* version of DOS. If we do not specify a specific version, the features and functions are available in all three. See Figures 1-1 through 1-4 for a summary of the changes made in each DOS version.

Function/Feature Command/Utility	DOS Version									
	1.0	1.1	2.0	2.1	3.0	3.1	3.2	3.3	4.0	5.0
3.5-Inch Diskettes							■	+	■	+
5.25-Inch Diskettes	■	++	■	■	++	■	■	■	■	■
<32MB Fixed Disks			■	■	■	■	■	■	■	■
>32MB Nonpartitioned Fixed Disks									■	■
>32MB Partitioned Fixed Disks								■	■	■
/? for command help										■
ANSI Device			■	■	■	■	■	■	++	■
APPEND Command									■	■
APPEND Utility								■	++	■
ASSIGN Utility			■	■	■	■	■	■	+	■
ATTRIB Utility			■	■	■	■	■	++	+	+
BACKUP Utility			■	■	■	■	■	++	+	■
BASIC Utility	■	■	■	■	■	■	■	■	+	■
BASICA Utility	■	■	■	■	■	+	+	+	+	■
Batch Files	■	■	■	■	■	■	■	■	■	■
BREAK Command		■	■	■	■	■	■	■	■	■
BREAK Statement			■	■	■	■	■	■	■	■
BUFFERS Statement			■	■	■	■	■	■	++	-
CALL Command								■	■	■
CHCP Command								■	■	■
CHDIR Command			■	■	■	■	■	■	■	■
CHKDSK Utility	■	■	++	■	■	■	■	■	++	■
CLS Command	■	■	■	■	■	■	■	■	■	■
COMMAND Utility	■	■	++	■	■	■	■	■	++	■
COMP Utility	■	■	■	■	■	■	■	■	+	+
COPY Command	■	■	++	■	■	■	■	■	+	■
COUNTRY Statement			■	■	■	■	■	++	■	■
CTTY Utility			■	■	■	■	■	■	■	■
DATE Command	■	■	■	■	■	■	■	+	+	■
DEBUG Utility	■	■	++	■	■	■	■	■	+	■
DEL Command	■	■	■	■	■	■	■	■	++	■

Figure 1-1

DOS Function versus Version Summary (part 1 of 4). Key to symbols:

Blank　　Not available in this release.

■　　　Available in this release.　　　++　　Significant improvement in this release.

+　　　Improved in this release.　　　-　　Reduced in this release.

Note: Version information is based on IBM's version of DOS. Some features may be slightly different for Microsoft's version of DOS.

Function/Feature Command/Utility	DOS Version									
	1.0	1.1	2.0	2.1	3.0	3.1	3.2	3.3	4.0	5.0
DEVICE Statement			∎	∎	∎	∎	∎	∎	∎	∎
DEVICEHIGH Statement										∎
DIR Command	∎	∎	∎	∎	∎	∎	∎	∎	+	++
DISKCOMP Utility	∎	∎	∎	∎	∎	∎	∎	∎	+	∎
DISKCOPY Utility	∎	∎	∎	∎	∎	∎	∎	∎	+	∎
DISPLAY Device								∎	∎	∎
DOS Statement										∎
DOSKEY Utility										∎
DOSSHELL Utility									∎	++
DRIVER Device							∎	∎	∎	∎
DRIVPARM Statement							∎	∎	∎	∎
ECHO Command			∎	∎	∎	∎	∎	∎	∎	∎
EDIT Utility										∎
EDLIN Utility	∎	∎	+	∎	∎	∎	∎	∎	∎	∎
ERASE Command	∎	∎	∎	∎	∎	∎	∎	∎	++	∎
EXE2BIN Utility	∎	∎	∎	∎	∎	∎	∎	∎	∎	∎
EXIT Command			∎	∎	∎	∎	∎	∎	∎	∎
Expanded Memory Support									∎	++
Extended Memory Support					∎	∎	∎	∎	+	++
FASTOPEN Utility								∎	++	-
FC Utility										∎
FCBS Statement						∎	∎	∎	∎	-
FDISK Utility			∎	∎	∎	∎	∎	++	++	∎
FILESYS Utility									∎	
FIND Utility			∎	∎	∎	∎	∎	∎	∎	+
FOR Command			∎	∎	∎	∎	∎	∎	∎	∎
GOTO Command			∎	∎	∎	∎	∎	∎	∎	∎
GRAFTABL Utility	∎	∎	∎	∎	∎	∎	∎	+	+	∎
GRAPHICS Utility			∎	∎	∎	∎	∎	∎	++	++
FORMAT Utility	∎	∎	+	∎	∎	∎	+	+	++	++
HELP Utility										∎
HIMEM Device										∎
IF Command			∎	∎	∎	∎	∎	∎	∎	∎
IFSFUNC Utility									∎	
INSTALL Statement									∎	∎
INT 21H Program Services	∎	+	++	+	++	++	+	++	++	+
International Support			∎	∎	∎	∎	∎	++	+	∎

Figure 1-2
DOS Function versus Version Summary (part 2 of 4).

Function/Feature Command/Utility	DOS Version									
	1.0	1.1	2.0	2.1	3.0	3.1	3.2	3.3	4.0	5.0
JOIN Utility					■	■	■	■	■	■
KEYB Utility			■	■	■	■	■	++	■	■
LABEL Utility			■	■	■	■	■	■	+	■
LASTDRIVE Statement						■	■	■	■	■
LOADHIGH Command										■
MEM Utility									■	■
Menu Driven Installation									■	++
MIRROR Utility										■
MKDIR Command			■	■	■	■	■	■	■	■
MODE Utility	■	+	+	+	+	+	+	++	++	■
MORE Utility			■	■	■	■	■	■	+	■
Networks						■	■	■	■	■
NLSFUNC Utility								■	■	■
PATH Command			■	■	■	■	■	■	■	■
PAUSE Command	■	■	■	■	■	■	■	■	■	■
PRINT Utility			■	■	■	+	■	■	■	■
PRINTER Device								■	■	■
PROMPT Command			■	■	■	■	■	■	■	■
QBASIC Utility										■
RAMDRIVE Device										■
RECOVER Utility	■	■	■	■	■	■	■	■	■	■
REM Command	■	■	■	■	■	■	■	■	■	■
REM Statement									■	■
RENAME Command	■	■	■	■	■	■	■	■	■	■
REPLACE Utility								■	■	■
RESTORE Utility			■	■	■	■	■	++	+	■
RMDIR Command			■	■	■	■	■	■	■	■
SET Command			■	■	■	■	■	■	■	■
SETVER Utility										■
SHARE Utility					■	■	■	■	+	■
SHELL Statement			■	■	■	■	■	■	■	■
SHIFT Command			■	■	■	■	■	■	■	■
SMARTDRV Device										■
SORT Utility			■	■	■	■	■	■	■	■
STACKS Statement								■	■	■
Standard I/O			■	■	■	■	■	■	■	■

Figure 1-3
DOS Function versus Version Summary (part 3 of 4).

Function/Feature Command/Utility	DOS Version									
	1.0	1.1	2.0	2.1	3.0	3.1	3.2	3.3	4.0	5.0
SUBST Utility						■	■	■	■	■
SWITCHES Statement									■	■
SYS Utility	■	■	+	■	■	■	■	■	+	■
TIME Command	■	■	■	■	■	■	■	+	+	■
Tree Structured Directories			■	■	■	■	■	■	■	■
TREE Utility			■	■	■	■	■	■	++	■
TRUENAME Command									■	■
TYPE Command	■	■	■	■	■	■	■	■	■	■
UNDELETE Utility										■
UNFORMAT Utility										■
VDISK Device			■	■	■	■	■	■	+	
VER Command	■	■	■	■	■	■	■	■	■	■
VERIFY Command	■	■	■	■	■	■	■	■	■	■
VOL Command			■	■	■	■	■	■	■	■
XCOPY Utility							■	■	■	■
XMA2EMS Device									■	■
XMAEM Device									■	

Figure 1-4
DOS Function versus Version Summary (part 4 of 4).

Basic DOS Concepts

This chapter introduces the concepts that you should know in order to use DOS and provides you with information to help you use your application programs. It is important that you become familiar with these concepts, as they provide the groundwork for the remaining topics covered in this book. Do not hesitate to review this chapter anytime you want to brush up on these concepts.

DOS provides many functions and features. Some are used only by your application programs and therefore, as a computer user, you do not need to understand them. Other DOS services do require your understanding. Use this analogy: You do not need to know how your car's engine works in order to drive the car, but you must understand the purpose of the gas pedal, brake, and steering wheel.

DOS is one of the most important programs you will use on your computer. It acts as a central controller for your computer and serves you in two major ways:

1. Your applications require help from DOS to perform their functions. Without DOS, they would not be able to work.

2. DOS provides many housekeeping functions necessary to keep your computer working effectively.

Learning about DOS does not have to be a hard task. Try making it a game. Experiment with DOS as you use your computer, and if you do not know how something works, read about it and then try it again. DOS will warn you before you do anything that might cause you to hurt your computer or lose information.

Do not expect to become a DOS expert overnight. Learning how to use any powerful tool takes time. In the meantime, you can still use DOS very effectively.

In this chapter we will discuss the following topics:

- Diskettes and Fixed Disks
- Data Files
- Directories
- Application Programs
- The DOS Shell
- DOS Commands and Utilities

Note: The discussions in this book assume that you are familiar with the basic parts and operation of a personal computer. The documentation that comes with your copy of DOS includes a brief introduction to personal computers, a description of the various parts that make up a PC, and a description of their uses or functions. If you are a new computer user you should take the time now to review this information. Many manufacturers also provide an introductory tutorial program to help familiarize you with your computer. You should work through the computer tutorial if one is provided.

DISKETTES AND FIXED DISKS

WHY YOU NEED DISKETTES AND FIXED DISKS

The major function of a computer is to take certain information (referred to as *data*) and change it into new information. A simple example is to take a list of numbers, compute their sum, and print that sum out. Of course, this could be done on an inexpensive pocket calculator; a computer is normally used to do much more complex changes. Since the data on a computer can be of great importance, you need a place to save it. On computers, you normally use diskettes or a fixed disk to do this.

Diskettes go into the *diskette drives* on your computer. You can change the diskette that is in the drive whenever you want, so the amount of information you can store on diskettes is unlimited. If you need to store more information, you just use another diskette.

This unlimited capacity of diskettes is one of their most appealing characteristics. Unfortunately, one of their most unappealing characteristics is that each diskette holds only a relatively small amount of data. For most newer personal computers diskettes can hold, depending on their type, 360,000 (360KB), 720,000 (720KB), 1,200,000 (1.2MB), 1,440,000 (1.44MB), and recently 2,880,000 (2.88MB) characters (called *bytes*) of information. If you consider that many modern application programs are over 2 million bytes long, you can see that it could take three or more diskettes to hold a single application. For example, DOS 5.0 takes three 720KB diskettes. This is one of the major reasons to have a fixed disk in your computer. Fixed disks start at 20 million bytes and go up to hundreds of millions of bytes.

Another reason you would want to use a fixed disk is for speed. Fixed disks are between ten and one hundred times faster than diskettes.

You may ask, "Why would anyone use diskettes when they can use a fixed disk?" There are several reasons why you might choose to use diskettes:

Cost   Fixed-disk drives are generally much more expensive than diskette drives (often ten times more). Diskette-only computers are generally much less expensive than fixed-disk computers.

Capacity   Although each fixed disk holds more than a single diskette does, you can have hundreds of diskettes, whose total capacity is far larger than that of a fixed disk.

Security   Diskettes can be removed from your computer and locked up in a safe place. The fixed disk stays inside your computer. Anyone who has access to your computer can access your data. Also, if your computer is lost by theft or destroyed by fire, for example, you still have your data on your diskettes.

> **Note:** In Chapter 13, "Data Integrity," we discuss several DOS utilities that help you protect the contents of your fixed disk. Their names are BACKUP, MIRROR, RECOVER, RESTORE, UNDELETE, and UNFORMAT. If you are a fixed-disk user, we highly recommend you read this chapter and follow its advice to ensure that your data on your computer's fixed disk is protected.

Exchange   Diskettes can be removed from your computer and moved to another computer. If you have more than one computer, diskettes make a convenient way for you to exchange data between your computers.

Your computer's hardware documentation and setup programs provide extensive information on how to use diskettes and diskette drives. They also explain the precautions you should follow to protect the data on your diskettes. Additional information on using diskettes and diskette drives is included in the documentation you received with your copy of DOS. If you are unfamiliar with using diskettes or diskette drives, we highly recommend that you review this information before you use your computer. The time you spend now will be repaid many times over later as you use your computer.

Both diskette and fixed-disk drives are selected by using a single-character name referred to as a *drive letter.* Drive letters start with A for the first drive, B for the second, and so on, all the way to Z for the last drive. Thus your computer can have up to twenty-six diskette and/or fixed-disk drives. Normally, you follow a drive letter with a colon (:), such as A:.

APPLICATIONS

Your computer cannot do anything without software to control it. This book deals mostly with a particular piece of software, the DOS operating system. DOS by itself can be used to do useful work, but it cannot do all the things that you might want to use your computer for. That job is left up to the numerous application programs available in the computer software market. Applications such as word processors, spreadsheets, database managers, graphics packages, networks, and utilities exist. Each is tailored to meet specific customer needs. Some applications provide combinations of these functions to satisfy customers with broader needs.

Many applications provide the same kind of support. For example, many word processing packages are available. They differ in price, function, and ease of use. Selecting the best applications for your needs is often difficult, but many books and magazines exist to help you make informed decisions.

To use an application, you must install it and set it up on your system. The steps needed to do this depend on the complexity of the application, on whether your computer has a fixed disk or diskettes, and on what other applications are already installed on your computer.

Each application is started with a specific procedure, which is described in the application's documentation. Often a command name is provided that you just type at the DOS Command Prompt. For example, a word processor application titled "NewWord" might use the command name "NW." It is also possible to add your application to the DOS Shell's list of applications. Once you have done this, you can start your application simply by choosing it from a menu list provided by the DOS Shell. You will learn how to do this in Chapter 6.

Once an application starts, it takes over your computer. You are now working with the application, not DOS. DOS is still there, but it is hidden from you by the application. When you eventually choose to exit from your application, DOS will reappear.

Depending on the particular application, your computer screen may or may not look like the DOS screens. Each application developer has tried to find the best way to make the application easy for you to use. Since the nature of different applications can be quite different, their appearance may also be quite different. This should not surprise you. Again, using automobiles for comparison, a station wagon looks quite different from a sports car, but each is a type of automobile.

What all this means is that in order to use your application, you also need to learn how it works. Understanding DOS alone is not enough. The computer software industry is realizing that this extra learning requirement is hard for its customers to deal with. Therefore, over time, you can expect that the differences in application appearance will disappear.

To help make this happen faster, IBM has published a set of guidelines (or conventions), called *Common User Access (CUA),* for application programmers to use. When followed, these guidelines will allow applications from different manufacturers to look and work alike. IBM plans to use these guidelines for all of its future computer software products. The DOS Shell follows the CUA guidelines.

DOS also provides you with a set of utilities. A utility is a special kind of application designed to do only a very simple, but important, job. These utilities are normally used only when you need to do one of these special jobs.

DATA FILES

Earlier, we mentioned that you will want to save your data on diskettes or a fixed disk. But if you just saved all of your data in one place, you could never sort it out to find it later. It would be like putting all the documents of a business in one file folder in a single file drawer.

DOS provides a way to put different information in different groups. The most basic way DOS does this is by using files. The name *file* comes from the business term for storing paper records. Each file holds information about a fairly small subject. A file can contain more than one thing. You might store all records about a particular customer in one file. Records for other customers would be stored in different files. DOS files can also hold many different types of information. See Figure 2-1 for an illustration of the DOS file concept.

Each office file is usually identified with the customer name or number. DOS also needs to identify files. This is done by giving them a filename. You (or your application programs) give files their names. We will talk more about filenames later in this section.

Just as in business, where you might group several related documents in a single file folder, DOS lets you put more than one file on a diskette or fixed disk. This can be quite convenient. You could put all of the files for a client named Smith on one diskette and all of the files for a client named Jones on another. To look up the information later, you just need to put the correct diskette in the computer's diskette drive.

Using diskettes in this way is very common. You can buy all sorts of boxes to hold diskettes. Some boxes work like a Rolodex®; others work like phone books. There are special file drawers to hold diskettes, special envelopes to mail diskettes, and even special safes to protect diskettes. If you plan to keep a large number of diskettes, we suggest you check your local office-supply source for these items.

Because a fixed disk cannot be removed from your computer, the concept of grouping the related files on different diskettes cannot be used with a fixed disk. You will see how to group files on fixed disks in the next section.

As you add more and more files to a diskette, it becomes harder to remember what is on the diskette. DOS provides services to let you look at the contents of your diskettes. It also lets you look at (or view) the contents of your files, move or copy them from one disk to another, delete files you

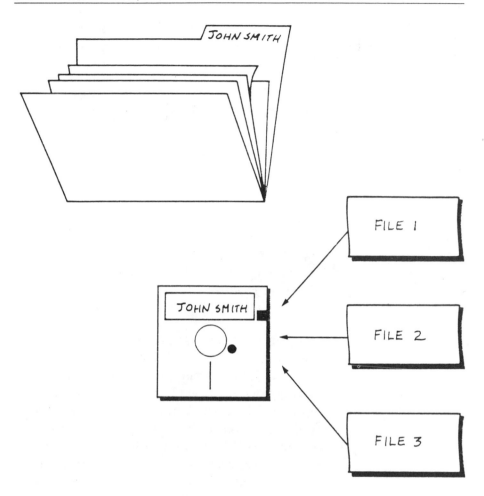

Figure 2-1
DOS File Concept

no longer need, change the name of a file to a new and better name, and print the files out on paper.

Certain application programs create files that contain information that can be understood only by your computer. If you view or print these files with DOS, the results look like gibberish. If this happens, you need to use your application to view or print the file. Any file can be moved, copied, deleted, or renamed via DOS.

When you choose a name for a file, there are some rules you must follow. DOS filenames can consist of one or two parts. The first part, called the *filename* (or *name* for short), can be from one to eight letters long. The sec-

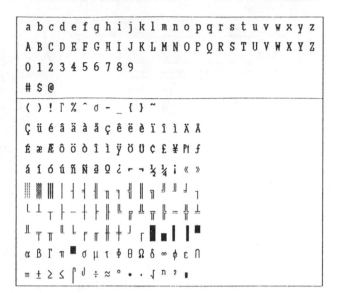

Figure 2-2
Valid DOS Filename
and Filename Exten-
sion Characters

ond part, called the *filename extension* (or *extension* for short), can be up to three letters long. You do not need to provide the filename extension; it is optional. If the filename extension is present, it must be separated from the filename with a period (.) character. You cannot put any spaces in any part of a DOS filename. For example, MYFILE.DOC is a valid DOS filename with both a filename and a filename extension.

DOS will let you type filenames and extensions that are longer than eight and three characters. If you do, DOS will simply ignore any characters after these limits. This is called *filename truncation*. For example, if you typed the name ALONGFILENAME.ALONGEXTENSION, DOS would treat it as if you had typed ALONGFIL.ALO.

DOS filenames can use most characters that you can type on your keyboard. There are a few exceptions. The characters shown in Figure 2-2 are allowed in either the filename or filename extension. If you use a character not listed, such as a comma (,), DOS might produce an error message. See Figure 2-3 for a list of invalid characters.

Figure 2-3
Invalid DOS
Filename and File-
name Extension
Characters

Blank . : , ; = + > < ¦ " / \ [ ] * ?

> **Note:** Even though all the characters shown in Figure 2-2 are valid, we recommend using only the characters in the first group. DOS treats lowercase letters the same as uppercase letters. Therefore, you can enter letters in either case.

Often, people have trouble picking filenames. They are concerned that somehow they have not picked the "right" name. You should not let this trouble you. When you need to pick a filename, just use what first comes to mind. If you think of a better name, DOS will let you change it. We will show you how to do this later in this book.

We recommend that when you pick a filename extension, you try to use it consistently. For example, if you choose to use the extension .DOC for your word processing documents, you should try to always use .DOC for each document you create. This will help you look up documents later. Many of your application programs will do this for you. For example, the Lotus 1-2-3® spreadsheet normally uses the extension .WKS.

DOS WILDCARD FILENAMES

For many DOS functions, you can refer to more than one file at a time. This is done by using a feature called *wildcard characters*. There are two wildcard characters, * and ?. These characters can be used in either the filename or the filename extension. They allow you to select more than one file. You do this by providing a sample name (including the wildcards); DOS will find all files that match this sample name.

The ? character is used to represent any single character. If you use the filename FILE?, then this name will match filenames such as FILE, FILE1, or FILEA. It will not match names such as FILE123 and FILLMORE. You can use more than one ? in the sample name. Some examples are FILE????, FILE.???, or A???DOC.

The * character is used to represent any remaining characters. If you use the filename FILE*, then this name will match filenames such as FILE, FILE1, FILEA, and FILE123. In other words, FILE* matches any filename that starts with FILE. It still will not match FILLMORE. You can use only one * in the name and one * in the extension. The sample name FILE???? acts exactly like FILE*. What really happens is DOS internally changes any * to as many ?s as are needed. The sample name *.* matches all files. The sample name *.XXX matches all files with an extension of XXX. The sample name FILE.* matches all files with the name FILE and any extension.

The next section discusses disk directories. If your computer does not have a fixed disk, then you may skip this section. We still recommend that you read it, however, because directories are supported on diskettes as well as on fixed disks.

DIRECTORIES

As mentioned earlier, when you use a fixed disk, you cannot group related files exactly as you do with diskettes. You will now see how files are grouped on fixed disks.

In an office with a large number of files, the files are usually kept in one or more file drawers. To aid in looking up the files, the drawers are labeled to identify the types of files in them. A commonly used method is to break up the files based on first letters — such as A–J, K–R, S–Z.

DOS supports a feature like a file drawer for fixed disks, called a *directory*. The term *directory* is used because of the similarity with a phone directory or building directory. DOS files can be grouped in directories just as paper files are grouped in a file drawer (see Figure 2-4). To identify the contents of a directory, DOS allows you to assign a directory name. Directory names follow the same rules as filenames. Normally, the filename extension

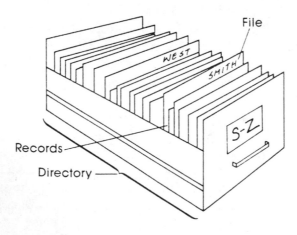

Figure 2-4
File Drawer Example

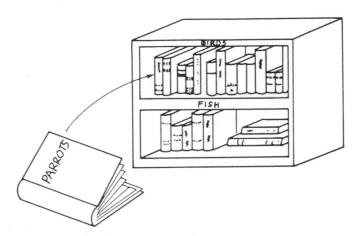

Figure 2-5
Library Example

part of the name is not used. When you use directories, files on related subjects can be grouped together in the same directory.

Another way to look at files and directories is to consider a library. A file would correspond to a book. Each book has a title (like a filename). Because a library has many books, they are divided into groups. For example, a book on robins and a book on parrots would be grouped under a category of "birds." Many levels of groupings are possible. For example, birds and fish could be grouped under "animals," and animals could be grouped with plants under "life" (see Figure 2-5).

To find the book on parrots, you would be told to do the following:

1. Go to the section on life.

2. Find the book section about animals.

3. Find the book shelf about birds.

4. Find the book about parrots.

You might write down these directions quickly as:

Life:Animals:Birds:Parrots

DOS provides a similar multilevel feature called *tree structured directories*. The term *tree* comes from how the levels look when written down. Just as the roots or branches of a tree spread out from the trunk, DOS directories spread out from the *root directory*. As you go down the tree, you go through *subdirectories* and reach *files* at the bottom. See Figure 2-6 for a picture of a directory tree as DOS shows it.

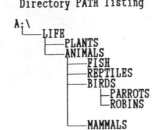

```
Directory PATH listing
A:\
  └──LIFE
        ├──PLANTS
        └──ANIMALS
              ├──FISH
              ├──REPTILES
              ├──BIRDS
              │     ├──PARROTS
              │     └──ROBINS
              │
              └──MAMMALS
```

Figure 2-6
Sample DOS TREE
Command Output

Just as in the library example, it is convenient to have a quick way to write directory names. DOS provides this. In DOS, each name is separated by a backslash (\) character. The backslash is used like the colon in the library path example.

If you had a disk with the same directory structure as the library on your C: fixed-disk drive, the parrot book would be referred to by

C:\LIFE\ANIMALS\BIRDS\PARROTS

This notation is referred to as a *file path* (or more often as just a *path*). It consists of three parts:

Drive   The name of the diskette or fixed-disk drive that contains the file. In this example C: is the drive name.

Directory path   The name of the directory or sequence of directories that contain the file. In this example \LIFE\ANIMALS\BIRDS is the directory path.

Filename   The name of the file. In this example PARROTS is the filename.

This example shows what is called a *fully qualified path* (because it includes the drive, directory path, and filename). You do not always have to type all three of these parts. In many cases only the filename is required. If any of the three parts is left out, then the path is a *partially qualified path*. Having to type a fully qualified path every time you want to reference a file would begin to get tedious. DOS provides you with two shortcuts:

1. The current drive

2. The current directory

By choosing a current drive, you tell DOS that whenever it sees a file path without the drive letter, you wish DOS to use the current drive. For example, if A: were the current drive and you entered the filename PARROTS, then DOS would act as if you had typed A:PARROTS.

By choosing a current directory, you tell DOS that whenever it sees a file path without a directory path, you want it to use the current directory. For example, if \LIFE\ANIMALS\BIRDS were the current directory and you entered the filename PARROTS, then DOS would act as if you had typed \LIFE\ANIMALS\BIRDS\PARROTS. The first backslash ("\") indicates that you are starting from the root directory and not from the current directory.

Each drive has a separate current directory. This means that you can change the current directory of one drive without affecting any other drive.

If the current drive is C: and the current directory for drive C: is \LIFE\ANIMALS\BIRDS, then the following file paths all refer to the same file:

PARROTS

C:PARROTS

\LIFE\ANIMALS\BIRDS\PARROTS

C:\LIFE\ANIMALS\BIRDS\PARROTS

If your current drive is A: and you want to refer to the PARROTS book on C:, you will have to type C:PARROTS. Since C: has a separate current directory, it does not matter what the current directory for A: is. If the current drive is C: but the current directory is, for example, \LIFE\PLANTS\TREES, you will have to type \LIFE\ANIMALS\ BIRDS\PARROTS.

DOS allows one more type of shortcut. Notice that in the example just given, the \LIFE directory is shared in common. You can take advantage of this when typing file paths. For example, if \LIFE were the current directory, you could type just ANIMALS\BIRDS\PARROTS to refer to the PARROTS book. Since the first (leading) backslash is missing, DOS adds the current directory to the front of what you type. Therefore, to DOS, it is as if you had typed \LIFE\ANIMALS\BIRDS\PARROTS. This is why you can just type PARROTS and yet really mean \LIFE\ANIMALS\BIRDS\PARROTS.

DOS filenames must be unique within the same directory. Only one file in a given directory can be named PARROTS. If this were not true, DOS could not determine which file you wanted when you typed the name PARROTS. However, this is not true across directories. You could have a

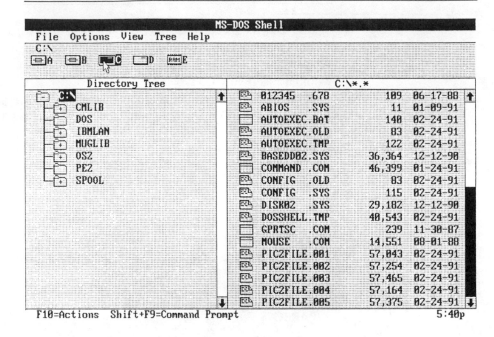

Figure 2-7
File System Sample
Screen

file named PARROTS in any other directory without a conflict. For example, DOS can tell the file \LIFE\PARROTS from the file \LIFE\ANIMALS\BIRDS\PARROTS.

Later, as you learn more about using DOS, you will see more examples of how these concepts are used, so do not be concerned if you are still somewhat unsure about these concepts.

In DOS, each diskette or fixed disk drive has a separate directory tree starting at a root. Normally, people set up multiple directories only on fixed disks. On diskettes, most people just use the root directory to hold all files.

When you use the DOS Shell, DOS provides you a view of these directories, as shown in Figure 2-7. On the left you see the disk directory tree. On the right are the files that are contained in the current directory (in this example the root directory). The fact that the DOS Shell shows you the directory structure of your diskettes and fixed disks is one way the DOS Shell makes DOS easy to use.

THE DOS SHELL

The DOS Shell is a way for you to communicate with DOS. It is intended to be significantly easier than using the DOS Command Line. The DOS Shell provides several features that help make DOS easier to use:

● Menu selection of your application programs as well as DOS commands and utilities.

● A visual display of the tree structure of your disks.

● The ability to pick files and directories from displayed lists by simply pointing to them.

● Menu selection of the most important DOS file and directory functions.

● Easily accessible help information about the activity you are currently doing.

The DOS Shell assists you in performing the most important day-to-day DOS tasks. It is quite possible that you will never need to use any other part of DOS.

We cover the DOS Shell in detail in Chapters 3, 4, 5, and 6. In these chapters, we provide a series of lessons that allow you to learn as you go in a step-by-step approach.

DOS COMMANDS AND UTILITIES

DOS commands and utilities also allow you to perform your day-to-day DOS tasks. Many of these commands perform functions that can also be done from the DOS Shell. Others provide important functions not available from the DOS Shell. For this reason, it is important that you understand what commands and utilities exist so that you can use them when necessary. In DOS versions before DOS 4.0, the DOS Command Prompt was the only way to ask DOS to do work for you. Beginning with DOS 4.0, the normal method to communicate with DOS is through the DOS Shell. Because some of the services DOS provides can be accessed only from the DOS Command Line, you may need to become familiar with its use. The DOS Command Line is also available from within the DOS Shell.

You may wonder why DOS provides commands and utilities for functions that are available from the DOS Shell. There are several reasons:

1. In earlier DOS versions, the DOS Shell was not provided; therefore, the commands and utilities were the only way to do these functions.

2. You will find that you perform certain tasks every day. It would be helpful if you could set up "canned" ways to do these tasks. DOS allows you to do this with what are called *batch files* (see "DOS Batch Files," Chapter 9, for more information). Once you have created a batch file to perform a task, the file may be added to the DOS Shell.

3. Some people will prefer to use the Command Line to access these commands and utilities instead of the DOS Shell.

We cover the DOS commands and utilities in detail in Chapters 8 through 13.

3 Using the DOS Shell

The DOS Shell is designed to simplify your day-to-day use of the computer. It allows you to quickly organize and maintain your computer's files and programs so that you can spend more time doing your work. You will soon see how simple and effective it is to use.

The DOS Shell allows you to organize your computer programs into lists or groups. This is similar to the way restaurant menus are organized, with separate lists for appetizers, main courses, and drinks within one main menu.

The DOS Shell provides advanced file and directory support features that are not available when you use the DOS Command Prompt. It allows you to create, delete, view, move, and copy both files and directories. Extensive online help is readily available to assist you when you use the Shell.

DOS 5.0 SHELL CHANGES

The Shell was not supported in DOS 3.3. It was first introduced in DOS 4.0 and was updated for release in DOS 5.0. This book covers the operation of the Shell in both DOS 4.0 and 5.0. We strongly encourage DOS 4.0 users to take advantage of the enhancements in DOS 5.0 by upgrading their operating systems.

DOS 4.0 Shell users will find that the DOS 5.0 Shell's operation is similar. In many cases, the screen layout and operation are identical. However, the DOS 5.0 Shell contains many enhancements and features not available in DOS 4.0. If you are familiar with the DOS 4.0 Shell, the following section summarizes some important differences in the DOS 5.0 Shell. If you are a first-time DOS user, it is not important that you understand these differences.

However, we do recommend that you read this section for a better understanding of the Shell's features.

Terminology Changes

Action bars are now called *menu bars*. The File System is now called the *File List*. The File Arrange pull-down panel is called *View*. The File View function is called *View File Contents*. The Start Programs screen is called the *Program List*.

New Task Swapper Enhancement

Multiple applications (up to 13) can now be run in a suspend and resume state. You can switch between these applications by pressing a key (see Lesson 11 in Chapter 4).

File List Enhancements

The File List is enhanced to support direct manipulation of files using the mouse pointer. You can move a file by simply dragging it from one directory to another directory or drive (see Lesson 16 in Chapter 5). In addition, you can start a program by dragging and dropping a data file on top of it (see Lesson 16 in Chapter 5).

The Shell's directory and file capacity limits are expanded and now support large-disk environments. A new screen arrangement is available, allowing you to display the Program and File Lists at the same time (see Lesson 1 in Chapter 4).

The File Associate function now supports the association of both data files with programs and programs with data files (see Lesson 15 in Chapter 5).

A new File Search function is available, allowing you to locate all occurrences of a file on a disk (see Lesson 10 in Chapter 5).

New File Options selections allow you to sort files in descending order, display hidden and system files, and activate a confirmation panel for mouse operations (see Lesson 2 in Chapter 5).

The View File Contents display is enlarged and supports single-line scrolling (see Lesson 12 in Chapter 5).

A new Tree pull-down panel allows you to control the amount of information displayed in the directory tree (see Lesson 4 in Chapter 5).

The Reading Disk Information panel is enhanced to display the current count of directories and files (see Lesson 1 in Chapter 5).

The drive icon display in graphics mode displays network and RAM drives (see Lesson 1 in Chapter 5).

The filename entry field no longer supports advanced wildcard options (see Lesson 9 in Chapter 5).

Program List Enhancements

The Program Manager's group capacity is increased to support more than 16 items per group and multiple levels of subgroups (see Lesson 1 in Chapter 6). The Disk Utilities Subgroup is redefined to include Quick Format, Undelete, Editor, and QBasic. Many of the Program Startup Commands (PSCs) are replaced by help-assisted data entry panels. Some PSCs are no longer supported. Password length is increased to 20 characters. User-defined help text length is reduced to 256 characters. Menu title length is reduced to 23 characters. The Program Startup Commands are reduced to 256 characters (see Lesson 2 in Chapter 6).

Help Text Enhancements

Help now appears in both the Program and File List menu bars as a pull-down panel and includes several new selections. The help text panel display is enlarged, allowing you to view more text (see Lesson 2 in Chapter 4).

New Repaint Screen Enhancement

The new Repaint Screen function allows you to restore the current Shell screen if it is disrupted by another program.

New Run Command Enhancement

The new Run Command function allows you to pass commands to DOS for execution similar to the DOS 4.0 Shell's Command Prompt (see Lesson 15 in Chapter 5).

Enhanced Video Mode Support

Additional video modes are available to support 43- and 50-line text-mode displays and 34-, 43-, and 60-line graphics-mode displays. You can now change to a different video mode without leaving the shell (see Lesson 6 in Chapter 4).

Enhanced Color Selection

Five additional preset color palettes are now available for your selection (see Lesson 5 in Chapter 4).

Enhanced Interaction Techniques	Two new methods for selecting files are available for your use (see Lesson 7 in Chapter 5). The appearance and operation of the scroll bar is similar (see Lesson 3 in Chapter 4). Additional hotkeys are available for your use (see Lesson 2 in Chapter 4).
Command Prompt Changes	You can no longer change the Command Prompt starting default directory from the Shell's directory tree (see Lesson 10 in Chapter 4).
Shell Function Level Control Changes	You can no longer deactivate, exit to DOS, or access to Menu Maintenance, date display, Program List operation, File List operation, sound, or Command Prompt Access.

DOS 5.0 SHELL ORGANIZATION

The first DOS 5.0 Shell screen display contains the file and program lists.

The file list allows you to perform many of the more common file and directory operations that are used to maintain your computer. The file operations include display, move, copy, delete, view, rename, and open (start) functions. The directory operations include display, create, rename, and delete functions.

The program list allows you to add your own program selections to a group or menu. Each menu group or subgroup can contain both programs and other subgroups of programs. The Shell is supplied with four different selections already installed on your Main Group screen (see Figure 3-1). Each of these selections is discussed in detail in the lessons in the following chapters.

Command Prompt	This program allows you to quickly access the DOS Command Prompt.
Editor	This program allows you to view and edit files.
MS-DOS QBasic	This program allows you to develop your own application programs using the BASIC programming language.
Disk Utilities (Program List Subgroup)	This menu group entry displays a list of the more common disk utility programs. These utilities allow you to copy a diskette, back up and restore your disk, prepare new diskettes for use by the computer, and recover deleted files.

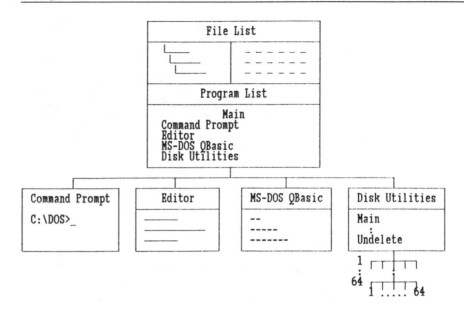

Figure 3-1
DOS 5.0 Shell Organization After Installation

DOS 4.0 SHELL ORGANIZATION

DOS 5.0 users should skip to the next section, "The Shell and Your Display Screen," and continue.

The first DOS 4.0 Shell screen displayed contains the main group of programs. From this main group, you may add up to 16 different selections, which can consist of programs and/or subgroups of programs.

The Shell is supplied with four different selections already installed on your Main Group screen. The DOS Utilities selection is a menu subgroup of additional program selections (see Figure 3-2).

Change Colors This program allows you to select one of four different color palettes for the display of the Shell's screens.

File System The file list, as in the DOS 5.0 Shell, allows you to perform many of the more common file and directory operations used to maintain your computer.

DOS Utilities (Start Programs Menu Subgroup) This menu group entry displays a list of the more common DOS utility programs. These utilities allow you to set the current date and time, back up and restore your disk, copy and compare diskettes, and prepare new diskettes for use by the computer.

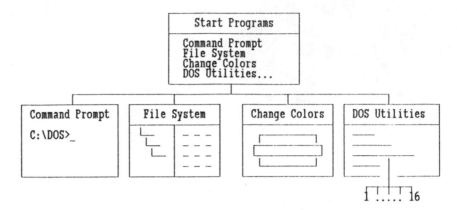

Figure 3-2
DOS 4.0 Shell Organization After Installation

Command Prompt	This program allows you to quickly access the DOS Command Prompt.

THE SHELL AND YOUR DISPLAY SCREEN

The Shell screens may be displayed in text mode or in graphics mode. Generally, text mode is selected on computers equipped with an IBM Monochrome or Color Graphics Adapter (CGA), whereas Graphics mode is selected on computers equipped with an IBM Enhanced Graphics Adapter (EGA), Video Graphics Array Adapter (VGA) or Extended Graphics Array Adapter (XGA).

With DOS 4.0, the highest quality video mode, based on the type of video adapter used by your computer, is automatically selected at installation time.

If you are using DOS 5.0, the Shell is enhanced to allow you to select from eight different video modes without leaving the Shell (see Lesson 6 in Chapter 4). All of the Shell's functions can be used in any of these video modes. Each video mode offers specific advantages (see Figure 3-3).

Text-mode displays are faster than those in graphics mode and provide a high level of compatibility with many terminate-and-stay-resident (TSR) programs, such as 3270 communication programs. In addition, text mode will operate on all IBM-compatible display adapters.

Graphics-mode displays are usually more attractive than text-mode and are better suited for use with a mouse pointing device. All computers compatible with the IBM Personal System/2s may operate the Shell in your choice of text or graphics mode. For your convenience, the tutorial in the

Video Mode	Number Lines	Supported By DOS 5.0 DOS 4.0		Text Density	Text Clarity
Text	25	Yes	Yes	Low	High
Text	43	Yes	No	Medium	Medium
Text	50	Yes	No	High	Low
Graphic	25	Yes	Yes	Low	High
Graphic	30	Yes	Yes	Low	High
Graphic	34	Yes	No	Medium	Medium
Graphic	43	Yes	No	High	Low
Graphic	60	Yes	No	High	Low

Figure 3-3
Shell Video Modes Comparison

following chapters includes lessons that support both text- and graphics-mode features.

Figure 3-4 shows how a Shell screen displayed in text mode differs from one in graphics mode.

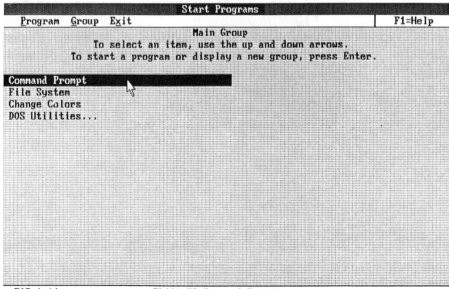

Figure 3-4
Text and Graphics Mode Screen Comparison

THE SHELL AND YOUR MOUSE

The Shell is designed to operate with the keyboard or mouse. In fact, the Shell will operate with most commercially available mice.

If you are using DOS 5.0, you need to make sure that the MOUSE.COM device driver (newer than version 6.2) is loaded before starting the Shell.

If you are using DOS 4.0 and have an IBM mouse, you should use the mouse driver supplied with the Shell. Non-IBM mice must support the Microsoft INT 33H mouse API to be successfully used with the Shell.

We highly recommend that you learn to use both the mouse and the keyboard. In many cases, you will find that the mouse dramatically increases your productivity. However, all Shell functions can be accomplished with just the keyboard.

The mouse allows you to manipulate the information displayed on the screen with a mouse pointer. The mouse is designed to operate on a flat surface such as a desktop. As you roll or move the mouse on the desktop, an arrow appearing on the display screen moves in proportion. This allows you to point at information such as filenames or symbols (often called *icons*) (see Figures 3-5 and 3-6). In addition, mice typically have a selection button that allows you to choose or make decisions about the information at which you are pointing (see Figure 3-7).

Some people find a mouse much simpler to operate than a keyboard. Keyboards typically contain over a hundred buttons, whereas a mouse may have from one to three. Even if your mouse has more than one button, the Shell will use only the first button, which is called the *Mouse Select button*.

The DOS 4.0 Shell provides a special option that allows you to change the button definitions from right to left. If the Shell's /LF option is active, your mouse buttons are automatically reassigned.

If you are operating the Shell in graphics mode, the tip of the mouse pointer is the selection area (see Figure 3-8). Only if the tip is actually on top of the desired text or on the same row will the proper selection be made when you press the Mouse Select button.

If you want to point at all positions on the display screen, move the mouse pointer off the bottom of the display, leaving only the tip visible. If

Figure 3-5
Graphics Mouse
Pointer Positioned on
Drive C: Icon

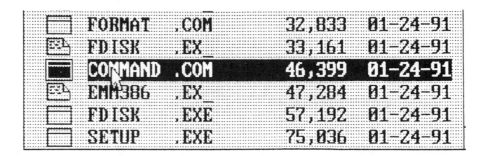

Figure 3-6
Mouse Pointer Positioned on Filename

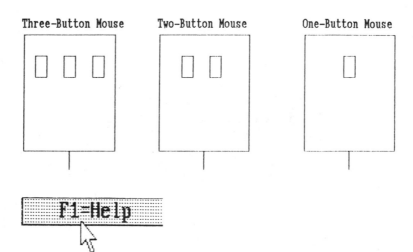

Figure 3-7
Traditional Mouse Configurations

Figure 3-8
Mouse Pointer Tip in Graphics Mode

you do not see the mouse pointer, move the mouse around and the pointer should reappear.

If you have a text-mode display, the mouse pointer appears as a block character, as shown in Figure 3-9. The movement of the pointer on the screen is not as smooth as it is in graphics mode. The mouse pointer jumps from one character position to another. In order to select or point in text mode, you must position the pointer on top of the desired text or on the same row.

Throughout the mouse instructions in the lessons that follow, you are requested to click the mouse pointer. This simply means that you position the mouse pointer on top of the desired text or icon and press the Mouse Select button once, while still pointing at the desired location. You will notice that a clicking sound occurs when you press the select button.

Figure 3-9
Text-Mode Mouse Pointer

```
  KEYB       COM     14592    5-31-88    8:00a
> KEYBOARD   SYS     23383    5-31-88    8:00a
  MODE       COM     23047    5-31-88    8:00a
  PRINTER    SYS     18969    5-31-88    8:00a
  REPLACE    EXE     19534    5-31-88    8:00a
```

ABOUT THE TUTORIAL

The next chapter contains a series of lessons designed to teach you the basic operations of the Shell. Before you can begin this tutorial, you should be familiar with the basic DOS concepts also discussed in Chapter 2, "Basic DOS Concepts."

You will find the Shell is easy to use, but it does take practice before it can be used effectively. Again, it is like driving a car: You must first understand the basic operations of the car, and then practice some, before driving becomes second nature. These lessons are designed to teach you the fundamentals necessary to quickly become an effective Shell user. You will learn by performing typical DOS tasks.

The lessons are divided into three chapters, beginning with Chapter 4, "Basic Shell Operations." That chapter contains 12 task-oriented lessons designed to teach basic operations including starting, stopping, and selecting programs. The 16 lessons in Chapter 5, "Performing File and Directory Operations," teach basic file and directory operations. The Shell lessons conclude with Chapter 6, "Performing Start Programs Maintenance," which contains nine lessons teaching you how to add, change, and delete programs and groups of programs from Shell menus. Chapter 7, "Using the DOS Editor," which follows the Shell lessons, contains three lessons designed to teach you the basic operations of the DOS Editor. Chapters 8, 9, and 10 discuss many of the DOS commands and utilities that you can add to Shell menus.

You are encouraged to complete all of the lessons for a better understanding of the Shell and its uses.

Each lesson contains step-by-step instructions for using DOS 5.0 with both the mouse and keyboard. Differences between the DOS 4.0 and 5.0 Shells are identified where appropriate in each lesson. The lessons are designed to use the knowledge and data acquired from the previous lesson, so you should complete the lessons in the order that they appear.

These lessons are designed so that both first-time and experienced users will be able to benefit from them. If you have previous experience with DOS, you will find that you will move more quickly through the lessons.

> **Note:** As before, the action symbol will be displayed to the left of any line where you are expected to take action.

4 Basic Shell Operations

When you complete this chapter, you will be able to perform the following basic Shell operations:

1. Start the Shell

2. Ask the Shell for Help

3. Use a Mouse to Scroll Graphics-Mode Lists

4. Use a Mouse to Scroll Text-Mode Lists

5. Change the Screen Colors

6. Change the Display Mode

7. Change the Screen View

8. Prepare a Diskette for Use

9. Copy a Diskette

10. Use the Command Prompt

11. Use the Task Swapper

12. Exit from the Shell

LESSON 1: START THE SHELL

When you complete this lesson, you will be able to start the Shell.

 To start the Shell, turn both the computer and display on.

Before the Shell appears, your computer will automatically perform an internal systems check. If any problems are detected, the computer will display a message on the screen. In some cases, a series of error numbers may appear and remain on the screen without starting the Shell. These numbers indicate the type of problem found. You should turn your computer and display off and try again. If you continue to get the same results, consult with your dealer to determine the nature of the problem. This procedure will require approximately 30 seconds to complete before the first Shell screen appears.

 Carefully look at the screens shown in Figures 4-1 through 4-4. Find the screen that comes closest to matching the one on your display. Make sure that you remember the type of display mode (text or graphics) that you are using. You will need this information to complete Lessons 3 and 4.

DOS will automatically display this first screen each time you turn your computer on or restart the system by pressing the Ctrl+Alt+Del keys at the same time.

Figure 4-1
First DOS 5.0 Command Prompt Display (Text Mode)

```
Microsoft(R) MS-DOS(R) Version 5.00
             (C) Copyright Microsoft Corp 1981-1990.
C:\DOS> _
```

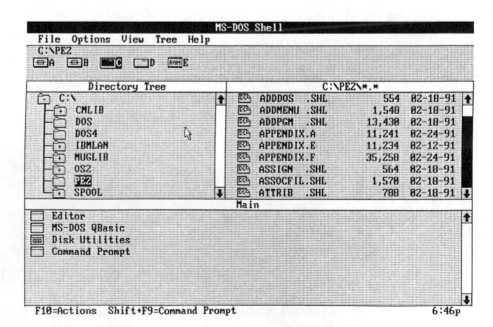

Figure 4-2
First DOS 5,0 Shell Screen Display (Graphics/Text Mode)

```
05-26-88                    Start Programs                   11:21 pm
Program  Group  Exit                                       | F1=Help
                             Main Group
             To select an item, use the up and down arrows.
           To start a program or display a new group press Enter.
Command Prompt
File System
Change Colors
DOS Utilities




F10=Actions                        Shift+F9=Command Prompt
```

Figure 4-3
First DOS 4.0 Shell
Screen Display (Text
Mode)

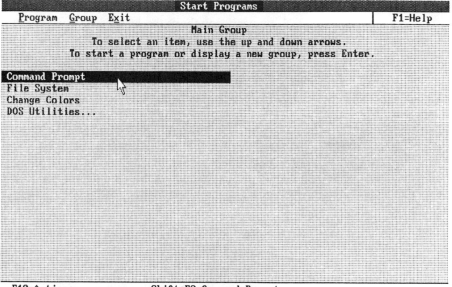

Figure 4-4
First DOS 4.0 Shell
Screen Display
(Graphics Mode)

 If your screen matches the text-mode Command Prompt display, you must type DOSSHELL and then press Enter (↵) to begin the Shell each time you turn your computer on.

You have now started the Shell and determined the video mode!

 You can stop at the end of any lesson in this tutorial. To do so, you simply turn both the computer and display off. Otherwise, continue with the next lesson.

LESSON 2:
ASK THE SHELL FOR HELP

When you complete this lesson, you will be able to ask the Shell for help.

DOS 5.0 is enhanced, allowing you to access Help in the Program List, File List, and View File Contents menu bars as a pull-down panel. Contextual help, which describes the function or operation of the current active screen area, is available only by pressing F1 on the keyboard.

> **Note 1:** We provide both keyboard or mouse interaction techniques throughout the lessons. If you do not have a mouse, simply skip the instructions labeled Mouse. If a mouse is installed on your computer, we recommend that you try both the keyboard and mouse techniques. You will soon see how much easier it is to operate the Shell with the mouse compared to the keyboard.
>
> **Note 2:** If your system unit beeps on the press of the arrow key, make sure that the NumLock keyboard function is off. Some keyboards are equipped with an LED NumLock light indicating that NumLock is on. The NumLock keyboard feature allows use of the numeric keypad for data entry operations.
>
> **Note 3:** When you are using DOS 4.0, the contextual help pop-up panel is displayed on the first press of the F1 key using the mouse or keyboard. You access all help functions by pressing or selecting the function keys located at the bottom of the Help pop-up panel (Figure 4-5). If any of these keys are pressed while the help panel is displayed, they will perform the assigned functions of Help-on-Help, Keys help, and help index.
>
> **Note 4:** Press Alt+F1 on keyboards that do not have an F11 function key.

Figure 4-5
DOS 4.0 Help Panel
Function Key Line

```
  Esc=Cancel    F1=Help    F9=Keys    F11=Index
```

KEYBOARD

 Press the Alt or F10 key once to switch to the menu bar.

 Using the right arrow, highlight the Help command on the menu bar.

 Press the Enter (↵) key once.

> **Note:** Notice that a certain character in each menu bar and pull-down panel command is underscored or highlighted. These characters are called *mnemonics*. If the mnemonic character is typed, the command is immediately performed. You may use mnemonics whenever they appear. In some cases, hotkeys (accelerator keys) are displayed within the pull-down panel to the far right of a selection's text (e.g., Alt+F4 in the Exit pull-down panel). Usually, these keys may be pressed at any time, whether or not the pull-down panel is displayed, to perform the assigned function.

MOUSE

 Move the mouse pointer on top of the Help command displayed in the menu bar on the second screen line from the top of the display. Make sure that the tip of the mouse pointer arrow is on top of the text characters.

 Press the Mouse Select button once.

When you select a menu bar command, a pull-down panel is displayed. The first selection in the pull-down panel is automatically highlighted. In general, once a pull-down is displayed, you use the up or down arrows to highlight the desired selection. Enter (↵) is used to accept and process the current highlighted selection. The left and right arrows are used to display adjacent pull-down panels. Pressing the Alt or Esc key, or clicking the Mouse Select button (outside of the pull-down panel area) removes the current pull-down panel.

You should see the display of the Help pull-down panel, as shown in Figure 4-6.

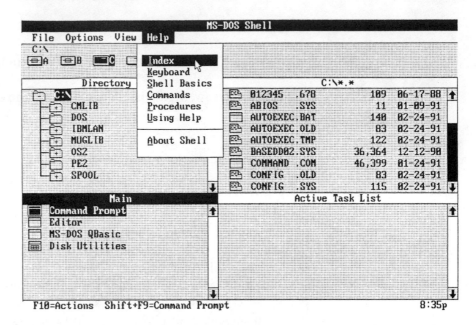

Figure 4-6
DOS 5.0 Help Pull-
Down Panel

While you are in any of the Shell's screens, you may use the Help pull-down panel to access any of the following types of help.

Help index   Is optionally accessed from the Help pull-down panel or after contextual help is displayed on the screen. The help index is similar to an index found in the back of a book. When you wish to cross-reference a subject or task, you may request the index and select the desired topic.

Keyboard (Keys help)   Is optionally accessed from the Help pull-down panel or from the Index after contextual help is displayed on the screen. The Keys help text describes the keys and assigned functions that are active throughout the Shell.

Shell Basics help   Is optionally accessed from the Help pull-down panel or after contextual help is displayed on the screen. The Shell Basics text helps you get started using the Shell.

Commands help   Is optionally accessed from the Help pull-down panel or from the Index after contextual help is displayed on the screen. The Commands help text describes the functions available in the File List, Program List, and View Screen menus.

Procedures help   Is optionally accessed from the Help pull-down panel or from the Index after contextual help is displayed on the screen. The Procedures help text discusses all of the different procedures required to operate the shell.

Using Help (Help- Is optionally accessed from the Help pull-down panel
on-Help)   or from the Index after contextual help is displayed on the screen. The Using Help text describes the operation of the Shell's help system.

About Shell   Is optionally accessed from the Help pull-down panel or from the Index after contextual help is displayed on the screen. The About Shell help text displays the current Shell version number and copyright notice.

If you select any of these functions, a Help text pop-up panel appears.

KEYBOARD

 Use the up or down arrow to highlight the Using Help command.

 Press Enter (⏎) to display the Using Help text.

MOUSE

 Point to the Using Help command.

 Press the Mouse Select button once.

The Help pull-down panel is removed, and the Using Help panel is displayed. (See Figure 4-7.)

When you read the last sentence of the Using Help text, you will notice that the help text extends beyond the viewing area of the panel. In order to continue reading the text, you need to scroll the contents of the panel. This is easy to do using either the keyboard or mouse. However, in this lesson, you will use only the keyboard to scroll the information. The next lesson will teach you how to scroll information using the mouse.

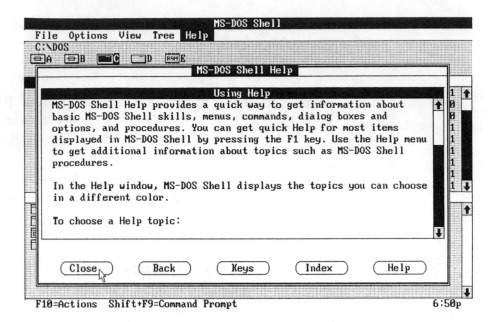

Figure 4-7
Using Help Pop-Up
Panel Display

KEYBOARD

 Press the PgDn key once.

Read the help text.

KEYBOARD OR MOUSE

 Press the PgDn key once again.

You should see the next page of the Using Help text. (See Figure 4-8.) Notice that a list of additional topics is displayed with "How to Learn About MS-DOS Shell" highlighted. You can select any of these cross-referenced help topics to display additional information.

KEYBOARD

 Use the Tab key or Shift+Tab to highlight "Requesting Help Directly."

 Press Enter (↵) .

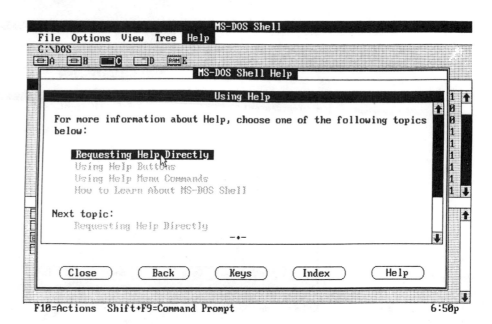

Figure 4-8
Help Text Scrolled
Using PgDn Key

MOUSE

 Point to "Requesting Help Directly."

 Press the Mouse Select button once.

The Using Help text is updated to display the Requesting Help Directly text. (See Figure 4-9.) Most help text displays are cross-referenced to other helps in this manner.

Notice the buttons located at the bottom of the Help pop-up panel in Figure 4-9. You can use any of these buttons while the panel is displayed to perform the following functions.

Close	Is used to exit the help support.
Back	Is used to redisplay the last help after selecting a cross-referenced help topic.
Keys	Is used to access Keyboard help.
Index	Is used to access Index help.
Help	Is used to access Using Help text.

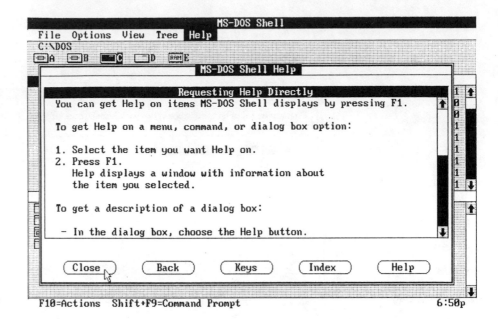

Figure 4-9
Requesting Help
Directly Text Display

KEYBOARD

 Use the Tab key or Shift+Tab to highlight the Index button.

> **Note:** Notice that a cursor appearing as an underscore identifies the active button selection.

 Press Enter (↵) .

MOUSE

 Point to the Index button.

 Press the Mouse Select button once.

The Requesting Help Directly text is removed and the Help index is displayed. Notice that the first topic in the index is highlighted for selection.

KEYBOARD

 Use the PgDn or PgUp keys to locate "Welcome to DOS Shell."

> **Note:** Lessons 3 and 4 will teach you how to use the mouse to quickly scroll information that appears in a list.

Notice that the topic highlight is no longer visible once you locate the Welcome to MS-DOS Shell text.

KEYBOARD

 Use the Tab or Shift+Tab keys to highlight the "Welcome to DOS Shell" text.

Press Enter (⏎) .

MOUSE

 Point to "Welcome to DOS Shell."

 Press the Mouse Select button once.

The Index is updated to display the Welcome to DOS Shell text.

At this point, you should understand the basic operation of the Shell's help mechanism. You are encouraged to browse through the help topics before continuing.

You may remove or cancel the Help panel at any time. Once the Help panel is removed, you can continue from the same place you were at before the help display.

KEYBOARD

 Press the Esc key once to cancel the Help function.

MOUSE

 Point at the Close text.

 Press the Mouse Select button twice to cancel the help function.

The Help panel is removed and the original screen is restored. You have used the Shell's Help function!

 Again, remember that you can stop at the end of any lesson in this tutorial. To do so, simply turn both the computer and display off. Otherwise, continue with the next lesson.

LESSON 3:
USE A MOUSE TO SCROLL
GRAPHICS-MODE LISTS

When you complete this lesson, you will be able to use the Shell's special graphic-mode features to quickly scroll information that appears in a list.

If you are using DOS 4.0 and your screen is displayed in text mode as identified in Lesson 1, or you do not have a mouse, then skip this Lesson and continue with Lesson 4.

The Shell is implemented according to the user interface conventions outlined in IBM and Microsoft's Common User Access (CUA) specification. This specification is designed to standardize the appearance and operation of applications on IBM Personal System/2–compatible computers.

> **Note:** When you are using DOS 4.0, scroll bars contain both single and double arrows. Clicking the mouse pointer on top of the double arrow pages the data in the direction of the arrow. When you move the slider bar with the mouse pointer, an outline box the same size as the slider bar moves with the mouse pointer, leaving the slider bar in place. Once you release the Select button, the outline box disappears, the slider bar moves to the new location of the outline box, and the list is immediately updated to reflect the new area being viewed.

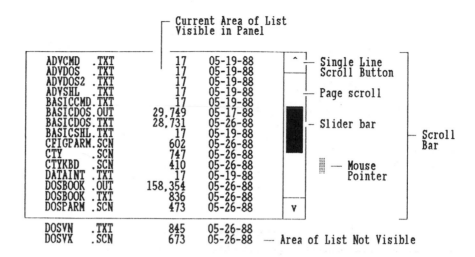

Figure 4-10
DOS 5.0 Scroll Bar

The scroll bar is an advanced list scrolling feature designed for use with the mouse. (See Figure 4-10.) It is displayed when a list of data can extend beyond the current visible screen area.

DOS 5.0 implements CUA graphics-mode user interface conventions in both text and graphics mode. This means that all mouse and keyboard interaction techniques are consistent across all of the supported display modes.

The scroll bar permits quick scrolling of the information appearing on the left side of the bar.

By placing the mouse pointer on the single arrow and pressing or clicking the Mouse Select button, you can scroll the data a line at a time in the direction of the arrow. (See Figure 4-11.)

MOUSE

Point to the Help command on the menu bar.

Press the Mouse Select button once.

Point to the Index button.

Press the Mouse Select button once.

The Help pull-down panel is removed and the Index help panel is displayed

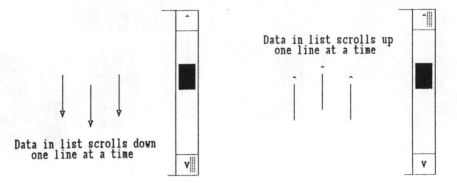

Figure 4-11
Clicking Mouse on
the Scroll Bar Single
Arrow

 Position the mouse pointer on the single down arrow at the bottom of the scroll bar.

MOUSE

 Press the Mouse Select button to scroll the index list one line at a time.

Clicking the mouse pointer inside the scroll bar above or below the slider bar pages the data up or down. (See Figure 4-12.)

MOUSE

 Position the mouse pointer inside the scroll bar below the slider bar.

 Press the Mouse Select button to scroll the index list down one page at a time.

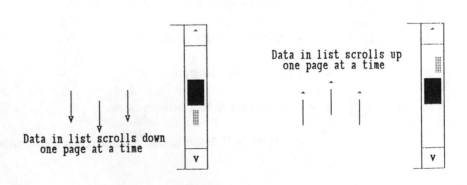

Figure 4-12
Clicking Mouse to
Page Data

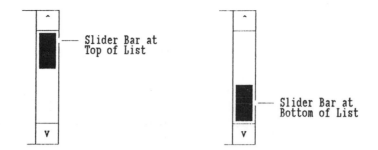

Figure 4-13
Slider Bar Showing
Current Location in
List

Notice that the white bar in between the up and down arrows moves when you scroll text. This is called the *slider bar*. It shows what portion of the list you are currently viewing and the length of the list.

For example, if the slider bar is at the top, then you are viewing the beginning of the list. Likewise, if the slider bar is at the bottom, then you are viewing the last entries in the list. (See Figure 4-13.)

In some cases, the slider bar fills the entire area in between the up and down arrows. (See Figure 4-14.) This indicates that the entire list is visible. Therefore, the list cannot be scrolled.

When the slider bar is not full size, you may directly move the bar by using the mouse pointer.

When you do this, the screen is automatically updated to show the new list area that you are viewing. This is one of the most powerful scrolling features available in the Shell.

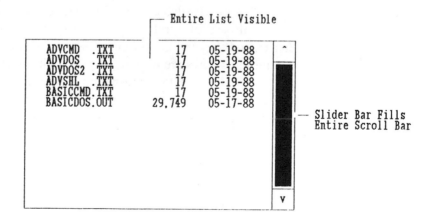

Figure 4-14
Slider Bar Display of
Entire List

MOUSE

 Using the Help index, place the mouse pointer on top of the slider bar.

 Press and hold the Mouse Select button down.

 Move the mouse pointer up and down within the scroll bar.

The slider bar moves with the mouse pointer, and the screen is updated. When you release the mouse button, the list reflects the relative scroll bar position. As you can see, the scroll bar is a powerful tool for quickly viewing information in a list. Throughout the rest of the tutorial, you should use the scroll bar whenever it appears.

LESSON 4:
USE A MOUSE TO SCROLL TEXT-MODE LISTS

When you complete this lesson, you will be able to use the Shell's special text mode feature to scroll information that appears in a list.

If you are using DOS 5.0, do not have a mouse, or are using DOS 4.0 in graphics mode as identified in Lesson 1, skip to the next lesson.

With DOS 4.0, displays that appear in text mode provide a subset of the list scrolling features available in graphics mode. This subset consists of the label More: followed by scroll arrows. These arrows are displayed when a list of data extends beyond the current visible screen area. (See Figure 4-15.)

The scrolling arrows are designed for use with the mouse pointer. They allow you to quickly scroll the information appearing in the list.

By placing the mouse pointer on one of the single arrows and pressing or clicking the Mouse Select button, you can scroll the data a line at a time in the direction of the arrow. (See Figure 4-16.)

MOUSE

 Select F1=Help.

 Select F11=Index.

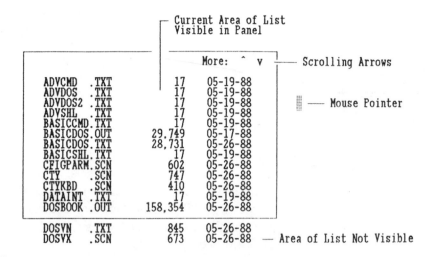

Figure 4-15
DOS 4.0 Text Mode
Scrolling Arrows

 Position the mouse pointer on top of the single down arrow.

 Press the Mouse Select button to scroll the index list.

If you continue to hold the Select button, the list will automatically scroll. When you find the selection you want, release the button and the scrolling will stop.

If the entire list is currently visible, the More: scroll arrows do not appear.

You have now used the Shell's text-mode direction indicators! Throughout the rest of the tutorial, you should feel free to use the More: scroll arrows whenever they appear.

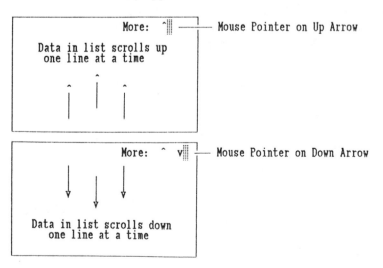

Figure 4-16
Clicking the Mouse
on a Single Arrow
Scrolls the List in the
Arrow Direction

LESSON 5:
CHANGE THE SCREEN COLORS

When you complete this lesson, you will be able to choose a new set of screen colors.

The DOS 5.0 Shell provides a simple function that allows you to select screen colors from eight different color sets. The Change Colors function is accessed from the Options pull-down panel.

Before you begin, it is important that you remove any displayed help panel by pressing the Esc key or selecting Close.

The DOS 4.0 Shell provides a simple program that allows you to select a set of screen colors from four different color sets. The Change Colors program is accessed from the Shell's Main Group display.

KEYBOARD

 Press the Alt or F10 key once to switch to the menu bar.

 Using the right arrow, highlight the menu bar command Options.

 Press the Enter (↵) key once.

MOUSE

 Move the mouse pointer on top of the menu bar command Options.

 Press the Mouse Select button once.

The Options pull-down panel is displayed. Notice the Colors command at the bottom of the panel.

KEYBOARD

 Use the Up or Down Arrow key to highlight the Colors command.

 Press Enter (↵).

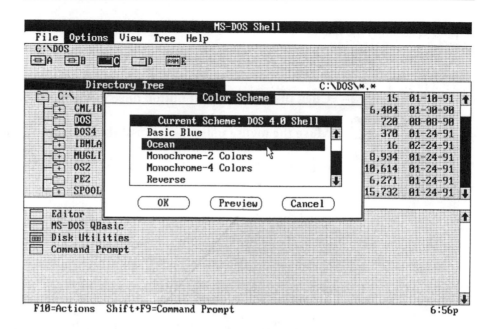

Figure 4-17
DOS 5.0 Change
Color Scheme Pop-
Up Panel Display

MOUSE

 Point to the Colors command.

 Press the Mouse Select button once.

The Options pull-down panel is removed and the Color Scheme pop-up panel is displayed. (See Figure 4-17.)

The Color Scheme pop-up panel shows you the current color used throughout the Shell. Eight different sets of screen colors are provided with the Shell. When you select a new set, you can preview the colors before accepting the selection.

KEYBOARD

 Use the up or down arrow to highlight a new color set.

 Use the Tab or Shift+Tab keys to select the Preview button.

 Press Enter (↵) .

MOUSE

 Move the mouse pointer on top of a new color set.

 Click the Mouse Select button once to highlight the new selection.

 Move the mouse pointer on top of the Preview button.

 Click the Mouse Select button once.

The screen is temporarily repainted using the new color selection. The Color Scheme pop-up panel is still displayed. You are encouraged to preview all of the Shell's color selections before saving a new set.

KEYBOARD

 Use the Tab or Shift+Tab keys to select the OK button.

 Press Enter (↵) to save the new color set.

MOUSE

 Move the mouse pointer on top of the OK button.

 Click the Mouse Select button once.

You have selected and saved a new set of screen colors!

LESSON 6:
CHANGE THE DISPLAY MODE

When you complete this lesson, you will be able to choose a new video display mode.

DOS 4.0 does not support this function. If you are using DOS 4.0, we recommend that you skip to the next lesson.

The DOS 5.0 Shell provides a simple function that allows you to select from eight different video display modes. The Change Display function is accessed from the Options pull-down panel.

KEYBOARD OR MOUSE

 Switch to the menu bar.

 Select the Options pull-down panel.

The Options pull-down panel is displayed. Notice the Display command at the bottom of the panel.

KEYBOARD OR MOUSE

 Select Display.

The Options pull-down panel is removed and the Screen Display Mode pop-up panel is displayed. (See Figure 4-18.)

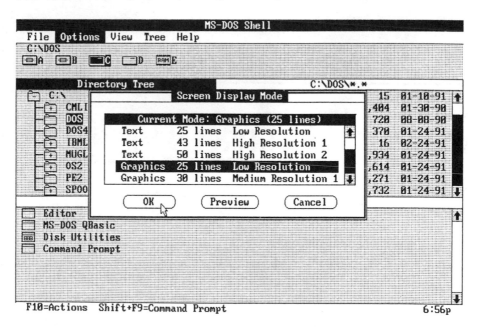

Figure 4-18
DOS 5.0 Change
Screen Mode Pop-Up
Panel Display

The Screen Display Mode pop-up panel shows you the current video mode used throughout the Shell. Eight different video modes are provided with the Shell. When you select a new mode, you can preview the display appearance before accepting the selection.

KEYBOARD OR MOUSE

 Select the new video display mode.

 Switch to the button area.

 Select the Preview button.

The screen is temporarily repainted using the new video display mode. The Screen Display Mode pop-up panel is still displayed. You are encouraged to preview all of the Shell's display mode selections before saving a new mode.

KEYBOARD OR MOUSE

 Select the OK button to save the new display mode.

You have selected and saved a new video screen display mode!

LESSON 7: CHANGE THE SCREEN VIEW

When you complete this lesson, you will be able to change the screen view.

The DOS 4.0 Shell defaults to the Start Programs list as the first screen view. However, once the file system is selected you can change the view using the Arrange pull-down panel. If you are using DOS 4.0, we recommend that you skip to the next lesson.

The DOS 5.0 Shell's View pull-down panel contains commands that allow you to rearrange the screen display or view.

KEYBOARD OR MOUSE

 Switch to the menu bar.

 Select the View pull-down panel.

The View pull-down panel is displayed. The first three selections display various views of the File List, which are discussed in the lessons in Chapter 5, "Performing File and Directory Operations." The current screen view is displayed using the Program/File List selection. Since this is the current displayed view, you cannot select it again. Therefore, it is dithered, is grayed, or appears in a halftone color. Selections that are currently invalid appear in this manner throughout the Shell. The last screen view selection displays the Program List without the File List.

KEYBOARD OR MOUSE

 Select Program List.

The View pull-down panel is removed and the Program List screen is displayed without the File List, as shown in Figure 4-19. Notice that the

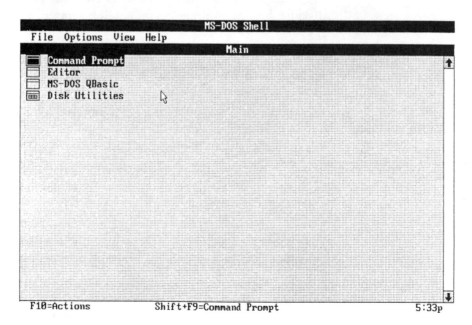

Figure 4-19
DOS 5.0 Program List
Screen View

Tree command no longer appears in the menu bar on the second line of the screen display. This command is used by the File List only and is removed from the menu bar when the Program List is active. The remaining lessons in this chapter use the Program List screen view.

You have selected and saved a new screen view!

LESSON 8:
PREPARE A DISKETTE FOR USE

When you complete this lesson, you will be able to prepare a new diskette for use.

When a diskette is new, DOS is not capable of reading or writing information to the surface of the diskette. You must prepare (or format) the diskette surface before DOS can write and read information. This is similar to preparing a slick surface before it can be painted. The Shell provides a special command that formats the surface of the diskette, allowing DOS to write and read information on the diskette.

This lesson requires the use of a new blank diskette. You may use an old diskette, but any information on it will be erased.

KEYBOARD

 Use the Up or Down Arrow keys to highlight Disk Utilities.

 Press Enter (↵) to display the Disk Utilities subgroup menu.

MOUSE

 Point at "Disk Utilities," then press the Mouse Select button twice rapidly.

> **Note:** This is called *double clicking*. Each button press must be performed as quickly as possible with no delay from one click to the other. The Shell counts the time between the clicks to determine if you are actually performing two single-click operations or one double-click operation. If the Disk Utilities screen does not display after double clicking, you should try again until you get the desired results.

The Main group in the Program List is removed and the Disk Utilities subgroup menu is displayed.

KEYBOARD

 Highlight, then select Format from the Disk Utilities program list by pressing Enter (↵) .

MOUSE

 Point at Format, then double click the Select button.

As discussed in Chapter 3, "Using the DOS Shell," the Disk Utilities program list is a subgroup list. Both programs and other subgroups may be selected from a subgroup. In graphics mode, an icon appears to the right of each selection in the subgroup. The symbol or icon appearing next to the Disk Utilities selection is used to indicate that a subgroup is displayed when selected. The icon appearing next to each of the other selections in the Main group is used to indicate that a program is executed when selected. (See Figure 4-19.) In text mode, icons are not displayed; however, the subgroup selections are enclosed in left and right brackets (e.g., [Disk Utilities]).

> **Note:** When you are using DOS 4.0, only programs may be selected from a subgroup.

Once the Format selection is made, a pop-up panel appears. (See Figure 4-20.) The entry field automatically defaults to drive A:. However, you may specify any drive you want.

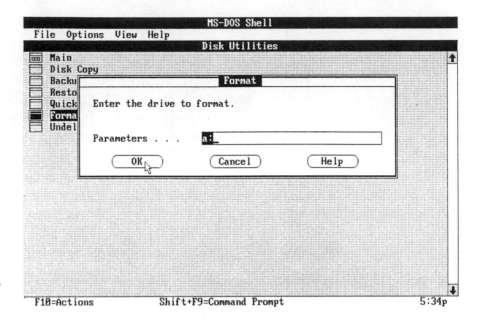

Figure 4-20
Pop-Up Display After
Format Selection

> **Warning:** Be careful to specify the drive that contains the disk you wish to format. Once the format process begins, any existing information on the disk is immediately lost! See Chapter 9, "More DOS Concepts," for information concerning the Unformat command.

KEYBOARD

 Press Enter (⏎) to accept the default drive A: selection.

MOUSE

 Point at the OK text, then click the Select button once.

The Shell screen disappears and the initial DOS Format screen is displayed. (See Figure 4-21.)

The selections in the Disk Utilities subgroup are not an inherent part of the DOS Shell. Therefore, you will notice that the screen changes color and that both the help and mouse pointer are no longer active after you select a Disk Utility. Of course, once you complete the utility's operation and return to the Shell, these functions are immediately restored. Programs that you add to a DOS Shell group will function in a similar manner. In some cases, you may add a program that does contain help and/or mouse support. These program features usually operate as expected when accessed from a Shell group.

KEYBOARD

 Following the instructions on the screen, insert your blank diskette in drive A:.

 Press Enter (↵) to begin formatting the diskette.

> **Note:** If you use an old diskette, formatted by another version of DOS, you will be warned that the disk cannot be Unformatted. You should answer Yes when prompted to proceed. DOS 5.0 includes a new command that allows you to unformat a disk originally formatted with DOS 5.0 and restore the previous contents, but disks formatted with earlier versions of DOS cannot be unformatted.

During the format of the diskette, you will see the percentage complete displayed on the screen, as shown in Figure 4-22.

Figure 4-21
Initial DOS 5.0 Format
Screen Display

```
Insert new diskette for drive A:
and press ENTER when ready...
```

Figure 4-22
Percentage of
Diskette Formatted

```
Insert new diskette for drive A:
and press ENTER when ready...
Checking existing disk format
Saving UNFORMAT information
Verifying 1.44M
51 percent of disk formatted
```

```
Insert new diskette for drive A:
and press ENTER when ready...
Checking existing disk format
Saving UNFORMAT information
Verifying 1.44M
Format complete
Volume label (11 characters, Enter for none)? TUTORIAL_
```

Figure 4-23
Enter Volume Label

At the completion of the format, you are prompted for a Volume label. This optional label may contain up to 11 characters. (See Figure 4-23.)

KEYBOARD

Type TUTORIAL.

Press Enter (↵) .

Immediately after you press Enter (↵), information concerning the amount of available disk storage space is displayed. It is not important that you fully understand this information. However, the number just before the "bytes available on disk" line indicates the maximum number of characters that may be stored on the disk. (See Figure 4-24.)

KEYBOARD

Type N for "No."

Press Enter (↵) .

```
Insert new diskette for drive A:
and press ENTER when ready...
Checking existing disk format
Saving UNFORMAT information
Verifying 1.44M
Format complete
Volume label (11 characters, Enter for none)? TUTORIAL
1457664 bytes total disk space
1457664 bytes available on disk
    512 bytes in each allocation unit
   2847 allocation units available on disk
Volume Serial Number is 123H-4AY
Format another (Y/N)? _
```

Figure 4-24
Format Operation
Complete

A message appears on the screen requesting you to "Press any key to return to the MS-DOS Shell." In this case, continuing will return you to the Shell Disk Utilities screen.

 Press Enter (↵) to return to the Shell.

You have prepared a diskette for use! All diskettes must be prepared in this manner before information may be read or written. Remember to be careful when specifying the drive to format, for any existing information will be lost.

LESSON 9: COPY A DISKETTE

When you complete this lesson, you will be able to make copies of a diskette.

You should periodically make an extra copy of diskettes containing valuable information in case your master copy is damaged or lost. This program selection is designed to simplify the diskette copying process. Its operation is similar to that of the Disk Utilities selection used to format the diskette in the last lesson.

This lesson requires the use of a blank diskette and the diskette supplied with DOS labeled "Install 1." You may use an old diskette instead of a new blank diskette. However, any information on it will be replaced by the copy process.

KEYBOARD OR MOUSE

 Select the Disk Copy entry from the Disk Utilities program list.

Once the Disk Copy selection is made, a pop-up panel appears. (See Figure 4-25.) The entry field automatically defaults to drive A: as the source and drive B: as the destination; however, you may specify any drives you want.

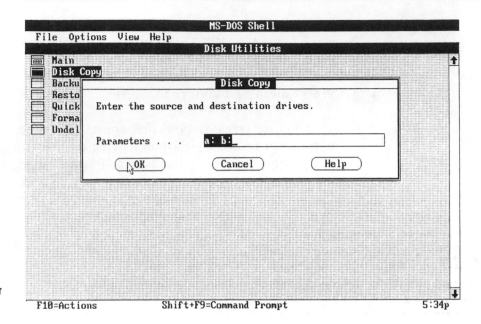

Figure 4-25
Pop-Up Display After
Disk Copy Selection

> **Warning:** Only diskettes, not fixed disks, may be Disk Copied.
> Be careful to specify the correct source and destination drives.
> Once the copy process begins, any existing information currently
> on the destination disk is immediately lost forever!

KEYBOARD OR MOUSE

  Press or click on the OK key to accept the default selections.

The Shell screen disappears and the initial DOS Diskcopy screen is displayed. (See Figure 4-26.)
As with the Format screen in the last lesson, the Diskcopy screen is not
an inherent part of the DOS Shell. Therefore, you will notice that the screen

Figure 4-26
Initial DOS Diskcopy
Screen Display

```
Insert SOURCE diskette in drive A:
Insert TARGET diskette in drive B:
Press any key to continue . . .
```

changes color and that both the help and mouse pointer are no longer active. Of course, once you complete the utility's operation and return to the Shell, these functions are immediately restored.

KEYBOARD

 Following the instructions on the screen, insert the DOS Install 1 diskette in drive A: and a blank diskette in drive B:.

> **Note:** If your computer contains one diskette drive, you will first insert the source diskette. The Disk Copy command will automatically prompt for the target diskette. You will have to switch the source and target diskettes with a single drive system several times before the copy is complete.

 Press Enter (↵) to begin copying.

All of the information contained on the diskette in drive A: will be copied to the diskette in drive B:. Messages describing the type of diskette and format of information being copied are displayed on the screen. In some cases, portions of a diskette are unusable; a message indicating read errors on the source diskette or the amount of the new diskette that cannot be used is displayed and updated. (See Figure 4-27.)

If the target diskette in drive B: is new, it will be automatically formatted before the copy begins. (See Figure 4-28.)

In some cases, surface errors may be detected on the target diskette. If this occurs, an error message indicating that the target diskette may be unusable is displayed. You should insert a new diskette in the target drive, then press Enter (↵) to begin the copy process again.

When the copy is complete you will see the messages shown in Figure 4-29.

Figure 4-27
Messages Indicating
Errors Found on
Source Diskette

```
Insert SOURCE diskette in drive A:
Insert TARGET diskette in drive B:
Press any key to continue . . .
Copying 80 tracks
18 Sectors/Track, 2 Side(s)
Unrecoverable read error on drive A:
Side 0, track 0
```

Figure 4-28
Target Diskette For-
mat Message

```
Insert SOURCE diskette in drive A:
Insert TARGET diskette in drive B:
Press any key to continue . . .
Copying 80 tracks
18 Sectors/Track, 2 Side(s)
Unrecoverable read error on drive A:
Side 0, track 0
Formatting while copying
```

Figure 4-29
Successful DISKCOPY
Without Error and For-
mat Messages

```
Insert SOURCE diskette in drive A:
Insert TARGET diskette in drive B:
Press any key to continue . . .
Copying 80 tracks
18 Sectors/Track, 2 side(s)
Volume Serial Number is 123H-4AY
Copy another diskette (Y/N)? _
```

KEYBOARD

 Type N for "No."

 Press Enter (⏎) .

A message appears on the screen requesting you to "Press any key to return to MS-DOS Shell." In this case, continuing will return you to the Shell Disk Utilities screen.

 Press Enter (⏎) to return to the Shell.

You have copied your DOS Install diskette! Once again, we recommend that you make a copy of all diskettes containing important information or programs.

Remember to be careful when specifying the source and target drives. Any existing information on the target diskette will be immediately lost.

The Shell will continue to display the current subgroup menu until you display a different one. You can easily redisplay a previous group.

KEYBOARD

 Select "Main" or press the Esc key once.

MOUSE

 Select "Main."

The Disk Utilities subgroup is removed and the Main subgroup is displayed.

You have redisplayed a subgroup!

LESSON 10:
USE THE COMMAND PROMPT

When you complete this lesson, you will be able to access and return from the Command Prompt.

The Shell supplies most of the functions that you need to operate your computer. However, you may find it necessary to use the DOS Command Prompt to access some of the less common DOS functions not available in the Shell.

There are several different ways to access the Command Prompt from the Program List screen. Notice that the first program selection in the Main group is the Command Prompt. (See Figure 4-30.) In addition, at the bottom of the screen in the function key area you find "Shift+F9=Command Prompt." This provides a fast way to access the Command Prompt using the keyboard. Either method may be used to access the same DOS Command Prompt.

KEYBOARD OR MOUSE

 Select the Command Prompt entry from the Main group in the Program List.

The display screen immediately changes color and the DOS Command Prompt is displayed. As with the Diskcopy screen in the last lesson, the Command Prompt screen is not an inherent part of the DOS Shell. Therefore, both the help and mouse pointer are no longer active. Once you return to the Shell, these functions are immediately restored.

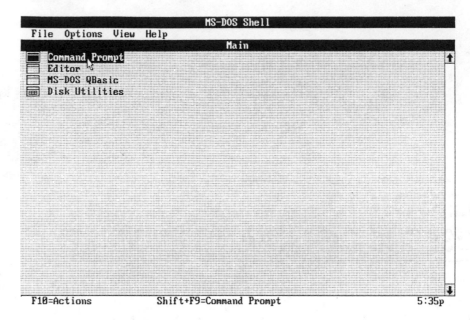

Figure 4-30
Command Prompt
Selection Is Highlight-
ed in DOS 5.0

Chapters 8, 9, and 10 discuss many of the commands that may be executed from the DOS Command Prompt. At this point, it is not necessary to understand these commands. We will use the DOS DIR command to demonstrate the operation of the Command Prompt, as shown in Figure 4-31.

KEYBOARD

 Insert the DOS Install 1 diskette in drive A:.

 Using the keyboard type DIR A:.

 Press Enter (↵) .

> **Note:** Do not be alarmed if the initial information displayed on the Command Prompt screen disappears when you execute a DOS command.

Figure 4-31
Initial Command
Prompt Display

```
Microsoft(R) MS-DOS(R) Version 5.00
            (C) Copyright Microsoft Corp 1981-1990.
C:\DOS> _
```

```
KEYB      COM    14592   5-31-88   8:00a
KEYBOARD  SYS    23383   5-31-88   8:00a
MODE      COM    23047   5-31-88   8:00a
PRINTER   SYS    18969   5-31-88   8:00a
REPLACE   EXE    19534   5-31-88   8:00a
SELECT    DAT    22454   5-31-88   8:00a
SELECT    EXE    99798   5-31-88   8:00a
SELECT    HLP    27562   5-31-88   8:00a
SELECT    PRT     1330   5-31-88   8:00a
SHARE     EXE    10308   5-31-88   8:00a
SYS       COM    11495   5-31-88   8:00a
VDISK     SYS     6399   5-31-88   8:00a
XCOPY     EXE    17110   5-31-88   8:00a
XMA2EMS   SYS    28143   5-31-88   8:00a
XMAEM     SYS    19367   5-31-88   8:00a
EGA       CPI    49075   5-31-88   8:00a
LCD       CPI    10615   5-31-88   8:00a
4201      CPI     6404   5-31-88   8:00a
4208      CPI      664   5-31-88   8:00a
5202      CPI      425   5-31-88   8:00a
012345    678      109   5-31-88   8:00a
DOSSHELL  BAT      292   5-31-88   4:34p
        34 File(s)       8192 bytes free
C:\DOS>_
```

Figure 4-32
DIR Listing of Install 1
Diskette

The DIR command displays the list of files and directories on drive A:. The light on the diskette drive is active, and the directory list displays on the screen. (See Figure 4-32.)

In the next chapter of lessons, we will use the Shell's File List function to explore a much more elegant method of displaying what the diskette contains.

You can return to the Shell at any time.

KEYBOARD

 Type EXIT.

 Press Enter (↵).

The Shell reloads and displays the Main group screen. You have now used the DOS Command Prompt and returned to the Shell!

LESSON 11:
USE THE TASK SWAPPER

When you complete this lesson, you will be able to use the Task Swapper.

DOS 4.0 does not support this function. If you are using DOS 4.0, we recommend that you skip to the next lesson.

The DOS 5.0 Shell allows you to run more than one program at a time. This function is called the Task Swapper. When it is active and you start a program, most of the Shell is removed from memory, leaving just the Task Swapper and DOS kernel in memory. This means that your computer's memory is free for use by the program you just started. When switching between programs, the Task Swapper automatically copies an image of the current program and its data to a temporary file on your disk. This file is saved until you swap back, at which point the image in the file is loaded back into memory and you continue in the program at the same point you left. Therefore, it is important that you have enough disk space available to support the temporary files created to save memory images of your programs when you switch between them. Both text- and graphics-mode programs are supported and can be mixed in the Task List.

Warning: You should not use communication programs that must remain resident in memory with the Task Swapper (e.g., 3270 Emulator). Communication sessions are disconnected when the program is swapped from memory. However, in some cases, if you start the communication program before the Shell is loaded, you may use the Task Swapper for other programs. In this case, less memory is available, because the communications program is loaded below the Shell.

You start the Task Swapper from the Options pull-down panel.

KEYBOARD OR MOUSE

 Switch to the menu bar.

 Select the Options pull-down panel.

The Options pull-down panel is displayed. Selecting the Enable Task Swapper command activates the multiple program support. Whenever the Task Swapper is active a diamond (◆) character appears to the left of the selection.

KEYBOARD OR MOUSE

 Select "Enable Task Swapper."

The Options pull-down panel is removed and the Program List screen is redisplayed with an Active Task List to the right, as shown in Figure 4-33. Notice that the Active Task List is empty.

When programs are started from the Program or File List, they are automatically added to the Active Task List. Up to 13 different programs can be

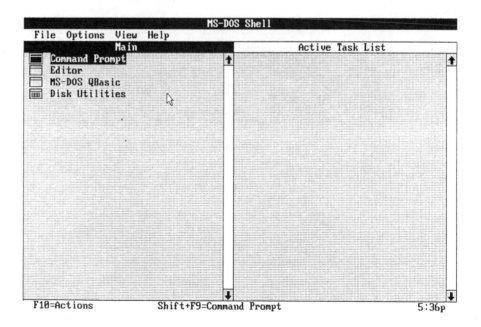

Figure 4-33
DOS 5.0 Active Task
List Screen Display

started at the same time and accessed from this list. You can even run multiple copies of the same program at the same time.

KEYBOARD

 Use the Tab or Shift+Tab keys to switch to the Main group panel area.

> **Note:** When you switch between panel areas, the title of the current active panel area is highlighted.

KEYBOARD OR MOUSE

 Select "Editor."

Once "Editor" is selected, the Active Task List is updated with the program name and a pop-up panel appears requesting the name of a file to edit. (See Figure 4-34.) In this lesson, you will accept the panel without specifying a file.

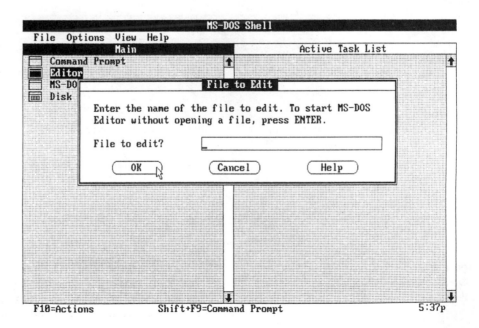

Figure 4-34
Editor Pop-Up Panel
Display

KEYBOARD OR MOUSE

 Select "OK."

The Shell's screen display is replaced by the Editor's first screen. You use this same method to start other programs from the Shell's Program List.

You can only switch back to the Shell using the keyboard once a program is active on the display screen. Three different key sequences are available to switch between programs and the Shell:

Alt+Tab	When you press and release Alt+Tab once, the last program running is swapped back into memory and the current program image is saved to disk. When only one program is running from the Shell, you can use this key to swap back and forth to the Shell. If you continue to hold the Alt key down, after pressing the Tab key, the screen is cleared and a title of the last program run appears at the top of the screen. Another press of the Tab key while continuing to hold the Alt key down displays each of the program titles that are running. When you locate the program that you want to run, release the Alt key to complete the task swap. This feature enables you to move directly from the current program to another.
Ctrl+Esc or Alt+Esc	When you press and release Ctrl+Esc, the current program image is saved to disk and the Shell is redisplayed. You cannot use this key sequence when the Shell is displayed.

KEYBOARD

 Press and hold the Ctrl key, then press the Esc key and release both keys.

The Editor display is removed and the Shell is redisplayed. You may switch back to the Editor by pressing the Alt+Tab keys, or you can select the Editor from the Active Task List display.

> **Note:** If an insufficient amount of disk space is available to save the image of the current running program and data, an error message is displayed. You must erase files to free disk space before you can swap back to the Shell or another running program.

KEYBOARD OR MOUSE

 Select "Editor" from the Active Task List.

The Editor is redisplayed. When you are finished with a program in the Active Task List, you should save any data, then exit the program. Programs that terminate are automatically removed from the Shell's Active Task List. However, you can terminate a running program from the Shell by highlighting the program to be deleted in the Active Task List, then pressing the Del key or selecting the Delete command from the File pull-down panel.

Warning: Data not saved by a program is lost when you use the Shell to terminate and delete the program from the Active Task List.

KEYBOARD OR MOUSE

 Switch to the Shell.

 Highlight the Editor selection in the Active Task List.

KEYBOARD

 Press the Del key once.

MOUSE

 Select the File pull-down panel.

 Select Delete.

The Shell displays a Warning pop-up panel, as shown in Figure 4-35.

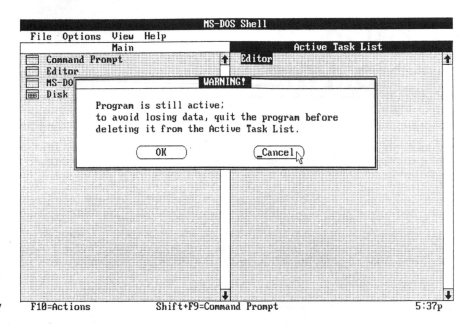

Figure 4-35
Program Delete from
Task List Warning
Pop-Up Panel Display

KEYBOARD OR MOUSE

 Select "OK."

The Warning pop-up panel is removed, the Editor is terminated, and the Editor selection is removed from the Active Task List. Any temporary files created by the Shell to save your program's memory image are automatically erased when you terminate a program in the Active Task List. You cannot switch to a program that is removed from the Active Task List until it is started again.

The Shell remembers that the Task Swapper is active every time you start your system. If you want to deactivate the Task Swapper, you select the Enable Task Swapper command in the File pull-down panel. The Task Swapper function toggles on or off each time it is selected.

> **Warning:** If a running program fails when using the Task Swapper, you should exit the Shell and restart the computer to avoid possible stability problems with DOS 5.0.

LESSON 12:
EXIT FROM THE SHELL

When you complete this lesson, you will know how to exit from the Shell properly before turning your computer off.

Throughout the previous lessons, you were instructed simply to turn the computer and display off when you were ready to stop the lessons. As we progress to the more advanced lessons, you must properly exit the Shell prior to turning the computer off. This will prevent the unnecessary accumulation of temporary Shell data files.

In order to exit the DOS 5.0 Shell, you must select the Exit command located in the File pull-down panel.

> **Note:** In DOS 4.0, the Exit Shell command is accessed from the menu bar Exit pull-down panel.

KEYBOARD OR MOUSE

 Select File.

 Select Exit.

When you successfully exit to DOS, you will see the DOS Command Prompt, as shown in Figure 4-36. This screen is similar to the DOS Command Prompt display taught in Lesson 10. However, it is important not to confuse the selection of the DOS Command Prompt with exiting the Shell. When exiting the Shell, you cannot type EXIT at the Command Prompt to return to the Shell. In order to start the Shell after exiting, you must type DOSSHELL at the Command Prompt.

> **Note:** Any programs running with the Task Swapper must be terminated before you can exit to DOS.

Figure 4-36
Exit to DOS Com-
mand Prompt

`C:\DOS>`

KEYBOARD

 Type DOSSHELL.

 Press Enter (↵).

If the Shell's Main group of programs appears again, you have successfully exited and started the Shell again! It is strongly recommended that you
exit the Shell in this manner prior to turning your computer and display off.

Note: You can exit to DOS from the Shell by pressing the F3
exit hotkey. This key is active whenever a pop-up panel is not
displayed in the Shell. Once the key is pressed, the Command
Prompt immediately appears.

---

5 Performing File and Directory Operations

When you complete this chapter, you will be able to perform the following Shell operations:

1. Display Drive Contents

2. Sort Files

3. Create a Directory

4. Change a Directory Tree Display

5. Delete a Directory

6. Rename a Directory

7. Delete a File

8. Copy a File

9. Find a File

10. Search for Files

11. Show Shell Information

12. View a File

13. Rename a File

14. Print a File

15. Start a Program

16. Direct Mouse Manipulation

This series of lessons teaches file and directory maintenance operations. In order to successfully complete the lessons in this chapter, you must first complete the lessons in Chapter 4, "Basic Shell Operations."

LESSON 1:
DISPLAY DRIVE CONTENTS

When you complete this lesson, you will know how to display the contents of a disk drive.

The DOS 5.0 Shell's View pull-down panel provides four different screen arrangements or views of your computer's file and directory structure. In this lesson, you will choose the Single File List selection in the View pull-down panel to display the files and directories stored on your disk(s).

Note: When using DOS 4.0, you display the File List by selecting the File System entry from the Main Group. There are a few minor differences between the DOS 5.0 and 4.0 Single File List screens. The DOS 4.0 directory path is displayed on the screen line below the available drives, and the time is displayed on the top right corner of the screen.

KEYBOARD OR MOUSE

 Select View.

 Select the Single File List entry.

The Single File List view is displayed on the screen showing the available drives, directory tree, and files. Your screen should look similar to the screen shown in Figure 5-1. Notice that the filenames are automatically displayed in alphabetical order.

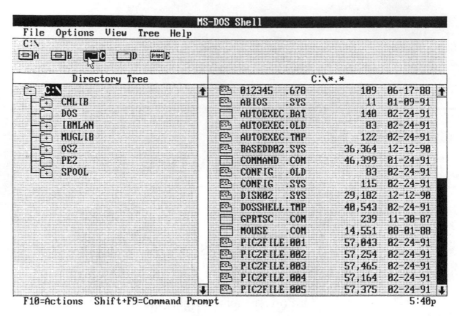

Figure 5-1
Display After the Disk
Read Is Complete

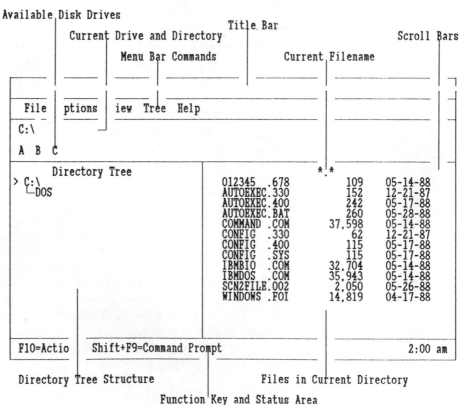

Figure 5-2
DOS 5.0 Single File List
Drive Display

> **Note:** Do not be concerned if your drive, files, and directory structures are different from those displayed in Figure 5-1. Your display accurately reflects the information currently on your disk.

Before continuing, it is important to understand the layout of the File List display. (See Figure 5-2.)

The Single File List screen areas are listed here for your reference. We recommended that you carefully read the definitions. However, it is not important that you fully understand the function of each area. We cover each of these areas in more detail throughout the remaining portion of this Lesson.

AVAILABLE DISK DRIVES

This area displays all of the drives that are currently available to your computer. This includes diskettes, fixed disks, VDISKS (or RAM drives), and network drives. From 2 to 26 different drives may be displayed at once. When your computer contains only one diskette drive, DOS automatically displays drive A: and a logical drive B:. In order to select logical drive B:, you must insert the drive B: diskette in drive A:. DOS will share the single diskette drive between drive A: and B:.

If your screen is displayed in graphics mode, different drive icons are used to depict diskette, fixed disks, and network drives. (See Figure 5-3.) In this example, diskette icons are used for drives A: and B:, fixed-disk icons are used for drives C: and D:, RAM drives for drives E: and F:, and network drives for drive Q:. The display of different icons to represent the types of available drives is available only in graphics mode.

> **Note:** When using DOS 4.0, drives displayed without drive lights are used as network or RAM drive icons. (See Figure 5-3.)

Figure 5-3
DOS 5.0 and 4.0 Available Drives in Graphics Mode

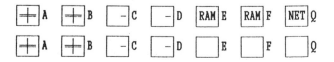

Figure 5-4
DOS 5.0 and 4.0
Available Drives in
Text Mode

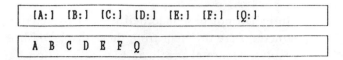

Text mode drive displays do not use icons; therefore, they are less informative concerning the nature of the available drives. (See Figure 5-4.) In this example, no indication of diskette, fixed disk, or network drives is available.

TITLE BAR

The DOS 5.0 Shell title bar (Figure 5-5) always indicates when the Shell is active.

> **Note:** When you use DOS 4.0, aside from the obvious display of the File List title, this screen area may optionally display the computer's current date and time.

CURRENT DRIVE AND DIRECTORY

The display area immediately below the drive list contains the current drive and directory. This information is displayed in the traditional Command Prompt format, as shown in Figure 5-6. In this example, C: represents the current drive and \DOS represents the current directory. Whenever you select a new drive or directory for display, this information is updated.

Figure 5-5
DOS 5.0 and 4.0 Title
Bars

```
 04-23-91                    Start Programs                    11:32 am
```

Figure 5-6
DOS 5.0 and 4.0 Current Drive and Directory

```
C:\DOS
```

SCROLL BAR

This screen area is used to display the scroll bar for the file list area. The scroll bar may be used to scroll the information contained in the list located to the left. See Lessons 3 and 4 in Chapter 4 for a detailed description of the interaction of the list scrolling support.

MENU BAR COMMANDS

The File List menu bar operates similarly to the Programs List menu bar. However, some of the available commands are different. (See Figure 5-7.)

The File pull-down panel contains commands that are used to manipulate both files and directories. (See Figure 5-8.)

The Options pull-down panel contains commands that affect the display of file information and the interaction of file manipulation. (See Figure 5-9.)

Figure 5-7
DOS 5.0 and 4.0 File List Menu Bar Commands

```
File  Options  View  Tree  Help
```

```
File  Options  Arrange  Exit          F1=Help
```

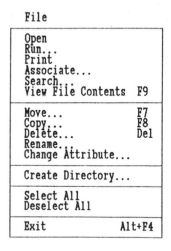

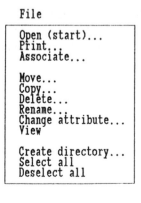

Figure 5-8
DOS 5.0 and 4.0 File Pull-Down Panels

Figure 5-9
DOS 5.0 and 4.0
Options Pull-Down
Panels

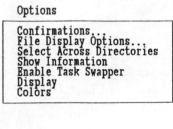

```
Options

Confirmations...
File Display Options...
Select Across Directories
Show Information
Enable Task Swapper
Display
Colors
```

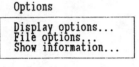

```
Options

Display options...
File options...
Show information...
```

Figure 5-10
DOS 5.0 View and
DOS 4.0 Arrange Pull-
Down Panels

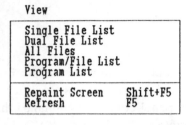

```
View

Single File List
Dual File List
All Files
Program/File List
Program List

Repaint Screen    Shift+F5
Refresh           F5
```

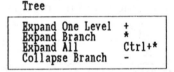

```
Arrange

Single file list
Multiple file list
System file list
```

Figure 5-11
DOS 5.0 Tree Pull-
Down Panel

```
Tree

Expand One Level   +
Expand Branch      *
Expand All         Ctrl+*
Collapse Branch    -
```

The View pull-down panel contains commands that change the arrangement of the screen information. (See Figure 5-10.)

The DOS 5.0 Tree pull-down panel contains commands that change the amount of information displayed in the directory tree. (See Figure 5-11.)

The DOS 5.0 Help pull-down panel replaces the DOS 4.0 F1=Help function key and provides an array of different help support, as discussed in Lesson 2 of Chapter 4. (See Figure 5-12.)

The DOS 4.0 Exit pull-down panel contains commands that return control to the Start Programs screen or allow you to continue with the File List. (See Figure 5-13.)

Figure 5-12
DOS 5.0 Help Pull-
Down Panel

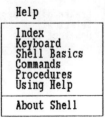

```
Help

Index
Keyboard
Shell Basics
Commands
Procedures
Using Help

About Shell
```

Figure 5-13
DOS 4.0 Exit Pull-
Down Panel

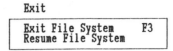

```
Exit

┌─────────────────────────────┐
│ Exit File System      F3    │
│ Resume File System          │
└─────────────────────────────┘
```

Figure 5-14
File-Mask and Match-
ing Filenames in List

```
┌──────────────────────────────────────────┐
│               FRED.*                       │
│  FRED    .678      109    05-14-88         │
│  FRED    .330      152    12-21-87         │
│  FRED    .400      242    05-17-88         │
│  FRED    .BAT      260    05-28-88         │
└──────────────────────────────────────────┘
```

CURRENT FILENAME

The information displayed in the title field represents the type of filenames that appear in the file list area immediately below the title. This field is also called the *file-mask*. The characters that appear in this field may include all of the valid filenames and DOS filename wildcards. See Chapter 2, "Basic DOS Concepts," for more information concerning DOS filename wildcards. Only files that match the specified file-mask will appear in the file list. (See Figure 5-14.)

In Figure 5-14, FRED.* is the file-mask title. All filenames that match FRED with any type of extension (as is requested by the *) appear in the file list. You will learn how to use the file-mask in Lesson 9 of this chapter.

DIRECTORY TREE STRUCTURE

The screen area containing the Directory Tree structure provides an overview of the current drive's organization. (See Figure 5-15.) This is one of the Shell's most powerful features. See Chapter 2 for more information concerning the directory tree.

In Figure 5-15, the current directory is the root of the tree, as is indicated by the highlight. There are two subdirectories, DOS and WORD, immediately below the root. The WORD subdirectory contains another subdirectory called DOCUMENT. The tree display is intended to simplify

Figure 5-15
Directory Tree Struc-
ture

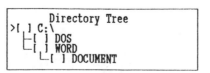

```
          Directory Tree
>[ ] C:\
   ├─[ ] DOS
   └─[ ] WORD
        └─[ ] DOCUMENT
```

Figure 5-16
Filename List

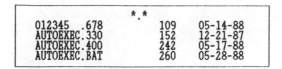

```
                         *.*
012345  .678             109    05-14-88
AUTOEXEC.330             152    12-21-87
AUTOEXEC.400             242    05-17-88
AUTOEXEC.BAT             260    05-28-88
```

directory interaction by making the disk drive's directory structure visible. For example, if you were to list the files contained in the DOCUMENT directory using the traditional Command Prompt, you would type DIR C:\ WORD\ DOCUMENT*.* and then press Enter (↵). To accomplish the same using the Shell, you would simply highlight DOCUMENT.

> **Note:** When using DOS 4.0, you must highlight the directory name, then press Enter (↵) to display a directory's files. In DOS 5.0, you only highlight the directory name and the Shell automatically displays the files.

FILES IN CURRENT DIRECTORY

The files in the current directory appear to the right of the Directory Tree structure. To the right of each filename appears the associated extension, size, and date information. (See Figure 5-16.) In this example, using the *.* file-mask title, all filenames and extensions are displayed. The fourth filename in the list is AUTOEXEC with an extension of BAT, a size of 260 characters, and a creation date of 05-28-88.

FUNCTION/STATUS KEY AREA

This screen area displays the status and function keys that are currently active. (See Figure 5-17.) In this example, if you select Shift+F9=Command Prompt, the DOS Command Prompt is displayed. If you exit the Command Prompt, you return to the same screen displayed before beginning the command prompt.

Figure 5-17
File List Function Key
Area

```
F10=Actions                    Shift+F9=Command Prompt
```

With a little practice, using these features will become second nature. In the remainder of this lesson, you will learn how to change drives.

KEYBOARD OR MOUSE

 Insert your working copy of the DOS Install 1 diskette in drive A:.

KEYBOARD

 Press the Tab (|←) key until the available disk drives area is highlighted.

 Using the right arrow, highlight drive A:.

 Press Enter (↵) to read drive A:.

MOUSE

 Point at the drive A: letter.

 Click the Mouse Select button once.

The message "Reading Disk Information" should appear, followed by the display of the DOS Install diskette directory structure and filenames. This message is usually displayed for 3 to 15 seconds, depending on the number of files and directories stored on your disk. After the "Reading Disk Information" is removed, the display is updated with the current disk's information. (See Figure 5-18.)

The Shell internally saves (buffers) different drive lists. This feature is provided to enable you to copy files from one drive to another. For example, when you first start the File List, the current drive, (in this example, A:) will be automatically buffered into memory. Until a different drive is read, the second Shell buffer is unused. (See Figure 5-19.)

If you display another drive such as C:, the Shell stores drive C:'s image in the unused memory buffer. Both the initial drive A: buffer and the C: buffer are stored at the same time. (See Figure 5-20.)

If you display a third drive such as D:, then the Shell replaces the oldest drive image in memory with the new drive. In this case, drive A: is replaced with drive D:. (See Figure 5-21.)

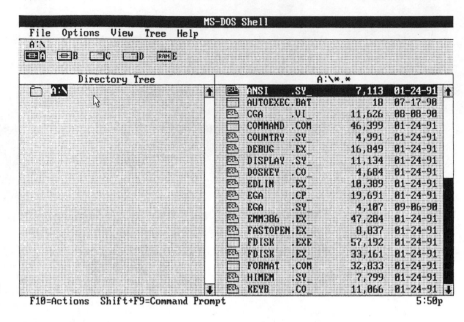

Figure 5-18
DOS Install Diskette in
Drive A:

Figure 5-19
Shell Memory Buffers
After Initial Start of
File List

Shell Memory Buffer One	Shell Memory Buffer Two
First Disk Read of Drive A:	Not Used

If you display a fourth drive such as A: again, then the Shell replaces the oldest image, which now is C:, with drive A:. (See Figure 5-22.)

The only exception to the rule of drive buffering is when you read a drive again that is already displayed on the screen. Following the examples just given, if drive A: is currently displayed and you select drive A: to read it

Figue 5-20
Shell Memory Buffers
After Second Disk
Read

Shell Memory Buffer One	Shell Memory Buffer Two
First Disk Read (Drive A:)	Second Disk Read (Drive C:)

Figure 5-21
Shell Memory Buffers
After Third Disk Read

Shell Memory Buffer One	Shell Memory Buffer Two
Third Disk Read (Drive D:)	Second Disk Read (Drive C:)

Figure 5-22
Shell Memory Buffers
After Fourth Disk
Read

Shell Memory Buffer One	Shell Memory Buffer Two
Third Disk Read (Drive D:)	Fourth Disk Read (Drive A:)

again, the current drive A: buffer is refreshed from the disk. This occurs even though drive D: is the oldest buffered image. Of course, at any time you may toggle back and forth between the two buffered drives. You will notice that the Shell does not have to read the disk again to display a currently buffered drive.

The Shell's multiple drive buffering feature enables you to copy files from one disk drive to another. In addition, the Shell's performance is greatly enhanced when switching between buffered drive images. In those cases where you are accessing a drive over the network, the drive image buffering dramatically increases performance.

If you have more than one diskette drive and/or a fixed disk, you should try changing drives a few times to get the feel of the drive buffering feature.

You can stop at the end of any lesson in this tutorial. Otherwise, continue with the next lesson. Make sure that you place your working copy of the DOS Install diskette in a safe place. You will use this diskette in future lessons.

LESSON 2: SORT FILES

When you complete this lesson, you will be able to sort the Shell's file display.

The file list may be sorted by name, extension, date, and size in disk and in ascending or descending order. The disk order sort is a special feature that places the files in the actual order in which they appear in the disk directory. This unsorted order increases file display performance when large numbers of files are listed. The Shell defaults to sorting files by name.

In this lesson, you will change the sort order from name to size.

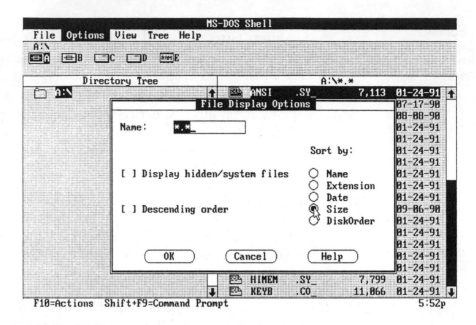

Figure 5-23
Display Options Pop-
Up Panel

KEYBOARD OR MOUSE

 Switch to the menu bar.

 Select the Options pull-down panel.

 Select File Display Options.

The Options pull-down panel disappears and the Display Options pop-up panel appears. (See Figure 5-23.)

> **Note:** The Display hidden/system files and Ascending/Descending order options are supported in DOS 5.0 only. You toggled these selections on or off by tabbing to the selection, then pressing the spacebar.

KEYBOARD

 Press the Tab (|←) key once to highlight the Sort selection.

Using the up and down arrows, highlight the Size selection.

 Press Enter (↵).

MOUSE

 Point at the Size text.

 Click the Mouse Select button once.

 Point at "OK" and click the Mouse Select button once to change the Sort order.

The Display Options pop-up panel is removed and the file list is sorted by size. Notice that the smallest files appear at the top of the list. (See Figure 5-24.)

You have sorted your files by size! You should try the other sort options for experience before continuing with the next lesson.

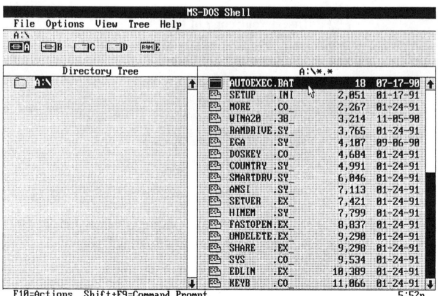

Figure 5-24
DOS Install Diskette
Sorted by Size

LESSON 3: CREATE A DIRECTORY

When you complete this lesson, you will be able to create a directory using the Shell.

As discussed in Chapter 2, directories provide a useful way of categorizing files or programs. The Shell provides the ability to quickly create a directory below any existing directory in the tree structure display. In this lesson, you will create two directories on the working copy of the DOS Install diskette created in Chapter 4.

> **Note:** It is important that you use the copy of the DOS Install diskette that you made earlier. The original diskette is write-protected and should not be modified by adding a directory.

KEYBOARD OR MOUSE

 Insert your copy of the DOS Install 1 diskette in drive A:.

 Display drive A:.

> **Note:** In the last lesson you changed the file list sort order. Make sure that you display the file list in the Name sort order before continuing.

Notice that the DOS Install 1 diskette contains only the root directory. All new directories may exist only below the root directory. All disks always contain a root directory.

The first directory that you create will be called SHELL.

KEYBOARD OR MOUSE

 Switch to the menu bar.

 Select the File pull-down panel.

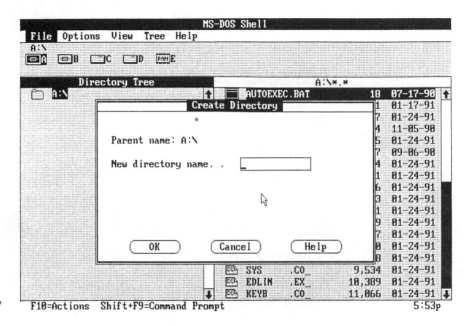

Figure 5-25
Create Directory
Pop-Up Panel Display

As discussed in Lesson 1 of this chapter, both file and directory commands are located in the File pull-down panel.

KEYBOARD

Select the Create Directory command by pressing the letter *e* mnemonic.

The File pull-down panel is removed and the Create Directory pop-up panel is displayed. (See Figure 5-25.)

You can use from 1 to 11 different characters to create the directory name, but you can use only valid DOS filename characters, as was discussed in Chapter 2.

KEYBOARD OR MOUSE

Type SHELL.

Press Enter (↵).

The Create Directory pop-up panel is removed and the Directory Tree is updated with the new directory. (See Figure 5-26.)

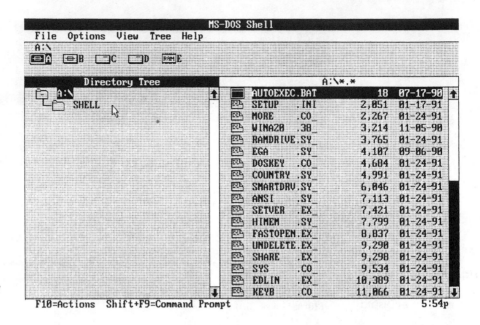

Figure 5-26
New SHELL Directory
Display

The second directory that you create will be called BACKUP. This directory will be located below the SHELL directory. The Shell creates new directories below the current directory. In order to create BACKUP below the SHELL directory, you must first make SHELL the current directory.

KEYBOARD

 Using the Tab (|←) key, switch to the Directory Tree structure.

 Using the up and down arrows, highlight the SHELL entry in the list.

> **Note:** When using DOS 4.0, you must press Enter (↵) to display the contents of a new directory selection.

MOUSE

 Point at the SHELL text in the Directory Tree.

 Click the Mouse Select button once.

Both the current directory and file list areas are updated. Notice that your new SHELL directory does not contain any files. Until you copy or move files into this directory it will be empty. A highlight always appears on the current selected directory name. Only one directory may be active at a time.

Now, you are ready to create the new BACKUP directory.

KEYBOARD OR MOUSE

Switch to the menu bar.

Select the File pull-down panel.

Select "Create Directory."

Type BACKUP.

Press Enter (⤶).

The Create Directory pop-up panel is removed and the Directory Tree is updated with the new directory. (See Figure 5-27.) You have created two new directories!

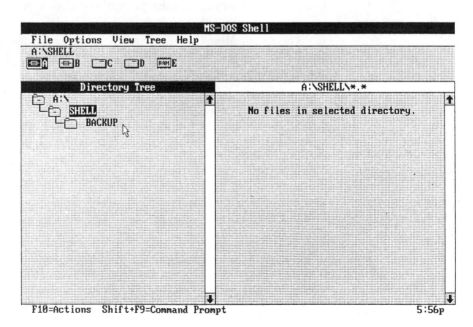

Figure 5-27
New BACKUP Directory Display

LESSON 4:
CHANGE A DIRECTORY TREE DISPLAY

When you complete this lesson, you will be able to change the directory tree display.

DOS 4.0 does not support this function. If you are using DOS 4.0, we recommend that you skip to the next lesson.

The DOS 5.0 Shell was enhanced to support a series of directory tree functions that allow you to dynamically tailor the amount of information displayed in the directory tree. This lesson is more effective when you have a large number of directories to display; however, you can use the subdirectories created in the last lesson.

KEYBOARD OR MOUSE

 Switch to the menu bar.

 Select the View pull-down panel.

 Select the Refresh command to read the disk again.

The four options in the Directory Tree pull-down panel allow you to change the amount of information currently displayed in the Directory Tree panel area. When a disk is read, the Shell displays only the first level of subdirectories that appear immediately below the root directory. In many cases, there are many other secondary subdirectories located below the first level of directories. You will find that it is confusing when a large number of subdirectories are displayed at once. You can use the following commands to expand or reduce the number of subdirectory layers displayed in the current directory tree area.

Expand One Level Displays only subdirectories that appear immediately below the current directory.

Expand Branch Displays all subdirectories that appear below the current directory.

Expand All Displays all subdirectories in the entire tree directory.

Collapse Branch   Removes the display of all directories up to the current directory.

You will display the entire tree.

KEYBOARD OR MOUSE

 Switch to the menu bar.

 Select the Tree pull-down panel.

The Tree pull-down panel is displayed.

KEYBOARD OR MOUSE

 Select "Expand All."

The Directory Tree display area on the screen is updated and the entire tree of the disk is visible. (See Figure 5-28.)

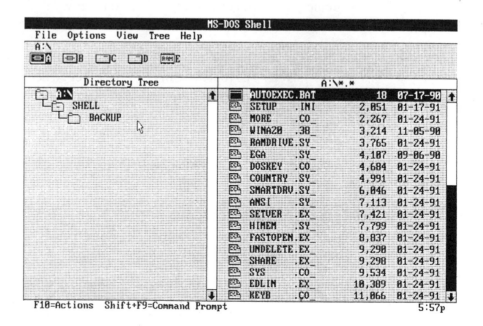

Figure 5-28
Expanded Directory
Tree Display

> **Note:** Notice that each directory in the tree is preceded by an icon or set of brackets. These directory symbols are blank or contain either a plus or minus sign. When you place the mouse pointer on top of a minus sign and click the Mouse Select button once, subdirectories below this point in the directory branch are removed from the display. When you place the mouse pointer on top of a plus sign and click the Mouse Select button once, subdirectories appearing inside this directory are displayed.

You have changed the Shell's directory tree display!

LESSON 5:
DELETE A DIRECTORY

When you complete this lesson, you will be able to delete a directory using the Shell.

As part of disk maintenance, you may find it necessary to delete unused directories from time to time. The Shell will delete the directory only if it is empty and displayed as the current directory. In this lesson, you will delete the BACKUP directory created in Lesson 3 of this chapter.

> **Note:** The root directory (\) may never be deleted.

KEYBOARD OR MOUSE

 Display BACKUP as the current directory.

Since you have not copied or moved files into the BACKUP directory, it is empty. (See Figure 5-29.)

KEYBOARD

 Press the Del key.

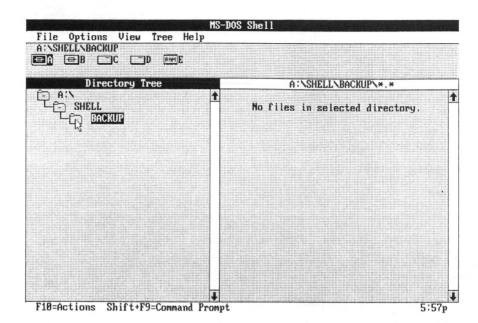

Figure 5-29
BACKUP as the Current Directory

MOUSE

 Select the File pull-down panel.

 Select "Delete."

Both file and directory operations share the same Delete command.

The DOS 5.0 Shell determines if you are performing a directory or file function by the last active panel area. In this case, the Directory Tree was the last active panel area before you switched to the menu bar.

> **Note:** When using DOS 4.0 and files are marked, a file operation is assumed even if the file area is not the last active panel area.

The File pull-down panel is removed and the Delete Directory Confirmation pop-up panel appears. (See Figure 5-30.)

The Delete Directory Confirmation pop-up panel displays the actual DOS path of the directory you have selected for deletion. If the directory is correct, you will select "Yes" to complete the deletion.

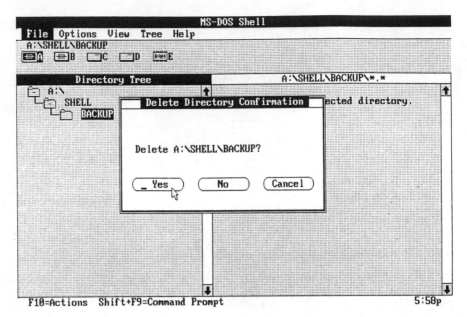

Figure 5-30
Delete Directory
Confirmation Pop-Up
Panel Display

> **Note:** When you are using DOS 4.0, the Delete Directory pop-up panel contains two numbered options—to delete the directory or not. You can select either option by using the mouse pointer or by pressing the number assigned to the option.

KEYBOARD OR MOUSE

Select "Yes."

The Delete Directory pop-up panel is removed and the BACKUP directory is deleted from the Directory Tree. In addition, BACKUP is removed from the current directory display. The next directory entry in the chain is always displayed as the new current directory after the delete.

You have now deleted a directory!

LESSON 6:
RENAME A DIRECTORY

When you complete this lesson, you will be able to rename a directory using the Shell.

This is one of the Shell's many functions not available from the Command Prompt. In past versions of DOS, once a directory name was created, you could not rename the directory using DOS. In this lesson, you will rename the SHELL directory to SHLBCKUP.

> **Note:** The root directory (\) may never be renamed.

The Shell can rename only the current directory.

KEYBOARD OR MOUSE

 Display the SHELL directory as the current directory.

 Switch to the menu bar.

 Select the File pull-down panel.

Both file and directory operations share the same Rename command.

KEYBOARD OR MOUSE

 Select "Rename."

The File pull-down panel is removed and the Rename Directory pop-up panel appears. (See Figure 5-31.)

The Rename Directory pull-down panel displays the current directory name and prompts for the new name. You can enter only valid DOS filename characters.

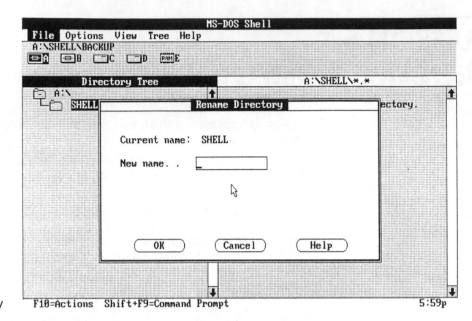

Figure 5-31
Rename Directory
Pop-Up Panel Display

KEYBOARD OR MOUSE

 Type SHLBCKUP.

 Press Enter (↵).

The Rename Directory pop-up panel is removed and the new SHLBCK-UP directory name appears in the Directory Tree and the current directory display area. You have now renamed a directory!

LESSON 7: DELETE A FILE

When you complete this lesson, you will be able to delete files using the Shell.

The Shell's Delete function provides a quick method of deleting files on a disk. Great care must be taken to use this function correctly! You could easily erase all of the files on a disk with a few keystrokes. In this lesson, you will delete files located on the working copy of the DOS Install diskette that you created in the last chapter.

The traditional DOS Command Prompt requires you to type the name of the file for deletion. The Shell provides a special feature that allows you to mark or select one or more files appearing in the file list area. This considerably increases your productivity by eliminating the need for you to type the name of each file you delete.

> **Note:** The file selection feature is used to perform file delete, copy, move, view, start, and associate functions. Each of these are discussed in the remaining lessons of this chapter.

KEYBOARD OR MOUSE

 Insert your copy of the DOS Install 1 diskette in drive A:.

 Display drive A:.

Figure 5-32 shows the DOS Install diskette in drive A:. Once a file is marked, it remains selected until the file operation is complete or you intentionally unmark or deselect the file. This is also true for files in the list that are not currently visible. As a good rule of thumb, you should use the "Deselect all" files command before performing any file function to ensure that there are no unintentional files selected.

> **Note:** If "Deselect all" is dithered, grayed, or appears in halftone color, it is not currently active. In this case, it means either that no files are currently marked or that the list of available files was not the last active screen area and you should skip to the next instruction in this lesson.

KEYBOARD OR MOUSE

 Switch to the file list screen area.

Switch to the menu bar.

 Select the File pull-down panel.

 Select "Deselect all."

Once you select "Deselect all," the File pull-down panel disappears, and any file that is selected is automatically deselected. This action should become second nature before you perform any file operation. When you use DOS 5.0, only the files marked on the current drive are affected by "Deselect all."

NORMAL AND EXTENDED SELECTION MODES

The DOS 5.0 Shell supports two different methods of selecting files, called the *Normal* and *Extended Selection Modes*. When the keyboard is in Extended Selection Mode, "ADD" appears in the bottom right corner of the display screen, as shown in Figure 5-32. This mode is toggled on or off by pressing and holding the Shift key, then pressing the F8 key once. When the keyboard is operating in Normal Mode, "ADD" is not displayed. If you use the Normal Selection Mode, the current highlighted file is automatically selected for an operation and cannot be unselected. However, Extended Selection Mode supports selecting more than one file at a time for an operation. If you use Extended Selection Mode, the file currently highlighted is selected by pressing the spacebar. This file remains selected when the cursor is repositioned to another file. However, if more than one file is selected and you switch to Normal Selection Mode, all of the files currently selected are deselected in the event of any other file selections. Mouse operations support the Extended Selection Mode when you press and hold the Ctrl key while selecting files. Once again, if you release the Ctrl key and select another file, the current file is selected and all other files are unselected.

The DOS 5.0 Shell supports Range Selection of contiguous files in both Extended and Normal Selection Modes. When you use the keyboard, press and hold the Shift key, while you use the Up or Down Arrow key to select a contiguous list of files for an operation. The mouse functions in the same manner, while you press and hold the Shift key move the mouse pointer over the contiguous files that you want to select. You can combine Range and Extended Selection Mode in a single file list.

> **Note:** The DOS 4.0 Shell supports only the Extended Selection Mode. This mode is always active and does not require you to press Shift+F8. In addition, the mouse always supports multiple selections and does not require you to press and hold the Ctrl key while selecting multiple files. Therefore, the ADD message is not displayed.

All remaining lessons in this chapter use the Extended Selection Mode.

KEYBOARD

 Press Shift+F8 to toggle Extended Selection Mode on.

The Extended Selection Mode ADD message appears on the bottom right corner of the display screen, as shown in Figure 5-32. You are now ready to select FASTOPEN for deletion.

KEYBOARD

 Using the Tab (|←) key, switch to the files in the current directory panel area.

 Using the up and down arrows, highlight the FASTOPEN program.

 Press the spacebar once to mark or select FASTOPEN.

MOUSE

 Point at FASTOPEN.

 Click the Mouse Select button once.

Notice that a mark has appeared to the left of the filename. If your screen is displayed in text mode, a > is used. If your screen is displayed in graphics mode, the icon changes color. (See Figure 5-32.)

If you select a wrong file, it may be deselected by selecting the same file

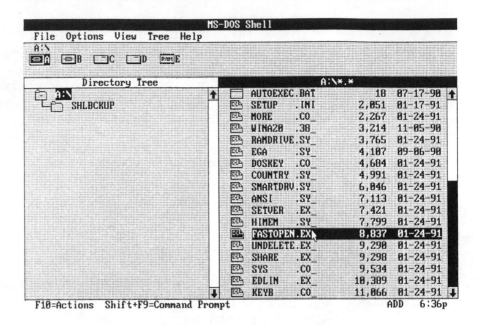

Figure 5-32
FASTOPEN Selected
for Deletion

again using the same method. You were instructed to select the FASTOPEN program; this was wrong. You need to deselect FASTOPEN, and select COUNTRY and FDISK.

KEYBOARD

 Press the spacebar while highlighting FASTOPEN.

 Highlight and mark the COUNTRY program with the spacebar.

 Highlight and mark the FDISK program with the spacebar.

MOUSE

 Point at FASTOPEN.

 Press and hold the Ctrl key, then click the Mouse Select button once.

 Point at COUNTRY.

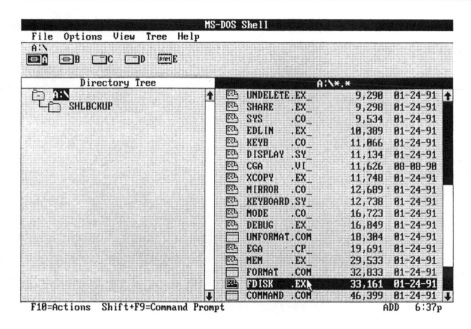

Figure 5-33
COUNTRY and FDISK
Selected for Deletion

 Click the Mouse Select button once.

 Point at FDISK.

 Press and hold the Ctrl key, then click the Mouse Select button once.

The FASTOPEN program is deselected, while COUNTRY and FDISK are selected. (See Figure 5-33.)

> **Note:** There is no limit to the number of different files that may be selected for operation.

Once the desired files are selected, you can begin the deletion.

KEYBOARD OR MOUSE

 Switch to the menu bar.

 Select the File pull-down panel.

 Select Delete.

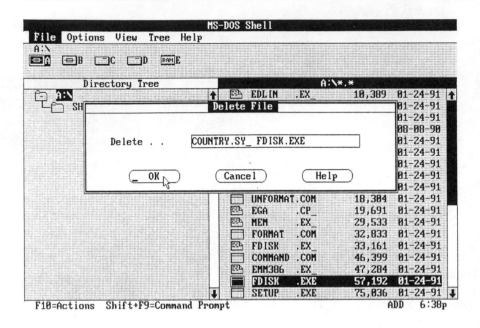

Figure 5-34
Delete File Pop-Up
Panel Display

> **Note:** You can press the Del key once to directly initiate the file Delete command without displaying the File pull-down panel.

The File pull-down panel is removed and the Delete File pop-up panel appears. (See Figure 5-34.)

The files selected for deletion appear in the Delete File pop-up panel. If these files are correct, you will accept the panel. Any marked filenames that appear as default values in an entry field such as this may not be changed.

When you are using DOS 4.0, entry fields use the direction symbols. You may scroll the information in the field by using the respective left or right arrows, or by placing the mouse pointer on top of this direction symbol and pressing the Select button. This type of entry field provides a convenient method of entering a large number of characters without cluttering the screen. All of the information you enter in the field is processed as expected.

KEYBOARD OR MOUSE

 Press Enter (↵).

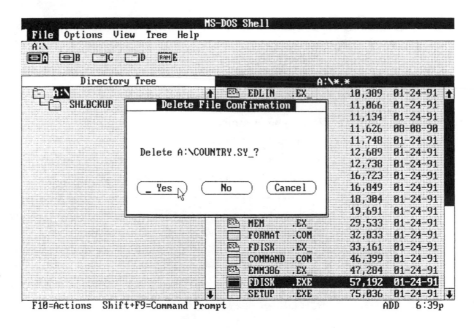

Figure 5-35
Delete File Confirmation Pop-Up Panel Display

The Delete File pop-up panel is removed and the Delete File confirmation pop-up panel appears. (See Figure 5-35.) This panel is similar to the Delete Directory panel. You will chose the option to delete for both files.

KEYBOARD OR MOUSE

 Select "Yes" to delete this file.

The Deleting file field changes to FDISK.

 Select "Yes" to delete this file.

The Delete File Confirmation pop-up panel, COUNTRY, and FDISK filenames are removed from the screen.
You have deleted files!

LESSON 8: COPY A FILE

When you complete this lesson, you will be able to copy files using the Shell.

This is perhaps the single most popular Shell command. In this lesson, you will copy a series of files from the root directory of the DOS Install diskette to the SHLBCKUP subdirectory that you created in an earlier lesson.

> **Note:** If you use DOS 4.0, you should use the 4201.CPI file in place of the MORE.CO file and the 5202.CPI file in place of the SETUP.INI file throughout the remaining lessons.

KEYBOARD OR MOUSE

 Display the files on the copy of the DOS Install 1 diskette in drive A:.

 Select the following files in the root directory:

1. AUTOEXEC.BAT

2. FORMAT COM

 Switch to the menu bar.

 Select the File pull-down panel.

 Select the Copy command in the File pull-down panel.

The Copy File pop-up panel is displayed with a list of the selected files and a prompt for the target directory. (See Figure 5-36.)

KEYBOARD OR MOUSE

 Position the cursor on the To: entry field.

 Type A:\SHLBCKUP. (See Figure 5-37.)

 Press Enter (↵).

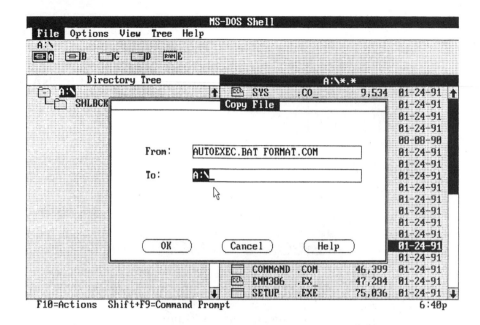

Figure 5-36
Copy File List Panel
Display

The Copy File list panel is removed and the Copy File in process panel is displayed. The From: field is updated as each file is copied. The panel is removed when the list of files is copied.

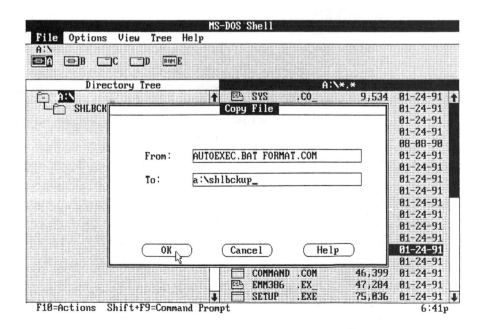

Figure 5-37
Specification of the
To Field

> **Note:** It is possible to change the target name of a file during the copy process. This can be accomplished when only one file is marked. The new filename is typed into the To field after the target path (e.g., To: A:\SHLBCKUP\FILENAME.NEW_>). This allows you to copy and rename a file in the same directory (e.g., CONFIG.SYS to CONFIG.BAK).

There is a simpler method available for you to specify the target name of the file copy. This method uses a special feature that is activated in the File Options pop-up panel.

KEYBOARD OR MOUSE

 Switch to the menu bar.

 Select the Options pull-down panel.

The Options pull-down panel is displayed. Notice the Select Across Directories option.

SELECT ACROSS DIRECTORIES

When the option to select across directories is not active, any files you mark are automatically unmarked when you display another directory's files. This prevents you from selecting another directory as the target for a copy. When Select Across Directories is activated, you are able to mark files for some operation on one directory and then display another directory's files without the Shell automatically unmarking your selected files. This is one technique used with the mouse to select a target directory for a file copy or move operation without having to type the target path.

> **Note:** When using the DOS 4.0 Shell, "Select Across Directories" is displayed when you select "File Options" in the Options pull-down panel. Highlight the selection, then press the spacebar to toggle on. You must reset this option each time you start the Shell.

KEYBOARD OR MOUSE

 Highlight "Select Across Directories."

 Press Enter (↵).

The Options pull-down panel is removed. You are now ready to perform another copy of files.

KEYBOARD OR MOUSE

 Mark the following files in the root directory:

1. MORE   CO

2. SETUP   INI

> **Note:** If you use DOS 4.0, the MORE.CO_ and SETUP.INI files do not exist. You should use the 4201.CPI file in place of the MORE.CO_ file and the 5202.CPI file in place of SETUP.INI file throughout the remaining lessons.

KEYBOARD OR MOUSE

 Switch to the Directory Tree panel area.

 Display the SHLBCKUP directory.

Figure 5-38 shows the SHLBCKUP directory.

KEYBOARD OR MOUSE

 Switch to the file list area.

 Switch to the menu bar.

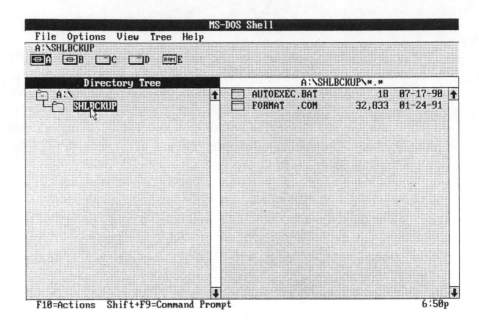

Figure 5-38
SHLBCKUP Directory
Display

     Select the File pull-down panel.

     Select Copy.

The File pull-down panel is removed and the Copy File list panel is displayed. Notice that both the files you selected and the target directory are already displayed. (See Figure 5-39.) This option works only when files are already located in the destination directory. The file operations are only active when the file list is the last active panel area.

KEYBOARD OR MOUSE

     Press or select Enter (↵).

You have copied multiple files! (See Lesson 16 for other techniques used to copy and move files.)

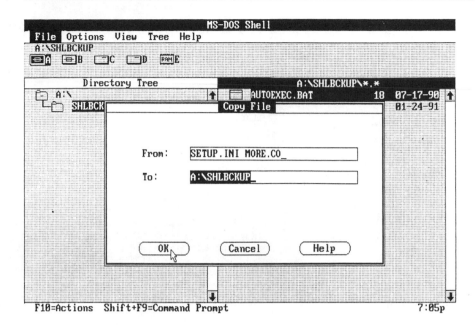

Figure 5-39
Completed Source
and Target

LESSON 9: FIND A FILE

When you complete this lesson, you will be able to find a file anywhere on a disk.

The Shell provides a special screen called the All Files view. When you use DOS 4.0, the All Files list is called the System File list. This screen displays all of a disk's files in one list regardless of the directory structure. It is a very powerful feature! Some of its uses include the ability to quickly locate all duplicate files on a disk for deletion, to copy all files on a disk to another disk for backup, and to locate a specific file or group of files.

In this lesson, you will use the All Files selection to locate all copies of the SETUP.INI program.

KEYBOARD OR MOUSE

 Switch to the menu bar.

```
                         MS-DOS Shell
     File  Options  View  Tree  Help
    A:\
    ═╗A  ═╗B  □C  □D  RAM E

                                    *.*
                 ┌────┐  AUTOEXEC.BAT    18   07-17-90   11:88a ↑
    File         ┌────┐  AUTOEXEC.BAT    18   07-17-90   11:88a
      Name : AUTOEXEC.BAT  SETUP   .INI   2,851  01-17-91    4:28p
      Attr :    ...a       SETUP   .INI   2,851  01-17-91    4:28p
    Selected     A    C    MORE    .CO_   2,267  01-24-91    6:50p
      Number:    2    1    MORE    .CO_   2,267  01-24-91    6:50p
      Size  : 80,558       WINA28  .38    3,214  11-85-90    1:37p
    Directory              RAMDRIVE.SY_   3,765  01-24-91    7:21p
      Name : \             EGA     .SY    4,107  09-86-90    5:81p
      Size :   572,943     DOSKEY  .CO_   4,684  01-24-91    6:18p
      Files:        34     SMARTDRV.SY_   6,846  01-24-91    7:21p
    Disk                   ANSI    .SY_   7,113  01-24-91    7:89p
      Name : DISK 1        SETVER  .EX_   7,421  01-24-91    7:81p
      Size :   730,112     HIMEM   .SY_   7,799  01-24-91    7:14p
      Avail:    94,208     FASTOPEN.EX_   8,837  01-24-91    6:21p
      Files:        38     UNDELETE.EX_   9,290  01-24-91    6:14p
      Dirs :         2     SHARE   .EX_   9,290  01-24-91    7:83p
                           SYS     .CO_   9,534  01-24-91    7:86p ↓
     F10=Actions  Shift+F9=Command Prompt                    7:86p
```

Figure 5-40
All Files View Display

 Select the View pull-down panel.

 Select "All Files."

The All Files screen is displayed. (See Figure 5-40.)
Two different techniques can be used to locate the desired file. The first is to sort the files by name and then scroll down the list until you find the desired file(s).

KEYBOARD OR MOUSE

 Switch to the menu bar.

 Select the Options pull-down panel.

 Select "File Display Options."

Figure 5-41 shows the Display Options pop-up panel.

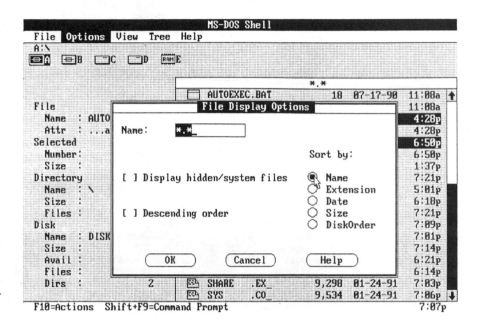

Figure 5-41
Display Options Pop-
Up Panel Display

KEYBOARD OR MOUSE

 Sort the files by name.

 Press Enter (↵) to accept the sort order.

The Display Options pop-up panel is removed and the files are sorted by name. Now, let's find the file.

KEYBOARD OR MOUSE

 Switch to the file list panel area.

 Scroll the file list until you highlight the first SETUP.INI file.

If you are using DOS 5.0 and the file list area is active, you can press a valid filename character to immediately display the next file that begins with the same character. When the last file in the list that begins with the character pressed is highlighted, the Shell starts at the beginning of the file list.

```
┌──────────────────────────────────────────────────────────────────┐
│                          MS-DOS Shell                              │
│  File  Options  View  Tree  Help                                   │
│ A:\                                                                │
│ ▣A   ▣B   ▢C   ▢D   RAM▣                                          │
│                                          *.*                       │
│  File                  ▤ KEYBOARD.SY_   12,738  01-24-91   7:19p ↑ │
│   Name  : SETUP.INI    ▤ MEM     .EX_   29,533  01-24-91   6:45p   │
│   Attr  : ...a         ▤ MIRROR  .CO_   12,689  01-24-91   6:13p   │
│  Selected      A   C   ▤ MODE    .CO_   16,723  01-24-91   6:49p   │
│   Number:      1   1   ▤ MORE    .CO_    2,267  01-24-91   6:58p   │
│   Size  :     78,291   ▤ MORE    .CO_    2,267  01-24-91   6:58p   │
│  Directory             ▤ RAMDRIVE.SY_    3,765  01-24-91   7:21p   │
│   Name  : \            ▤ SETUP   .EXE   75,036  01-24-91   8:14p   │
│   Size  :    572,943   ▤ SETUP   .INI    2,051  01-17-91   4:28p   │
│   Files :         34   ▤ SETUP   .INI    2,051  01-17-91   4:28p   │
│  Disk                  ▤ SETVER  .EX_    7,421  01-24-91   7:01p   │
│   Name  : DISK 1       ▤ SHARE   .EX_    9,298  01-24-91   7:03p   │
│   Size  :    730,112   ▤ SMARTDRV.SY_    6,846  01-24-91   7:21p   │
│   Avail :     94,208   ▤ SYS     .CO_    9,534  01-24-91   7:06p   │
│   Files :         38   ▤ UNDELETE.EX_    9,298  01-24-91   6:14p   │
│   Dirs  :          2   ▢ UNFORMAT.COM   18,304  01-24-91   6:13p   │
│                        ▤ WINA20  .38     3,214  11-05-90   1:37p   │
│                        ▤ XCOPY   .EX_   11,748  01-24-91   7:08p ↓ │
│  F18=Actions  Shift+F9=Command Prompt                      7:08p   │
└──────────────────────────────────────────────────────────────────┘
```

Figure 5-42
Highlight First
SETUP.INI File

Because the list is sorted by name, all occurrences of SETUP.INI appear together. Notice that the first copy of SETUP.INI is located in the root, as indicated by the drive and current directory display. (See Figure 5-42.)

KEYBOARD OR MOUSE

Press the down arrow once to highlight the second SETUP.INI file.

Notice that this copy of SETUP.INI is located in the SHLBCKUP directory, as indicated by the drive and current directory display.

In some cases, the disk being displayed in the All Files view contains hundreds or thousands of files. Even with the list sorted by name, it would be time-consuming to search for a specific file. The Shell provides a special feature that eliminates the need to visually search the file list for a specific file.

KEYBOARD OR MOUSE

Switch to the menu bar.

Select the Options pull-down panel.

 Select "File Display Options."

The Options pull-down panel is removed and the Display Options pop-up panel appears. (See Figure 5-41.)

The Name: field can be used to specify the type of files to be displayed in the file list area. This entry field supports use of the traditional DOS filename and wildcard conventions. For example, entering M*.* would display all files that begin with a letter M.

> **Note:** When you use DOS 4.0, several advanced Shell filename search features are included for your convenience. For example, entering the tilde character in the first position of ~M*.* displays all files *except* those that contain a letter M as the first character. In addition, entering *M*.* displays all filenames that contain a letter M somewhere in the filename. These special features are not supported when you use the DOS Command Prompt.

KEYBOARD OR MOUSE

 Position the cursor on the Name: entry field.

 Type SETUP.INI.

 Press Enter (⏎).

The Display Options panel is removed and the file list area is updated with only files that match the Name: field. (See Figure 5-43.) You have used both techniques to find all occurrences of a file!

Before you continue, make sure that you change the Display Options Name: field back to *.*.

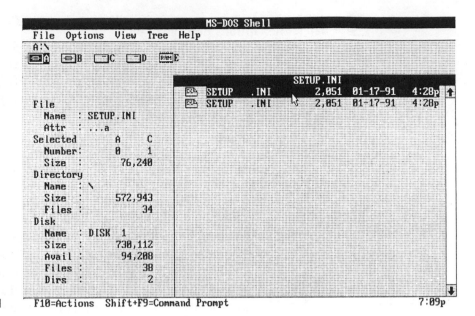

Figure 5-43
SETUP.INI Displayed
Using the Name Field

LESSON 10: SEARCH FOR FILES

When you complete this lesson, you will be able to find a file anywhere on a disk.

DOS 4.0 does not support this function. If you are using DOS 4.0, we recommend that you skip to the next lesson.

The DOS 5.0 Shell supports an additional file search function that displays all of a disk's files in one list regardless of the directory structure. This function is similar to the All Files view; however, the drive and disk information is not displayed.

KEYBOARD OR MOUSE

 Switch to the menu bar.

 Select the File pull-down panel.

 Select Search.

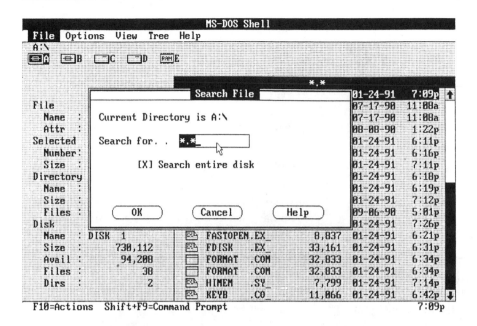

Figure 5-44
Search File Pop-Up
Panel Display

The Search File pop-up panel is displayed. (See Figure 5-44.)

You can optionally search the entire disk or only the current directory. In this lesson, you will use the Search File selection to locate all copies of the SETUP.INI program across the entire disk.

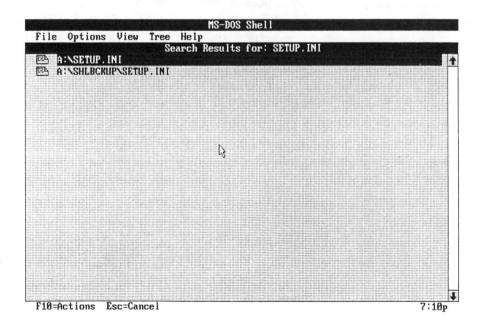

Figure 5-45
Search Results Pop-
Up Panel Display

KEYBOARD OR MOUSE

 Switch to "Search for."

 Type SETUP.INI.

 Press Enter (↵).

Figure 5-45 shows the Search Results display. Notice that every occurrence of SETUP.INI displays the entire file path. You can mark and perform file operations on any of the files appearing in the Search Results list.

You have used the file Search feature to find all occurrences of a file!

LESSON 11: SHOW SHELL INFORMATION

When you complete this lesson, you will be able to display information concerning your computer.

The Shell's All Files view screen provides an extensive display of disk, file, and directory information. (See Figure 5-46.)

The File information includes display of the current highlighted filename, extension, and attribute. The file attribute field may contain any combination of four different attributes. (See Figure 5-47.)

The "Selected" drive information identifies the drive image(s) currently stored in the Shell's memory. The total number of files marked for operation

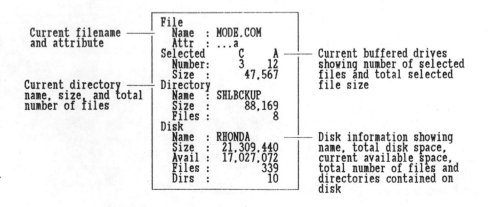

Figure 5-46
Shell Information Display

```
          Read Only File                    Hidden File
┌─────────────────────────┐      ┌─────────────────────────┐
│File                     │      │File                     │
│   Name : MODE.COM       │      │   Name : MODE.COM       │
│   Attr : r...           │      │   Attr : .h..           │
            System File                     Archived File
┌─────────────────────────┐      ┌─────────────────────────┐
│File                     │      │File                     │
│   Name : MODE.COM       │      │   Name : MODE.COM       │
│   Attr : ..s.           │      │   Attr : ...a           │
```

Figure 5-47
Current File Attribute
Information

```
       Single Drive Buffer              Multiple Drive Buffers
│Selected          A              │Selected       C    A
│   Number:       12              │   Number:     3   12
│   Size  :   47.567             │   Size  :   56.890
```

Figure 5-48
Current Buffered
Drive Information

```
┌────────────────────────
│Disk
│   Name  : RHONDA
│   Size  :   21,309,440
│   Avail :   17,027,072
│   Files :          339
│   Dirs  :           10
```

Figure 5-49
Current Displayed
Disk Information

is displayed for each buffer image. (See Figure 5-48.) In addition, the cumulative size of marked files for both buffered drive images is displayed. Use this information to determine the amount of disk space freed when deleting files, or the amount of space required at a copy target.

The Disk fields contain information about the current displayed buffer image. This includes the volume name (or identification) assigned to the disk during formatting, total size capacity, total space currently available, and total number of files and directories on the disk. (See Figure 5-49.)

The Shell's information display appearing in the All Files view screen is updated as you select files for operation. The same information may be viewed in the Single File List, Dual File List, and Program/File Lists by selecting "Options" from the menu bar and then selecting "Show Information."

KEYBOARD OR MOUSE

 Switch to the menu bar.

 Select the View pull-down panel.

 Select "Dual File List."

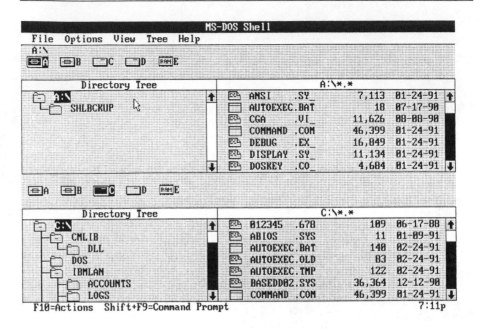

Figure 5-50
Dual File List Display

The View pull-down panel is removed and the Dual File List screen is displayed. (See Figure 5-50.)

The Dual File List screen is capable of simultaneously displaying two different drives or two views of the same drive. This screen is used primarily to compare file lists in different drive directories. The Shell's information pop-up panel displays information for the current drive panel area.

KEYBOARD OR MOUSE

 Switch to the upper Directory Tree panel area.

 Switch to the menu bar.

 Select the Options pull-down panel.

 Select "Show Information."

The Options pull-down panel is removed and the Show Information panel is displayed. (See Figure 5-51.)

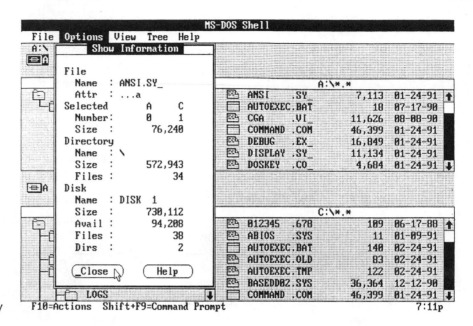

Figure 5-51
Show Information
Pop-Up Panel Display

Since this is a noninteractive pop-up panel, you must remove the Show Information pop-up before continuing to interact with the File List.

KEYBOARD OR MOUSE

 Press or select "Close."

The Show Information pop-up panel is removed.

> **Note:** You may display the lower Directory Tree information by switching to the lower Directory Tree before displaying the information panel.

You have displayed the Shell's information panel!

LESSON 12: VIEW A FILE

When you complete this lesson, you will be able to display the contents of a file.

The Shell's File View function supports the display of a file's contents. Only one file may be marked for viewing at a time.

> **Note:** You may not change the information in the file using this option. You may only view it.

KEYBOARD OR MOUSE

Switch to the file list panel area.

Select AUTOEXEC.BAT.

Switch to the menu bar.

Select the File pull-down panel.

Select "View File Contents."

The file view screen appears with the AUTOEXEC.BAT file contents displayed in ASCII. (See Figure 5-52.) The DOS 5.0 Shell is enhanced to display more data on each screen page. In addition, you can now switch between ASCII and HEX display modes from the View pull-down panel in the View File Contents menu bar.

The contents of the file may also be viewed in hexadecimal format. This format is provided to view non-ASCII file contents, such as an executable program. You may toggle back and forth between the ASCII and hexadecimal displays by pressing the F9 function key.

> **Note:** Whenever you toggle between the hexadecimal and ASCII modes, the file display is reinitialized to the top of the file.

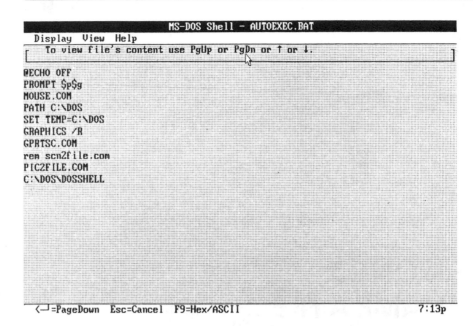

Figure 5-52
AUTOEXEC.BAT Contents in ASCII

KEYBOARD OR MOUSE

 Press or select F9 to display the AUTOEXEC.BAT file in hexadecimal.

Figure 5-53
AUTOEXEC.BAT Contents in HEX

Figure 5-53 shows the contents of the AUTOEXEC.BAT file in hexadecimal format.

When you are viewing a large file, you may press the PgDn or PgUp keys to quickly browse the contents of the file.

KEYBOARD OR MOUSE

 Select Esc to cancel view.

You have viewed a file's contents!

LESSON 13: RENAME A FILE

When you complete this lesson, you will be able to rename files using the Shell.

The same Rename command is used for both directory and file operations. If the file list is the last active panel area, a file rename is assumed. The Rename command supports the ability to select more than one file at a time to rename. In this lesson, you will rename the ANSI file to A.SYS.

> **Note:** When you use DOS 4.0 and Rename is chosen with a file marked, the Shell assumes that you are performing a file rename. If no files are marked, the Shell assumes that you are renaming a directory.

KEYBOARD OR MOUSE

 Display the root as the current directory.

 Switch to the file list panel area.

 Select ANSI.

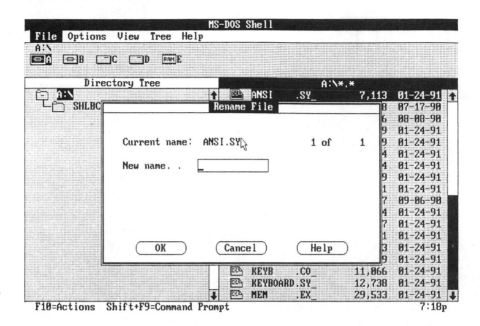

Figure 5-54
Rename File Pop-Up
Panel Display

 Switch to the menu bar.

 Select the File pull-down panel.

 Select "Rename."

The File pull-down panel is removed and the Rename File pop-up panel appears. (See Figure 5-54.)

The Rename File pop-up panel displays the current filename and prompts for the new name. Only valid DOS filename characters may be used.

KEYBOARD OR MOUSE

 Type A.SYS.

 Press Enter (↵).

The Rename File pop-up panel is removed and the new A.SYS filename appears in the file list in place of ANSI.

You have renamed a file!

LESSON 14: PRINT A FILE

When you complete this lesson, you will be able to print files using the Shell.

The Shell's Print command sends or submits selected files to the DOS Background Print function. If you do not have a printer configured in your system, you will not be able to use this Shell command. In this case, skip to the next lesson.

If a printer is configured on your system, turn it on. In this lesson, you will select AUTOEXEC.BAT and SETUP.INI files for printing.

KEYBOARD OR MOUSE

 Switch to the file list panel area.

 Select AUTOEXEC.BAT and SETUP.INI.

 Switch to the menu bar.

 Select the File pull-down panel.

 Select "Print."

Note: If the Print command cannot be selected, you must add PRINT.COM to your AUTOEXEC.BAT file or run PRINT.COM before using the Shell's Print command. Or, you can switch to the Shell Command Prompt by pressing Shift+F9 and then issue the PRINT command without modifying your AUTOEXEC file.

The File pull-down panel is removed and the Print File pop-up panel appears.

Each selected file is submitted to the DOS Background Print facility for printing. The Print File pop-up panel is automatically removed if all of the files are successfully submitted. If you exceed the number of files that the

PRINT queue can hold at once, an error message appears. You can cancel submission of the remaining files or wait until enough files in the queue are printed, then submit the remainder. If your printer is properly configured on your system, the submitted files will immediately begin to print.

You have submitted files to the printer!

LESSON 15: START A PROGRAM

When you complete this lesson, you will be able to start a program from the Shell's File List.

In Chapter 4, you learned how to start programs from the Shell Start Programs screen and the Command Prompt. In this lesson, you will learn three new techniques for starting programs from the Shell's file list. For purposes of this lesson, you will start the MEM.EXE program located on your working DOS diskette.

The first way to start programs from the file list is accomplished by highlighting the file to run in the file list and then pressing Enter (↵).

If your display is in graphics mode, you may have noticed the two different icons that appear in the file list. Each file list entry is preceded by one of these icons to indicate if it is a data file or a program. The icon appearing in front of the AUTOEXEC.BAT and COMMAND.COM files is the one used to indicate that the entry is a program. The icon appearing in front of the SETUP.INI file indicates that the file contains data. (See Figure 5-55.)

In this lesson, you will start the MEM.EXE program from your fixed disk or working diskettes.

KEYBOARD OR MOUSE

 Locate the MEM.EXE file on your disk.

 Switch to the file list panel area.

 Scroll the file list until you highlight MEM.EXE.

```
┌─────────────────────────────────────────────┐
│                 C:\PE2\*.*                  │
├─────────────────────────────────────────────┤
│  🗐  MOVE      .SHL      2,334   02-18-91  ▲│
│  ▭  PE2       .EXE     76,240   03-30-87   │
│  🗐  PE2       .HLP      7,754   08-16-85   │
│  🗐  PE2       .PRO      4,767   05-27-88   │
│  🗐  PEZLONG   .PRO      7,256   08-16-85   │
│  🗐  PREPCP    .SHL        672   02-24-91   │
│  🗐  PRINT     .SHL      1,779   02-18-91   │
│  🗐  PROMPT    .SHL        552   02-18-91   │
│  🗐  PRTDIR    .SHL        538   02-18-91  ▼│
└─────────────────────────────────────────────┘
```

Figure 5-55
Program and Data
File Icons

KEYBOARD

 Press Enter (↵).

MOUSE

 Point at the MEM.EXE text and double click.

The display screen is cleared and the MEM.EXE program begins execution. When MEM.EXE has completed the display of system memory, control returns to the Shell. A prompt is displayed at the screen bottom, allowing you to view the screen prior to displaying the screen you left in the Shell. (See Figure 5-56.)

KEYBOARD OR MOUSE

 Press Enter (↵).

The Shell screen that you left is redisplayed.

Figure 5-56
MEM.EXE Program
Display

```
655360 bytes total memory
654336 bytes available
538832 largest executable program size
393216 bytes total extended memory
393216 bytes available extended memory
Press Enter (<─┘) to return to File List.
```

ASSOCIATE PROGRAMS AND DATA FILES

The second way to start a program from the File List is accomplished by creating an association between a program and data filename extension. You must first select the program(s) to be associated.

KEYBOARD OR MOUSE

 Switch to the file list panel area.

 Locate the QBASIC.COM program on your fixed disk or working DOS diskette.

 Mark the QBASIC.COM program for operation.

> **Note:** When you use DOS 4.0, you will mark BASIC.COM.

 Switch to the menu bar.

 Select the File pull-down panel.

 Select "Associate."

The Associate File pop-up panel is displayed. The QBASIC.COM program is shown as the program, and the cursor is positioned in the Extensions entry field. (See Figure 5-57.) This field supports the definition of 20 different filename extensions. Each extension entered is associated with the filename displayed in the panel. Once the association is complete, any attempt to start a data file with the same extension will automatically invoke the associated program. You will associate one filename extension with the QBASIC.COM program.

KEYBOARD OR MOUSE

 Type BAS.

 Press Enter (↵).

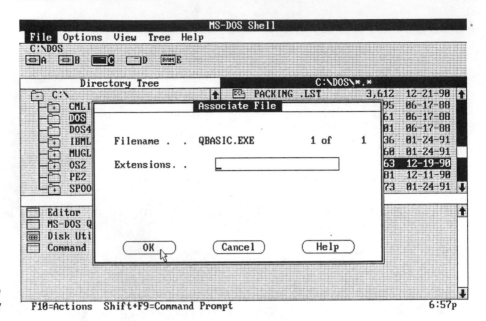

Figure 5-57
Associate Prompt File
Pop-Up Panel Display

> **Note:** A single space should appear between each extension entered (e.g., DAT BAT DOC). Do not include the traditional extension period. Up to 20 different extensions and/or filenames may be associated. For example, 10 different programs could each be associated with two unique extensions, or 20 different programs with one unique extension, and so forth.

The Associate File pop-up panel is removed and QBASIC will be automatically executed whenever a BASIC program with a .BAS extension is executed. The BASIC program will be passed as a parameter.

You will start a BASIC program to demonstrate how file association works.

KEYBOARD OR MOUSE

 Locate the MONEY.BAS or MORTGAGE.BAS program on your disk.

KEYBOARD

 Highlight MONEY.BAS or MORTGAGE.BAS.

 Press Enter (⏎).

MOUSE

 Point at MONEY.BAS or MORTGAGE.BAS.

 Double click the Mouse Select button.

At this point, it is not necessary to actually start the MONEY.BAS or MORTGAGE.BAS program. However, it is important to understand that this option may be applied to any program such as an editor or spreadsheet with unique data file extensions. (See the next lesson for other techniques used to start programs.)

LESSON 16: DIRECT MOUSE MANIPULATION

When you complete this lesson, you will be able to use the mouse to quickly and effectively start a program with a data file, move files on the same drive, or copy files to another drive without using the intermediate menu bar pull-down panels. This method of using the mouse pointer to drag and drop files is called *direct manipulation*. This is one of the most powerful enhancements made to DOS 5.0. Your system must have a mouse to complete this lesson. If you do not have a mouse, we recommend that you skip to the next lesson.

DOS 4.0 does not support this function. If you are using DOS 4.0, we recommend that you skip to the next lesson.

START PROGRAMS USING DIRECT MANIPULATION

In earlier lessons, you learned a quick way to start a program with the mouse by double clicking the Mouse Select button while the mouse pointer is on top of the file. This form of direct manipulation is expanded in DOS 5.0 to allow you to drag and drop a data file on top of an executable program. The data file is passed as a parameter to the executable program. You will use the MONEY.BAS file used in the last lesson.

MOUSE

 Point at the MONEY.BAS program on your disk.

 Press and continue holding the Mouse Select button.

 Move the mouse pointer or drag the file away from the program name on the display.

Notice that the mouse pointer has changed its shape. (See Figures 5-58 and 5-59.) Whenever you are dragging a file, the mouse pointer will indicate that a direct manipulation operation is in process by changing the mouse pointer shape. As you move the mouse pointer around the screen, you may see the pointer change shapes several times. Whenever the mouse pointer is located over an area of the screen where you cannot drop the file(s) you are dragging, an invalid icon replaces the mouse pointer. Conversely, when the mouse pointer is over an area of the screen where the file(s) could be dropped, a valid icon replaces the mouse pointer. In addition, the status line

Figure 5-58
Graphics Mode
Direct Manipulation
Mouse Pointer
Shapes

Invalid Drop   Valid Document Drop   Valid Program Drop   Valid Multiple Drop

Figure 5-59
Text Mode Direct
Manipulation Mouse
Pointer Shapes

Invalid Drop   Valid Drop

at the bottom of the screen is updated to describe valid and invalid drops during the drag operation. It is important that you do not release the Mouse Select button until you are ready to perform the appropriate function. Once you release the Mouse Select button, the mouse pointer returns to normal and the direct manipulation is performed or canceled.

MOUSE

 Position the mouse pointer over QBASIC.COM.

 Release the Mouse Select button.

You may have to practice this several times to become proficient. When you are successful, a valid icon appears when the mouse pointer is on top of QBASIC.COM. Once you release the Mouse Select button, QBASIC.COM is executed with the MONEY.BAS program. You can use this same technique to start and pass a data file to the Editor.

MOVE FILES USING DIRECT MANIPULATION

DOS 5.0 supports another form of direct manipulation, which is used to move a file(s) from one directory to another on the same disk. This is very quick and easy to do with direct manipulation!

MOUSE

 Display a disk with multiple directories using the Single File view display.

 Point at a file in one directory on the disk.

 Press and continue holding the Mouse Select button.

 Drag the file to another directory displayed in the Directory Tree panel area.

 Release the Mouse Select button.

If a valid drop pointer is displayed, the file is immediately moved to the new directory. You can practice this again by moving the file back to the original directory.

COPY FILES USING DIRECT MANIPULATION

The last direct manipulation enhancement in DOS 5.0 supports the copy of a file from a directory on one disk drive to the current directory on another disk drive. This operation is very similar to the direct manipulation move operation that you just performed.

MOUSE

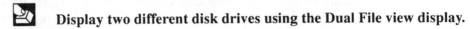 **Display two different disk drives using the Dual File view display.**

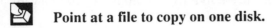 **Point at a file to copy on one disk.**

Press and continue holding the Mouse Select button.

Drag the file to the other disk drive displayed in the drive list area.

Release the Mouse Select button.

If a valid drop pointer is displayed, the file is immediately copied to the current directory on other drive's disk.

You have successfully started a program and moved and copied a file using direct manipulation!

You have completed the last lesson in this chapter. You should proceed with the next chapter for a better understanding of how to maintain and use the Program List in the Shell.

6 Performing Start Programs Maintenance

When you complete this chapter, you will be able to perform the following Shell operations:

1. Add a Program to a Group

2. Change a Program in DOS 5.0

3. Change a Program in DOS 4.0

4. Copy a Program in a Group

5. Delete a Program in a Group

6. Add a Group

7. Change a Group

8. Delete a Group

9. Reorder a Group

This series of lessons teaches the advanced program and group maintenance operations. In order to complete these lessons successfully, you must first complete the lessons in Chapter 4, "Basic Shell Operations."

LESSON 1: ADD A PROGRAM TO A GROUP

When you complete this lesson, you will be able to add programs to a group list.

Each of the selections appearing in the Disk Utilities subgroup was originally created using the commands available in the Program List menu bar pull-down panels located at the top of the display screen.

The Program List menu bar operates like the File List menu bar, as was discussed in the last chapter. However, some of the available commands are different. (See Figure 6-1.)

The File pull-down panel contains commands that are used to manipulate both programs and groups. (See Figure 6-2.)

> **Note:** If you use DOS 4.0, the Start, Add, and Change commands are called *Open, New,* and *Properties* in DOS 5.0. The lessons in this Chapter are oriented for DOS 5.0. If you are using DOS 4.0, you will need to substitute the proper commands to successfully complete the lessons in this chapter. Differences between DOS 5.0 and 4.0 are discussed as appropriate throughout the remaining lessons.

The Options, View, and Help pull-down panel commands perform the same functions explored in the File List lessons in the previous chapter. (See Figure 6-3.)

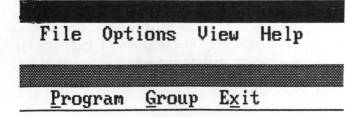

Figure 6-1
DOS 5.0 and 4.0 Program List Menu Bar Commands

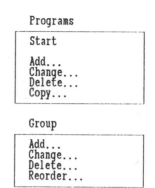

Figure 6-2
DOS 5.0 and 4.0 Program List Menu Bar Pull-Down Panels

The View pull-down panel contains commands that change the arrangement of the screen information. (See Figure 6-3.)

The DOS 5.0 Help pull-down panel replaces the DOS 4.0 F1=Help function key and provides an array of different help support, as discussed in Lesson 2 of Chapter 4. (See Figure 6-3.)

The DOS 4.0 Exit pull-down panel contains commands that return control to the Start Programs screen or allow you to continue with the File List.

In this lesson, you will add a new selection to the Disk Utilities subgroup to prepare a system diskette for use. This is similar to the Format command taught in Chapter 4. However, this selection will copy all of the necessary DOS programs to a diskette, enabling it to "boot," or start, the computer. This type of diskette is useful when you have a program that you wish to run from a diskette. Once the diskette is prepared using this new selection, you may copy a program on the diskette to run. This diskette can be configured to automatically start DOS and your program when it is inserted in drive A: and the computer is turned on.

Since you are adding a selection to the Disk Utilities menu, you must first display the menu. In general, the commands on the File or Program pull-down panel affect the currently displayed program or group list.

Figure 6-3
DOS 5.0 Options, View, and Help Pull-Down Panels

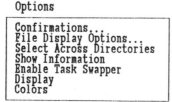

KEYBOARD OR MOUSE

 Display the Disk Utilities program list.

 Switch to the menu bar and select the File pull-down panel.

You may have noticed the three dots (...) that appear after some of the selections in the Shell. This indicates that another pop-up panel will be displayed after you make the selection.

KEYBOARD OR MOUSE

 Select "New."

The New Program Object pop-up panel is displayed. This panel allows you to indicate if the new entry is another group of programs or a program item to be executed when selected. (See Figure 6-4.)

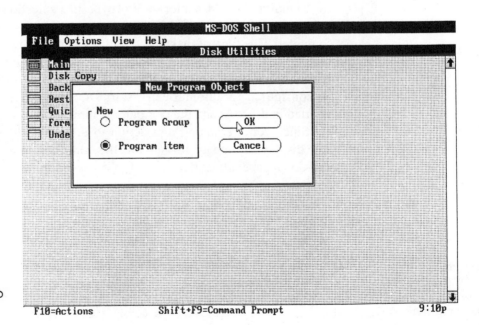

Figure 6-4
New Group or Program Object Pop-Up Panel Display

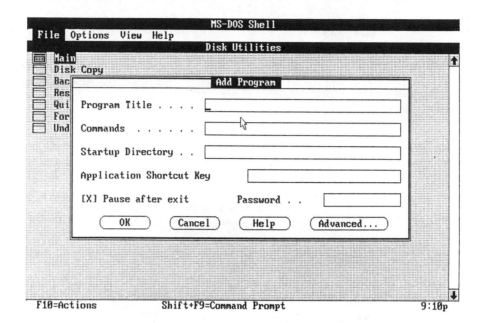

Figure 6-5
Add Program Entry
Field Panel

KEYBOARD OR MOUSE

 Select "Program Item."

 Select "OK."

A panel is displayed containing blank entry fields for the new selection, as shown in Figure 6-5. The first two entry fields in the panel are required. The remaining are optional.

> **Note:** Whenever multiple entry fields appear in the same panel, you press the Tab (|←) or Enter (↵) key to move between the fields.

The first entry field is the title that appears in the program list.

KEYBOARD OR MOUSE

 Type Format System Diskette in the Title entry field.

Press the Enter (⏎) key once to advance to the Commands field.

The second field is used to tell the Shell which commands are necessary to run your program when you select the title from the program list.

KEYBOARD OR MOUSE

 Type FORMAT A: /s in the Commands entry field.

At this point, you have completed all of the information necessary to create a new selection in the Disk Utilities subgroup. Now, you must save the information in the panel.

KEYBOARD OR MOUSE

 Save the panel.

The panel is automatically removed as soon as you save the information. In addition, the program list is updated to include your new entry. You may now use your new entry to prepare system diskettes that contain the components of DOS necessary to start the computer. Try it!

 You can stop at the end of any lesson in this tutorial. Otherwise, continue with the next lesson.

LESSON 2:
CHANGE A PROGRAM IN DOS 5.0

When you complete this lesson, you will be able to change a program in a group list.

The advanced features of program selection in DOS 5.0 are very different from DOS 4.0. If you are using DOS 4.0, skip to the next lesson.

In this lesson, you will change the Format System Diskette entry that you created in the last lesson. Currently, this program selection is set to format a diskette in drive A: only. You will add a prompt panel that will allow you to specify a different drive each time this entry is selected.

User-defined prompt panels are one of the Shell's most powerful features. These panels are used to pass variable information to the program commands. Each prompt panel is restricted to one title, instruction line, prompt, and entry field. Each program selection may have up to 9 different prompt panels. However, most program selections use no more than 3 prompt panels, depending on the type and amount of information being passed to the program.

KEYBOARD OR MOUSE

 Display the Disk Utilities program list.

KEYBOARD

 Using the up and down arrows, highlight the Format System Diskette selection. Be careful not to press Enter (⏎)!

MOUSE

 Point at the Format System Diskette selection and click once.

KEYBOARD OR MOUSE

 Switch to the menu bar and select the File pull-down panel.

 Select the Properties command.

The Add Program pop-up panel is displayed containing the information that you entered in the last lesson. (See Figure 6-6.)

You will now position the cursor on the Commands entry field.

KEYBOARD

 Press Tab (|←) or Enter (⏎) once.

```
                          MS-DOS Shell
    File  Options  View  Help
                          Disk Utilities
    Main
    Disk Copy
    Bac        ┌──────────── Add Program ────────────┐
    Res        │                                     │
    Qui        │  Program Title . . . . Format System Diskette │
    For        │                                     │
    Und        │  Commands  . . . . . . FORMAT A: /s_ │
               │                                     │
               │  Startup Directory . .              │
               │                                     │
               │  Application Shortcut Key           │
               │                                     │
               │  [X] Pause after exit    Password . .      │
               │                                     │
               │  ( OK )   ( Cancel )   ( Help )   ( Advanced... ) │
               └─────────────────────────────────────┘

    F10=Actions           Shift+F9=Command Prompt              9:11p
```

Figure 6-6
Change Program
Item Properties Entry
Field Panel

MOUSE

 Point at the text you entered in the Commands field and click once.

KEYBOARD OR MOUSE

 Press the Home key once, then use the left and right keyboard arrows to move the cursor to the drive letter appearing after the word FORMAT in the Commands field.

 Press the Delete key until the information appearing after the FOR-MAT command is erased.

In the simplest form, a prompt panel can be created by placing %1 in the Commands entry field at the desired position, as shown in Figure 6-7.

When the Format System Diskette selection is made with %1 in the Commands entry field, a default title and entry field appear. (See Figure 6-8.)

This prompt panel is general in its request for information. It would be better if the prompt panel specifically requested the type of information necessary to complete the action successfully. The Shell provides a series of

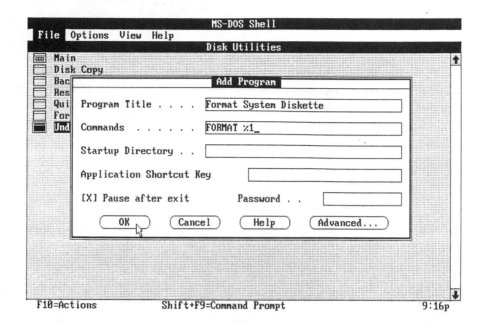

Figure 6-7
Simplest Form of a
Prompt Panel Com-
mand

advanced features that allow you to create custom prompt panels with user-defined titles, instructions, and prompts.

You can define up to nine different prompt panels in a single program selection using %n, where n is a whole number representing a variable from

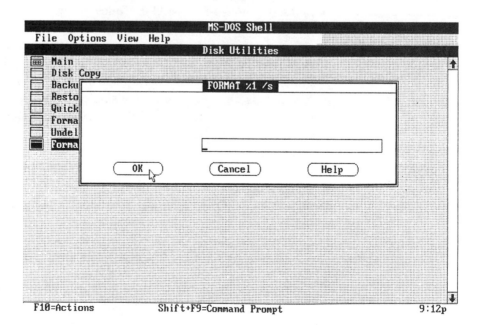

Figure 6-8
Pop-Up Display After
Format Selection

1 to 9. Only one variable may be associated per prompt panel entry field. The first occurrence of a variable in the Commands entry field displays a prompt panel. The same variable may appear subsequently within the same string of program startup commands. Once a variable has been assigned to a prompt panel, the information you enter in the resulting entry field is automatically associated with the variable. Wherever this variable appears in the string of commands, your data entry is automatically substituted. This may sound complicated at first; however, you will soon see how easy and powerful it is to use prompt panel variables.

Example: Commands . . FORMAT %1:

In this example, a prompt panel appears and allows you to specify the desired drive. If you type the letter B, then the Shell internally passes FOR-MAT B: to DOS for execution. Notice that a colon appears immediately after the prompt panel brackets. Once you accept the panel by pressing Enter (↵), the %1 is replaced by your data entry.

You can enter multiple commands for execution in the Commands entry field. These commands are executed in the order entered when the associated program item is selected. You must separate each command by a semicolon that has a leading and trailing space.

Example: Commands . . FORMAT %1: ; DIR %1:

In this example, you are prompted for a drive to format. If you type B and press Enter (↵), FORMAT B: followed by DIR B: is passed to DOS for execution. The prompt panel is displayed only on the first occurrence of %1; therefore, you will have to enter the drive letter only once. The diskette in drive B: will be formatted, then a directory listing will be displayed before you return to the Shell. This example demonstrates the ability to enter multiple commands for execution from a single program item selection. You may enter up to 255 characters of different commands (counting the separator semicolons for each menu selection).

Any DOS batch file command may be included in your program startup commands with the exception of the GOTO statement. In addition, if you use the batch file variable %n, n must be alphabetic. Remember that the Shell uses its own variables, which include %1 to %9. It is important not to confuse the Shell's variables with those that are processed directly by DOS. For example, if you included FOR %H IN (FILE1) DO DIR in your commands, %H would process as a DOS variable as expected. However, if FOR %1 IN (FILE1) DO DIR is used in your commands, the Shell would attempt to process the %1 variable, which would not produce the desired results.

Batch files may be placed directly in the program startup commands. However, you must use the DOS batch file CALL statement (e.g., CALL G.BAT). If you do not use the CALL statement, any additional commands appearing after the batch file in the startup commands will not be executed. You will immediately return to the Shell after the batch file is executed.

Example: Commands . . CALL A.BAT ; B.BAT ; DIR

In this example, A.BAT is executed as expected; however, control is immediately returned to the Shell after executing B.BAT without executing the DIR command.

In the remainder of this lesson, you will change the Format System Diskette selection to prompt the user with a customized prompt panel.

KEYBOARD OR MOUSE

 Type %1: /S after FORMAT in the Commands entry field.

 Select OK.

The Change Program Item Properties panel is removed and a new pop-up panel appears prompting you for the title, instructions, prompt text, and entry field default value. (See Figure 6-9.) The title is limited to 23 characters and the instruction line to 200 characters. The prompt message limit is 19 characters, and the default parameter limit is 64 characters.

KEYBOARD

 Type "Format System Diskette" in the Window Title entry field.

 Type "Insert blank diskette in drive to be formatted." in the Program Information entry field.

 Type "Enter drive letter" in the Prompt Message entry field.

 Type "A" in the Default Parameters entry field.

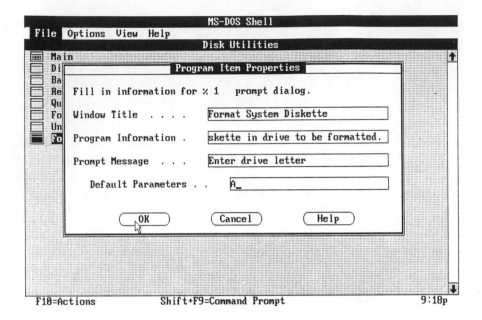

Figure 6-9
Advanced Prompt
Panel Commands

> **Note:** Special Default Parameter commands are available that
> allow you enhance your program item selections.
> - **%f** Automatically defaults to the last filename selected in the
>   file list.
> - **%l** Automatically defaults to the last filename or data typed
>   into the program item's prompt panel entry field.

Your entry field should appear similar to the one shown in Figure 6-9.
Once you complete the entry fields, you must save the panel information.

  KEYBOARD OR MOUSE

Select "OK" to save.

The panel is automatically removed as soon as you save the information.

KEYBOARD OR MOUSE

  Select "Format System Diskette."

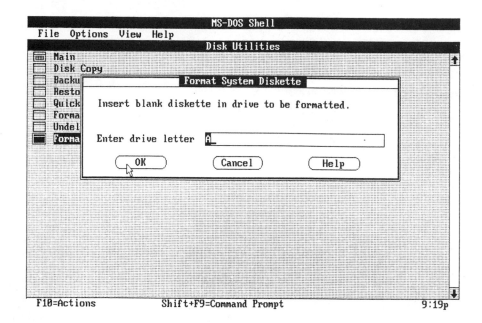

Figure 6-10
Program Pop-Up
Panel

The pop-up prompt panel should appear as shown in Figure 6-10.
You may now use your new program entry to prepare system diskettes that are initialized with DOS.

Warning: You must be careful when specifying the drive letter to format. Once the format process actually begins, all existing information on the disk is lost! Be especially careful not to inadvertently format your fixed disk.

The DOS 5.0 Program List is enhanced to support optional features that allow you to tailor the environment of each program item selection. When you add or change a program item selection, you can access these features from the Program Item Properties pop-up panel.

 KEYBOARD OR MOUSE

Display the Disk Utilities program list.

KEYBOARD

 Using the up and down arrows, highlight "Format System Diskette." Be careful not to press Enter (↵)!

MOUSE

 Point at "Format System Diskette" and click once.

KEYBOARD OR MOUSE

 Switch to the menu bar and select the File pull-down panel.

 Select the "Properties."

The Add Program pop-up panel is displayed containing the information that you entered in this last lesson. (See Figure 6-11.)

Before continuing, notice the additional entry fields that appear below the Commands entry field in Figure 6-11. You can use the Startup Directory field to define your program's beginning drive and directory. When you use this field, you can reset the starting drive and directory during the execution of your program item startup commands by using the multiple command option discussed in the next lesson. As a rule, you should always explicitly state the beginning drive and directory where your program is located.

You can use the Application Shortcut Key field to associate a hotkey combination with a program item selection. This hotkey immediately transfers control to the associated program item selection when the Task Swapper is enabled and the program item selection is active. When you press a valid hotkey, you can transfer control from the Shell or any application that supports swapping. You define the hotkey combination by pressing and holding Shift, Ctrl, or Alt, then pressing a character. When you define a valid key combination, it appears in the Application Shortcut Key entry field. The key combinations listed below are reserved and cannot be used as a hotkey combination.

Ctrl+H	Shift+Ctrl+H
Ctrl+I	Shift+Ctrl+I
Ctrl+M	Shift+Ctrl+M

Ctrl+[Shift+Ctrl+[

Ctrl+5 *   Shift+Ctrl+5 *

* 5   on the keypad only

In some cases, you may find it useful to use the Pause After Exit feature. This will allow you to see any messages displayed by the program item selection before you return to the Shell. Once you are satisfied with the operation of your program selection, you may want to toggle this feature off.

You can use the Password entry field to restrict access to program item selections appearing in the Program List. You will use this optional feature in Lesson 8.

Notice the Advanced properties selection that appears at the bottom of the panel in Figure 6-11. You will select this function to display the advanced environment commands associated with the Format System Diskette program item selection.

KEYBOARD OR MOUSE

 Select the Advanced button.

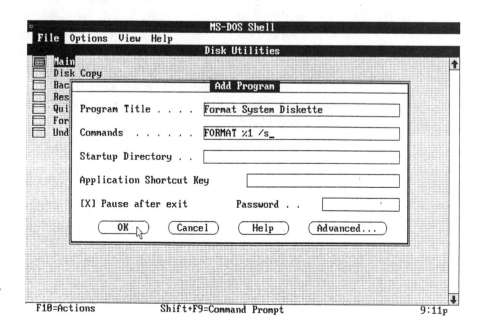

Figure 6-11
Change Program
Item Properties Entry
Field Panel

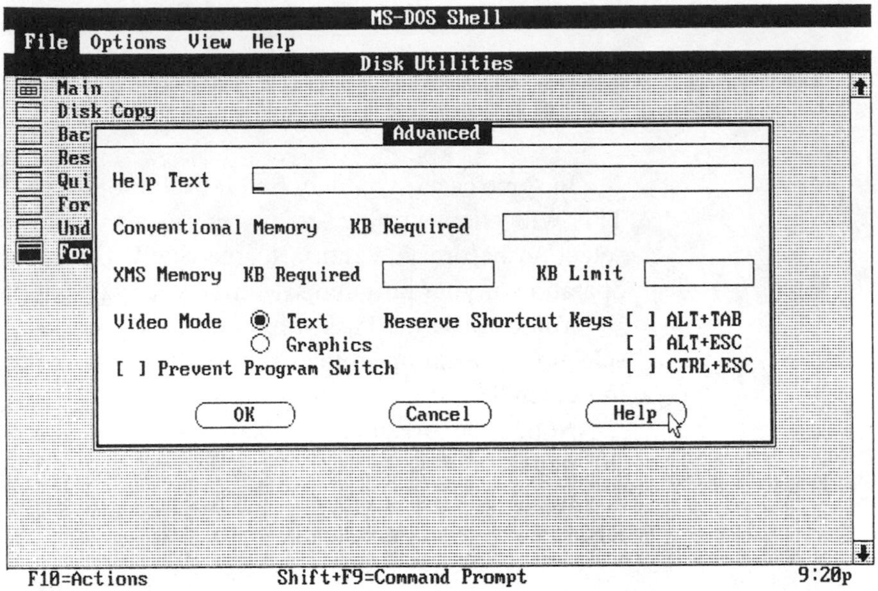

Figure 6-12
Advanced Program
Item Selection Pop-
Up Panel Display

The Add Program pop-up panel is removed, and the Advanced panel is displayed (as shown in Figure 6-12). All of the fields appearing in this panel are optional.

The Help Text entry field may contain up to 255 characters of help text. You may type any text you want in this field. We recommend that the text you enter discuss the purpose and operation of the associated selection. Both program and group entries share this same optional feature. Once the help is entered and saved, you can display it by highlighting the title and pressing F1. Your text is automatically wordwrapped and displayed without breaking words on different lines. However, you can start a new line by typing a carat followed by an M.

Example: Help Text [A new line appears where ^M is placed]

In this example, a new line will start wherever the ^M characters appear in the help text.

The Conventional Memory KB Required entry field is used to specify the minimum amount of memory required to run a program. The Shell always passes all of the conventional memory available to an application when the application is executed. If a program requires more memory than is available, an error message is displayed and control returns to the Shell.

This feature does not limit the amount of memory passed to a program. The default value is 128KB.

The XMS features are used to control the amount of extended memory that an application can access. In order to use these features, applications must be written to the Lotus-Intel-Microsoft-AST extended memory specification (XMS standard).

The XMS Memory KB Required entry field operates like the Conventional Memory KB Required entry field. If a program requires more memory than is available, an error message is displayed and control returns to the Shell. The default value is 0KB. The XMS memory is saved on disk when a task swap occurs. This increases the amount of time required between task swaps. In order to improve performance, you should only use this option if necessary.

The XMS Memory KB Limit entry field is used to set the maximum amount of extended memory that an application can use. Many applications that support extended memory automatically take all of the available XMS memory whether it is needed or not. You can use this option to restrict the amount of memory that these applications use. If you set this option to 0, no XMS memory is available to the program selection. However, if you set this option to –1, all available XMS memory is available for the application.

Both the Conventional and XMS Memory features are active only when the Task Swapper is enabled.

The Video Mode Graphics option is used for all display monitors except the CGA display. The Video Mode Text option is used only with CGA displays.

The Reserved Shortcut Keys (ALT+TAB, ALT+ESC, and CTRL+ESC) used by the Shell's Task Swapper to switch between tasks can be deactivated. In some cases, other application programs use one or more of these key combinations. When you toggle these off, the Shell passes the key combination to the running application. You should be careful not to deactivate all of these keys or you will not be able to swap back to the Shell without quitting a task.

The Prevent Program Switch is used to deactivate the swapping of an executing program. In some cases, communication programs will crash when their execution is interrupted by the Task Swapper. You should toggle this feature on if you experience problems with an application after task swapping.

It is not important that you use these optional features at this point. However, you should become familiar with the available functions.

KEYBOARD OR MOUSE

Select Cancel.

 The Advanced pop-up panel is removed and the Program List is displayed.

 You have successfully changed a program and explored many of the DOS 5.0 Shell's advanced features!

LESSON 3:
CHANGE A PROGRAM IN DOS 4.0

When you complete this lesson, you will be able to change a program in a group list.

 The advanced features of program selections in DOS 4.0 are very different from DOS 5.0. If you are using DOS 5.0, skip to the next lesson.

 In this lesson, you will change the Format System Diskette entry that you created in Lesson 1 of this chapter. Currently, this program selection is set to format a diskette in drive A: only. You will add a prompt panel, which will allow you to specify a different drive each time this entry is selected.

 User-defined prompt panels are one of the Shell's most powerful features. These panels are used to pass variable information to the program commands. Each prompt panel is restricted to one title, instruction line, prompt, and entry field. Each program selection may have up to 250 different prompt panels. However, most program selections use no more than 3 prompt panels, depending on the type and amount of information being passed to the program.

KEYBOARD OR MOUSE

Display the Disk Utilities program list.

KEYBOARD

Using the up and down arrows, highlight "Format System Diskette." Be careful not to press Enter (⏎)!

MOUSE

Point at "Format System Diskette" and click once.

KEYBOARD OR MOUSE

Switch to the menu bar and select the Program pull-down panel.

Select the Change command.

The Add Program pop-up panel is displayed containing the information that you entered in the last lesson. (See Figure 6-13.)
You will now position the cursor on the Commands entry field.

KEYBOARD

Press Tab (|←) or Enter (↵) once.

MOUSE

Point at the text you entered in the Commands field and click once.

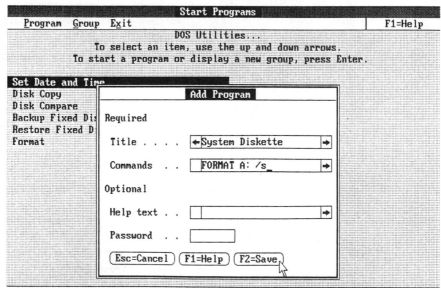

Figure 6-13
Change Program
Entry Field Panel

KEYBOARD OR MOUSE

 Use the right and left keyboard arrows to move the cursor to the drive letter appearing after the word FORMAT in the Commands field.

 Press the Delete key until the information appearing after the FORMAT command is erased.

In its simplest form, a prompt panel can be created by placing two brackets in the Commands entry field at the desired position, as shown in Figure 6-14.

When the Format System Diskette selection is made with the prompt brackets as shown in the Figure 6-14, a default title, instruction line, prompt, and entry field appear. (See Figure 6-15.)

This prompt panel is general in its request for information. It would be better if the prompt panel specifically requested the type of information necessary to complete the action successfully. The Shell provides a series of Program Startup Commands (PSCs) that allow you to create custom prompt panels with user defined titles, instructions, and prompts.

The PSCs are listed here for your reference. We recommend that you carefully read each definition. However, it is not important that you fully

```
                          Start Programs
   Program  Group  Exit                           │ F1=Help
                          DOS Utilities...
             To select an item, use the up and down arrows.
             To start a program or display a new group, press Enter.

 Set Date and Time
 Disk Copy            ┌──────────────── Add Program ────────────────┐
 Disk Compare         │                                             │
 Backup Fixed Dis     │ Required                                    │
 Restore Fixed D      │                                             │
 Format               │   Title . . . .  [◄System Diskette     ►]   │
                      │                                             │
                      │   Commands  . .  [FORMAT []_            ►]   │
                      │                                             │
                      │ Optional                                    │
                      │                                             │
                      │   Help text . .  [                     ►]   │
                      │                                             │
                      │   Password  . .  [          ]               │
                      │                                             │
                      │  (Esc=Cancel) (F1=Help) (F2=Save)           │
                      └─────────────────────────────────────────────┘

 F10=Actions  Esc=Cancel  Shift+F9=Command Prompt
```

Figure 6-14
Simplest Form of a Prompt Panel Command

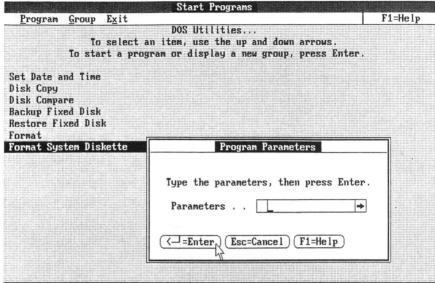

Figure 6-15
Pop-Up Display After
Format Selection

understand the function of each command. We will actually use the more common PSCs later in this lesson.

- [] Defines a default prompt panel. From 0 to 250 different prompt panels may be defined for each program selection.

    Example: Commands . . FORMAT []

    This example creates a prompt panel entry field in which you may type the drive letter to format. If you type B: and press Enter (↵), FORMAT B: is passed to DOS for execution.

- [/T"Title Text"] Defines a new title that replaces the default Program Parameters title appearing in the prompt panel. You may enter up to 40 characters in between the quote marks immediately following /T.

    Example: Commands . . [/T"Format System Diskette"]

    In this example, "Format System Diskette" will appear as a title at the top of the prompt panel.

- [/I"Instruction Text"] Defines a new instruction line that replaces the default "Type the parameters, then press Enter" appearing in the prompt panel. You may enter up to 40 characters in between the quote marks immediately following /I.

Example: Commands . . [/I"Insert diskette in drive and specify"]

In this example, "Insert diskette in drive and specify" will appear as an instruction line below the title in the prompt panel.

- [/P"Prompt Text"] Defines a new prompt line that replaces the default "Parameters . ." appearing in the prompt panel. You may enter up to 20 characters in between the quote marks immediately following /P.

Example: Commands . . [/P"drive letter . ."]

In this example, "drive letter . ." will appear as the prompt immediately before the panel's data entry field.

- [/F"Drive:\Path\Filename"] Used to verify an existing filename at the specified drive and path. You may enter up to 76 characters in between the quote marks immediately following /F. This option is often used to verify if the proper program diskette is inserted in a particular drive.

Example: Commands . . [/F"A:DW4.EXE"]

In this example, the Shell verifies that the DW4.EXE program exists on drive A: before leaving the Shell to execute the program.

- [%n] Where n is a whole number representing a variable from 1 to 10. If variables are used they must appear immediately after the left bracket as the first entry. Only one variable may be associated per prompt panel entry field. The first occurrence of a variable in the Commands entry field must be defined in between the prompt brackets. Subsequent occurrences of the same variable may appear outside the prompt brackets within the same string of Program Startup Commands. Once a variable has been assigned to a prompt panel, the information you enter in the resulting entry field is automatically associated with the variable. Wherever this variable appears in the PSC outside of the prompt brackets, your data entry is automatically substituted. This may sound complicated at first; however, you will soon see how easy and powerful it is to use prompt panel variables.

Example: Commands . . FORMAT [%1]:

In this example, a prompt panel appears and allows you to specify the desired drive. If you type the letter B, then the Shell internally passes FORMAT B: to DOS for execution. Notice that a colon appears immediately after the prompt panel brackets. Once you accept the panel by pressing Enter (↵), the brackets and everything in between are replaced by your data entry.

● %n Here n is a whole number representing a variable from 1 to 10. This is the same variable just described. In this case, the variable does not appear inside the prompt panel brackets. It is important, however, that the first occurrence of this variable in a PSC appear inside the brackets.

Example: Commands . . FORMAT [%1]:‖DIR %1:

In this example, you are prompted for a drive to format. If you type B and press Enter (↵), FORMAT B: followed by DIR B: is passed to DOS for execution. Only one set of prompt panel brackets is defined; therefore, you will have to enter the drive letter only once. The diskette in drive B: will be formatted, then a directory listing will be displayed before you are returned to the Shell. This example demonstrates the ability to enter multiple commands for execution from a single program list selection. The command separator (‖) is created by pressing F4. You may enter up to 500 characters of different commands (including the separator bars for each menu selection).

● [/D"Text String"] Defines an initial default value. In some cases, there is an answer to an entry field that is usually correct. This command allows you to specify this initial or default value. You may enter up to 128 characters in between the quotes as the entry field's default value. The prompt panel appears with this default value in the entry field. If the value is correct, you simply press Enter (↵). Otherwise, you may enter a new value before accepting the panel.

Example: Commands . . FORMAT [%1/D"B"]:‖DIR %1:

In this example, the letter B appears in the prompt panel entry field as the default value. If you press Enter (↵), FORMAT B: and DIR B: are passed to the DOS for execution. We recommend that you supply default values whenever possible to simplify user interaction.

● [/D"%n"] Here n is a whole number representing a variable from 1 to 10. This variation of the command just discussed allows you to specify a variable's current value as the default value. It is important to use only those variables that have been initialized earlier in the same command string.

Example: Commands . . FORMAT [%1]:‖DIR [/D"%1"]:

In this example, you are prompted for the drive to be formatted, followed by another prompt for a drive's directory listing. The second prompt contains the drive letter entered in the first prompt as a default value. Of course, you may change or accept the default entry.

- [/R] If this command is present, the default value in the prompt panel's entry field is immediately erased or cleared when the first character is typed into the entry field. This is a nice editing touch, which can be used to increase your productivity by eliminating unnecessary editing or erasure of the default value.

    Example: Commands . . DISKCOPY [/D"A: B:"/R]

    In this example, a prompt panel appears with a default source and target drive. If you begin to type a new source entry the entire default value is immediately erased and the first character you typed appears in the field. Any additional typed characters appear in the field as expected.

- [/L"n"] Here n is a whole number variable from 0 to 128 representing the length of the prompt panel's entry field. This feature allows you to tailor the length of the entry field to the maximum necessary. If this is not used, the prompt panel's entry field defaults to 128 characters in length. In some cases, you may not want an entry field to appear in the prompt panel. If you set the length to zero, the field will not appear; however, you must press Enter (↵) to accept the prompt panel. This technique is useful for providing special instructions prior to execution of the program selection.

    Example: Commands. . . [/I"Insert program diskette in drive A"/L"0"]

    In this example, the prompt panel instructing the user to insert a program diskette in drive A: appears. No entry field appears. The user must press Enter (↵) to continue.

- [/M"e"] This command is designed to be used with a prompt panel containing a filename entry field. Once you type the filename and press Enter (↵), the Shell checks to determine if the filename exists. If the file is not found, the Shell displays an error message and displays the prompt panel again. You must enter a filename that already exists or press Esc to cancel the prompt panel.

    Example: Commands . . COPY A:[/M"e"] B:

    In this example, the entry field prompts for the filename to copy from drive A: to drive B:. If you enter a filename that does not exist on drive A:, the Shell will display the same prompt panel again. To continue, you must supply an existing filename or press Esc to cancel the operation.

- [/C"%n"] Here n is a whole number representing a variable from 1 to 10. This feature allows you to pass values assigned to a variable in between different selections in the group list. This is useful when you create a series of different program selections that normally are selected one after the other.

Example: Commands . . SPELLCHK [/C"%3"]

For the purposes of our example, the previous program selection was an editor that assigned the %3 variable to a filename for editing. This option will only work if you have used the editor selection since you turned the computer on. When the SPELLCHK selection is made, the prompt panel entry field contains the filename that was associated during the editor selection. Of course, this default value may be changed as necessary.

● /# The Shell replaces this command with the drive letter from which the Shell was started followed by a colon. **This command must be used outside the brackets.**

Example: Commands . . DISKCOPY /# B:

In this example, if the current drive is A:, it will be copied to drive B:.

● /@ The Shell replaces this command with the path where the Shell was started. This command must be used outside of the brackets. It is important to note that the substituted path does not end or begin with a (\) slash.

Example: Commands . . COPY /#\/@*.* B:

In this example, if the current drive is A: and the path is \SUB1\SUB2, then the command that is passed to DOS for execution is COPY A:\SUB1\SUB2*.* B:.

All of the Program Startup Commands can be mixed as necessary.

With the exception of the GOTO statement, any DOS batch file command may be included in your PSC. In addition, if you use the batch file variable %n, n must be alphabetic. Remember that the Shell uses its own variables, which include %1 to %10. It is important not to confuse the Shell's variables with those that are processed directly by DOS. For example, if you included FOR %H IN (FILE1) DO DIR in your PSC, %H would process as a DOS variable as expected. However, if FOR %1 IN (FILE1) DO DIR is used in a PSC, the Shell would attempt to process the %1 variable, which would not produce the desired results.

Batch files may be placed directly in the PSC. However, you must use the DOS batch file CALL statement (e.g., CALL G.BAT). If you do not use the CALL statement, you will not return to the Shell once the program entry is started.

In some cases, you may find it useful to place a DOS batch file PAUSE statement as the last command in the PSC. This will allow you to see any messages displayed by the PSC commands before returning to the Shell. Once you are satisfied with the operation of your PSC, you may want to remove the PAUSE statement.

In the remainder of this lesson, you will change the Format System Diskette selection to prompt the user with a customized prompt panel.

KEYBOARD

 Using the up and down arrows, highlight the Format System Diskette selection.

MOUSE

 Point at the Format System Diskette selection and click once.

KEYBOARD OR MOUSE

 Switch to the menu bar and select the Program pull-down panel.

 Select the Change command.

The Change Program pop-up panel is displayed containing the information that you entered. (See Figure 6-16.)

You will now position the cursor on the Commands entry field.

KEYBOARD

 Press Tab (|←) or Enter (↵) once.

MOUSE

 Point at the text you entered in the Commands field and click once.

```
                         Start Programs
   Program  Group  Exit                              F1=Help
                         DOS Utilities...
            To select an item, use the up and down arrows.
         To start a program or display a new group, press Enter.

  Set Date and Time
  Disk Copy              ┌──────── Change Program ────────┐
  Disk Compare           │                                │
  Backup Fixed Di        │  Required                      │
  Restore Fixed D        │                                │
  Format                 │  Title . . . .  ┌Format System Diskette→┐
  Format System D        │                                │
                         │  Commands  . .  ┌.FORMAT []         →┐
                         │                                │
                         │  Optional                      │
                         │                                │
                         │  Help text . .  ┌               →┐
                         │                                │
                         │  Password  . .  ┌        ┐       │
                         │                                │
                         │ (Esc=Cancel) (F1=Help) (F2=Save)│
                         └────────────────────────────────┘
  F10=Actions   Esc=Cancel   Shift+F9=Command Prompt
```

Figure 6-16
Change Program
Entry Field Panel

KEYBOARD OR MOUSE

Use the right and left keyboard arrows to move the cursor to the first bracket appearing after the word FORMAT in the Commands field. (See Figure 6-17.)

You will edit this field by placing the cursor into insert mode. This will allow you to type characters in between the two brackets without overtyping the right bracket character.

KEYBOARD OR MOUSE

Press the Insert key once.

> **Note:** When insert mode is active in graphics mode, the cursor is a vertical line; in text mode, the cursor is a large block character. Insert mode may be toggled on and off by pressing the Ins key.

Now you are ready to specify the new prompt panel.

```
                        Start Programs
    Program  Group  Exit                           │  F1=Help
                      DOS Utilities...
             To select an item, use the up and down arrows
          To start a program or display a new group, press Enter.

Set Date and Time
Disk Copy       ┌──────────────── Change Program ────────────────┐
Disk Compare    │                                                │
Backup Fixed Di │  Required                                      │
Restore Fixed D │                                                │
Format          │  Title . . . .    [Format System Diskette]→    │
Format System D │                                                │
                │  Commands  . .    [FORMAT []_            ]→     │
                │                                                │
                │  Optional                                      │
                │                                                │
                │  Help text . .    [                      ]→    │
                │                                                │
                │  Password  . .    [          ]                 │
                │                                                │
                │  (Esc=Cancel) (F1=Help) (F2=Save)              │
                │                                                │
                └────────────────────────────────────────────────┘

 F10=Actions  Esc=Cancel  Shift+F9=Command Prompt
```

Figure 6-17
Cursor Positioned
After the FORMAT
Command

KEYBOARD OR MOUSE

 Type /D"A"/T"Format System Diskette"/I"Insert blank diskette in drive and specify"/P"drive letter . ."/L"1" in between the two brackets.

 Using the right arrow key, position the cursor after the right bracket.

 Type : /s immediately after the bracket.

Your entry field should appear similar to the one shown in Figure 6-18. Once the new PSC has been entered, you must save the panel information.

KEYBOARD OR MOUSE

 Press F2 to save.

The panel is automatically removed as soon as you save the information.

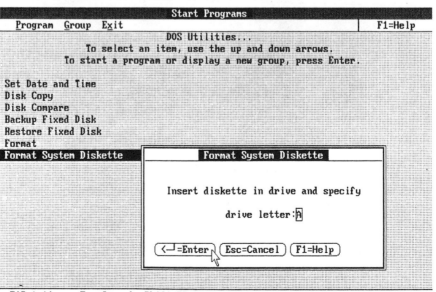

Figure 6-18
Advanced Prompt
Panel Command

KEYBOARD OR MOUSE

  Select the "Format System Diskette."

The pop-up prompt panel should appear as shown in Figure 6-19.

Figure 6-19
Program Pop-Up
Panel

You may now use your new program entry to prepare system diskettes that are initialized with DOS.

> **Warning:** You must be careful when specifying the drive letter to format. Once the format process actually begins, all existing information on the disk is lost! Be especially careful not to inadvertently format your fixed disk.

LESSON 4: COPY A PROGRAM IN A GROUP

When you complete this lesson, you will be able to copy an existing program entry in a group list.

This convenient feature allows you to quickly assemble new program lists from existing lists without rekeying selections. Selections may be copied from any group to another group or even to the same group. Only programs may be copied not subgroups. Once the copy process begins, the on-screen instructions change to assist you with the completion of the copy process in the status line at the bottom of the screen.

> **Note:** When you use DOS 4.0, the instructions are located in top screen panel area. All program entries appearing in any group may be copied with the exception of the Main Group's Command Prompt, File System, Change Colors, and Disk Utilities selections.

In this lesson, you will copy to the Main Group the new program entry, Format System Diskette, that you created in the Disk Utilities subgroup.

KEYBOARD OR MOUSE

 Display the Disk Utilities program list.

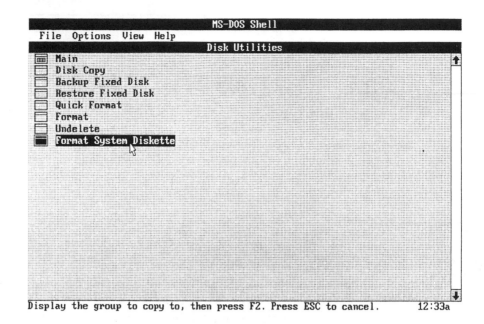

```
                              MS-DOS Shell
         File  Options  View  Help
                              Disk Utilities
         ⊞  Main                                              ↑
         ☐  Disk Copy
         ☐  Backup Fixed Disk
         ☐  Restore Fixed Disk
         ☐  Quick Format
         ☐  Format
         ☐  Undelete
         ⊞  Format System Diskette



                                                             ↓
Display the group to copy to, then press F2. Press ESC to cancel.    12:33a
```

Figure 6-20
New Copy Instruc-
tions

 Highlight the Format System Diskette selection. (See Figure 6-20.)

 Switch to the menu bar and select the File pull-down panel.

 Select the Copy option.

Notice that the File pull-down panel disappears and the screen instructions immediately change after selection of the Copy command. (See Figure 6-20.)

Following the new screen instructions, you must locate the destination group. In this example, the Main Group is your destination for the copy.

KEYBOARD OR MOUSE

 Display the Main Group.

Once the Main Group screen is displayed, you may complete the copy process.

> **Note 1:** After the selection is made in the copy process, you may move freely through the group structures in order to locate the Destination menu. If necessary, you may cancel the copy process by pressing the Esc key.
>
> **Note 2:** When you use DOS 4.0, press F3 to cancel.

KEYBOARD

 Press the F2 key to save.

The Main Group screen is updated with the new selection and the screen instructions change, as shown in Figure 6-21.

All new program selections are always added to the end of the current program list. You may use the File or Group pull-down panel's Reorder function to move the selection to the desired location within the group.

You have copied a program selection!

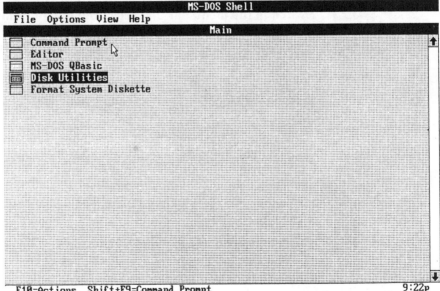

Figure 6-21
Destination Screen of
Program Copy

LESSON 5:
DELETE A PROGRAM IN A GROUP

When you complete this lesson, you will be able to delete a program from a group list.

In this lesson, you will delete the new selection that you copied to the Main Group in the last lesson. The original entry will still exist in the Disk Utilities group list.

KEYBOARD OR MOUSE

 Display the Main Group program list.

 Highlight the Format System Diskette program selection. Make sure that you do not press Enter (↵) to start. (See Figure 6-22.)

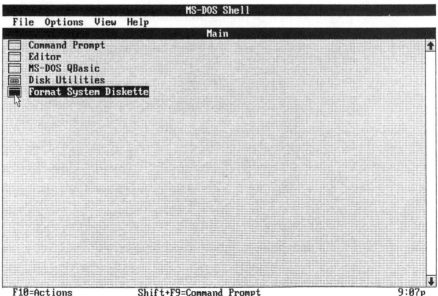

Figure 6-22
Highlight Program
Selection to Delete

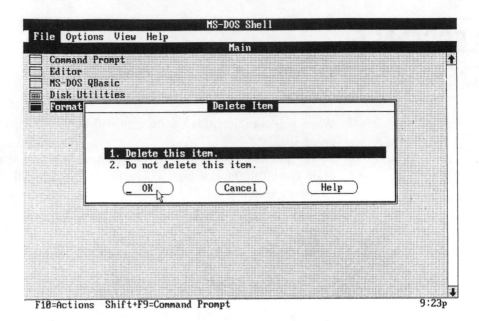

Figure 6-23
Confirm Deletion of
Program Selection

KEYBOARD OR MOUSE

 Switch to the menu bar and display the File pull-down panel.

 Select Delete.

The delete confirmation pop-up panel appears. If you are using DOS 5.0, you can press the Del key to bypass the File pull-down panel.

KEYBOARD OR MOUSE

 Select "Delete this item," as shown in Figure 6-23.

After confirming the deletion, the pop-up panel is removed and the Format System Diskette selection is removed from the screen.

You have deleted a program selection!

LESSON 6: ADD A GROUP

When you complete this lesson, you will be able to add a new subgroup.

Adding a subgroup to the Main Group is similar to adding a program to a group. In this lesson, you will add a Word Processing subgroup to the Main Group.

> **Note:** When you use DOS 4.0, additional groups or subgroups may be added only to the Main Group screen.

KEYBOARD OR MOUSE

 Display the Main Group program list.

 Switch to the menu bar and select the File pull-down panel.

 Select the New command.

The New Program Object pop-up panel is displayed. This panel allows you to indicate whether the new entry is another group of programs or a program item to be executed when selected. (See Figure 6-24.)

KEYBOARD OR MOUSE

 Select "Program Group."

 Select "OK."

The Add Group panel is displayed with blank entry fields, as shown in Figure 6-25. This panel is very similar to the Add Program panel discussed in Lesson 1 of this chapter. The required and optional entry fields are clearly marked.

The Add Group Title field is identical to the Add Program Title field.

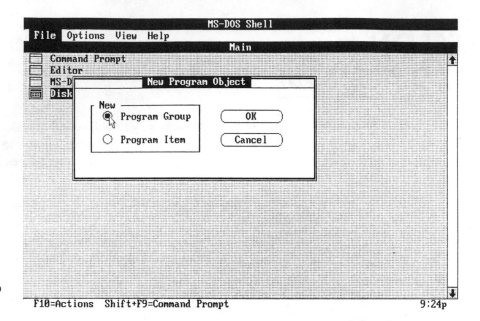

Figure 6-24
New Group or Program Object Pop-Up Panel Display

Note: When you use DOS 4.0, three dots (...) are automatically added to the end of the group title. This clarifies which entries are actual programs and which are groups of programs.

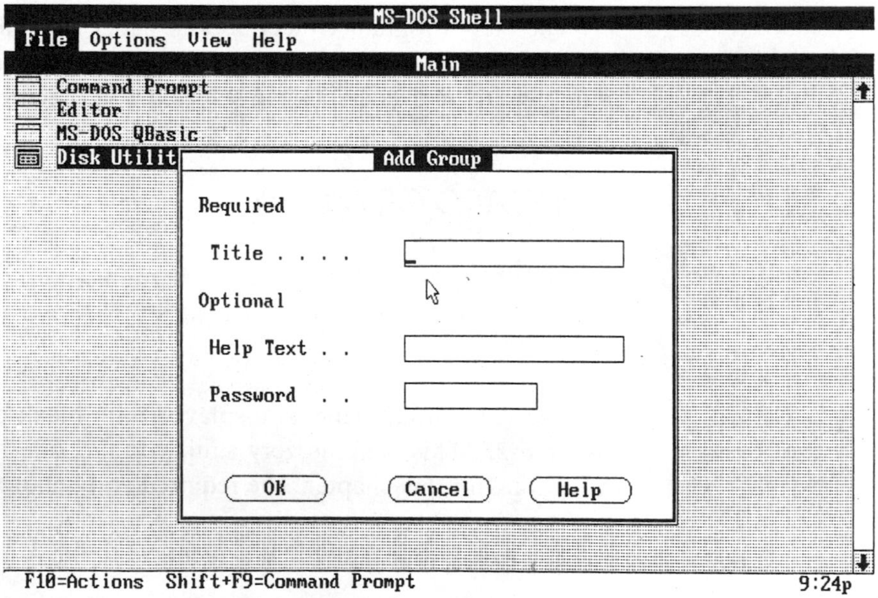

Figure 6-25
Add Group Entry Field Panel

KEYBOARD OR MOUSE

 In the Title entry field, type Word Processing.

When you use DOS 4.0, a filename field appears immediately below the Title field. This field provides a convenient method for you to assign the name of the file that contains your new list of programs. You may specify any name you desire.

> **Note:** If you are using DOS 4.0, position the cursor on the file-name entry field by pressing Tab (|←), then type WORD.

KEYBOARD OR MOUSE

 Position the cursor to the Help Text entry field.

The Help Text entry field may contain up to 255 characters of help text. You may type any text you want in this field. We recommend that the text you enter discuss the purpose and operation of the associated selection. Both group and program entries share this same optional feature. Once the help is entered and saved, you can display it by highlighting the title and pressing F1. Your text is automatically wordwrapped and displayed without breaking words on different lines. However, you can start a new line by typing a carat followed by an M.

KEYBOARD OR MOUSE

 Type "This is the Word Processing subgroup. Selection of this entry displays a list of programs used for word processing."

 Position the cursor to the Password entry field.

The Password entry field may contain up to 20 characters of text. You may type any text you want in this field. Both group and program entries share this same optional feature. Each group and program selection may have a unique password.

It is important that you remember the text entered. If you lose the text, you will not be able to operate or change this selection.

KEYBOARD OR MOUSE

 Type DOS for your password.

At this point, you have completed all of the entries in the Add Group pop-up panel.

Once you save the information, the Add Group pop-up panel is removed and the new Word Processing selection appears in the Main Group.

KEYBOARD OR MOUSE

 Save the panel.

If you select the Word Processing subgroup, a blank program list is displayed.

KEYBOARD OR MOUSE

 Select "Word Processing."

A pop-up panel appears prompting for the assigned password. (See Figure 6-26.) This is a nondisplay entry field. All of the editing keys function as expected.

KEYBOARD OR MOUSE

 Type DOS, then press Enter (↵).

If you correctly enter the password, the Word Processing screen is displayed. Notice that the program list is empty. You may now copy program selections from other groups or add new selections as desired. Since this group is entitled Word Processing, we recommend that you add editors, word processors, and spell checking programs. You have added a new group and assigned a password!

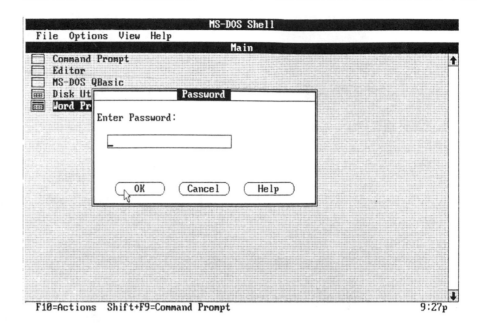

Figure 6-26
Password Pop-Up
Panel Prompt

LESSON 7: CHANGE A GROUP

When you complete this lesson, you will be able to change a subgroup entry.

In this lesson, we will change the Word Processing entry that you created in the last lesson. Currently, this group selection requires the entry of a password. We will eliminate the need to enter a password before displaying this group's program list.

> **Note:** When you use DOS 4.0, be careful to select the proper menu bar command when operating on groups and programs. If you have highlighted a group entry, you must use the menu bar Group pull-down panel commands. If you have highlighted a program entry, you must use the menu bar Program pull-down panel commands. The only exception to this rule are the Add and Reorder pull-down commands.

KEYBOARD OR MOUSE

 Display the Main Group.

 Highlight the Word Processing subgroup entry. Do not select it!

 Switch to the menu bar and select the File pull-down panel.

 Select the Properties command.

Since you are attempting to change a selection that has an assigned password, you must first enter the current password.

KEYBOARD OR MOUSE

 Type DOS, then press Enter (↵).

The Change Group panel is displayed, containing the information that you entered in the last lesson. (See Figure 6-27.)

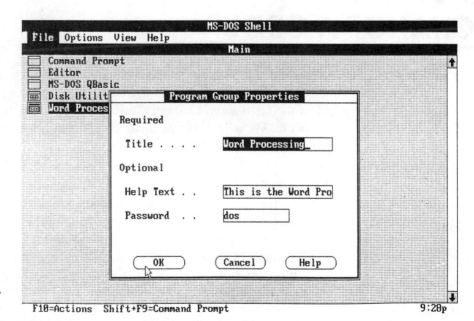

Figure 6-27
Change Group Entry
Field Panel

KEYBOARD OR MOUSE

 Position the cursor on the Password entry field.

 Press the Del key until the password field is empty.

 Save the panel.

The panel is automatically removed as soon as you save the information.

KEYBOARD OR MOUSE

 Select the Word Processing entry.

The password prompt panel should not appear, and the Word Processing program list should be immediately displayed.

You have changed a group selection!

LESSON 8: DELETE A GROUP

When you complete this lesson, you will be able to delete a subgroup from the Main Group display.

In this lesson, you will delete the Word Processing group selection that you created and modified in the previous lessons.

KEYBOARD OR MOUSE

 Display the Main Group program list.

 Highlight the Word Processing subgroup selection.

 Switch to the menu bar and display the Group pull-down panel.

 Select "Delete."

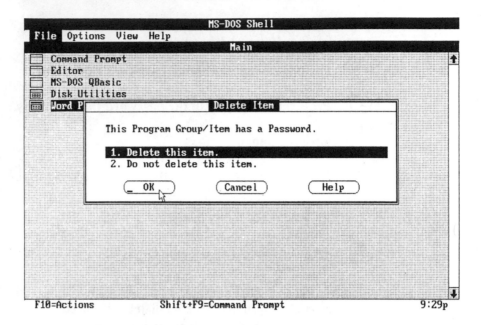

Figure 6-28
Confirm Deletion of
Group Selection

The Delete Confirmation pop-up panel appears. (See Figure 6-28.)

KEYBOARD OR MOUSE

Select "Delete this item."

After the deletion is confirmed, the pop-up panel is removed and the
Word Processing selection is removed from the screen.

You have deleted a group selection!

LESSON 9: REORDER A GROUP

When you complete this lesson, you will be able to reorder selections in a
group list.

This convenient feature allows you to quickly reorder programs in a group. Once the reorder process begins, the screen instructions change to assist you with the completion of the reorder.

In this lesson, you will move the Main Group's Command Prompt selection to the bottom of the program list.

KEYBOARD OR MOUSE

 Display the Main Group program list.

 Highlight the Command Prompt entry. Do not select it!

 Switch to the menu bar and select the File pull-down panel.

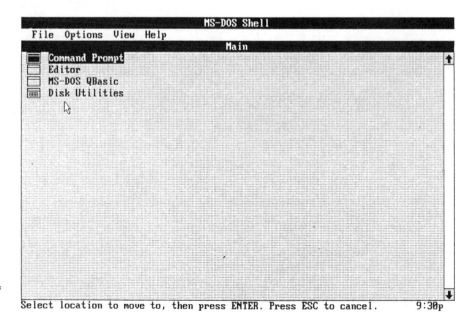 **Select the Reorder option.**

The pull-down panel disappears and the screen instructions immediately change after selection of the Reorder command. (See Figure 6-29.)

Following the instructions, you must highlight the current entry position in the group list where you wish the Command Prompt entry to appear.

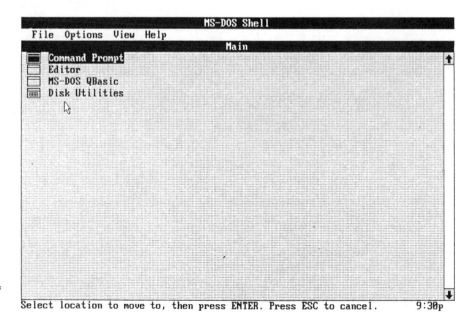

Figure 6-29
Destination Screen of
Program Reorder

KEYBOARD

 Using the up and down arrows, highlight the selection at the bottom of the program list.

 Press Enter (↵) to move the Command Prompt selection to the highlighted position.

MOUSE

 Point at the text of the last selection and double click.

The Main Group screen is updated with the Command Prompt selection relocated to the bottom of the list. Notice that all of the other selections move up to fill the vacant position left by the last position of the Command Prompt entry in the list.

You have reordered a group!

You have completed the last Shell lesson!

At this point, you should understand the basic application of the Shell's function. We strongly encourage you to use the skills that you have acquired throughout these lessons right away. The remainder of this book discusses many of DOS's advanced features. For some, it will not be necessary to continue past this point. However, we recommend that you read the remaining chapters anyway to get a better understanding of the functions and operation of DOS.

Using the DOS Editor

When you complete this chapter, you will be able to perform the following Editor operations:

1. Starting the DOS Editor

2. Using the Editor Help

3. Editing a New Text File

This series of lessons teaches you how to use the new DOS 5.0 Editor. This is the first version of DOS that is supplied with a full-screen editor. Skip this chapter if you are not using DOS version 5.0. If you have completed the DOS Shell lessons in the previous chapters, you will find that the Editor operates similarly.

LESSON 1:
STARTING THE DOS EDITOR

When you complete this lesson, you will be able to start and quit the DOS Editor. In addition, you will be familiar with the Editor's screen display and pull-down panels.

You can start the DOS 5.0 Editor from the DOS Shell or Command Prompt. If you are starting the DOS Editor from the Shell, use the following instructions.

MOUSE

 Place the mouse pointer on the EDIT.COM file in the DOS directory.

 Double click the Mouse Select button.

If you are starting the DOS Editor from the Command Prompt, use the following instructions.

KEYBOARD

 Change to the DOS subdirectory.

 Type EDIT and then press Enter (↵)

The first Editor screen appears as shown in Figure 7-1. Notice that the default filename is displayed in the second line of the screen display.

Before you continue, it is important to understand the layout of the Editor display. (See Figure 7-2.)

The Editor screen areas are listed here for your reference. We recommend that you carefully read the definitions. However, it is not important that you fully understand the function of each area. We cover each of these areas in more detail throughout the remaining portion of this lesson.

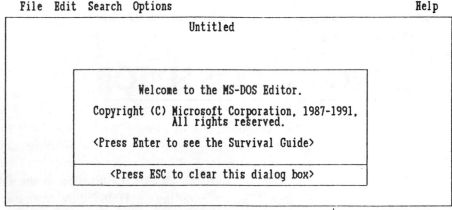

Figure 7-1
First Editor Screen Display

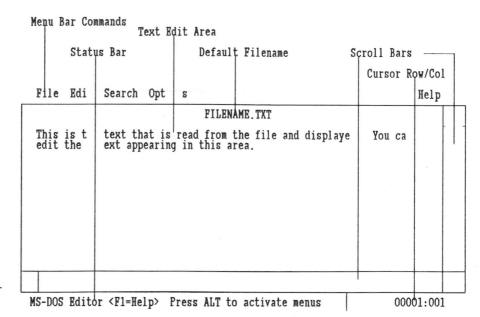

Figure 7-2
Layout of the First Editor Screen Display

Default Filename   This screen area displays the current text filename.

Text Edit Area   This is where you view and edit text.

Instruction Line   Directions instructing you in the operation of the Editor are displayed in this line.

Scroll Bars   This screen area is used to display the scroll bars for the text edit area. The scroll bar may be used to scroll the information contained in the list located above or to the left. See Lessons 3 and 4 in Chapter 4, "Basic Shell Operations," for a detailed description of the interaction of the scroll bar.

Menu Bar Commands   The Editor menu bar operates similarly to the Shell's menu bars. However, the available commands are different. The File pull-down panel contains commands that are used to read, create, save, and print files. (See Figure 7-3.) The Edit pull-down panel contains commands that allow you to copy, paste, or delete text. (See Figure 7-4.) The Search pull-down panel contains commands that allow you to find and replace text in the file. (See Figure 7-5.) The Options pull-down panel contains commands that allow you to change the screen colors and tab settings and set the directory path of the Editor's help text

File

```
New
Open
Save
Save As
```
```
Print
```
```
Exit
```

Figure 7-3
File Pull-Down Panel

Edit

```
Cut        Shift+Del
Copy       Ctrl+Ins
Paste      Shift+Ins
Clear      Del
```

Figure 7-4
Edit Pull-Down Panel

Search

```
Find
Repeat Last Find    F3
Change
```

Figure 7-5
Search Pull-Down
Panel

Options

```
Display
Help Path
```

Figure 7-6
Options Pull-Down
Panel

Help

```
Getting Started
Keyboard
```
```
About
```

Figure 7-7
Help Pull-Down Panel

file. (See Figure 7-6.) The Help pull-down panel provides several different types of help text support. (See Figure 7-7.)

You have successfully started the DOS Editor!

 You can stop at the end of any lesson in this tutorial. To do so, you simply turn both the computer and display off. Otherwise, continue with the next lesson.

LESSON 2: USING THE EDITOR HELP

When you complete this lesson, you will be able to use the Editor's help support.

You can access contextual help from any screen in the Editor. Help is also available from the menu bar. You can view help by pressing the key sequences described in Figure 7-8 or by clicking the right mouse button once.

When the Editor is first started, you are prompted for access to the Survival Guide help.

KEYBOARD OR MOUSE

 Press Enter to see the Survival Guide.

The Survival Guide pop-up panel is removed and replaced with the Survival help text. (See Figure 7-9.)

Figure 7-8
Keys Used to Access
Help

Key Sequence	Assigned Function
F1	Help on menus and commands
Shift+F1	Help on getting started

```
 File  Edit  Search  Options                              Help
┌──────────────────────────────────────────────────────────────┐
│                          Untitled                              │
│ MS help text screen goes here                                  │
│                                                                │
│                                                                │
│                                                                │
│                                                                │
│             Getting Started                                    │
│                                                                │
│             Keyboard                                           │
│                                                                │
│                                                                │
│                                                                │
└──────────────────────────────────────────────────────────────┘
            <ESC=Cancel>                |          00001:001
```

Figure 7-9
Editor Survival Guide
Help Display

You can use the Tab or Shift+Tab keys to select a desired topic. Once the topic is selected, press Enter (↵) to display the associated help text.

KEYBOARD OR MOUSE

 At this point you should review the help text before continuing.

You have successfully viewed the Editor's help!

LESSON 3: EDITING A TEXT FILE

When you complete this lesson, you will be able to use the Editor to change a text file.

REMOVE HELP

KEYBOARD

 Press the Esc key once to cancel help.

The help text is removed and replaced with a blank untitled document file. In this lesson, you will open the DOSSHELL.INI file to add a new set of color selections. This new selection will be available from the DOS Shell.

KEYBOARD OR MOUSE

 Switch to the menu bar and select the File pull-down panel.

 Select the Open command.

```
 File  Edit  Search  Options                              Help
┌────────────────────────────────────────────────────────────┐
│                          Untitled                            │
│    ─    ┌──────────────────────────────────────────┐        │
│         │ Filename:  ┌─────────────────────┐        │        │
│         │            │ *.INI               │        │        │
│         │            └─────────────────────┘        │        │
│         │ C:\                                        │        │
│         │                                            │        │
│         │          Files            Dirs/Drives      │        │
│         │  ┌──────────────────┐  ┌───────────────┐   │        │
│         │  │ DOSSHELL.INI     │  │ DOS           │   │        │
│         │  │ QBASIC.INI       │  │               │   │        │
│         │  │                  │  │               │   │        │
│         │  │                  │  │               │   │        │
│         │  └──────────────────┘  └───────────────┘   │        │
│         │                                            │        │
│         │      <OK>      <Cancel>      <Help>         │        │
│         └──────────────────────────────────────────┘        │
└────────────────────────────────────────────────────────────┘
 MS-DOS Editor <F1=Help>  Press ALT to activate menus    │    00001:001
```

Figure 7-10
Drive, Directory, and
Filename Selection
Pop-Up Panel

The Open pop-up panel is displayed containing a directory of your drive. (See Figure 7-10.)

KEYBOARD OR MOUSE

Position the cursor in the Filename field.

KEYBOARD

Type *.INI and then press Enter (↵).

You need to view the directories on your disk until you locate the DOSSHELL.INI file. When the appropriate directory is located the files appear as shown in Figure 7-10.

KEYBOARD OR MOUSE

Select the different directories in the Dirs/Drives panel area until you locate the DOSSHELL.INI file.

> **Note:** When you use the mouse, double click on the directory name to display the files located in the directory.

```
 File  Edit  Search  Options                                    Help
┌──────────────────────────────────────────────────────────────────┐
│                          DOSSHELL.INI                              │
│ ***************  WARNING  *********************                     │
│ This file may contain lines with more than 256                     │
│ characters. Some editors will truncate or split                    │
│ these lines. If you are not sure whether your                      │
│ editor can handle long lines, exit now without                     │
│ saving the file.                                                   │
│                                                                    │
│ Note: The editor which is invoked by the                           │
│       MS-DOS 5.0 EDIT command can be used                          │
│       to edit this file.                                           │
│ ***************  NOTE  ************************                     │
│ Everything up to the first left square bracket                     │
│ character is considered a comment.                                 │
│ ***********************************************                     │
│ [savestate]                                                        │
└──────────────────────────────────────────────────────────────────┘
 MS-DOS Editor <F1=Help>  Press ALT to activate menus    |      00001:001
```

Figure 7-11
DOSSHELL.INI Text File

KEYBOARD

 Position the cursor on top of the DOSSHELL.INI file.

 Press Enter (⏎).

MOUSE

 Position the mouse pointer on top of the DOSSHELL.INI file.

 Double click the Mouse Select button.

The Open pop-up panel is removed and the DOSSHELL.INI file is loaded into memory. (See Figure 7-11.)

MOVING THE CURSOR

When you type text, it appears at the cursor position. You can move the cursor with the mouse or keyboard.

KEYBOARD

 Use the Arrow keys described in Figure 7-12 to move the cursor around the screen and through the text.

Key Sequence	Assigned Function
Left Arrow or Ctrl+S	Moves cursor one character left.
Right Arrow or Ctrl+D	Moves cursor one character right.
Up Arrow or Ctrl+E	Moves cursor one line up.
Down Arrow or Ctrl+X	Moves cursor one line down.
Ctrl+Left Arrow or Ctrl+A	Moves cursor one word left.
Ctrl+Right Arrow or Ctrl+F	Moves cursor one word right.
Home	Moves cursor to beginning of line.
End	Moves cursor to end of line.
Ctrl+Enter	Moves cursor to left most character of next line.
Ctrl+Q+E	Moves cursor to top of current window.
Ctrl+Q+X	Moves cursor to bottom of current window.
Ctrl+Home or Ctrl+Q+R	Moves cursor to beginning of file.
Ctrl+End or Ctrl+Q+C	Moves cursor to end of file.

Figure 7-12
Keys Used to Move
the Cursor

MOUSE

 Place the mouse pointer in the middle of the screen.

 Click the Mouse Select button once.

Notice that the cursor is repositioned when the Arrow keys or Mouse Select button is pressed. To continue this lesson, you need to move the cursor to the bottom of the file.

KEYBOARD

 Press Ctrl+End.

The screen is updated and the bottom of the file is displayed.

SCROLLING TEXT

You will locate the text shown in Figure 7-13 by using the keys described in Figure 7-14 to scroll the text file up.

KEYBOARD

 Press the PgUp key until you locate the selection = line above the title = Turquoise line.

```
    File  Edit  Search  Options                              Help
┌──────────────────────────────────────────────────────────────────┐
│                          DOSSHELL.INI                              │
│                                                                    │
│      selection =                                                   │
│      {                                                             │
│            title = Turquoise                                       │
│            foreground =                                            │
│            {                                                       │
│                base = black                                        │
│                highlight = brightwhite                             │
│                selection = brightwhite                             │
│                alert = brightred                                   │
│                menubar = brightwhite                               │
│                menu = black                                        │
│                disabled = white                                    │
│                accelerator = brightwhite                           │
│                dialog = black                                      │
└──────────────────────────────────────────────────────────────────┘
 MS-DOS Editor <F1=Help>  Press ALT to activate menus    │      00001:001
```

Figure 7-13
DOSSHELL.INI Text File

Key Sequence	Assigned Function
Ctrl+Up Arrow or Ctrl+W	Scrolls text up one line.
Ctrl+Up Down or Ctrl+Z	Scrolls text down one line.
Page Up	Scrolls text up one page.
Page Down	Scrolls text down one page.
Ctrl+Page Up	Scrolls text left one screen.
Ctrl+Page Down	Scrolls text right one screen.

Figure 7-14
Keys Used to Scroll
Text

SELECTING TEXT

Now you will copy text to the internal clipboard buffer starting with the **selection =** line down through the second brace (}) after the **cursor = bright-green** line using the keys described in Figure 7-15.

KEYBOARD OR MOUSE

Move the cursor to the selection = **line.**

Key Sequence	Assigned Function
Shift+Left or Shift+Right	Selects character to cursor left or right.
Shift+Up or Shift+Down	Selects characters on line above or below cursor.
Shift+Ctrl+Left Arrow	Selects word left of arrow.
Shift+Ctrl+Right Arrow	Selects word right of arrow.

Figure 7-15
Keys Used to Select
Text

KEYBOARD

 Press and continue holding the Shift key.

 Press the Down Arrow key until the second brace (}) after the cursor = bright-green **line is selected or highlighted.**

MOUSE

 Place the mouse pointer on top of the line containing selection =.

 Hold the Mouse Select button down while moving the mouse pointer down until the second brace (}) after the cursor = bright-green **line is selected or highlighted.**

You may have to practice several times before you successfully select or highlight the text to be copied. Once you are successful, you will copy the selected text to the clipboard.

KEYBOARD OR MOUSE

 Switch to the menu bar and select the Edit pull-down panel.

 Select the Copy command.

The Edit pull-down panel is removed and the selected text is copied to the clipboard.

PASTING TEXT

You will copy the clipboard text to the line located above the **associations =** line of text near the bottom of the text file. You can use the keys described in Figure 7-16 to cut and paste text.

Figure 7-16
Keys Used to Cut and
Paste

Key Sequence	Assigned Function
Del	Deletes selected text.
Shift+Del	Copies or cuts selected text to internal buffer.
Shift+Ins	Copies or pastes stored text to cursor position.

KEYBOARD OR MOUSE

 Position the cursor on the brace (}) located just above the line containing associations = near the bottom of the file.

 Switch to the menu bar and select the Edit pull-down panel.

 Select the Paste command.

The Edit pull-down panel is removed and the text stored in the clipboard is copied to the current cursor position.

> **Note:** If you are not successful, you should select the Exit command in the File pull-down panel without saving your changes and try again.

If you are successful, you have added another copy of the last color selection to the Shell.

INSERTING AND REPLACING TEXT

In this lesson, you will modify the new color selection that you added to the Shell. You will start by changing the title of the new entry.

KEYBOARD OR MOUSE

 Position the cursor on the letter *T* in "Turquoise" in the new section you just copied.

 Use the keys described in Figure 7-17 to replace "Turquoise" with "My new color selection".

Key Sequence	Assigned Function
Backspace or Ctrl+H	Deletes character left of cursor.
Del or Ctrl+G	Deletes character at cursor.
Ctrl+T	Deletes contiguous characters right of cursor.
Ctrl+Y	Deletes line at cursor position.
Ctrl+Q+Y	Deletes from cursor position to end of line.
Shift+Tab	Deletes leading spaces in current line.
Ins or Ctrl+V	Toggles from character overwrite to insert mode.
Ctrl+P then Ctrl+key	Insert special text character.

Figure 7-17
Keys Used to Delete
or Replace Text

```
foreground =                              background =
{                                         {
      base = black                              base = brightcyan
      highlight = brightwhite                   highlight = blue
      selection = brightwhite                   selection = black
      alert = brightred                         alert = brightwhite
      menubar = black                           menubar = brightyellow
      menu = black                              menu = brightyellow
      disabled = white                          disabled = brightyellow
      accelerator = white                       accelerator = brightyellow
      dialog = black                            dialog = brightyellow
      button = black                            button = brightwhite
      elevator = black                          elevator = brightwhite
      titlebar = black                          titlebar = brightwhite
      scrollbar = black                         scrollbar = black
      borders = black                           borders = black
      drivebox = black                          drivebox = brightcyan
      driveicon = black                         driveicon = brightcyan
      cursor = black                            cursor = brightgreen
}                                         }
```

Figure 7-18
New Sample
DOSSHELL.INI Color
Selection

```
black            brightblack
blue             brightblue
red              brightred
cyan             brightcyan
magenta          brightmagenta
green            brightgreen
brown            brightbrown
white            brightwhite
```

Figure 7-19
Available
DOSSHELL.INI Color
Choices

CHANGING THE SHELL'S COLORS

You can create your own color selection by reassigning the colors in the DOSSHELL.INI file. You should save an extra copy of the DOSSHELL.INI file before starting. A new color sample is described in Figure 7-18. You can create your own Shell colors by using the color choices described in Figure 7-19.

USING BOOKMARKS

You can define temporary bookmarks within your data files by using the keys defined in Figure 7-20.

Figure 7-20
Keys Used to Set
Bookmarks

Key Sequence	Assigned Function
Ctrl+K then 0, 1, 2, or 3	Set bookmark.
Ctrl+Q then 0, 1, 2, or 3	Go to set bookmark.

Figure 7-21	Key Sequence	Assigned Function
Keys Used to Search for Text	Ctrl+Q or Ctrl+F	Search for text.
	F3	Repeat find.

SEARCHING FOR TEXT

You can search for matching text strings by using the keys defined in Figure 7-21.

SAVING TEXT FILE CHANGES

You can easily save your changes at any time.

KEYBOARD OR MOUSE

 Switch to the menu bar and select the File pull-down panel.

 Select the Exit command.

The File pull-down panel is removed and a pop-up panel is displayed prompting you to save changes made.

 Select "Yes."

The file is saved and the Editor is exited. You can use the DOS Shell's change color option to select and display the new color selection.

You have successfully created a new text file using the DOS Editor!

You have completed the last lesson in this chapter. You should proceed with the next chapter for a better understanding of how to use the DOS Command Line and DOS Utilities.

Using DOS Commands and Utilities

In this chapter we will introduce you to the command and utility programs that come with DOS. By using these commands and utilities you can perform many of your day-to-day DOS tasks. As was mentioned earlier, you can perform many of these same tasks with the DOS Shell, whereas you can perform others only with a command or utility.

The diskettes that come with DOS contain many files. Some of the files contain the code that makes up the DOS program as well as its commands and utilities. Other files contain data that tells DOS how to work.

In this chapter we will discuss the following topics:

- Entering Commands at the DOS Command Prompt

- Getting Help for DOS Command Parameters

- DOS Commands

- DOS Utilities

ENTERING COMMANDS AT THE DOS COMMAND PROMPT

You start commands, utilities, and application programs by typing their name as the first part of a "command line" at the DOS Command Prompt. DOS then determines if the name represents a command, a utility, or an application. A command line requests DOS to run a command, utility, or application program. To you, a user of DOS, these commands, utilities, and application programs appear very similar, but they are not exactly the same.

Commands are built into DOS, whereas utilities and applications are kept in files outside of DOS. Utilities differ from applications in that they come with DOS. Applications must be purchased separately.

One of the utilities provided with DOS is called COMMAND.COM. This utility, which is started automatically when you start your computer, contains the computer code that provides the DOS commands.

You tell DOS what you want to do by typing on the keyboard. Before you can tell DOS what you want to do, however, you have to wait for DOS to tell you it is ready to accept a command line. DOS does this by displaying the DOS Command Prompt. The normal DOS Command Prompt is the current drive and current directory followed by the > character. DOS displays the Command Prompt when it is ready for you to tell it what to do. In other words, DOS prompts you to tell it what to do.

> **Note:** You can change or customize your DOS Command Prompt. See the section "Displaying and Changing Your DOS Prompt String" for more information on how the DOS Command Prompt works.

Once you see the DOS Command Prompt, you tell DOS what to do by typing in a command line that names the command, utility, or application you want to work with. After the name, you provide additional parameters, if they are required. There are several ways that you can supply these parameters:

Command Line Options   When you enter the command, utility, or application name, you also enter all of the other information that will be necessary to do what you want. Most DOS commands and utilities use this method.

Line Interactive   After you enter the name of the command, utility, or applications, you wait to be asked questions that you respond to. Some DOS commands and utilities use this method (e.g., DATE and TIME). Some applications also use this method.

Through a Profile or Control File   When you enter the command, utility, or application name, you also enter the name of a file that indicates what you want done. There is usually a default name that is used in these situations. For example, the GRAPHICS program uses the default profile named GRAPHICS.PRO.

Full-Screen Interactive   After you enter the name of the command, utility, or application, you wait to be asked questions that you respond to. A few DOS utilities use this method (e.g., FDISK). Many applications use this method. Some full-screen applications, as well as the DOS Shell, allow you to work with the mouse as well as the keyboard.

As the individual commands and utilities are described below and in the chapters that follow, you will be told how to interact with them.

FILENAMES, OPTIONS, AND SWITCHES

We have already described the various ways of specifying the filenames and directories you will be working with. If you would like to review them, see "Data Files" (Chapter 2). Most of the DOS commands and utilities require you to enter one or two filenames, although some do not require any. Here are a few simple examples:

- The VER command does not require any parameters at all. It simply displays the DOS version.

- The DIR command does not require any parameters either. If you do not tell DIR which file or files you are interested in, it will show you all the files. However, if you do tell DIR which file or files you are interested in, it will show you only those files.

- The TYPE command requires only one filename, which is the name of the file you want to be displayed.

- The COPY command requires at least two filenames, the file that you want to copy from and the file that you want to copy to.

When you are using many of the utilities, you will supply additional information other than filenames. Some commands work with just directories (e.g., MKDIR, CHDIR, and RMDIR), and some utilities work only with entire drives (e.g., FORMAT and CHKDSK). Each command or utility has its own way of being told what to do.

In addition to drives, directory names, and filenames, some of the commands and utilities can be controlled through what we call *switches*. A switch is simply another parameter you enter to change or control what the command or utility does for you. In DOS, a switch is always preceded by the slash character (/) and can be one or more characters long. For example, the MEM switches /PROGRAM and /DEBUG control the type of information the MEM utility shows you. Switches are almost always optional.

The DOS Command Prompt is displayed by the COMMAND.COM (or just COMMAND) utility. When you enter a command to DOS, you are talking to the COMMAND.COM utility. If COMMAND recognizes what you have entered as one of its own commands, it will run the command you have entered. If COMMAND does not recognize what you have entered as one of its own commands, it will search your computer's fixed disk or diskette drives looking for a file that has the same name as the command that you have entered. If such a file is found, COMMAND reads the computer code contained in the file into memory and runs it. Command uses the DOS PATH to find the file. See "The PATH Command" (Chapter 9) for more information on the DOS PATH.

HELP WITH COMMANDS

As we discuss the DOS commands, you will see that some have complicated formats with several parameters — including dates, times, filenames, directory names, and device names. Many of the commands have one or more switches. Remembering all of this information can be difficult, especially if you use these commands infrequently. This will be even more difficult when you learn about the remaining DOS commands.

When you need a refresher on how to use a command you can look up the command in a book like this one. It would be convenient if DOS itself could provide you with help on using these commands like the help provided by the DOS Shell. DOS 3.3 and DOS 4.0 do not provide command help. DOS 5.0 does provide help in two similar ways.

1. On any DOS command, you can use the /? switch. /? provides a brief description of the command and all of its parameters and switches. For example, to get help on DATE, you could use the command

```
C:\>date /?
Displays or sets the date.

DATE [date]

DATE with no parameters displays the current date setting and
prompts for a new one.  Press ENTER to keep the same date.
C:\>
```

and to get help on DIR, you could use the command

```
C:\>dir /?
Displays a list of files in a directory.

DIR [pathname] [/P] [/W] [/O[:sortorder]] [/A[:attributes]] [/S] [/B] [/L]

   pathname       The directory and/or files to list.
   /P             Pause after each screenful of information.
   /W             Use wide list format.
   /S             Display files in the specified directory and all subdirectories.
   /B             Use bare format (filenames only).
   /L             Use lower case.
   /O             List files in sorted order.
   sortorder    N name                  S size
                E extension             D date and time
                G group subdirectories  - prefix to reverse order
   /A             Display files with specified attributes.
   attributes   D subdirectories        R read-only files
                H hidden files          A files ready for archive
                S system files          - prefix meaning "not"

Switches may be preset in DIRCMD environment variable.  Override
preset options by prefixing any switch with -, e.g., /-W.
C:\>
```

2. You can use the HELP command. "HELP commandname" displays the same information as "commandname /?" does. You may chose to use either form of help. If you use HELP and leave off the commandname, HELP displays a short summary of every DOS command.

THE BASIC INTERPRETER

Listed here are the files on the DOS diskettes that are associated with the BASIC interpreter. Not all releases of DOS will contain all of these files.

BASIC.COM   This program starts a subset of the Advanced BASIC Interpreter.

BASICA.COM   This program starts the Advanced BASIC Interpreter. Extensive documentation is available for the BASIC interpreter. Examples of this are the BASIC Reference and BASIC Handbook publications available from IBM. The full use of the BASIC interpreter is beyond the scope of this book.

To use this program, simply type BASICA and press Enter. If you know the name of the BASIC program that you want to run, you can enter that as well. For example,

BASICA MORTGAGE

will run the MORTGAGE.BAS program that is supplied with DOS. To exit the BASIC interpreter, type SYSTEM and press Enter.

QBASIC.EXE   Like BASIC and BASICA, this program provides access to the BASIC interpreter. However, the QBASIC functionality is far more robust. It provides an environment that is much more supportive of program development. QBASIC was introduced with DOS 5.0.

QBASIC provides a menu-driven interface that provides push-button access to help for instant statement syntax and a full-screen interface to edit your BASIC program with.

There are a few parameters you might need to know to use the QBASIC program:

filename   This parameter tells QBASIC what program file you want to work with. If any other parameters are specified, they must come before the filename on the QBASIC command line.

/B   This tells QBASIC that you want to work in monochrome mode, even if you have a color display.

/EDITOR   This tells QBASIC that you want to work with EDIT, the full-screen text file editor. This is different from using the full QBASIC program that will handle syntax check and execution of BASIC programs.

/G   This tells QBASIC to maximize the performance of accesses to a Color Graphics Adapter display. You may notice some "snow" on the screen when using this mode.

/H   This tells QBASIC to put your display into the highest possible resolution mode so that you get the most lines possible to display at one time.

/MBF   This tells QBASIC to treat IEEE-format binary numbers as Microsoft Binary Format numbers.

/NOHI   This tells QBASIC not to use high-intensity characters on the display.

/RUN   This tells QBASIC to run the filename that you have specified on the QBASIC command.

QBASIC.HLP   This file contains the help text for the QBASIC program.

QBASIC.INI   This file contains information that tells QBASIC how it should run. It contains preferences that can be set through the Options menu selection.

MORT-GAGE.BAS and other .BAS files   A sample BASIC program. There may be several different files ending in the extension .BAS. Each of these is a sample BASIC program.

CONTROLLING YOUR COMPUTER'S INTERNAL CLOCK

Once your computer is up and running, it can keep track of the current date and time. DOS uses the current date and time to time-stamp some of the actions that you or your applications perform with fixed disks and diskettes. Many of your applications will also use the current date and time to keep track of your activities within the application, or to automatically put the date and time on reports that are generated.

DOS will time-stamp the following fixed disk and diskette activities:

- When you create the volume label of a disk

- When you change the volume label of a disk

- When you create a file

- When you change the contents of the file

- When you create a subdirectory

The CHKDSK utility will display the date and time at which the disk and diskette volume labels were created or changed. The DIR command will display the date and time for files and subdirectories.

DISPLAYING AND CHANGING THE COMPUTER'S DATE

The computer's date is changed with the DATE command. There are two ways that you can use the date command:

1. Enter just the DATE command. DOS will display the current date and then prompt you to enter the new date. This is also how you can find out what the current date is. At the DATE Prompt, you can enter a new date, or just press Enter (↵). If you just press Enter, the current date will not be changed.

```
C:\>DATE
Current date is Sun  6-26-1988
Enter new date (mm-dd-yy):

C:\>DATE
Current date is Sun  6-26-1988
Enter new date (mm-dd-yy): 6-27-1988

C:\>_
```

With the first DATE command in this example, we just looked at the current date and pressed Enter. The second DATE command was used to change from June 26, 1988 to June 27, 1988.

The characters "mm-dd-yy" are DOS's way of telling you in what order to enter the new date.

MM   This means that DOS is expecting two month digits. Of course, 01 stands for January, 02 for February, and so on, up to 12 for December. The numbers 01 to 09 can be shortened to just 1 to 9, the 0 in front is not required.

DD   This means that DOS is expecting two day-of-the-month digits. This number must be appropriate for the month that is being entered; January will accept from 1 to 31, February will accept from 1 to 28 (29 in leap years), and so on.

YY   This means that DOS is expecting two year digits. The two digits are the last two digits of the current year, 88 means 1988. DOS will also accept four-digit numbers, so either 88 or 1988 can be used. When you use two year digits, DOS will accept dates from January 1, 1980 (1-1-80) through December 31, 1999 (12-31-99). When you use four year digits, DOS will accept dates from January 1, 1980 (1-1-1980) through December 31, 2099 (12-31-2099).

As you can see in the example, DOS also displays an abbreviation of the day of the week when it displays the current date. DOS does not allow you to enter the day of the week when you enter a new date.

Day of Week	DOS Abbreviation
Sunday	Sun
Monday	Mon
Tuesday	Tue
Wednesday	Wed
Thursday	Thu
Friday	Fri
Saturday	Sat

2. Enter the new date at the same time you enter the DATE command. If you use this method, DOS will not display the current date and will not prompt you to enter a date.

```
C:\>DATE 6-26-88
C:\>_
```

In this example, the computer's date was changed from June 27, 1988, back to June 26, 1988.

In these two examples, the hyphen (-) character was used to separate the month, day, and year numbers. You could also use the slash (/) or the dot (.) characters when entering the new date, but DOS will use the hyphen character when it displays the date.

DOS will not permit you to enter a new date that is not acceptable, such as 6-50-88 (June 50, 1988). If you try to enter an invalid date like this, DOS will display an error message and prompt you to enter a new date.

```
C:\>DATE 6-50-88

Invalid date
Enter new date (mm-dd-yy): 6-26-1988

C:\>_
```

In the United States, we write dates as June 26, 1988. In other words, we write the month first, followed by the day of the month, followed by the year. Because of this, when DOS is running in the United States, it displays dates as month-day-year. This is also the order in which DOS is expecting you to enter a new date. Not all countries write dates the same way as the United States does, so in other countries, DOS will display the date in a different order. In these countries the "mm-dd-yy" characters that DOS displays will be changed so that you know in what order to enter the new date.

```
C:\>DATE 6-26-88

Invalid date
Enter new date (dd-mm-yy): 26-6-1988

C:\>_
```

In this example, we are trying to set the date to July 26, 1988 while running DOS in Germany. Germany uses the day-month-year format. When DOS looked at what we entered, it believed we were trying to set the month to 26. Since this is not an acceptable value, it generated the error. When we enter the date in the correct format, it works properly.

Of course, DOS does not really know what country you are working in. It believes what the COUNTRY statement in the CONFIG.SYS file says.

DISPLAYING AND CHANGING THE COMPUTER'S TIME

The computer's time is changed with the TIME command. There are two ways in which you can use the time command:

1. Enter just the TIME command. DOS will display the current time and then prompt you to enter the new time. This is also how you can find out what the current time is. At the TIME Prompt, you can enter a new time, or just press Enter (↵). If you just press Enter, the current time will not be changed.

```
C:\>TIME
Current time is  6:15:09.29p
Enter new time:

C:\>TIME
Current time is  6:15:22.19p
Enter new time:  7:15:22p

C:\>_
```

The first TIME command was just used to find out what time it was. After DOS displayed the current time, we pressed Enter. This did not change the current time. The second TIME command was used to change the time. After DOS displayed the time, we entered a new time and pressed Enter.

In the United States, DOS will always display the time as hours:minutes:seconds:hundredths. In other countries, DOS may use other characters to separate the hours, minutes, seconds, and hundredths. When you enter a new time, you should enter it using the same characters that DOS uses when the time is displayed.

2. Enter the new time at the same time you enter the TIME command. If you use this method, DOS will not display the current time and will not prompt you to enter a time.

```
C:\>TIME  6:15p
C:\>_
```

In this example, the computer's time was changed to 6:15 PM.

Command	Time Set To
TIME 16	16:00:00.00
TIME 16:15	16:15:00.00
TIME 16:15:22	16:15:22.00
TIME 16:15:22.19	16:15:22.19

Figure 8-1
DOS Time Padding

In the preceding examples, DOS used a 12-hour clock. In other countries, DOS may use a 24-hour clock. This is often referred to as *Military Time* in the United States. When you use a 24-hour clock, the A.M. hours (from midnight to noon) are numbered from 0 to 12 and the P.M. hours (from noon to midnight) are numbered from 13 to 24.

Regardless of the format that DOS uses to show you the time, you can enter the new time as either 12- or 24-hour-clock time. To enter the new time in 12-hour format, follow the new time with either "a" or "p". The "a" indicates an A.M. (morning) time and the "p" indicates a P.M. (afternoon) time. You cannot put blanks between the time and the A.M./P.M. indicator. To enter the new time in 24-hour format, just enter the hour number and DOS will figure out if it is A.M. or P.M.

When you are entering the new time, you only need to enter as many of the parts (hours, minutes, seconds, hundredths) of the time as necessary. DOS will fill in all of the unspecified parts with zero. (See Figure 8-1.)

DOS will not permit you to enter a new time that is not acceptable (e.g., 16:75 or 4:75 P.M.). If you try to enter an invalid time, DOS will display an error message and will prompt you to enter a new time.

```
C:\>TIME 16:75

Invalid time
Enter new time: 16:57

C:\>_
```

WHICH FILES ARE HERE?

The DIR command gives you the ability to get a list of the files and directories that are in a directory.

As an example, DIR with no parameters might display

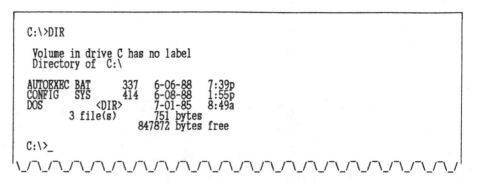

```
C:\>DIR

 Volume in drive C has no label
 Directory of  C:\

AUTOEXEC BAT      337   6-06-88   7:39p
CONFIG   SYS      414   6-08-88   1:55p
DOS           <DIR>     7-01-85   8:49a
       3 file(s)          751 bytes
                      847872 bytes free

C:\>_
```

In general, DIR displays the following information:

- Partition Volume Label

- Partition Volume Serial Number (DOS 4.0 and higher only)

- Name of the Directory Being Listed

- Filename

- Filename Extension

- Directory Indicator

- File Size

- Last Modified Date

- Last Modified Time

- Number of Names Displayed

- Total Bytes in Files Displayed (DOS 5.0 and higher only)

- Number of Free Bytes in the Partition

The format of the date and time may change depending on the country you are in.

After you enter DIR \DOS /P, the screen looks like this:

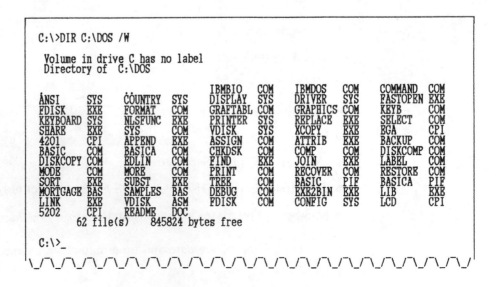

```
.                <DIR>      07-01-85    8:49a
                 <DIR>      07-01-85    8:49a
COMMAND   COM     37637     06-17-88   12:00p
ANSI      SYS      9148     06-17-88   12:00p
COUNTRY   SYS     12838     06-17-88   12:00p
DISPLAY   SYS     15741     06-17-88   12:00p
DRIVER    SYS      5274     06-17-88   12:00p
FASTOPEN  EXE     16302     06-17-88   12:00p
FORMAT    COM     22923     06-17-88   12:00p
GRAFTABL  COM     10271     06-17-88   12:00p
GRAPHICS  COM     16733     06-17-88   12:00p
KEYB      COM     14759     06-17-88   12:00p
KEYBOARD  SYS     23360     06-17-88   12:00p
NLSFUNC   EXE      6910     06-17-88   12:00p
PRINTER   SYS     18946     06-17-88   12:00p
REPLACE   EXE     17199     06-17-88   12:00p
SHARE     EXE     10285     06-17-88   12:00p
SYS       COM     11472     06-17-88   12:00p
VDISK     SYS      6376     06-17-88   12:00p
XCOPY     EXE     17087     06-17-88   12:00p
EGA       CPI     49052     06-17-88   12:00p
4201      CPI      6404     06-17-88   12:00p
APPEND    EXE     11170     06-17-88   12:00p
Press any key to continue . . .
_
```

You can request a more condensed form of display by using the /W switch. When you use /W, only the filename and filename extension are shown. DIR will also present five columns of names.

```
C:\>DIR C:\DOS /W

 Volume in drive C has no label
 Directory of  C:\DOS

                            IBMBIO   COM   IBMDOS   COM   COMMAND  COM
ANSI      SYS   COUNTRY  SYS   DISPLAY  SYS   DRIVER   SYS   FASTOPEN EXE
FDISK     EXE   FORMAT   COM   GRAFTABL COM   GRAPHICS COM   KEYB     COM
KEYBOARD  SYS   NLSFUNC  EXE   PRINTER  SYS   REPLACE  EXE   SELECT   COM
SHARE     EXE   SYS      COM   VDISK    SYS   XCOPY    EXE   EGA      CPI
4201      CPI   APPEND   EXE   ASSIGN   COM   ATTRIB   EXE   BACKUP   COM
BASIC     COM   BASICA   COM   CHKDSK   COM   COMP     COM   DISKCOMP COM
DISKCOPY  COM   EDLIN    COM   FIND     EXE   JOIN     EXE   LABEL    COM
MODE      COM   MORE     COM   PRINT    COM   RECOVER  COM   RESTORE  COM
SORT      EXE   SUBST    EXE   TREE     COM   BASIC    PIF   BASICA   PIF
MORTGAGE  BAS   SAMPLES  BAS   DEBUG    COM   EXE2BIN  EXE   LIB      EXE
LINK      EXE   VDISK    ASM   FDISK    COM   CONFIG   SYS   LCD      CPI
5202      CPI   README   DOC
          62 file(s)    845824 bytes free

C:\>_
```

Here are some hints on using the DIR command:

- DIR with no filename or filename extensions is the same as DIR *.*

- DIR NAMEONLY is the same as DIR NAMEONLY.*

- To show only files that do not have an extension, use DIR NAMEONLY.

- DIR .EXT is the same as DIR *.EXT

> **Note:** DOS 3.3 and DOS 4.0 users can use the FIND filter (Try DIR ¦ FIND "<DIR>") to get DOS to show only the DIR entries in a directory. DOS 5.0 users can use the /A:d parameter to tell DIR to list only directory names.

There have been several enhancements in the DIR command for DOS 5.0:

- You can now tell DIR the attributes of the files and directories that you want displayed. To do this, you use the /A: switch and select from the following attribute list:

  A Display only files with the Archive attribute set (modified since the last time the file was backed up).

  –A Display only files without the Archive attribute set (not modified since the last time the file was backed up).

  D Display only directory names (no files).

  –D Display only filenames (no directories).

  H Display only files with the Hidden attribute set.

  –H Display only files without the Hidden attribute set.

  R Display only files with the ReadOnly attribute set.

  –R Display only files without the ReadOnly attribute set.

  S Display only files with the System attribute set.

  –S Display only files without the System attribute set.

  You can also combine the attribute values to reduce the displayed information even further.

```
C:\>DIR /A:HR-D

 Volume in drive C has no label
 Directory of  C:\

IBMBIO   COM    33302 01-29-91   1:02a
IBMDOS   COM    36994 01-29-91   1:02a
         2 file(s)      70296 bytes
                      1252352 bytes free

C:\>_
```

In this example, the DIR command displays only files with the Hidden and ReadOnly attributes set.

● You can now tell DIR how you want the displayed information sorted. To do this, you use the /O: switch and select from the following sort control list:

D   Sort by date and time of last modification. The oldest entries will occur before newer entries.

–D   Sort by date and time of last modification. The newest entries will occur before older entries.

E   Sort alphabetically (A occurs before Z) by filename extension.

–E   Sort backwards (Z occurs before A) by filename extension.

G   Group all directory names before any filenames.

–G   Group all filenames before any directory names.

N   Sort alphabetically (A occurs before Z) by filename.

–N   Sort backwards (Z occurs before A) by filename.

S   Sort by increasing file size (smallest file before larger files).

–S   Sort by decreasing file size (largest file before smaller files).

As with the attribute control, you can combine sort orders. DIR will sort the list by the first sort control you specify and then sort matches by the second, by the third, and so on.

If you enter just the /O without an additional order control string, the directory output will be sorted by filename and then by filename extension.

```
C:\>DIR FILE*.*

 Volume in drive C has no label
 Directory of  C:\
FILEA    2         10 02-17-91    1:41p
FILE     1          9 02-17-91    1:41p
FILE     2          9 02-17-91    1:41p
FILEA    1         10 02-17-91    1:41p
         4 file(s)        38 bytes
                    12974080 bytes free

C:\>DIR FILE*.* /O:SNE

 Volume in drive C has no label
 Directory of  C:\
FILE     1          9 02-17-91    1:41p
FILE     2          9 02-17-91    1:41p
FILEA    1         10 02-17-91    1:41p
FILEA    2         10 02-17-91    1:41p
         4 file(s)        38 bytes
                    12974080 bytes free

C:\>_
```

In this example, we first look for all files that match FILE*.*, and find that there are four files. They are not in any particular order in the directory. Next, we look for the same files, but we ask DIR to sort the output first by file size, then by filenames, and finally, by filename extensions.

- You can now tell DIR to process subdirectories from where it starts. This is similar to the subdirectory processing of the ATTRIB and TREE commands. If DIR starts at the root directory, it will process all of the directories on your disk. You tell DIR to process subdirectories by using the /S switch.

- You can tell DIR that you do not want the titles and the summary information that it normally provides. To do this, you use the /B switch.

    When you use the /B switch, the line-by-line output from DIR is also changed. Only the names and name extensions are displayed (not the file size, modification date and time, and so on), and the name and extension are put together with the period character separator (e.g., FILENAME.EXT) rather than the normal DIR output (e.g., FILENAME EXT). This allows you to begin the creation of a batch file by using the DIR command and redirecting the output to a file. After the file is created, you can edit the file to enter the commands you want to use on each file.

- You can tell DIR that you want entries which have not been sorted to be displayed in lowercase letters (*a* rather than *A*). To do this, you use the /L switch.

- You can use the DOS environment to set up a standard set of parameters that you want DIR to use each time you enter the DIR command. You do this with the SET command. Simply SET DIRCMD=parameters, where "parameters" is any set of the switches just described.

If you use the SET DIRCMD technique, you can still override the standard parameters by specifying the opposite parameter on the DIR command line. For instance, if you have SET DIRCMD=/O:NE to sort by filename first and then by filename extension, you can still enter the command DIR /O:EN to sort by filename extension first, followed by sorting by filename.

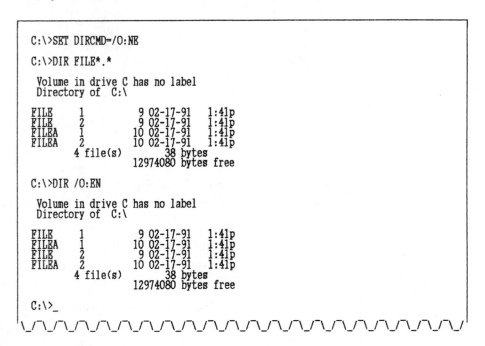

```
C:\>SET DIRCMD=/O:NE

C:\>DIR FILE*.*

 Volume in drive C has no label
 Directory of  C:\

FILE     1          9 02-17-91   1:41p
FILE     2          9 02-17-91   1:41p
FILEA    1         10 02-17-91   1:41p
FILEA    2         10 02-17-91   1:41p
        4 file(s)          38 bytes
                     12974080 bytes free

C:\>DIR /O:EN

 Volume in drive C has no label
 Directory of  C:\

FILE     1          9 02-17-91   1:41p
FILEA    1         10 02-17-91   1:41p
FILE     2          9 02-17-91   1:41p
FILEA    2         10 02-17-91   1:41p
        4 file(s)          38 bytes
                     12974080 bytes free

C:\>_
```

WHAT IS MY DIRECTORY LAYOUT?

The TREE utility gives you the ability to get a complete picture of what your fixed disk or diskette looks like. This is different from the DIR command, which lets you look at only the files and directories in a single directory of your fixed disk or diskette.

You can use the TREE utility to look at the disk organization in several ways:

1. You can look at all of the subdirectories. To do this, simply use the TREE command and tell it which drive you want to look at. Of course, if you want to look at the current drive, you do not need any parameters at all.

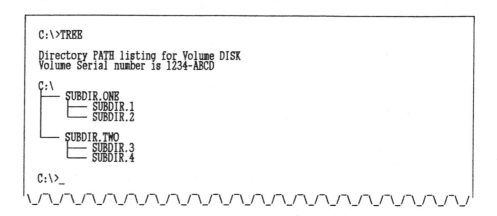

```
C:\>TREE

Directory PATH listing for Volume DISK
Volume Serial number is 1234-ABCD

C:\
├──── SUBDIR.ONE
│     ├─── SUBDIR.1
│     └─── SUBDIR.2
└──── SUBDIR.TWO
      ├─── SUBDIR.3
      └─── SUBDIR.4

C:\>_
```

2. You can look at all of the subdirectories and the files. As in 1, you do this by using the TREE command and telling TREE which drive you want to look at. But in this case, you tell TREE that you want to see the files also. To do this, add /F to what you type to start the TREE utility.

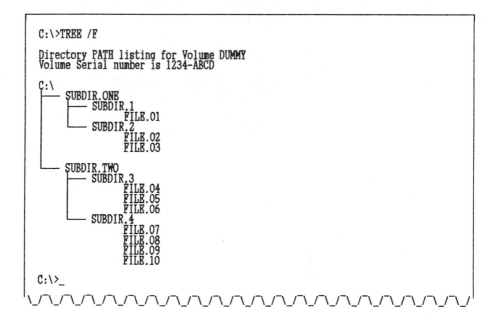

```
C:\>TREE /F

Directory PATH listing for Volume DUMMY
Volume Serial number is 1234-ABCD

C:\
├──── SUBDIR.ONE
│     ├─── SUBDIR.1
│     │       FILE.01
│     └─── SUBDIR.2
│             FILE.02
│             FILE.03
└──── SUBDIR.TWO
      ├─── SUBDIR.3
      │       FILE.04
      │       FILE.05
      │       FILE.06
      └─── SUBDIR.4
              FILE.07
              FILE.08
              FILE.09
              FILE.10

C:\>_
```

3. You can look at just some of the subdirectories. This is just like the first case, except that you tell TREE not to start at the root of the disk. Instead, you tell TREE where on the disk you want to start. The TREE utility will show you the subdirectories and files from that point on down into the disk.

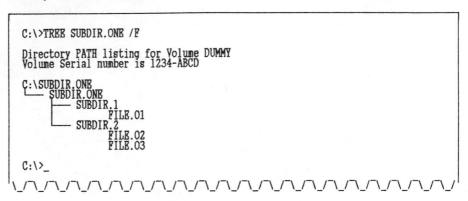

```
C:\>TREE SUBDIR.ONE /F

Directory PATH listing for Volume DUMMY
Volume Serial number is 1234-ABCD

C:\SUBDIR.ONE
└───SUBDIR.ONE
    ├──── SUBDIR.1
    │          FILE.01
    └──── SUBDIR.2
               FILE.02
               FILE.03

C:\>_
```

There is one other switch that the TREE utility allows, /A. This switch causes the TREE utility to use an alternate set of characters when displaying or printing out your disk's structure. This is provided for people who have printers that do not support the graphics characters that are normally used by TREE. It also helps for displays that have a code page loaded that does not support the block graphics characters. The /A switch can be used with all of the forms of TREE shown earlier.

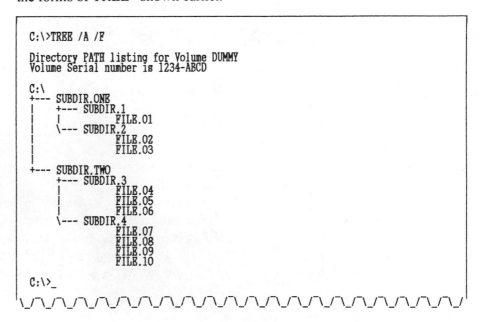

```
C:\>TREE /A /F

Directory PATH listing for Volume DUMMY
Volume Serial number is 1234-ABCD

C:\
+--- SUBDIR.ONE
|    +--- SUBDIR.1
|    |         FILE.01
|    \--- SUBDIR.2
|              FILE.02
|              FILE.03
|
+--- SUBDIR.TWO
     +--- SUBDIR.3
     |         FILE.04
     |         FILE.05
     |         FILE.06
     \--- SUBDIR.4
               FILE.07
               FILE.08
               FILE.09
               FILE.10

C:\>_
```

> **Note:** The TREE utility can produce many lines of output. Unlike the DIR command, the TREE utility does not support the /P switch. To see the TREE output one screen at a time, use the MORE filter. Try TREE \ /F ¦ MORE.

The TREE utility was enhanced to provide a pictorial view of your disk structure in DOS 4.0. Prior to that release, it would list only the directories and files on your disks. Previous releases would not allow you to specify the starting directory; you could process only an entire drive.

DISPLAYING AND CHANGING A FILE'S ATTRIBUTES

The ATTRIB command has three primary uses:

- Changing the Archive, Hidden, ReadOnly, and System attributes of your files.
- Showing you the Archive, Hidden, ReadOnly, and System attributes of your files.
- Finding files for you.

CHANGING FILE ATTRIBUTES

The ATTRIB utility is used to change the Archive and ReadOnly attributes of the files on your disks. Following is a description of these attributes:

Archive   The Archive attribute is used to indicate when a file has been changed. This attribute is turned on when a file is created and whenever the contents of a file are changed. It is not turned on when a file is renamed.

The DOS utilities BACKUP and XCOPY can use the Archive attribute as part of the selection criteria for which files they process. When you back up a file, its Archive attribute is turned off. So, by using the Archive attribute, you do not always have to back up all of the files on your disk. If you have a complete backup already, you can just back up the files that have been created or changed since the last backup was done.

ReadOnly   The ReadOnly attribute is used to tell DOS that you do not want the contents of a file changed. DOS will not allow a command, utility, or application to write into a file if the ReadOnly attribute is set.

The ATTRIB command uses the following parameters to enable you to control the files attributes:

+A   Turn on the Archive attribute. The Archive attribute is used by the XCOPY and BACKUP commands as a selection criteria for the files that it processes. It generally means that the file has been modified since the last time it was backed up.

–A   Turn off the Archive attribute.

+H   Turn on the Hidden attribute. The Hidden attribute is used by commands that search your directories. These commands, like DIR and ATTRIB, will not show you the hidden files. The files are there — they just do not always get shown to the user.

–H   Turn off the Hidden attribute.

+R   Turn on the ReadOnly attribute. The ReadOnly attribute prevents programs from writing into or deleting your files.

–R   Turn off the ReadOnly attribute.

+S   Turn on the System attribute. The System attribute is similar to the Hidden attribute, in that it is frequently used to prevent files from being processed or shown to the user. It has a slightly different meaning, in that it should only be turned on for files that are part of the DOS Kernel.

–S   Turn off the System attribute.

Note: The parameters +H, –H, +S, and –S were not available prior to DOS 5.0.

You can enter these parameters either before or after the filename on the ATTRIB command. You can change both the Archive and ReadOnly attributes at one time.

You can change the attributes of one file or many files. To change one file's attributes, just use the file's name. To change several files at once, use the * and ? filename matching characters.

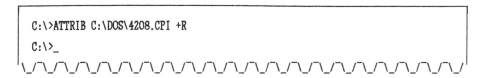

```
C:\>ATTRIB C:\DOS\4208.CPI +R
C:\>_
```

LISTING FILE ATTRIBUTES

Anytime you want to know what the Archive or ReadOnly attributes of your files are, you can use the ATTRIB utility to find out. You can look at the attributes for one file or many files. In the following example, we are listing the attributes of all of the Code Page Information (.CPI) files in the DOS subdirectory.

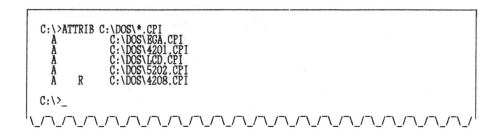

```
C:\>ATTRIB C:\DOS\*.CPI
    A              C:\DOS\EGA.CPI
    A              C:\DOS\4201.CPI
    A              C:\DOS\LCD.CPI
    A              C:\DOS\5202.CPI
    A       R      C:\DOS\4208.CPI
C:\>_
```

The output of ATTRIB shows you that the Archive attribute is turned on for all of the files shown and that the ReadOnly attribute is turned on for the file \DOS\4208.CPI. The ReadOnly attribute is turned on because we turned it on in the example on changing file attributes. The Archive attributes are all turned on because we have not done a backup of our fixed disk since we installed DOS.

ATTRIB's output is easy to understand. To the left of each file listed, the character A will appear if the Archive attribute is turned on. The character R will appear if the ReadOnly attribute is turned on, and so on. The A, H, R, and S characters will appear if all the attributes are turned on.

You should turn off the ReadOnly bit of the 4208.CPI file at this time. Use the command ATTRIB -R \DOS\4208.CPI and then list the attributes again to see what has changed.

FINDING FILES ON YOUR DISKS

The ATTRIB utility is very useful for searching for files on your disks. As the disk drives get larger, more and more files are being kept on them. We have seen some computers that have had over 50,000 files on their disks. With a large number of files, it is easy to forget where you put one. For a description of how to use ATTRIB to find the file you are looking for, see "The ATTRIB and DIR Commands."

LOOKING INSIDE A FILE

The TYPE command provides you with the ability to see the contents of a file. DOS will allow you to TYPE any file, but files that do not contain plain text will appear as gibberish.

To see what we mean, try typing your own AUTOEXEC.BAT and CONFIG.SYS files. When we typed our AUTOEXEC.BAT file, this is what we saw:

```
C:\>TYPE AUTOEXEC.BAT
@echo off
cls
set comspec=c:\dos\command.com
prompt [$p]
call \progs\setpath
call setappend
call setsubst
set include=c:\ibmc\include
set lib=c:\ibmc\small
set display=vdidy010
set tmp=d:\
set PCTERM@=00000000
rem c:\vdi\progs\init_vdi
c:\msmouse\mouse
call virtual d:

C:\>_
```

The contents of many AUTOEXEC.BAT and CONFIG.SYS files are different. Try this on your own computer to see what is in your files.

Some files contain a combination of text and nontext data. An example of this is the file BASIC.COM in the DOS subdirectory. Try typing this file. You should hear some beeps and there should be some text and other "things" on the screen. We do not recommend using TYPE to view files that contain nontext data.

> **Note:** Unlike the DIR command, the TYPE command does not support the /P switch. If you want to see only one screen of data at a time, use the MORE filter. Try TYPE filename ¦ MORE.

CLEARING THE DISPLAY

The CLS command is used to clear the screen. All the characters are replaced with blanks and the cursor is placed in the upper left-hand corner of the screen. Then the prompt is displayed and you are ready to enter your next command.

To clear the screen, just enter CLS and press Enter (↵).

COPYING FILES

The COPY command is used to copy files. This is similar to using a photocopier to make a copy of a file from a file drawer. The difference is that with the COPY command, you can copy only the whole file. With the photocopier, you can copy just the pages you want.

In general, you have to tell COPY the name of the original file you want to copy and the name of the new file you want to create. This is not quite all there is to it. You can make copies of several original files at one time, or you can combine several original files into one new file. You can also replace an existing file with a copy of another file.

The COPY command is actually very easy to use. The only difficulty is figuring out what you really want to do. Once you know that, you can easily get it done.

COPY ONE FILE

To copy a single file, you just need to know where the original file is and where you want to create the new file. Simply enter COPY, the name of the original file, and where you want the file copied to. Here are some examples:

```
C:\>COPY FILE.ONE B:
        1 File(s) copied
C:\>COPY FILE.ONE B:\
        1 File(s) copied
C:\>COPY FILE.ONE \ANOTHER.DIR\FILE.TWO
        1 File(s) copied
C:\>COPY \ANOTHER.DIR\FILE.TWO
        1 File(s) copied
C:\>COPY FILE.TWO FILE.ONE
        1 File(s) copied
C:\>_
```

The first COPY command will make a copy of the original file FILE.ONE in the current directory on drive B:. The second COPY command will make a copy of the original file FILE.ONE in the root directory of drive B:.

The third COPY command introduces a new ability. You can make a copy of a file and give the new file a different name. The fourth COPY command also introduces a shortcut in telling COPY what you want done. If you do not tell COPY where to put the copy of the original file, it will put the copy in the current directory of the current drive.

The last COPY command replaces FILE.ONE with FILE.TWO.

Warning: Since FILE.TWO was created from FILE.ONE, this is not a problem. However, if you tell COPY to replace a file, it will do just that. You cannot get the replaced file back. The data that was there is now gone forever.

When you copy a file, the new file will have the same size, date, and time as the original file. However, it will not have the same attributes as the original file. You will have to use the ATTRIB command to set the attributes on the new file (see "Displaying and Changing a File's Attributes" for more information).

The COPY command cannot copy files that have the Hidden or System attributes set. In other words, you cannot copy a file that you cannot see with the DIR command.

COPY SEVERAL FILES

To copy several files, you can use either several COPY commands or the * and ? filename matching characters (see "DOS Wildcard Filenames" for a description of the * and ? filename matching characters). Entering several commands may be your only choice, but if the filename matching characters can be used, it can make your life much easier.

For example, if you want to copy each of the files that have the filename THISFILE, you can use the original filename THISFILE.*. This tells COPY to copy each file that has the filename THISFILE, regardless of the filename extension. In the following example, the three files THISFILE.001, THISFILE.002, and THISFILE.003 will be copied to the C:\WASTED directory.

```
C:\>COPY THISFILE.* \WASTED
THISFILE.001
THISFILE.002
THISFILE.003
        3 File(s) copied

C:\>_
```

Likewise, you could copy each of the files that have the filename extension ABC. You would use the original filename *.ABC. This tells COPY to copy each file that has the filename extension ABC, regardless of the filename. In the following example, the files FILE0001.ABC and FILE0002.ABC will be copied to the C:\WASTED directory.

```
C:\>COPY *.ABC \WASTED
FILE0001.ABC
FILE0002.ABC
        2 File(s) copied

C:\>_
```

You could have tried to use the ? filename matching character for the last example but you might have gotten more than you wanted.

```
C:\>COPY FILE000?.* \WASTED
FILE0001.ABC
FILE0002.ABC
FILE0002.DEF
        3 File(s) copied

C:\>_
```

Here, the extra file FILE0002.DEF was copied. There is an easy way to prevent this from happening. Before you use the * and ? filename matching characters to copy files, use them with the DIR command. This way, you will get to see which files will be copied before you actually do the copy.

You can COPY using the filename matching characters and change the names of the files you copy. In this case, the meaning of the * and ? are somewhat different. They mean "Use the characters from the original filename or filename extension." You have to be careful of what you try to do. Watch:

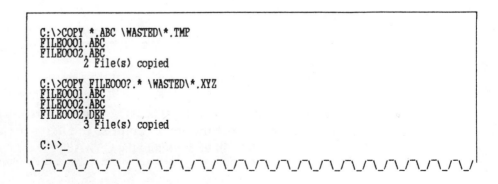

```
C:\>COPY *.ABC \WASTED\*.TMP
FILE0001.ABC
FILE0002.ABC
        2 File(s) copied

C:\>COPY FILE000?.* \WASTED\*.XYZ
FILE0001.ABC
FILE0002.ABC
FILE0002.DEF
        3 File(s) copied

C:\>_
```

The first COPY command copies files FILE0001.ABC and FILE0002.ABC to the directory C:\WASTED. The new filename tells COPY to keep the entire filename the same, just change the filename extensions. The filename extensions of the files are all changed to TMP, so the new names are FILE0001.TMP and FILE0002.TMP.

The second COPY command copies files FILE0001.ABC, FILE0002.ABC, and FILE0002.DEF to the directory C:\WASTED. The filename extensions of the files are all changed to XYZ, so the new names are FILE0001.XYZ, FILE0002.XYZ and FILE0002.XYZ. Whoops! Two of the new names are the same. First, FILE0001.ABC will be copied to C:\WASTED\ FILE0001.XYZ. Then FILE0002.ABC will be copied to C:\WASTED\ FILE0002.XYZ. We are OK so far. Now the problem! FILE0002.DEF is copied to C:\WASTED\FILE0002.XYZ. This replaces the copy of FILE0002.ABC.

Warning: Be careful when using the filename matching characters and changing the filenames at the same time. Think through what each of the new filenames and filename extensions will be before executing the COPY command.

The filename matching characters can only be used in the filename and the filename extension. They cannot be used in entering the directory names.

COPY ALL FILES

Copying all files is very similar to copying several files. There are two ways to copy all the files in one directory:

1. Use the *.* original filename. This tells COPY to copy each file that has any filename and any filename extension.

2. Use just the directory name. This tells COPY to copy every file in the directory.

Of course, copying every file with any filename and any filename extension is the same thing as copying all the files in the directory.

A shorthand way of telling COPY to copy all the files in the current directory is to use just the DOT name (.). The DOT name refers to the current directory:

```
C:\>COPY . \ANOTHER.DIR
FILE.001
FILE.002
FILE.003
        3 File(s) copied

C:\>_
```

In this example, the DOT was referring to the current directory of the current drive, or C:\. Some other ways of entering the same copy command would be:

1. COPY C:*.* \ANOTHER.DIR

2. COPY C:\ \ANOTHER.DIR

3. COPY *.* \ANOTHER.DIR

4. COPY . \ANOTHER.DIR

All four of these ways work equally well. You can use whichever one you please.

COPY SEVERAL FILES INTO ONE NEW FILE

So far, we have been discussing how you make a new file for each of the original files you are copying. Now we will show you how to combine several files into one new file. This is called *concatenation*.

Suppose you have two files, FILE.001 and FILE.002, that you want to put together into one new file named FILES.ALL. To do this, enter the COPY command and tell COPY to add the two files together to create one new file:

```
C:\>COPY FILE.001+FILE.002 FILES.ALL
FILE.001
FILE.002
        1 File(s) copied

C:\>_
```

By using the + symbol, you have told COPY to treat the two files together as the original file. Notice that COPY displayed the message "1

File(s) copied." This is because it treated the two files together as one original file.

You do not always have to list each of the original files that you want to copy. You can use the filename matching characters as explained earlier. You can also use the directory name if you want to combine all of the files in the directory. In both of these cases, you need to be careful. For instance, let's change the COPY command that we used in the last example:

```
C:\>COPY FILE.* FILE.ALL
FILE.001
FILE.002
FILE.ALL
Content of destination lost before copy
Content of destination lost before copy
        1 File(s) copied

C:\>_
```

The message "Content of destination lost before copy" indicates that COPY has noticed that the new file is also one of the original files. In this case, the copy may not have produced what you were expecting.

> **Warning:** If you are using filename matching characters, or if you are using the directory name to enter the original files for concatenation, you should put the new combination file in another directory or on another disk.

ADVANCED USES FOR COPY

There are two limitations to the COPY command:

1. You can copy from only one directory at a time. If you want to copy files from several directories, you will have to use separate COPY commands. The XCOPY (eXtended COPY) command may be able to simplify what you want to do. See "Copying Directory Structures" (Chapter 10) for more information.

2. You can copy only files that will fit on the target disk. If you are trying to copy a large file from one disk to another, you may want to use the BACKUP

and RESTORE commands. The BACKUP command allows you to copy a very large file from your fixed disk to several diskettes. The RESTORE command allows you to copy the backed up file parts to a new file on another fixed disk. See "Making Backups of Your Files" and "Restoring Files from Your Backups" for more information.

DELETING FILES

You will not want to keep every file on your disks forever. Two commands allow you to get rid of files on your disks: DEL (short for DELETE) and ERASE. Both of these commands perform the same function—they get rid of one or more files on your disks.

It is very easy to get rid of files, perhaps too easy. You simply enter the DEL or ERASE command and the name of the file you want to get rid of.

```
C:\>ERASE SOMEFILE
C:\>_
```

The file SOMEFILE is now gone. You cannot get it back. Very easy. Too easy! Be careful when using the DEL and ERASE commands; their effect is permanent. This is true even for DOS 5.0 users, who have access to the UNDELETE command. UNDELETE may be able to reclaim a file immediately after it is deleted, but once the file's directory entry or disk space has been reused, nothing will get the file back. If you have just deleted a file by mistake, see "Recovering Deleted Files" for instructions on how to try to get it back.

To make sure that you do not delete files by mistake, you should use the /P switch. Both DEL and ERASE will then ask you to confirm the deletion before it takes place.

```
C:\>ERASE FILE* /P
C:\FILE1,    Delete (Y/N)?n

C:\FILE2,    Delete (Y/N)?y

C:\>_
```

As with many other commands, you can get rid of several files with a single command. You can use the * and ? filename matching characters to do this.

```
C:\>ERASE SOMEFILE.*
C:\>_
```

All of the files with the filename of SOMEFILE are now gone. Permanently.

You can also erase all the files in a directory. When ERASE sees that you are erasing all of the files in a directory, it will ask you if you really want to do this.

```
C:\>ERASE ANYDIR
All files in directory will be deleted!
Are you sure (Y/N)?Q
All files in directory will be deleted!
Are you sure (Y/N)?Y

C:\>_
```

If you answer Y, then all the files will be erased. If you answer N, then the files will not be erased. The DEL and ERASE commands ask this question because it is fairly simple to enter the name of a directory when you meant to enter the name of a file. It is always better to be sure.

Warning: When you are erasing using filename matching characters, or are erasing entire directories, it is a good idea to use the DIR command first. This will give you a chance to see what is about to be deleted before you actually do the ERASE or DEL command. Afterwards, it is too late. You may not even be able to find out what was deleted. You can also use the /P switch with ERASE or DEL.

RENAMING FILES

Just as you will not want to keep files around forever, you may change your mind about what they should be named. You can use the RENAME command to change the filename and filename extension of one or more files.

Using RENAME is as simple as using any other DOS command. You enter the RENAME command, the original name of the file, and the new name of the file.

```
C:\>RENAME SOMEFILE.123 NEWNAME.123
C:\>RENAME NEWNAME.123 SOMEFILE.*
C:\>_
```

In this example, the first RENAME command changes the filename from SOMEFILE to NEWNAME. The filename extension, 123, stays the same. The second RENAME command changes the filename back to SOMEFILE. Again, the extension stays the same. However, this example shows you how to just change the name without having to reenter the filename extension.

In fact, you can use the filename matching characters with RENAME just as they are used with COPY. When these characters are used to enter original files, the RENAME command will use them to select which files are renamed. When they are used to enter the new filenames, the RENAME command will replace them with the corresponding original filename characters.

```
C:\>RENAME FILE000?.ABC *.DEF
C:\>_
```

If the files FILE0001.ABC, FILE0002.ABC, and FILE0003.ABC were found, they would be renamed to FILE0001.DEF, FILE0002.DEF, and FILE0003.DEF.

PRINTING FILES

There are two primary ways to print files with DOS:

1. Use COPY to copy the file to the printer.

2. Use PRINT to print the file on the printer.

If you use the COPY command, DOS and your computer cannot do anything else until all of the data has been copied to the printer. The COPY command may finish several seconds (or even minutes) before the file has been completely printed. This is because many printers have an internal area where they store the data to be printed. Even if you have this type of printer, it does not take a very large file to fill up the printer's buffer area. Once the buffer is full, your computer can send characters only as quickly as they are being printed.

DOS provides you with the capability to print files and documents on your printer without keeping your computer from doing other work. It can do this because your computer is so much faster than your printer is. To do this, use the PRINT extension to DOS. When you are printing files through the PRINT extension, DOS will occasionally ask PRINT to check to see if the printer is ready for more data to print. If it is, PRINT will read the data from the disk or diskettes and send it to the printer. It does this by borrowing the computer away from what you are doing for a very short time. Usually, you will not even notice this happening.

You enter PRINT commands for two primary reasons:

1. To tell DOS where you want your files printed.

2. To control which files you want to print on your printer.

STARTING PRINT

The first time you enter a PRINT command, part of the PRINT utility stays in your computer's memory as an extension to DOS. In order to tell PRINT how it should work, you can supply several switches the first time you enter a PRINT command:

/D:device   This is the device on which you want to print your files. Each time you turn your computer on, you can print on a different device, but you can specify the /D: switch only the first time you use the PRINT command. Everything you print with the PRINT command will go to that printer until you restart your computer.

    If you do not enter the /D:, DOS will prompt you to enter the name of the device you want to print on. If you simply press Enter (↵), the PRN device will be used. The other printer devices that DOS supplies are LPT1 (LPT1 and PRN are the same device), LPT2 and LPT3, AUX, COM1 (COM1 and AUX are the same device), COM2, COM3, COM4.

    Be careful with the device name you specify. If you enter a device name that does not exist, you will have to restart your computer to fix this mistake.

    If you do enter the /D: switch, it must be the first parameter on the PRINT command line.

/Q:count   This is the count of files that you have waiting to be printed at one time. It is the number of files that PRINT will keep in its queue of work to do. You can enter a count from 4 to 32. If you do not enter a count, DOS will use 10.

The rest of the switches that you can use with PRINT are used to tune PRINT's performance. For more information on tuning the performance of the PRINT command, see "PRINT." Please read this section before entering values other than the DOS defaults.

Again, these PRINT switches can only be entered the first time the PRINT command is used. When you installed DOS, a PRINT command may have been added to your AUTOEXEC.BAT file. If so, this PRINT command is used to set the switches just listed.

If you are working on a computer that is attached to a network server, there are restrictions on how you can use the PRINT command. You can use PRINT on a redirector station to print files from the server to your private printer. From a redirector station, you can use PRINT to print any files to a shared printer on the server, but the preferred method is to use the NET PRINT command. You cannot use PRINT on a server station at all, because the network gives you the ability to share your printers, which PRINT does not understand.

CONTROLLING WHAT IS PRINTED

Once PRINT is started, there are four functions you can perform with it:

1. You can list the files in the print queue. You do this by entering the PRINT command without any additional parameters.

```
C:\>PRINT

  C:\AUTOEXEC.BAT is currently being printed
  C:\CONFIG.SYS is in queue

C:\>_
```

2. You can add files to the print queue. You can do this by entering PRINT with the name of the file you want printed. If you want, you can add the /P switch, but PRINT will assume this is what you want to do.

   PRINT will always skip to the top of the next page before starting to print a new file. Unless you cancel files or terminate printing, the files will be printed in the order you add them to the queue (the order you PRINT them). You can add several files to the queue simply by listing all of their names on a single PRINT command.

```
C:\>PRINT MEMOS\SCHEDULE.TXT MEMOS\STATUS.TXT

  C:\SCHEDULE.TXT is currently being printed
  C:\STATUS.TXT is in queue

C:\>_
```

3. You can cancel files from the print queue. You do this by entering the PRINT command, the name of the file you want to cancel, and the /C switch.

```
C:\>PRINT DUMMY /C
File not in PRINT queue - C:\DUMMY

   C:MEMOS\SCHEDULE.TXT is currently being printed
   C:MEMOS\STATUS.TXT is in queue
C:\>PRINT MEMOS\STATUS.TXT /C

   C:MEMOS\SCHEDULE.TXT is currently being printed

C:\>_
```

The first PRINT command shows you what happens if you try to cancel a file that is not in the queue. PRINT displays an error message. There is one other message you could get in this situation, "PRINT queue is empty." In either case, your file was not found.

The next PRINT command successfully cancels the printing of MEMOS\STATUS.TXT.

4. You can terminate all PRINT activity. You do this by entering the PRINT command along with the /T switch. A more familiar description of this would be to purge the print queue. All files in the queue are thereby canceled. If a file is currently being printed, PRINT will print the message "All files cancelled by operator," skip to the top of the next page, and tell the printer to beep.

```
C:\>PRINT /T
PRINT queue is empty

C:\>_
```

If you want to use the printer that PRINT is using, you must either wait until PRINT is finished or use PRINT /T to terminate what PRINT is doing. If you or your applications try to use the printer that PRINT is using, an "Out of paper" or "Not ready writing device" error will occur. If this happens and you cannot wait, use PRINT /T.

Another obvious use of the /T switch is when you want to print a file and do not want to wait for PRINT to finish what is in the queue. To do this, you can use two PRINT commands, one to terminate printing and one to print the new file. You can also do this with just one command:

PRINT /T FILENAME.NEW

You can actually combine a series of filenames and switches to create a very complex request to PRINT. We recommend that you keep it simple and only do one type of operation with each PRINT command. You can still print or cancel several files with one command. This can be done by listing each file you want to print or cancel on one PRINT command. You can also use the * and ? filename matching characters with the PRINT command.

PRINT can only remember a small number of files at one time. Using the wildcard filename matching characters may cause the PRINT queue to become full. This will not cause PRINT a problem, but once the queue becomes full, PRINT will ignore any further matching files it finds. If this situation occurs, some files you are expecting to print will not be printed.

Since you may be doing something while PRINT is printing your files, it only has two ways of telling you what it is going on:

1. When PRINT encounters a problem with the printer, it will tell you this the next time you issue a PRINT command. A typical example   of this is when the printer runs out of paper. Another example is when the printer is not turned on.

```
C:\>PRINT C:\AUTOEXEC.BAT
Errors on list device indicate that it
may be off-line. Please check it.

  C:\AUTOEXEC.BAT is currently being printed

C:\>
```

2. When PRINT experiences a problem with the disk or diskette you are print- ing from, the following actions occur:

- The file PRINT has trouble reading is canceled (just as with /C).

- A message is printed indicating the problem that occurred with the disk or diskette. One example of this type of message is "Not ready error reading file B:\DOCUMENT.TXT." Other messages could occur.

- The printer skips to the top of the next page.

- If there are more files in the queue, PRINT starts printing them.

MAKING NEW DIRECTORIES

The MKDIR and MD commands are used to create subdirectories on your fixed disks and diskettes. They are very simple to use; you simply type the command and the name of the subdirectory that you want to create. You can create a new subdirectory on the current drive in the current directory. By entering an alternate drive and path, you can create a new subdirectory anywhere you want one. There is no difference between MKDIR and MD, one is just a shorter command for you to enter. Try entering the following commands:

```
C:\>MKDIR SUBDIR-1.1
C:\>MKDIR \SUBDIR-1.2
C:\>MKDIR C:SUBDIR-1.3
C:\>MKDIR C:\SUBDIR-1.4
C:\>_
```

The four MKDIR commands in the example above would create four subdirectories: SUBDIR.1, SUBDIR.2, SUBDIR.3, and SUBDIR.4. The commands show the four possible ways to enter a new subdirectory name:

1. A simple subdirectory name will create a subdirectory of the current directory on the current drive.

2. A subdirectory name that is preceded by a path will create a new subdirectory anywhere on the current drive.

3. A subdirectory name that is preceded by a drive will create a new subdirectory in the current directory of any drive.

4. A subdirectory name that is preceded by a drive and path will create a new subdirectory on any drive in any directory.

In this example, all four subdirectories would be created on the same drive and in the same directory, C:\.

When a new subdirectory is created, DOS automatically adds two names:

1. The DOT (.) <DIR> entry. DOS creates the DOT entry and points it to itself. In this way, you can use the "." name to refer to the current directory.

2. The DOTDOT (..) <DIR> entry. DOS creates the DOTDOT entry and points it to the new subdirectory's parent directory. In this way, you can use the ".." name to refer to the current directory's parent directory.

When you specify a new path with a new subdirectory name, the entire path must already exist. Otherwise, you must create the path one level at a time.

```
C:\>MKDIR SUBDIR-1.1\SUBDIR-2.1\SUBDIR-3.1
Unable to create directory

C:\>MKDIR SUBDIR-1.1\SUBDIR-2.1

C:\>MKDIR SUBDIR-1.1\SUBDIR-2.1\SUBDIR-3.1

C:\>_
```

In the preceding example, we first asked DOS to create SUBDIR-1.1\ SUBDIR-2.1\SUBDIR-3.1, but because SUBDIR-1.1\SUBDIR-2.1 did not already exist, DOS responded that it could not do what we asked. Then we created SUBDIR-1.1\SUBDIR-2.1, which was successful, and SUBDIR-1.1\ SUBDIR-2.1\SUBDIR-3.1, which was also successful.

If you try to create a subdirectory that already exists, DOS will respond with the message "Directory already exists." If you try to create a subdirectory when a file exists with the same name, DOS will respond with the message "Unable to create directory."

DOS has a fully qualified file specification limit of just 64 characters. If you try to create a directory whose fully qualified name is longer than 64 characters, DOS will respond with the message "Unable to create directory" (see page 20 for the definition of a fully qualified path).

If there are active SUBSTs, JOINs, or ASSIGNs, the subdirectories you create may not go where you expect them. See "Drive Letter Mapping Functions" for more information on these situations.

CHANGING THE CURRENT DIRECTORY

The CHDIR and CD commands are used to change the current directory you are working in. There is no difference between the CHDIR and CD commands; one is just a shorter command for you to enter.

DOS never requires you to change your current directory, but some applications can work only with files that are in the current directory. You may also want to change your current directory if you are going to use DOS to work with several files in one subdirectory. As long as you are working with files in the current directory, you do not need to enter a path when you are entering the filenames.

The CHDIR and CD commands will work on the current drive or any other drive that you enter. For each drive you have, there is a current directory. The following example demonstrates how to use CHDIR by using the subdirectories that we created in the MKDIR example.

```
C:\>CHDIR DUMMY
Invalid directory
C:\>CHDIR SUBDIR-1.1\SUBDIR-2.1\SUBDIR-3.1
C:\SUBDIR-1.1\SUBDIR-2.1\SUBDIR-3.1>CHDIR ..
C:\SUBDIR-1.1\SUBDIR-2.1>CHDIR ..
C:\SUBDIR-1.1>CHDIR \SUBDIR-1.2
C:\SUBDIR-1.2>CHDIR C:\SUBDIR-1.3
C:\SUBDIR-1.3>CHDIR \
C:\>_
```

Here is what happened during this example:

- The first CHDIR command attempted to change the current directory to a name that did not exist. DOS will not allow you to do this and responded with the message "Invalid directory." You will also get this message if you try to change the current directory to a filename rather than a subdirectory name.

- The second CHDIR command shows how you can change the current directory several levels at a time. Notice how the DOS Command Prompt changed to show you the new current directory. That is because our prompt is set to display the current drive and current directory. Each time we change the current directory, the prompt will change automatically.

- The third and fourth CHDIR commands show you how you can change quickly to parent directories by using the DOTDOT name. This could have been done with one command (CHDIR ..\..).

- The next three CHDIR commands show several alternate ways of entering the new subdirectory you want to go to.

  Every part of the path you enter must exist before you can make it the current directory. DOS will not create these parts for you unless you use the MKDIR command.

> **Note:** You can also use the CHDIR and CD commands to display what the current directory is. Even if your DOS Command Prompt displays the current directory, this can be useful to find out what the current directory of another drive is. Simply enter the CHDIR command and the drive that you want to know about.

REMOVING DIRECTORIES

The RMDIR and RD commands allow you to remove subdirectories that have been previously created. There is no difference between the RMDIR and RD commands, one is just fewer characters for you to type.

Before a subdirectory can be removed, it must be empty. This means that it must not have any files or subdirectories in it. You do not have to worry about this, because DOS will not allow you to remove a subdirectory that still contains files or subdirectories. Instead, DOS will respond with the message "Invalid path, not directory, or directory not empty." In general, if the DIR output of a directory shows only the DOT and DOTDOT entries, then you should be able to remove it. This is not always the case; some applications install hidden files or subdirectories. If the DIR shows only the DOT and DOTDOT entries and DOS still responds with "Invalid path, not directory, or directory not empty," DOS 3.3 and DOS 4.0 users will need to use a utility such as Norton Utilities to remove the subdirectory. DOS 5.0 users can use the ATTRIB command to turn off the hidden or system attributes (e.g., ATTRIB *.* -S -H), then the files can be deleted with the DEL or ERASE commands.

The DOT and DOTDOT entries are automatically created by DOS and cannot be removed by the user. A subdirectory can be removed as long as it contains only the DOT and DOTDOT entries.

The following example shows you how to remove the subdirectories that were created by the MKDIR examples just given. As in the MKDIR example, the four methods of entering the subdirectory name to be removed are shown.

```
C:\>RMDIR SUBDIR-1.1
Invalid path, not directory,
or directory not empty

C:\>RMDIR SUBDIR-1.1\SUBDIR-2.1\SUBDIR-3.1

C:\>RMDIR SUBDIR-1.1\SUBDIR-2.1

C:\>RMDIR SUBDIR-1.1

C:\>RMDIR \SUBDIR-1.2

C:\>RMDIR C:SUBDIR-1.3

C:\>RMDIR C:\SUBDIR-1.4

C:\>_
```

DOS will not allow you to remove the current directory of any drive. If you attempt to remove the current directory of a drive, DOS will respond with the message "Attempt to remove current directory."

If there are active SUBSTs, JOINs, or ASSIGNs, the subdirectories you remove may not be where you expect them. See "Drive Letter Mapping Functions" (Chapter 10) for more information on these situations.

WHAT'S IN MY COMPUTER'S MEMORY?

The MEM utility was introduced in DOS 4.0, and it allows you to see information about the memory in your computer. Prior to DOS 4.0, the only information available is that provided by the CHKDSK command (see "Using CHKDSK").

There can be one, two, or three types of memory in your computer:

1. Conventional memory. This is the memory that DOS and your applications normally use. The processor in your computer limits this to 1,048,576 bytes (1024KB or 1MB). Your computer needs part of this memory, so DOS and your applications are limited to just 655,360 bytes (640KB). This memory is available on all computers that DOS supports. All of the different parts of DOS can use this memory. All of your applications can use this memory also.

2. Extended memory. This type of memory was first introduced on the IBM Personal Computer AT. This memory is available only on computers that use the 80286, 80386, or 80486 processors. Extended memory is limited to 15,728,640 bytes (15MB) on 80286-based computers and 4,294,967,296 bytes (4GB) on 80386- and 80486-based computers. DOS and DOS applications can use only partially the extended memory of your computer. The portions of DOS that use extended memory are

- DOS itself when loaded into the High Memory Area (HMA).

- The VDISK.SYS device driver.

- The RAMDRIVE.SYS device driver.

- The SMARTDRV device driver (and some other disk cache programs).

- The EMM386.EXE, XMAEM.SYS, and XMA2EMS.SYS device drivers.

When you have used these device drivers to support EMS, DOS and your applications use more of your extended memory by making it look like expanded memory.

In addition, any application that is written to be an XMS or EMS client may use extended or expanded memory also. Some operating systems that support the full range of extended memory are

- Operating System/2®

- AIX

- XENIX®

3. Expanded memory. Many of the more advanced applications require more than just 640KB of memory. Expanded memory is a partial solution to this problem. Expanded memory is what looks like a small part of the computer's conventional memory area. By "tricking" the computer, the expanded memory adapters can provide up to 32MB of memory. There is one drawback, however—only a small portion of this memory can be worked with at one time. Several applications have been rewritten to be able to use expanded memory. In DOS 4.0, the functions VDISK.SYS, FASTOPEN, and BUFFERS can use expanded memory. In DOS 5.0, the functions RAMDRIVE.SYS, SMARTDRV.SYS, and FASTOPEN can use expanded memory.

For a thorough explanation of the different types of memory in your computer, see "Expanded Memory Support" (Chapter 11).

The MEM utility will show you information only for the types of memory that your computer has installed.

By using the different formats of the MEM command, you can get four different reports on what is happening with your memory:

1. **Summary report.** This is the basic memory report. It shows the amount of each type of memory your system has, how much is in use, and how much is left for DOS and your applications to use (see Figure 8-2).

The "bytes total memory" count is the amount of conventional memory that your computer contains. The "bytes available" count is the amount of conventional memory that is available for DOS and your applications to use. The "largest executable program size" count is the largest number of bytes of conventional memory that can be allocated in one piece.

The "bytes total EMS memory" count is the total amount of expanded memory that is available for DOS and your applications to use. The "bytes free EMS memory" count is the amount of expanded memory that is still left for DOS and your applications to use.

The "bytes total extended memory" count is the total amount of extended memory that is available for DOS and your applications to use. The "bytes available extended memory" count is the amount of extended memory that is still left for DOS and your applications to use.

```
 655360 bytes total conventional memory
 654336 bytes available to MS-DOS
 576688 largest executable program size

7602176 bytes total contiguous extended memory
      0 bytes available contiguous extended memory
      0 bytes available XMS memory
        MS-DOS resident in High Memory Area
```

Figure 8-2
DOS 5.0 MEM
Summary Report

2. Program report. This is the basic memory report plus a listing of the programs that currently own memory (see Figure 8-3). In addition to the basic memory report output, MEM also displays each piece of memory that is currently allocated to a program in your computer's conventional memory. MEM will also list the loaded device drivers and show how much space is being used by the configurable parts of DOS. To get this report, you need to enter the MEM command with the /PROGRAM switch. DOS 5.0 allows you to abbreviate /PROGRAM as just /P. See "Who's Using My Memory?" for a detailed description of what this report shows.

```
Address    Name        Size     Type
-------    --------    ------   ------
000000                 000400   Interrupt Vector
000400                 000100   ROM Communication Area
000500                 000200   DOS Communication Area

000700     IO          000AE0   System Data

0011E0     MSDOS       0013F0   System Data

0025D0     IO          0010F0   System Data
           SETVER      000180   DEVICE=
           HIMEM       000470   DEVICE=
           RAMDRIVE    0004A0   DEVICE=
                       000130   FILES=
                       000100   FCBS=
                       000200   BUFFERS=
                       0001C0   LASTDRIVE=
0036D0     MSDOS       000040   System Program

003720     COMMAND     000940   Program
004070     COMMAND     000040   Data
0040C0     COMMAND     000100   Environment
0041D0     MOUSE       000040   Environment
004220     MOUSE       002880   Program
006AB0     DOSSHELL    000060   Environment
006B20     GRAPHICS    0016F0   Program
008220     GPRTSC      0001A0   Program
0083D0     PIC2FILE    000560   Program
008940     DOSSHELL    001130   Program
009A80     DOSSWAP     000060   Environment
009AF0     DOSSWAP     0087F0   Program
0122F0     COMMAND     000050   Data
012350     COMMAND     000940   Program
012CA0     COMMAND     000200   Environment
012EB0     COMMAND     000050   Data
012F10     MEM         000050   Environment
012F70     MEM         0176F0   Program
02A670     MSDOS       075580   -- Free --

   655360 bytes total conventional memory
   654336 bytes available to MS-DOS
   576640 largest executable program size

  7602176 bytes total contiguous extended memory
        0 bytes available contiguous extended memory
        0 bytes available XMS memory
          MS-DOS resident in High Memory Area
```

Figure 8-3
DOS 5.0
MEM /PROGRAM
Report

3. **Debugging report.** This is the most extensive report that MEM can produce. In addition to the information displayed by the Program report, MEM will also display the device drivers that are internal to IBMBIO.COM. To get this report, enter the /DEBUG switch along with the MEM utility name. DOS 5.0 allows you to abbreviate /DEBUG as just /D. See "Who's Using My Memory?" (Chapter 12) for a detailed description of what this report shows.

> **Note:** The output of MEM /PROGRAM and MEM /DEBUG is often longer than the length of your computer's display. Use the MORE filter to pause between screenfuls. Try MEM /PROGRAM ¦ MORE.

4. **Classification report.** This is a very short, concise, and useful report. The individual pieces of memory allocated to your program are summed up so that there is just one line per program in your report (see Figure 8-4).

```
Conventional Memory :

    Name              Size in Decimal          Size in Hex
    ----------        --------------------     -------------
    IBMDOS            12992    ( 12.7K)         32C0
    SETVER              352    (  0.3K)          160
    HIMEM              1136    (  1.1K)          470
    EMM386             9408    (  9.2K)         24C0
    COMMAND            2624    (  2.6K)          A40
    DOSSHELL           2160    (  2.1K)          870
    DOSKEY             4128    (  4.0K)         1020
    COMMAND            2736    (  2.7K)          AB0
    FREE                 64    (  0.1K)           40
    FREE             619440    (604.9K)         973B0

Total  FREE :        619504    (605.0K)

Total bytes available to programs :                  619504    (605.0K)
Largest executable program size :                    619312    (604.8K)

    1441792 bytes total EMS memory
    1048576 bytes free EMS memory

    5505024 bytes total contiguous extended memory
          0 bytes available contiguous extended memory
    4292608 bytes available XMS memory
            IBM DOS resident in High Memory Area
```

Figure 8-4
DOS 5.0
MEM /CLASSIFY
Report

COMPARING FILES

The COMP command is used to compare one or more pairs of files to see if they contain the same information.

```
C:\>COMP FILE.1 FILE.2
Comparing FILE.1 and FILE.2...
Files compare OK

Compare more files (Y/N) ?N

C:\>_
```

This example compares the two files, FILE.1 and FILE.2 and finds them to be the same. The COMP command always asks if you would like to compare more files. If you enter N, then the COMP command returns to DOS. If you enter Y, then COMP asks you what files you want to compare. If you enter just the COMP command with no files, it will ask you the same questions:

```
C:\>COMP
Enter name of first file to compare:FILE.1
Enter name of second file to compare:FILE.2
Option :
Comparing FILE.1 and FILE.2...
Files compare OK

Compare more files (Y/N) ?N

C:\>_
```

Prior to DOS 5.0, COMP would not allow you to compare files that were of different sizes. If you tried to, it would display an error message and ask if you want to compare other files:

```
C:\>COMP FILE.1 FILE.2
Comparing C:FILE.1 and C:FILE.2...
Files are different sizes

Compare more files (Y/N) ?N

C:\>_
```

Starting with DOS 5.0, you can now tell COMP to compare only the first several lines of the files, even if they are of different sizes. For example, the command

COMP FILE.1 FILE.2 /N=27

would compare only the first 27 lines of the file. The /N=number switch is new in DOS 5.0.

If the COMP command finds differences, then it will display those differences so you know what and where they are:

```
C:\>COMP FILE.1 FILE.2
Comparing C:FILE.1 and C:FILE.2...
Compare error at OFFSET 1
File 1 = 62
File 2 = 42

Compare more files (Y/N) ?N

C:\>_
```

The files FILE.1 and FILE.2 are different. The second byte of FILE.1 is b. The second byte of FILE.2 is B. The message "Compare error at OFFSET 1" indicates that the files are not the same at the second byte. This OFFSET value is 1 rather than 2 because COMP numbers the characters starting with zero.

People usually count starting with the value 1. This is called Base One. Computers usually start counting with the value zero. This is called Base Zero. Fortunately, it is easy to convert between the two counting systems; for the same number of items, the Base One value is always one larger than the Base Zero number.

The values that are displayed are the hexadecimal values of the two different characters. These are the values that the computer sees when it looks at the two characters. As you can see, they are different values. After the COMP command has displayed 10 different places where the files are not the same, it will stop comparing that pair of files.

While the default is to display file differences in hexadecimal, DOS 5.0 adds three new switches that allow you to control how the file differences are displayed:

/A   Display differences in ASCII. Default is hexadecimal.

/D   Display differences in decimal. Default is hexadecimal.

/L   Display the line number where miscompares occur. Default is to display the byte offset into the file where miscompares occur.

Repeating the above example, this time with the /A and /L switches, you have:

```
C:\>COMP FILE.1 FILE.2 /A /L
Comparing C:FILE.1 and C:FILE.2...
Compare error at LINE 1
File 1 - b
File 2 - B

Compare more files (Y/N) ?N

C:\>_
```

Finally, one additional switch was added in DOS 5.0 — /C. This switch allows you to compare files without regard to the case in which the characters are recorded. This allows you to compare a file that is recorded with uppercase letters (A, B, C, . . . , Z) to a file that is recorded with lowercase letters (a, b, c, . . . , z) with errors. Normally, COMP would find that A and a are different; however, with the /C switch, you can make these characters look the same to COMP. Again, using the preceding example, you have:

```
C:\>COMP FILE.1 FILE.2 /C
Comparing C:FILE.1 and C:FILE.2...
Files compare OK

Compare more files (Y/N) ?N

C:\>_
```

Not all programs write just the number of bytes that are in a file. Some programs write 128 (or more) bytes at a time. The BASIC interpreter is one such program. This means that even if a program has only 10 bytes of data, it will write 128 bytes to the file. Only the first 10 bytes will be of any value; the other 118 bytes will be random garbage. The DIR command will show the file as being 128 bytes long. These types of programs use the character value 26 (hexadecimal value 1A), also called the *End-Of-File character*, to signal the end of data. For a 10-byte file, this would be the value of the 11th byte. When COMP is comparing this type of file, it will compare all 128 bytes. Because only the first 10 characters of the file are valid, COMP may find differences after the first 10 bytes.

In order to help you understand what is happening, COMP has another message, "EOF mark not found." This message is displayed when the last byte of the file is not the End-Of-File character. If the files compare exactly, then you do not care if this message is displayed. However, if there are differences in the last 128 bytes of the file and this message is displayed, then the files may actually be the same. Since you cannot tell if they are the same or not, treat them as if they are different.

```
C:\>COMP FILE.1 FILE.2

C:FILE.1 and C:FILE.2

EOF mark not found
Files compare OK
Compare more files (Y/N) ?N

C:\>_
```

In this example, the files FILE.1 and FILE.2 are the same. The last byte of the files was not the End-Of-File character.

You can also compare several pairs of files by using the ? and * filename matching characters or by just naming directories. This is very similar to the way that the COPY command works:

```
C:\>COMP SOME.DIR ANOTHER.DIR

C:SOME.DIR\FILE.1 and C:ANOTHER.DIR\FILE.1

EOF mark not found
Files compare OK

C:SOME.DIR\FILE.2 and C:ANOTHER.DIR\FILE.2

EOF mark not found
Files compare OK
Compare more files (Y/N) ?N

C:\>_
```

All of the files in the directory SOME.DIR will be compared with files in the directory ANOTHER.DIR. In this case, both files, FILE.1 and FILE.2, compared correctly.

If the file FILE.2 had not existed in the ANOTHER.DIR directory, COMP would have displayed the message "File not found - C:ANOTHER.DIR\ FILE.2."

If you are using DOS 5.0, you can use a more powerful command to compare files. FC, for File Compare, works very similarly to COMP, but it has more features. FC can compare files as a sequence of bytes or characters like COMP. It can also compare files as sequence of text lines.

FC can be used to compare binary files. Binary files contain data formatted in a format readable only by your computer. A program is a binary format file. FC will automatically compare files as binary files if they have an extension of BIN, COM, EXE, LIB, OBJ, or SYS. You may also request a binary compare on files with different extensions by using the /B switch.

Assume that the program PGM1.COM contains the following binary data:

```
0000 BA 80 01 B4 09 CD 21 CD-20 00 00 00 00 00 00 00    ......!. ...............
0010 00 00 00 00 00 00 00 00-00 00 00 00 00 00 00 00    ......................
0020 00 00 00 00 00 00 00 00-00 00 00 00 00 00 00 00    ......................
0030 00 00 00 00 00 00 00 00-00 00 00 00 00 00 00 00    ......................
0040 00 00 00 00 00 00 00 00-00 00 00 00 00 00 00 00    ......................
0050 00 00 00 00 00 00 00 00-00 00 00 00 00 00 00 00    ......................
0060 00 00 00 00 00 00 00 00-00 00 00 00 00 00 00 00    ......................
0070 00 00 00 00 00 00 00 00-00 00 00 00 00 00 00 00    ......................
0080 54 68 69 73 20 69 73 20-61 20 6D 65 73 73 61 67    This is a mes-
0090 65 0D 0A 24 00 00 00 00-00 00 00 00 00 00 00 00    sage..$.....
```

and that the program PGM2.COM contains the following binary data:

```
0000 BA 80 01 B4 09 CD 21 CD-20 00 00 00 00 00 00 00    ......!. ...............
0010 00 00 00 00 00 00 00 00-00 00 00 00 00 00 00 00    ......................
0020 00 00 00 00 00 00 00 00-00 00 00 00 00 00 00 00    ......................
0030 00 00 00 00 00 00 00 00-00 00 00 00 00 00 00 00    ......................
0040 00 00 00 00 00 00 00 00-00 00 00 00 00 00 00 00    ......................
0050 00 00 00 00 00 00 00 00-00 00 00 00 00 00 00 00    ......................
0060 00 00 00 00 00 00 00 00-00 00 00 00 00 00 00 00    ......................
0070 00 00 00 00 00 00 00 00-00 00 00 00 00 00 00 00    ......................
0080 54 68 69 73 20 69 73 20-61 6E 6F 74 68 65 72 20    This is another
0090 6D 65 73 73 61 67 65 0D-0D 24 00 00 00 00 00 00    message..$......
```

To compare these two files, you could use this command:

```
C:\>fc pgm1.com pgm2.com /b
Comparing files PGM1.COM and PGM2.COM
00000089: 20 6E
0000008A: 6D 6F
0000008B: 65 74
0000008C: 73 68
0000008D: 73 65
0000008E: 61 72
0000008F: 67 20
00000090: 65 6D
00000091: 0D 65
00000092: 0A 73
00000093: 24 73
00000094: 00 61
00000095: 00 67
00000096: 00 65
00000097: 00 0D
00000098: 00 0D
00000099: 00 24
C:\>
```

Notice that FC did not report any differences until position 89. At position 89 in PGM1 is a blank (or 20). In PGM2 it is an n (or 6E). The differences continue through position 99. After that the files are again the same, so FC does not report any differences.

FC can also be used to compare text files. Text files are files that can be read by people. FC will automatically compare files as text files unless they have an extension of BIN, COM, EXE, LIB, OBJ, or SYS. You may also request a text compare on files with different extensions by using the /L switch.

Assume that the file FILE.1 contains the following text:

This is file number 1

It has three text lines.
It has three text lines.
It has three text lines.

and that the file FILE.2 contains the following text:

This is file number 2

It has three text lines.
It has three text lines.
It has three text lines.

If you want to check to see if these two files are the same, you would enter

fc file.1 file.2

and FC would respond with

```
Comparing files FILE.1 and FILE.2
***** FILE.1
This is file number 1

***** FILE.2
This is file number 2
```

Notice that FC showed that only the first line of each file was   different.

In this example, both files had the same number of lines. FC can also compare files with differences in many lines. When it finds a different line it looks for lines further down in both files that are the same. It will only show the lines that are different between the parts that are the same.

Assume that the file FILE.1A contains the following text:

This is file number 1A

It has three text lines.
It has three text lines.
It has three text lines.

Plus 1 more.

This is the end of the file.

and that the file FILE.1B contains the following text:

This is file number 1B

It has three text lines.
It has three text lines.
It has three text lines.

Plus 2 more.
Plus 2 more.

This is the end of the file.

To compare these two files, you could use this command:

```
C:\>fc file.1a file.1b /l /n
Comparing files FILE.1A and FILE.1B
***** FILE.1A
    1:    This is file number 1A
    2:
***** FILE.1B
    1:    This is file number 1B
    2:
*****

***** FILE.1A
    6:
    7:    Plus 1 more.
    8:
***** FILE.1B
    6:
    7:    Plus 2 more.
    8:    Plus 2 more.
    9:
*****

C:\>
```

Notice that FC showed that the first lines were different, that FILE.1A had one line different from FILE.1B, and that FILE.1B had two lines different from FILE.1A.

FC supports several switches. We have already used the /L (for line or text comparison) and /B (for binary comparison) switches.

Some additional switches control how matching is done within a text line during a line comparison. The /C (for ignore case) switch instructs FC to ignore case differences. Thus the text "Hello!" and "hello!" would be considered the same. The /T (for tabs) switch instructs FC to treat a tab as a tab and not to expand the tab into spaces. Expanding tabs to spaces is the usual way tabs work. Each tab is expanded to enough spaces to make the character after the tab start on the next eight-column position (1, 9, 17, 25, and so on). The /W (for ignore extra spaces) switch instructs FC to treat any sequences of more than one blank as a single blank. This causes FC to ignore differences in spacing. Normally people consider the meaning of words to be the same independent of the spacing between the word or the case of the words. To compare files as people do, use the /C and /W switches together.

There are also some switches that control how FC "resynchronizes" after it finds line differences. The /# (where # is a number) switch controls how many identical lines must be found together before the file is resynchronized. The normal value is two. Thus it takes two identical lines to end a range of different lines. The /LB# (for line buffer, where # is a number) switch also results in a line or text comparison. The # value controls the size of a line area (or buffer) that FC uses to hold different lines while it looks for lines that are the same further down in the file. The normal size of this buffer is 100 lines. You can make it larger if you expect the file to have long ranges of lines that are different before identical lines begin again.

The /N (for number) switch causes FC to add line numbers before each displayed line. The /A (for abbreviate) switch causes FC to show only the first and last line of a range of different lines. Without /A, all lines that differ are displayed.

Like COMP, FC can use wildcard in the names. For example, you can compare all the files in A:\DOS directory to the files with the same names in C:\DOS directory with the command

fc a:\dos*.* c:\dos

Because you did not provide either the /L or /B switches, FC automatically selects the type of comparison, binary or text, on each file.

More DOS Concepts

This chapter introduces you to concepts that you should know in order to make the best use of DOS. It also provides you with information that helps you to make better use of your application programs. This information supplements the topics we introduced earlier. We discuss the following topics in this chapter:

- DOS Error Messages

- DOS Devices

- Using the DOS Keyboard

- DOS Batch Files

- File Redirection and DOS Filters

- Finding Programs and Data Files

As you become more familiar with DOS, you will find that you will want to take more advantage of these features. They can help make using DOS, especially via the DOS Command Line, much easier.

DOS ERRORS

COMMAND AND UTILITY ERRORS

From time to time you will experience error messages from DOS. These messages result from input errors on your part or unusual situations. Do not become alarmed when you get one of these errors. They are normally easily corrected.

Command input errors can be fixed just by retyping the command line. For example, if you entered

COPY FILE1 FILE2 /Q

COPY would report

Invalid switch - /Q

If you had meant to type A instead of Q, just change the Q to A.

Command execution errors can be a little trickier. You must decide what caused the error and how to correct the problem. For example, if you entered

COPY FILEA FILE2

COPY might report

File not found - FILEA

You might realize you meant to type FILE1 instead of FILEA. You can correct that mistake right away.

If you really expected FILEA to exist, you might need to check to see that your current disk or directory is what you expected it to be. FILEA might indeed exist, but in another directory or on another diskette or fixed-disk drive.

When you are using the DOS Shell, these messages are presented in a pop-up message box. For each one, you will be asked either to cancel the operation or to correct the operation and continue.

The reference book included with your copy of DOS may provide a chapter that describes all possible DOS error messages and what to do to correct them. You should look there for assistance.

CRITICAL ERRORS

Normally, when a DOS command or utility encounters an error situation, it will report the error and stop. Sometimes this can be inconvenient. For example, if an error occurs while saving a long document you just typed into a word processor, you could lose all the input you just typed. This can be extremely frustrating, to say the least.

DOS has a special type of error, called a critical error, which normally requires your immediate attention. These errors are usually correctable, so your application can continue without losing any of your work. An example is shown here:

Not ready reading drive A

Abort, Retry or Fail?

This error indicates that you need to put a diskette in drive A:. When you have done that, type r (for retry). If you did not really want to access the A: drive, you should type f (for fail).

Critical errors normally take on one of the following forms:

<error> reading drive <x>	**<error> writing drive <x>**
Abort, Retry, Ignore or Fail?	**Abort, Retry, Ignore or Fail?**
<error> reading device <x>	**<error> writing device <x>**
Abort, Retry, Ignore or Fail?	**Abort, Retry, Ignore or Fail?**

These errors can be explained as follows:

<error>   Indicates the type of error.

reading or writing   Indicates the operation that encountered the error.

<x>   Indicates the drive or device name with the error.

Abort, Retry, Ignore or Fail   Indicates the actions you can take.

Abort   Indicates that you want DOS to end the current command, utility, or application immediately. If you are sure you cannot correct the situation and you will not lose data, then you should select this choice.

Retry   Indicates that you want DOS to retry the operation that caused the problem. In some cases, the problem will correct itself. In others, you or another person must take action to remove the problem. You should use this choice if you have taken action to correct the problem.

Ignore   Indicates that you want DOS to ignore the problem and to continue. Ignoring a problem is rarely the best choice. It can result in loss of data. You should use this choice only when the other actions (Abort, Retry, or Fail) are inappropriate.

Fail   Indicates to DOS that you wish it to end the current request that the command, utility, or application is making. DOS will return an error to the running program. The program can then take appropriate corrective action. If you cannot take steps to correct the problem (see "Retry"), then this is generally the best choice.

On some errors only the <error> part is present. Also, you may not get all of the choices (Abort, Retry, Ignore, or Fail) on some critical errors.

The most commonly occurring critical errors are:

Write protect   Indicates that the diskette is write-protected and thus cannot be changed.

> **For 3.5-inch diskettes.**   If you want to use this diskette, remove it from the drive, open the write-protect door, put the diskette back in the drive, and then press r. If you do not want to use this diskette, press f.

> **For 5.25-inch diskettes.**   If you want to use this diskette, remove it from the drive, remove the write-protect tab, put the diskette back in the drive, and press r. If you do not want to use this diskette, press f. If the diskette does not have a write-protect tab, it cannot be written to, and you must choose f.

Not Ready   Indicates that a diskette is not in the drive or is in the drive incorrectly.

> If a diskette is not in the drive, put the desired diskette in the drive, then press r. If the desired diskette is already in the drive, remove the diskette from the drive and put it back in the drive correctly, then press r. If you do not have a diskette to put in the drive, press f.

FCB unavailable   Indicates that your application tried to access a FCB (an internal DOS data area) and could not find it. This can happen whenever the DOS SHARE feature is installed. SHARE may be installed if you have a fixed disk larger than 32MB.

> You should press f to exit from the situation. Later you will need to update your configuration to increase the FCBS value. Please see your DOS book for more information.

Sharing violation   Indicates that another user on your network is currently using a file you are trying to access. This error should only happen if you are a network user.

> If you want to use this file, wait awhile and then press r. If the error occurs again, then the file is still being used. You can wait and try again by pressing r. If you do not want to wait to use this file, press f.

Data error   Indicates that all or part of your fixed disk or a diskette has been damaged.

> To get out of the error, press f. You may get this error again if you keep using the same fixed disk or diskette. To fix the problem you need to recover your fixed disk or diskette. See Chapter 13 for more information.

No paper   Indicates that either there is no paper in your printer or the printer has an error.

   Put paper in the printer or fix the printer error and press r. To get out of the error, press f.

When you are using the DOS Shell, these critical error messages are presented in a pop-up message box. For each one, you will be asked to either cancel the operation or correct the operation and continue. There will not be any "Abort, Retry, Ignore or Fail" message when you are using the DOS Shell.

   The reference book included with your copy of DOS may provide a chapter that describes every possible DOS critical-error message and what to do to correct them. You should look there for assistance.

DOS DEVICES

DOS supports several different kinds of devices. You are already familiar with the display, keyboard, diskette, and fixed-disk devices. DOS also supports printers and asynchronous communications devices. Often, when you are using your applications or DOS commands, you will need to be able to identify these devices. You will do this by using a device name. A device name is similar to a filename. In fact, DOS does not let you create or use a file with the same name as a DOS device.

   DOS provides all the devices shown in Figure 9-1.

Device Name	Function
CON	DOS Console (Keyboard and Display)
NUL	Null device. Any information sent to this device is thrown away.
LPT1 PRN LPT2 LPT3	First printer Another name for your first printer Second printer Third printer
COM1 AUX COM2 COM3 COM4	First asynchronous (serial) port Another name for your first asynchronous (serial) port Second asynchronous (serial) port Third asynchronous (serial) port Fourth asynchronous (serial) port
A: - Z:	Diskette and fixed disk drives

Figure 9-1
DOS Standard
Devices

The CON device represents the computer's keyboard and display. You can input information directly from CON to some other location, such as a file. A common example of this is creating short batch files (to be discussed in the next section). For example, to create the batch file MYFILE.BAT you could use the command

copy con myfile.bat

While you are typing into the file, DOS will not present you with the DOS command line prompt. Just type each line and end each one with the Enter (↵) key. You may make changes in the line only before you press Enter to move to the next line. You can use the Backspace key to correct any typing errors. When you are done with all the lines, press the F6 key (which displays ^Z on the screen) and then Enter. This indicates to DOS that you have completed all of your typing. The F6 key is used to indicate an End-of-File on the CON device. DOS resumes displaying the DOS command line prompt to tell you it is done accepting input via the CON device name.

Another example of using the CON device is to display the contents of a file on the display. This is similar to the DOS TYPE command. To display the AUTOEXEC.BAT file you could use the command

copy autoexec.bat con

The NUL device is used to prevent output of information DOS normally displays. For example, the DOS COPY command shows each filename as it is copied. In a batch file, you might not want this information displayed. You can stop it by using the command

copy *.* a: >nul

The normal COPY output will not be displayed. Any error messages will still be displayed.

The PRN and LPTx devices represent up to three parallel printers. Parallel printers are printers that attach to your computer via a parallel (versus a serial) port. Most printers are parallel printers. The names PRN and LPT1 both represent your first parallel printer. You may use either name. The names LPT2 and LPT3 represent a second and third printer if you have them.

You can send output directly to a DOS printer. For example, to type directly from your keyboard to your first printer you could use the command

copy con prn

> **Note:** Nothing will print until you press the F6 key, indicating all of your input is done.

The AUX and COMx devices represent serial ports. You can use serial ports to talk to other computers or to serial printers or plotters. The names AUX and COM1 both represent your first serial port. You may use either name. The names COM2 through COM4 represent additional serial ports if you have them.

Do not attempt to use a printer that is not attached to your computer (by either a LPTx or COMx port). If you do, you may see one of the following three behaviors.

1. You get an error message immediately.

2. DOS pauses for a short while, nothing seems to happen, and nothing is printed. No error message is produced.

3. DOS pauses for a long time and seems to be locked up. If you wait long enough (at least a minute, sometimes longer), you will get an error message. You can try to get unstuck by pressing the Ctrl+Break keys.

The A: through Z: devices are your diskette and fixed-disk drives. To DOS they actually represent what are called *block device drivers*. Generally, block device drivers are used to access diskette and fixed-disk drives, but they can be used to access other devices such as tape drives, CD-ROMs, and so on. These names are used to select from up to twenty-six block device drivers.

You can add more devices to DOS by using installable device drivers. You do this by using the DEVICE statement in the CONFIG.SYS file. For more information see Chapters 11 and 12.

USING THE DOS KEYBOARD

First we will discuss how to use the keyboard editing features available under DOS 3.3 and DOS 4.0. Then we will discuss the features provided by the DOSKEY keyboard extension included with DOS 5.0.

When you enter command lines at the DOS command line prompt, you can make corrections or changes to what you type. Changes can be made only before you press the Enter key. To do this press the Backspace or Left Arrow keys to erase what you just typed so you can retype it. As you use Backspace or Left Arrow, you move towards the beginning of the line.

If your cursor is in the middle of a command line (versus at the end of it), you erase the character at the cursor by pressing the Del key. You can insert characters before the cursor by first pressing the Ins key and then typing your new characters. You can stop inserting by pressing Ins again. If you are not inserting, any new characters you type will replace the characters at the cursor.

When you press Enter, DOS begins to process the command line you entered. It also saves a copy of the command line in an area called the *command line template* (or *template,* for short). You can use this template as a starting point for the next command. This is quite convenient if you are typing similar command lines.

> **Note:** The template is stored in your computer's memory in an area that may be used by large applications. If you run a large application, you may find that the template is reset (or cleared), and thus you cannot copy from it. In this case you must retype the new command completely.

You can copy characters from the template to the command line by using several keys. The F1 or Right Arrow keys copy the next character. If you repeat these keys, you can copy the entire command. That is exactly what the F3 key does, so it is an easy way to get the entire previously entered command line. The F2 key copies from the template until it finds a character that is the same as the next character you type immediately after pressing the F2 key. F2 does not do anything until you press another key. F2 is useful for copying a part of the template, up to some special character.

As an example, say you wanted to copy three files to a different directory on a different disk drive, as follows:

C:\>copy myfile.1 a:\savedir

C:\>copy myfile.2 a:\savedir

C:\>copy myfile.3 a:\savedir

You can do this by first typing the command:

copy myfile.1 a :\savedir

When DOS completes copying that file and redisplays the DOS command line prompt, press the F2 key and then the 1 key. DOS will display the following:

C:\>copy myfile._

You then complete the change by pressing the 2 key and then F3 to copy the rest of the line. When you do this, DOS will display the following:

C:\>copy myfile.2 a:\savedir_

To start the command, press Enter. To enter the third copy command, just press F2, then 2, then 3, then finally F3 and Enter.

You can change something that is short in a previously entered command into something longer. For example, you change myfile.1 into myfile.dat as follows:

C:\>copy myfile.1 a:\savedir

C:\>copy myfile.dat a:\savedir

you would again press the F2 and 1 keys. Press the Del key once to remove the 1 (still not copied from the template) from the template. Next you press Ins to enter insert mode and type dat. To complete the line just press F3.

The Esc key erases the displayed command so that you can start from a blank line.

DOSKEY

DOS 5.0 provides an extension, called DOSKEY, that increases the ease of use of the DOS command line. DOSKEY is an extension to DOS. You must request it. If you wish to use DOSKEY, we suggest that you add it to your AUTOEXEC.BAT file (to be discussed later in this chapter) so that it will be available each time you start your computer. DOSKEY provides the same keyboard interaction of prior DOS versions (as described in the previous section) and adds some new features.

1. **Command line recall** Whenever you enter a command to DOS at the DOS Command Line, DOSKEY will save it. This is similar to the template described earlier, but DOSKEY can save more than one template. The maximum number of lines depends on how long they are. Longer lines result in fewer lines saved.

Under DOSKEY, commands are saved as they are entered from newest to oldest. When too many commands are saved, the oldest is replaced by a new command. You use the Up Arrow, Down Arrow, PgUp, and PgDn keys to move through the list of saved commands. Up Arrow retrieves the previous entered command in the list. Down Arrow retrieves the next command. Repeated pressing of these keys positions to the next command respectively. PgUp retrieves the first command in the list. PgDn retrieves the oldest command.

The F7 key shows all the saved commands. You can then select one of the lines by pressing F9. The F8 key selects lines that start with the text shown on the command line. You can erase all the saved commands by pressing Alt+F7.

2. **Extended editing keys** In addition to the F1, F2, F3, Ins, Del, Left and Right Arrow, and Backspace keys normally supported by DOS, DOSKEY adds several more. Home moves you to the start of the command line. End moves you to the end of the line. Ctrl+End erases the rest of the line from the current cursor position. Ctrl+Home erases the beginning of the line up to the cursor. Ctrl+Left Arrow moves you left one word. Ctrl+Right Arrow moves you right one word.

3. **Multiple commands on one DOS command line** DOSKEY allows you to type more than one command on a single command line. This can be convenient. To do this, just separate each command with the Ctrl+T keys. DOS will show a paragraph symbol (¶) between each command.

4. **Command line macros** DOSKEY supports macros. Macros are short names for a longer command line. Whenever DOS sees a macro name typed on a command line it is replaced with the macro's contents.

To create a macro you use the DOSKEY command with the format

DOSKEY name=command

where "name" is the macro name and "command" is the new macro contents.

For example, to create the macro SAVEDISK to back up your fixed disk you would enter

doskey savedisk=backup c:*.* a: /c /l:c:\logfile /f

To delete a macro, just set it to blank. For example, to delete the SAVEDISK macro you would enter

doskey savedisk=

DOSKEY allows some special control symbols to be used in macro definitions. These symbols all start with the $ character. The symbol letters may be upper- or lowercase.

$$ The $ character itself. Equivalent to the $ character typed at the DOS command line.

$*   Represents all of the parameters to the macro. Anything typed after the macro name when it is used replaces the $* in the macro's definition.

$n   Represents one of the parameters to the macro; N is 1 through 9.

$B   Pipes commands. Equivalent to the ¦ character typed at the DOS command line.

$G   Redirects output. Equivalent to the > character typed at the DOS command line. Use GG to get >>.

$L   Redirects input. Equivalent to the < character typed at the DOS command line.

$T   Separates to DOS commands within a single DOSKEY macro. Equivalent to Ctrl+T typed at the DOS command line.

For example, to create a macro that prints a sorted directory list you would enter

doskey pdir=dir $* $B sort $Gprn

To use the macro to print a sorted list of all .DAT files, you would enter

pdir *.dat

You use $* to get all the macro's parameters. You can use $1 through $9 to reference the parameters individually. For example, to change the PDIR macro so that you can select the printer device, you would enter

doskey pdir=dir $1 $B sort G2

To use this version to print a sorted list of all .DAT files, you would enter

pdir *.dat prn

You can get a list of your currently defined macros. To do this, use the command

doskey /macros

> **Note:** You cannot reference a macro inside of a batch file. If you do, DOS will not recognize the macro name and you will get an error message. However, you may create macros inside of batch files.

DOS BATCH FILES

Quite often you will find that you will need to use more than one DOS command to perform a certain task. If you need to do that task often, it would be convenient if DOS could somehow remember it. Batch files are special files that are used to store sequences of DOS commands. Once you have created it, you can use a batch file any time you need to perform one of these complicated tasks. This can save you a great deal of time.

Batch files can be used for many purposes. Some examples are:

- Shorthand for a long DOS command. For example, if batch file SAVEDISK contains the command line

    BACKUP C:*.* A: /S /L:C:\\LOGFILE /F

    you can back up your C: drive just by typing SAVEDISK. When you use DOSKEY, you can also use a macro as an alternative method for producing a shorthand for a long DOS command.

- Performing the same exact commands over and over. For example, if batch file SAVEDOCS contains the command lines

    COPY C:*.DOC A:

    ERASE C:*.DOC

    you can save all documents to diskette and then delete the documents by just typing SAVEDOCS.

- Performing the same steps each time you start your computer.

    DOS provides a special batch file, called AUTOEXEC.BAT, that it uses each time you start up your computer (either by turning it on or by pressing the Ctrl+Alt+Del keys). If you have an AUTOEXEC.BAT on the diskette or fixed disk that DOS starts from, DOS will run each command included in it.

For example, to load the DOSKEY feature each time you start your computer, your AUTOEXEC.BAT file should contain the command line

doskey

> **Note:** It is best to place the DOSKEY line at the end of the AUTOEXEC.BAT file but before any DOSSHELL line.

When you do not have an AUTOEXEC.BAT file, DOS automatically displays the DOS copyright and version messages and asks you to enter the date and time. If you have an AUTOEXEC.BAT file you should include the following commands at the start of it so that you continue to get asked for the date and time:

VER

DATE

TIME

If you do not want to be asked for the date and time, just omit the DATE and TIME commands.

● Performing different steps based on parameters. For example, if batch file DOIT contains the command lines

IF %1. == TYPE. TYPE %2 ¦ MORE

IF %1. == COPY. COPY %2 %3

IF %1. == PRINT. PRINT %2

IF %1. == DELETE. ERASE %2

you can choose the function this batch file performs based on what you type as a parameter. For example, DOIT TYPE MYFILE will display the file MYFILE and will automatically pause after each full screen of text.

> **Note:** Do not be concerned if you do not understand how the IF command works. We will explain it shortly.

Before you make a batch file to perform a complex task, we recommend you use the individual DOS commands first. In this way, you can make sure that you know and understand every required step of the task. If you type the batch file first, you may skip a necessary step.

Batch files are simple text files that you create by using the DOS COPY command or an editor such as EDIT or EDLIN. Each line in a batch file represents a command to DOS. All batch files have a filename extension of .BAT.

Simple text files are files that can be TYPEd directly. They contain no internal application data. They are often called just *text files* or *ASCII files*.

Batch files can be treated like most other files. They can be viewed, copied, deleted, renamed, or printed. They act like batch files only when you use them as a command. To start a batch file, just type its name (do not include the .BAT extension) at the DOS command line prompt. If they are needed, you can supply parameters to the batch file, as you can with any other DOS command.

Any DOS command or utility can be used from a batch file. Also, any application program can be started from a batch file. In fact, it is a standard part of an application's installation procedure for the application to create a batch file to start itself.

Batch files allow replaceable parameters, which is very convenient. This allows you to type parameters on the line that starts the batch file and have them temporarily change the batch file. You may have up to nine replaceable parameters. For example, if you had a batch file called ECHOIT.BAT with a line

@ECHO Batch File %0: %1,%2,%3,%4,%5,%6,%7,%8,%9

and you entered the command

echoit This is a test

you would see

Batch File echoit: This,is,a,test,,,,,

From this example, you can see that %0 is replaced with the batch filename "echoit." %1 through %4 are replaced with "This," "is," "a," and "test," respectively. %5 through %9 are replaced with nothing.

The %n values can occur anywhere in a line. They do not need to be used in order. Not every %n value needs to be used, as is shown here.

This %3 line %5 uses %4 five %1 replaceable %2 parameters

Please notice the @ before the ECHO command shown earlier. The @ tells DOS not to echo (show) the command on the computer screen as it is being processed. This @ is not normally used when the command is entered via the command line prompt.

BATCH FILE COMMANDS

Batch files also support additional DOS commands that do not work from the DOS command line prompt. These commands are used to preform special batch file functions.

In the descriptions that follow, the batch commands are shown in uppercase. You can type them in either upper- or lowercase.

ECHO

The ECHO command is used to control the display of the batch file contents. ECHO has several forms:

ECHO ON   Specifies that each line of the batch file following ECHO ON is to be displayed on the screen before it is processed. ECHO ON is set automatically when a batch file starts.

ECHO OFF   Specifies that each line of the batch file following ECHO OFF is not to be displayed on the screen before it is processed. ECHO OFF has the same effect as putting an @ before every command in the batch file.

ECHO message Causes the text of "message" to be displayed on the screen. "Message" can be anything and contain any characters (except ¦, >, and <). Messages are used to provide progress updates and help information.

When you first create a batch file, it is best to use ECHO ON. This will let you see how the batch file is working in case a problem occurs. Once you have worked out all problems (i.e., tested the batch file), you can use ECHO OFF. For example, to display progress messages, use

```
@ ECHO OFF
ECHO Beginning step 1 using %1
CALL STEP1 %1
ECHO Beginning step 2 using %2
CALL STEP2 %2
```

IF

The IF command is used to control the flow of a batch file. Often you will want to do different things based on what conditions are found. For example, if you made a batch file to delete a group of files, you would want to stop after the last file was deleted.

The IF command has several forms:

IF string1 == string2 command   Specifies that if string1 equals string2, then "command" is to be processed. String1 and string2 may not contain any blanks or other punctuation. This form of the IF command is especially useful if one of the strings is a replaceable parameter. For example, the command

> **IF %1. == QUIT. GOTO DONE**

tests to see if %1 is the word "QUIT."

If %1 is not "QUIT" (say, you entered XXX), then the command is interpreted as

> **IF XXX. == QUIT. GOTO DONE**

Since "XXX." does not equal "QUIT.," the GOTO command is not performed.

If %1 is not supplied, then the command is interpreted as

> **IF . == QUIT. GOTO DONE**

The "." is important. If you left it out and %1 was omitted, then the command is interpreted as

> **IF == QUIT. GOTO DONE**

and DOS will produce an error message.

You do not need to use a "."; it is just an example character. You may use another character.

The IF command is case sensitive. You should always test for both cases, as shown here:

> **IF %1. == QUIT. GOTO DONE**
>
> **IF %1. == quit. GOTO DONE**

IF EXIST path command   Causes DOS to check to see if the path exists. If it does, "command" is performed. The path may represent either a file or a directory. Wildcards may be used. This check is useful when certain setup or cleanup operations are needed. Because files may or may not exist from your past activity, you can test to see if these special activities are needed. For example, call batch file CLEANUP if the file named by %1 exists:

IF EXIST %1 CALL CLEANUP %1

To see if any document file exists and if one (or more) does, save it:

IF EXIST *.DOC CALL SAVEFILE *.DOC

IF ERRORLEVEL n command   Tests the result of the previous batch file command. If that line started a DOS utility or an application program, there may be an ERRORLEVEL to test. The following DOS utilities set ERRORLEVEL:

- BACKUP and RESTORE

- DISKCOMP and DISKCOPY

- FORMAT

- GRAFTABL

- KEYB

- REPLACE

- SETVER

- XCOPY

See your application documentation for more information.

> **Note:** The setting of ERRORLEVEL is only possible from DOS utilities or application programs. DOS commands cannot set ERRORLEVEL.

The n value is compared against the number returned by the application. If the ERRORLEVEL is greater than or equal to n, then the command is processed.

Normally, an ERRORLEVEL other than 0 indicates that an error occurred. For example, go to ERROR if application WORDPROC failed:

WORDPROC MYDOC

IF ERRORLEVEL 1 GOTO ERROR

The IF command has one other form, IF NOT ..., which reverses any of the tests just discussed. For example, if %1 is defined, perform batch file DOIT using %1:

IF NOT %1. == . CALL DOIT %1

If directory \MYDIR does not exist, make it:

IF NOT EXIST \MYDIR MKDIR \MYDIR

Go to OK if application WORDPROC worked:

WORDPROC MYDOC

IF NOT ERRORLEVEL 1 GOTO OK

The IF command can be combined, as shown here:

IF NOT %1. == . IF NOT EXIST %1 MKDIR %1

This command tests the directory name provided by %1 to see if it has been provided. If it has, the command tests to see if the name exists on disk. If the name does not exist, it is created.

GOTO

The GOTO command is used to transfer to another location in a batch file. It is often used in combination with the IF command. The GOTO command has the following form:

GOTO name

A label is on a line by itself and looks like:

:name

where "name" matches the name on the GOTO command.

The label must occur somewhere in the batch file, or DOS will produce an error message. The label name is not case sensitive. For example, go to label ERROR if file XYZ is not found:

IF NOT EXIST XYZ GOTO ERROR

> .
>
> .
>
> .

:ERROR

FOR

The FOR command is used to perform a command one time for each file that matches a specified selection mask (a sample name). This command is useful when you need to perform an action on every file in a directory. The FOR command has the following form:

FOR %%a IN (mask) DO command

The "a" of %%a can be any letter. The mask can be any valid DOS file path, including wildcards. It can be repeated. For example, to erase every file in the current directory (same as the ERASE *.* command):

FOR %%A IN (*.*) DO ERASE %%A

To display files A, B, C, and D:

FOR %%A IN (A B C D) DO TYPE %%A

To print every text file starting with "A":

FOR %%A IN (A*.TXT) DO PRINT %%A

For every document in the \MYDOC directory, run the MYBATCH batch file:

FOR %%A IN (C:\MYDOCS*.DOC) DO CALL MYBATCH %%A

> **Note:** The FOR command can be used outside of a batch file (e.g., at the DOS command line prompt). If you do so, use the form "%a" everywhere we have shown "%%a".

FOR %A IN (1 2 3) DO ECHO Its as easy as %A

CALL

The CALL command is used to run another batch file from within a batch file. The CALL command has the following form:

CALL name parameters

For example, to call batch file MYBAT using parameter %1:

CALL MYBAT %1

> **Note:** If you reference a batch file from within a batch file and you do not use the CALL command, the original batch file is stopped immediately. Any additional command lines in that batch file will not be processed.

REM

The REM command is used to place a remark in a batch file. Any text after the word REM is ignored. Remarks are used to document the function of the batch file. The REM command has the following form:

REM remark

Remark can contain any characters (except ¦, >, and <). For example, to explain the purpose of DELDIR batch file:

REM This batch file deletes all files in a directory and

REM then deletes the directory

ERASE %1

RMDIR %1

It is not an error to have a label that is not used by a GOTO command. Therefore, you can also create remarks in batch files by using labels. Remarks created this way are never displayed. Remarks created by using the REM command are displayed if ECHO is ON. For example, to explain the purpose of DELDIR batch file:

:This batch file deletes all files in a directory and

:then deletes the directory.

ERASE %1

RMDIR %1

PAUSE

The PAUSE command is used to optionally display a message and then wait for you to press a key. Often you will need to change diskettes during a batch file. You can use PAUSE to do this. PAUSE will display a message similar to "Press any key to continue . . . ." The PAUSE command has the following form:

PAUSE message

For example, to request a change of diskette:

PAUSE Insert diskette 1 in the A: drive

COPY A:*.* C:

PAUSE Insert diskette 2 in the A: drive

COPY A:*.* C:

> **Note:** IF ECHO is OFF, the message is not displayed. In this case you should do the following:

ECHO Insert diskette 1 in the A: drive

PAUSE

SHIFT

The SHIFT command is used to access more than nine command line parameters. Each time you use SHIFT, the contents of %2 move to %1, %3 moves to %2, and so on. The SHIFT command has the following form:

SHIFT

For example, assume %1 = A, %2 = B, %3 = C, and %4 through %9 = nothing:

@ECHO OFF

ECHO No shifts: %1 %2 %3 %4 %5 %6 %7 %8 %9

SHIFT

ECHO 1 shift : %1 %2 %3 %4 %5 %6 %7 %8 %9

SHIFT

ECHO 2 shifts : %1 %2 %3 %4 %5 %6 %7 %8 %9

SHIFT

ECHO 3 shifts : %1 %2 %3 %4 %5 %6 %7 %8 %9

displays the following lines:

No shifts: A B C

1 shift : B C

2 shifts : C

3 shifts :

BATCH FILE EXAMPLE

As mentioned earlier, to create simple batch files, you can use the DOS COPY command. To do this, copy from the device CON to the batch file. DOS will then let you type in each line of the batch file. You can make corrections only before you press Enter. DOS does not display the command line prompt until you are finished typing in all your lines. You indicate when you are done by using the F6 key.

Please feel free to enter this batch file on your computer. If you have a fixed disk, you should use drive C:. Make sure you copy each line exactly. Leave the line numbers ([##]) off from the front of each line; they are just to help with the explanations that follow.

[01] A:\>copy con \printdir.bat

[02] @echo off

[03] rem This batch file makes a directory listing, sorts it and

[04] rem then prints it.

[05] rem

[06] if exist \tempdir.out erase \tempdir.out

[07] :loop

[08] rem Test for more directories to sort and print

[09] if %1. == . goto done

[10] echo Sorting directory %1 . . .

[11] echo Sorted directory of %1 >>\tempdir.out

[12] dir %1 ¦ sort >>\tempdir.out

[13] rem Set to next parameter and repeat

[14] shift

[15] goto loop

[16] :done

[17] if exist \tempdir.out print \tempdir.out

[18] <F6>

[19] A:\>

> **Note:** <F6> means press the F6 function key.

A line-by-line explanation of the PRINTDIR batch file follows.

[01]	Tells DOS to copy the console to the file PRINTDIR.BAT.
[02]	Turns ECHO OFF for this batch file. The @ prevents DOS from echoing the ECHO OFF command.
[03]–[05]	Describes this batch file.
[06]	Checks to see if the file TEMPDIR.OUT already exists. If it does, then it is deleted. This prevents the printed directory listing from having information from any previous use of the PRINTDIR batch file.
[07]	Defines the label "loop."
[08]	Describes the purpose for the following IF command.
[09]	Tests to see if the %1 parameter is present. If it is not, then there are no more directories to sort and print, so the processing is complete.
[10]	Displays a progress message as each parameter is processed.
[11]	Adds the directory name to the output to separate multiple directories.
[12]	Creates the directory listing for a single directory, sorts it, and adds it to the TEMPDIR.OUT file.
[13]	Describes the purpose for the following SHIFT command.
[14]	Shifts the parameters so that the second, third, etc., parameter can be referenced, in turn, by %1.

[15]   Repeats the sorting loop until all supplied directory names are processed.

[16]   Supplies the label "done" to indicate the end of the batch file.

[17]   Checks to see if any output has been created (there will not be any if no directory names are supplied). If there is any output, it is printed.

[18]   Indicates to DOS the end of the batch file input.

[19]   Indicates DOS is ready for more commands.

To use the batch file to print a sorted directory of the root and C:\DOS directories, enter

A:\>printdir c:\ c:\dos

While PRINTDIR is running, it displays the following messages:

Sorting directory c:\ . . .

Sorting directory c:\dos . . .

ENVIRONMENT VARIABLES IN BATCH FILES

DOS provides a feature called the *DOS Environment,* which can remember things for you. Many DOS values are remembered in the DOS Environment. Some applications (the Microsoft C Compiler, for example) also use the DOS Environment. To check or change the DOS Environment, use the DOS SET command, which has the following form:

SET name=value

Both "name" and "value" are optional. If "name" is omitted, also omit the =.

If SET is entered by itself, the current DOS Environment is displayed. The DOS Environment looks like this:

COMSPEC=C:\DOS\COMMAND.COM

PATH=C:\DOS;C:\PE2;C:\DWS;C:\TOOLS

APPEND=C:\DOS;C:\PE2;C:\DWS

PROMPT=[$d Thhh $P]

If both name and value are present, a new value is added to the DOS Environment. For example:

> set myname=John Smith

adds MYNAME to the environment, as follows:

> **COMSPEC=C:\DOS\COMMAND.COM**
>
> **PATH=C:\DOS;C:\PE2;C:\DWS;C:\TOOLS**
>
> **APPEND=C:\DOS;C:\PE2;C:\DWS**
>
> **PROMPT=[$d Thhh $P]**
>
> **MYNAME=John Smith**

If you want to remove MYNAME from the DOS Environment, just leave off the value:

> **set myname=**

You can reference DOS Environment names in batch files. For example, the lines

> **@ECHO My Name is %myname%**
>
> **@ECHO My PATH is %path%**
>
> **@ECHO My PROMPT is %prompt%**

display the lines

> **My Name is John Smith**
>
> **My PATH is C:\DOS;C:\PE2;C:\DWS;C:\TOOLS**
>
> **My PROMPT is [$d Thhh $P]**

FILE REDIRECTION AND DOS FILTERS

FILE REDIRECTION

In the batch file examples in the previous section, we used the notation >>. This is an example of file redirection. You might ask, "What is file redirection?" It is a way of taking information normally displayed on your computer's screen and putting it somewhere else. The most commonly used places are another device, such as a printer, or a file. You can also use a file as input instead of the keyboard. This "redirection" is done by using the symbols <, >, >>, and ¦.

The notation < means "redirect keyboard input" (also called *standard input,* or *STDIN*). It causes your application to use a file instead of the keyboard. Remember that the COMP command asks you if you want to compare another diskette. Every time you use COMP, you have to answer this question. By using input redirection, you can avoid having to do this. This can be most useful when you put the COMP command in a batch file.

Assume the file named N contains the character n. If you entered the command

COMP FILE1 FILE2 < \ N

COMP would not ask you about another file. It would get its answer from the N file instead.

You can create this file by the following command:

COPY CON \ N

n

<F6>

> **Warning:** It is important to make sure that you answer all questions that might be asked by any program you redirect input to. If you do not, DOS will normally produce an error. Sometimes your computer will just seem to stop. If this happens, you need to press Ctrl+Break to continue.

The notation > means "redirect display output" (also called *standard output* or *STDOUT*). It causes your application to use a device or file instead of the screen. If you wanted to get a printed copy of a directory, you could enter

DIR >LPT1

This command causes the output of the DIR command to go to the printer instead of the screen. None of the DIR command's normal output is displayed, but error messages are still displayed. This makes sure you will see these important messages.

You can also direct the output to a file:

DIR >DIR.OUT

This can be very useful if you want to use this information somewhere else. For example, you might want to include it in some other file by using an editor application.

If you wanted the directory of several drives in a single file, you could do the following:

DIR A: >DIR.OUT

DIR B: >>DIR.OUT

DIR C: >>DIR.OUT

The notation > erases the file first, and the notation >> adds to the end of the file.

If you want to get a sorted directory listing, you can do the following:

DIR >TEMP

SORT <TEMP

DEL TEMP

This approach requires you first to create a temporary file and then to delete it later. DOS provides an easier way for you to do this. You can do the following:

DIR ¦ SORT

The notation ¦ (for Pipe) causes DOS to make a temporary file, run DIR and then SORT, and finally delete the temporary file. This is done by making the standard output of DIR the standard input of SORT.

Another way to supply an answer to a prompt is to use the ECHO command, as follows:

ECHO N ¦ COMP FILE1 FILE2

You might want to go back and review the PRINTDIR batch file example to see some more examples of file redirection.

DOS FILTERS

We have used a program called SORT in many examples. SORT is an example of a type of DOS command called a *filter*. This name is used because these commands take input from the standard input, make some change to it (or filter it), and then output the changes to the standard output. There are three DOS filters: FIND, MORE, and SORT. They are described in the following sections.

FIND

FIND is used to find lines that have certain text in them. For example, if you wanted a directory listing that showed only the subdirectories in the root directory of the C drive, you would enter

DIR C:\ ¦ FIND "<DIR>"

Because every subdirectory (and only subdirectories) in the output of the DIR command contains the string <DIR>, this combination will show only the directories.

The FIND command has the following form:

FIND switch(es) string file(s)

where "switch" is optional and controls how FIND works, "string" selects the found lines and "file" is optional. If file is missing, Standard Input is used. File may be repeated.

FIND supports the following switches:

/C   Reports the number of lines in the input that have the string. Normally FIND shows you the lines themselves.

/I   Specifies that the search is to be case insensitive. Normally FIND is case sensitive, which means you must type the string using the same capitalization as is used in the file. /I is supported only in DOS 5.0.

/N   Adds the line's file line number to the front of each found line.

/V   Reverses the search, thus reporting all lines which do not contain the string.

FIND can also look in files:

FIND "This is a test" FILE1

This acts the same as:

FIND "This is a test" <FILE 1

MORE

MORE is used to count output lines and stop every time the screen fills up. This is quite useful when viewing long files. The MORE command has the following form:

MORE

   To view the file MEMO you would enter

TYPE MEMO ¦ MORE

   You could also just enter

MORE <MEMO

SORT

SORT is used to sort input lines. This is quite useful to get a sorted directory listing.
   The SORT command has the following form:

SORT switch

where "switch" is optional and controls how SORT works.
   SORT supports the following switches:

/R   Sorts the report in descending order. Normally SORT uses increasing alphabetic order.

/+n   Sorts the report beginning at position n. SORT normally uses position 1. This can be used to sort on different information. For example, to sort by filename extension instead of filename, use:

    DIR ¦ SORT /+10.

Combining DOS Filters

You can combine DOS filters. As an example, to get a sorted directory displayed one screenful at a time, you could enter

   DIR A: ¦ SORT ¦ MORE

FINDING PROGRAMS AND DATA FILES

DOS frequently needs to find application programs or data files on your disks. When you are using directories, the program and data files can be located in any one of several different directories. To help find these files, DOS uses the PATH and APPEND commands.

PATH

The PATH command sets up a list of directories for DOS to look in to find programs. Programs are files that have extensions of COM or EXE. The PATH is also used to find batch files (which have an extension of .BAT).

The PATH command has the following form:

PATH directory;directory;...;directory

where directory specifies a directory on one of your disks. "Directory" should be fully qualified. You can have as many directories as will fit on the line.

When you type in a command at the DOS command line prompt, DOS performs a series of steps to find the program. Let's use an example. For this example assume the following conditions are true:

- The current drive is C:.

- The current directory of C: is the root (\).

- The current PATH value is

    C:\MSWORD;C:\LOTUS123;C:\DOS

    You want to run EDIT to edit CONFIG.SYS, so you enter

    C:\>edit config.sys

    DOS will now perform the following steps to find and run EDIT:

1. Search the root of C: for the file EDIT.*.

DOS uses EDIT.* so that it will find any instance of EDIT.COM, EDIT.EXE, or EDIT.BAT. DOS will make sure that it finds any form of the EDIT command. If more than one form exists, DOS will use the first one found in the order .COM, .EXE, and then .BAT.

DOS always searches the current drive/directory first. Because EDIT is in the DOS directory, it is not found.

2. Search the MSWORD directory of C: for the file EDIT.*. Because EDIT is in the DOS directory, it is not found.

3. Search the LOTUS123 directory of C: for the file EDIT.*. Because EDIT is in the DOS directory, it is not found.

4. Search the DOS directory of C: for the file EDIT.*. Because EDIT.COM is in the DOS directory, it is found. (Finally!)

5. DOS starts the EDIT.COM program.

> **Note:** If EDIT.COM had not been in the DOS directory, DOS would display the error message "Bad command or file." This message indicates that DOS cannot find your program file. If you get this message, you should check to see that all the directories that contain your installed applications are listed in the DOS PATH. You do not need to include every directory on your disk in your PATH. Only directories that contain programs (.COM, .EXE, or .BAT files) need to be included.

If the PATH contains references to diskette drives, this searching can take quite a while. If you know which diskette or directory a program is in, you can tell DOS to look only there. For example:

```
A:\>c:\dos\edit config.sys
```

will find EDIT in C:\DOS directly and edit the CONFIG.SYS file on drive A:.

To set a new PATH, you would enter

```
path c:\newdir;c:\msword;c:\lotus123;c:\dos
```

If you do not want a PATH, you would enter

```
path ;
```

To check to see what the current PATH is, you would enter

```
path
```

It is not directly possible to add a new directory to an existing PATH.

The entire PATH must be retyped. To avoid this you can create a simple batch file to change the PATH as follows:

C:\>copy con addpath.bat

@echo off

if not %1.==. path %1;%path%

echo The new PATH is %path%

<F6>

You can then add new directories to your path, as follows:

addpath c:\newdir

APPEND

The PATH command is used by DOS only to find programs. It can find files only with the extensions .COM, .EXE, or .BAT. Frequently your applications will need to find other files, such as help text, messages, profiles, or overlays. These files might have extensions such as .HLP, .MSG, .PRO, and .OVY.

The DOS APPEND command provides the ability to find these files very much the way PATH finds programs. PATH is always supported, but APPEND is optional, because it takes up some of your computer's memory. This was done to allow you to make a choice. APPEND is normally needed only if your computer has a fixed disk.

You normally set your APPEND path to be the same as your PATH path. If you use a directory only to find programs (.COM, .EXE, or .BAT files), then your APPEND path does not need to include it.

The APPEND command has the following form:

APPEND directory;directory;...;directory

where "directory" specifies a directory on one of your disks. "Directory" should be fully qualified. You can have as many directories as will fit on the line.

To set a new APPEND, you enter

append c:\newdir;c:\msword;c:\lotus123;c:\dos

If you do not want an APPEND, you enter

append ;

To check to see what the current APPEND is, you enter

append

As with the PATH, it is not directly possible to add a new directory to an existing APPEND. The entire APPEND must be retyped. To avoid this, you can create a simple batch file to change the APPEND as follows:

C:\>copy con addapnd.bat

@echo off

if not %1.==. append %1;%append%

echo The new APPEND is %append%

<F6>

You can then add new directories to your APPEND, as follows:

addapnd c:\newdir

> **Note:** The use of %append% is valid only on DOS 4.0 and DOS 5.0.

The APPEND command supports several switches that change its behavior. We do not recommend that you use them unless your application documentation indicates that you should. For more information about these switches see "Displaying and Changing Your Appended Directories."

ATTRIB AND DIR

The ATTRIB command can be used to find files on your disks. Unlike PATH and APPEND, ATTRIB works only when you use it. PATH and APPEND work after you use them.

ATTRIB provides two basic functions:

1. It displays or changes the attributes of a file. See "Changing File Attributes" for more information on this use of ATTRIB.

2. It finds any and all occurrence of a file anywhere on your disk. This feature is sometimes referred to as a WHEREIS command.

When you have a lot of files located in many different directories, you will find that it is hard to remember where you put a certain file. Looking for the file can be very difficult and could take a long time. DOS provides two ways to find these files. One is using the DOS 4.0 Shell's Global File List display or DOS 5.0 Shell's Search function. Another is by using ATTRIB.

If you want to find the file JOHNMEMO, you would enter

C:\>attrib johnmemo /s

The /S switch tells ATTRIB to look for JOHNMEMO in all subdirectories. Because the current directory is the root, this means the entire disk. If the current directory were not the root, you would need to enter

C:\DOS>attrib \johnmemo /s

ATTRIB will display a report similar to

C:\MYDOCS\JOHNMEMO

You can also use wildcards with ATTRIB. If you could not remember the name of a file but knew it was a document, you would enter

C:\>attrib *.doc /s

ATTRIB would display a report similar to

   C:\README.DOC

   C:\LETTERS\JOHN.DOC

   C:\LETTERS\RESUME.DOC

   C:\LETTERS\PAUL.DOC

   C:\LETTERS\CUTBACK.DOC

A **C:\MEMOS\NEWPLAN.DOC**

   C:\MEMOS\OLD\NEWPLAN.DOC

Once you see the list of documents, you remember that you wanted the NEWPLAN.DOC file in the MEMOS directory. This use of ATTRIB is a good reason to create file extensions that have meaning so that you can categorize your files.

> **Note:** The A on the left indicates that this file has changed since
> the last time you backed up your fixed disk. When you see a lot
> of files with an A, you should use BACKUP to save them. You
> can count the number of changed files on your disk by the fol-
> lowing command:
>
> **attrib *.* /s ¦ find /c " A "**

The " A " must be entered as a capital since ATTRIB shows it as a capital. If it is entered as " a " the count will always be zero.

When using DOS 5.0 only, the DIR command can also be used to find
any and all occurrences of a file anywhere on your disk.

If you want to find the file JOHNMEMO, you would enter

C:\\>dir \\johnmemo /s

As with ATTRIB, the /S switch tells DIR to look for JOHNMEMO in
all subdirectories. DIR shows the normal file size, date, and time information instead of ATTRIB's archive indicator.

10 More Use of DOS Commands and Utilities

In this chapter we will show you the DOS commands that are not limited to working with files only. These commands change the way DOS looks at the computer it is running on. These commands fall into four areas:

1. **Fixed-Disk and Diskette functions.** These commands and utilities perform functions on a disk or diskette. They do not work on files.

2. **Directory Functions.** These utilities work on all of the files in a directory or set of directories.

3. **Drive Letter Mapping Functions.** These utilities enable DOS and your applications to run with an imaginary set of fixed-disk and diskette drives. You can trick DOS into believing that there are more or fewer drives than there really are. You can also make DOS believe that one drive is really another.

4. **System Functions.** These commands and utilities change the environment that DOS and your applications run in.

FIXED-DISK AND DISKETTE FUNCTIONS

In this section, we will cover the following utilities:

DISKCOMP   Compares two diskettes of the same format to see if they are identical.

DISKCOPY   Makes an exact copy of a diskette on another diskette of the same format.

FORMAT   Formats (prepares) a diskette or fixed disk for use.

LABEL   Displays or sets the volume label of a disk.

SYS   Adds the DOS Kernel to a disk.

VOL   Displays the volume label of a disk.

These utilities perform functions on a fixed disk or diskette. They do not work on files. These utilities can only work on real drives. DOS will not allow them to access imaginary drives.

DISKETTE COMPATIBILITY

If you look at 5.25-inch and 3.5-inch diskettes, you can see that they are not the same. But if you look at two different 5.25-inch diskettes, or two different 3.5-inch diskettes, the difference is not as easy to spot.

There are several types of 5.25-inch diskettes, but we are interested in the three that are the most common:

1D   This is a single-sided, dual-density diskette. The original IBM Personal Computer used this type of diskette. The only real reason you would need one now is if you wanted to exchange data with someone that still had the old diskette drive. These diskettes were originally formatted to hold 160KB, but the 180KB format was introduced later.

2D   This is a two-sided, dual-density diskette. These diskettes first became available on a later model of the IBM Personal Computer. These diskettes were originally formatted to hold 320KB, but today the 360KB format is used almost exclusively.

This type of diskette can also be formatted and used as a 1D diskette.

2HC   This is a two-sided, high-capacity (quadruple-density) diskette. These diskettes first became available on the IBM Personal Computer AT. These diskettes are formatted to hold 1.2MB of data.

This type of diskette can be formatted and used as a 2D or 1D diskette, but there are several restrictions on this type of usage.

Figure 10-1
5.25-inch Diskette
and Drive Compati-
bility

Diskette Type	1D Drive	2D Drive	2HC Drive
1D	RWF	RWF	Read
2D	NO	RWF	Read
2HC	NO	NO	RWF

For each of the 5.25-inch diskette types, there is a corresponding diskette drive. In general, smaller-capacity diskettes can be read in drives that support larger-size formats. Figure 10-1 shows all of the rules for interchanging the 5.25-inch diskettes and drives.

An explanation of the terms in Figure 10-1 follows:

RWF   This type of diskette can be read from, written to, or formatted in this type of drive.

Read   We recommend only reading these diskettes in this type of drive.

NO   This type of diskette cannot be used in this type of drive.

To format a 1D diskette in a 2D or 2HC drive, you must use one of the format-size-limiting switches /1 or /F:. To format a 2D diskette in a 2HC drive, you must use one of the format-size-limiting switches, /4 or /F:.

If a 5.25-inch diskette is written to or formatted in a 2HC drive, it may not be readable by a 1D or 2D drive.

DOS currently supports three types of 3.5-inch diskettes:

1.0MB or 2HC   This is a two-sided, high-capacity (quadruple-density) diskette. These diskettes first became available on the IBM Convertible Personal Computer. These diskettes are formatted to hold 720KB of data. These IBM diskettes will have either "1.0MB capacity" or "double sided 2HC" printed on the sliding metal cover.

2.0MB or HD   This is a two-sided, high-density (quadruple-density) diskette. These diskettes first became available on the IBM Personal System/2 computers. These diskettes are formatted to hold 1.44MB of data. These IBM diskettes will have "2.0MB capacity" printed on the sliding metal cover. These IBM diskettes also have an extra rectangular hole across from the write-protect sliding switch.

4.0MB or ED   This is a two-sided, extra-high-density diskette. These diskettes are formatted to hold 2.88MB of data. These IBM diskettes will have "4.0MB capacity" printed on the sliding metal cover. Like the HD diskettes, these also have an extra rectangular hole across from the write-protect sliding switch; however, it is in a slightly different location. The diskette drive that accommodates these diskettes is sometimes referred to as a *media-sense drive,* in that it can tell if the diskette in the drive is a 1.0MB, 2.0MB, or 4.0MB.

There are numerous ways of indicating the diskette types. Check Figure 10-2 for some information that you might be able to find on your diskette labels.

For each of the 3.5-inch diskette types there is a corresponding diskette drive. As with 5.25-inch diskettes, smaller-capacity diskettes can be read in drives that support larger formats. Figure 10-3 shows all of the rules for interchanging the 3.5-inch diskettes and drives.

Figure 10-3 uses the same terms as Figure 10-1.

Figure 10-2
Diskette Cross-Reference Table

Formatted Capacity	Diskette Size	Diskette Type	Sides	Tracks	Sectors Per Track
160KB	5.25-inch	1D	1	40	8
180KB	5.25-inch	1D	1	40	9
320KB	5.25-inch	2D	2	40	8
360KB	5.25-inch	2D	2	40	9
720KB	3.5-inch	2HC/1.0MB	2	80	9
1.2MB	5.25-inch	2HC	2	80	15
1.44MB	3.5-inch	2.0MB	2	80	18
2.88MB	3.5-inch	4.0MB	2	80	36

Figure 10-3
3.5-inch Diskette and Drive Compatibility

Diskette Type	1.0MB Drive	2.0MB Drive	4.0MB Drive
1.0MB / 2HC	RWF	RWF	RWF
2.0MB / HD	NO	RWF	RWF
4.0MB / HD	NO	NO	RWF

> **Warning:** If you accidentally format a 2.0MB diskette in a 1.0MB drive, you will cause permanent damage to the diskette. The diskette should be discarded, as it will no longer be reliable.

FORMATTING YOUR DISKS

What Does FORMAT Do?

When you purchase diskettes, they are frequently not ready to be used. Before your computer can store data on them, they must be formatted. The FORMAT utility performs the following steps in order to prepare your diskettes for you, and DOS, to use:

1. It records patterns on the diskette that separate the diskette into small, manageable areas. These areas are called *sectors*. Each sector on most DOS diskettes contains 512 bytes (characters) of data. This is somewhat like building the floors in a hotel and then taking a floor in a hotel and building the walls for each room. Each area is labeled with a unique address (see "What the Diskette Looks Like" for more information on what the diskette looks like).

This pattern recording is referred to as *low-level formatting*. With DOS 5.0, this operation is not always performed, thereby saving you time during format operations.

2. If any areas of the diskette do not seem to work correctly, they are remembered so that later DOS does not try to store your data or programs in bad parts of your diskettes.

This portion of the format process is referred to as verifying the disk surface. As with the low-level formatting procedure described earlier, DOS 5.0 does not always require this step to be performed.

3. It records information at the beginning of your diskette that describes the diskette and provides the ability to start DOS from the diskette. This information is recorded in the first sector of the diskette and is called the *boot record*. This description tells DOS how to treat each diskette it works with. The description includes:

● Number of Bytes in Each Sector

● Number of Sectors Per Track

- Number of Tracks or Cylinders

- Number of Sides or Heads

- Number of File Allocation Tables

- Number of Allocation Units

- The Volume Serial Number

Other information is also recorded, but these fields pretty much describe the diskette format.

The code that is written to start DOS can only do so if the rest of the DOS files (IBMBIO.COM, IBMDOS.COM, and COMMAND.COM) are added to the diskette. This code is called the BOOT or LOADER code.

> **Note:** On some versions of DOS, the files IBMBIO.COM and IBMDOS.COM are named IO.SYS and MSDOS.COM.

4. It writes two copies of the **File Allocation Table (FAT)** to the diskette. The FAT is marked so that the areas of the diskette that do not work correctly are never allocated to one of your files.

5. It creates and writes the ROOT directory for the diskette.

6. If you have entered the /S switch, the files IBMBIO.COM, IBMDOS.COM, and COMMAND.COM will be copied to the diskette. This will allow you to start DOS from the formatted diskette. IBMBIO.COM and IBMDOS.COM are hidden files, so you will not be able to see them with a DIR command.

7. If you have entered the /B switch, the files IBMBIO.COM and IBMDOS.COM will be created on the diskette, but the DOS code will not be recorded. This allows you to put DOS onto the diskette at a later time with the SYS command.

8. If you have entered the /V switch, a volume label will be created in the root directory.

With DOS 5.0, if you enter the /Q switch, FORMAT will not perform the process of verifying the disk surface to ensure that all the sectors work correctly. This reduces the amount of time that FORMAT takes to process your disks. However, you can only use the /Q switch on disks that are known to work correctly. You should not use the /Q switch on any disk that DOS has reported errors on when processing.

Again, with DOS 5.0, if you enter the /U switch, FORMAT will not skip the low-level formatting procedure. Without the /U switch, FORMAT will normally just erase the root directory and clear the FAT, thus allowing you to use the REBUILD command to possibly recover some important data on a disk you accidentally formatted. With the /U switch, the data is completely destroyed, and there are no utilities available to get it back.

For all releases, if you are formatting a diskette to hold the DOS system files, and you have used the /S switch, DOS may prompt you as follows:

Insert DOS disk in drive A: and press ENTER when ready...

When this occurs, insert a bootable DOS diskette into drive A:. This message is displayed when DOS cannot locate the DOS system files elsewhere on your computer. Before formatting the new diskette, DOS will read the system files from the diskette you put in A: and then transfer them to your new diskette after the formatting is complete.

When you format a fixed disk, DOS does not work exactly the same. There are two main differences:

1. DOS and FORMAT will not recognize a disk until after the FDISK utility has been run. The FDISK utility breaks the disk into one or more partitions. The description of these partitions is recorded in the master boot record on the fixed disk. This is similar to the boot record of a diskette.

2. The FORMAT utility expects the partition to already have the markings that separate the disk into sectors. The FORMAT utility will not perform this operation. To do this, you need to run the diagnostics that are packaged with your computer.

Although FORMAT does not perform the sectoring of the fixed disk, it does go out and test each sector of the partition. As with diskettes, this is how DOS keeps you from putting data and programs on parts of the disk that do not work correctly.

When you format a partition or diskette that contains files, those files are no longer available. They are lost forever. The operations that FORMAT performs destroy all of the FAT and directory information that is necessary for DOS to find the data and read it into memory. This applies to both partitions and diskettes. If you have defined more than one partition on a disk, only the information in the partition you format will be lost.

Normal Diskette Formatting

You have a diskette that you want to use. You want to format it so that you can use it with your computer. It is the normal type of diskette for the diskette drive you are going to use, and you are not going to use this diskette to move data to another computer.

About 99 percent of the time, this scenario describes how you will use the FORMAT utility. In these cases, you simply put the diskette into the drive and tell DOS to FORMAT the diskette. You answer the questions that DOS may ask and you watch for any problems to occur. Simple! Easy!

If you are not trying to do what has just been described, skip to "Special Diskette Formatting" to find out what you need to do. The rest of this section describes the normal usage of the FORMAT utility.

> **Warning:** About the most important thing to remember with FORMAT is that once you have formatted a diskette (or fixed disk!), all of the data that was there is lost forever. Nothing that you can do will get it back. Remember this each time you format a diskette.

To format a diskette you will not be starting DOS from, simply enter FORMAT and the drive that you want to format in. If you do not use the /V: switch, FORMAT will ask you for a volume label later.

```
C:\>FORMAT A:
Insert new diskette for drive A:
and press ENTER when ready...

 Format complete
 Volume label (11 characters, ENTER for none)?NON-DOS

   xxxxxxxx bytes total disk space
   xxxxxxxx bytes used by system
   xxxxxxxx bytes available on disk

   xxxxxxxx bytes in each allocation unit
   xxxxxxxx allocation units available on disk

 Volume Serial number is 0B2F-19E5

 Format another (Y/N)?N

C:\>_
```

When you first start the FORMAT command, you see a message that says "1 percent of disk formatted." The percentage complete should continue to increase until the entire disk is formatted. At that time, the message "Format complete" is written over the "100 percent of disk formatted."

Formatting a system diskette (a diskette that you will start DOS from) is not very different. You simply add the /S switch when you enter the FORMAT command.

```
C:\>FORMAT A: /S

Format complete
Volume label (11 characters, ENTER for none)?SYSTEM
System transferred

    xxxxxxxx bytes total disk space
    xxxxxxxx bytes used by system
    xxxxxxxx bytes available on disk

    xxxxxxxx bytes in each allocation unit
    xxxxxxxx allocation units available on disk

  Volume Serial number is 227f-3E95

C:\>_
```

In this example, there is one more message, "System transferred," that was not in the last example. This is the indication that the DOS files have been copied over to the new diskette. If FORMAT cannot find the DOS files (IBMBIO.COM, IBMDOS.COM, COMMAND.COM), it will ask you for help by prompting you to put a DOS diskette into drive A:. Follow the directions so that these files can be copied to your newly formatted diskette.

Rather than waiting for DOS to ask for a volume label, you can use the /V: switch on the FORMAT command. The volume label you enter will become the new volume label. You do not have to worry about entering an illegal volume label. Anytime FORMAT sees an illegal volume label, it will tell you and ask for another one.

To format multiple diskettes at one time, simply answer Y to the "Format another (Y/N)?" message that appears. Remember that you cannot change the parameters between diskettes when formatting multiple diskettes.

DOS and FORMAT will not allow you to format imaginary drives. This includes the drives that are created through the ASSIGN and SUBST commands. It also includes drives that have been redirected to a network server. If you have used the JOIN command to join a physical drive into another drive, DOS will not let you format that drive either.

If FORMAT encounters a diskette error that it cannot circumvent, it will terminate. Before terminating, FORMAT will display a message that tells you what went wrong.

If you want to learn about the other 1 percent of the time you use FORMAT, read the next section now. By learning this now, you may save yourself from having to learn it later. Formatting of fixed disks is described later, in "Formatting Fixed Disks."

Special Diskette Formatting

The other uses of FORMAT are split between formatting diskettes and disks. Formatting disks is usually only done once — when you first get them. The use of FORMAT that remains is formatting diskettes to a size other than their maximum formatted capacity. This should done for only two reasons:

1. Because you do not have the right type of diskettes for the drive you are going to use. You would be better off if you believed that the formatting could not be done. We recommend that you resist the urge to do this as strongly as possible.

2. Because you want to move data from one computer to another and the computers do not have the same type of diskette drives.

In both of these cases, you will be formatting a diskette to less than what it was designed to hold.

Since early in DOS's history, if you told DOS to format a diskette, DOS would format it to the largest capacity the diskette could hold. Only if you wanted a smaller-capacity diskette created did you need to add switches to control the final size of the diskette.

As the number of diskette types has continued to grow, so has the complexity of reducing their formatted size. Having to make decisions on how many sides, how many sectors per track, and so forth, is more than the DOS user should have to cope with. For this reason, a new parameter, /F:, was introduced in DOS 4.0. You can use this parameter to specify the capacity you want the diskette to have, and FORMAT will then figure out the rest of the parameters.

Figure 10-4 shows the switches that would have been required to format the different diskette capacities under DOS 3.3. It also shows the /F: switch value that you need to use if you want to create the same size diskette. The

Diskette Type	Formatted Capacity	Old Switches Required	/F Value Required	Optional Switches
1D	160KB 180KB	/8	160	/S /V: /S /V: /F:180
2D	160KB 180KB 320KB 360KB	/1 /8 /1 /8	160 180 320	/S /V: /S /V: /S /V: /S /V: /F:360
2HC	160KB 180KB 320KB 360KB 1.2MB	/1 /8 /1 /4 /4 /8 /4	160 180 320 360	/S /V: /S /V: /S /V: /S /V: /S /V: /F:1220
1.0MB	720KB			/S /V: /F:720
1.0MB 2.0MB	720KB 1.44MB	Not Supported	720	/S /V: /S /V: /F:1440
1.0MB 2.0MB 4.0MB	720KB 1.44MB 2.88MB	Not Supported	720 1440	/S /V: /S /V: /S /V: /F:2880

Figure 10-4
Format Size Values versus Old Switches

figure also lists the optional switches that you can use to add a system or volume label.

The /B switch can be substituted for /S, but you cannot use both at the same time.

To reduce the formatted capacity of a diskette, simply add the /F:size parameter to the FORMAT command. Several synonyms are available for each size, and these can be found in Figure 10-5. If the diskette that you are trying to format cannot be formatted to the size you request, DOS will let you know by issuing the message "Parameters not compatible."

Format Size	Allowable /F: Values
160KB	160, 160K, 160KB
180KB	180, 180K, 180KB
320KB	320, 320K, 320KB
360KB	360, 360K, 360KB
720KB	720, 720K, 720KB
1.2MB	1200, 1200K, 1200KB, 1.2, 1.2M, 1.2MB
1.44MB	1440, 1440K, 1440KB, 1.44, 1.44M, 1.44MB
2.88MB	2880, 2880K, 2880KB, 2.88, 2.88M, 2.88MB

Figure 10-5
Synonyms for /F Values

Formatting Fixed Disks

Using FORMAT on disks is essentially the same as with diskettes. The main differences are:

- It takes much longer. The larger the disk, the longer FORMAT takes. Also, each time FORMAT encounters a bad area of the disk, it must spend extra time determining what parts of the disk are bad.

- There are only two options:

    1. You can create a system disk that will boot DOS when you turn your computer on. Just as with diskettes, you do this with the /S switch.

    2. You can specify the disk's new volume label with the /V: switch. If you do not enter the /V: switch and volume label, FORMAT will ask you to enter one. Again, this is done just as for diskettes.

- The FORMAT utility will ask you to enter the volume label of the disk that you want to format. You may think that this is unnecessary — after all, you did tell FORMAT what drive you wanted to format. But remember that the FORMAT operation could cause you to lose the entire contents of a very large disk. This "sanity check" has saved more than one fixed disk.

    If you have one fixed disk, you will almost always want to format it as a system disk. You may not want to make your only fixed disk a DOS system disk if you are also using another operating system such as XENIX, AIX, or Operating System/2. That way, you will not need a diskette to start DOS. This first fixed disk will always be drive C:. If you have two fixed disks, there is no need to format the second disk as a system disk. DOS will not boot from your second fixed disk. The only exception to this is when you have no DOS partitions defined on your first fixed disk.

    This example shows you how you would format drive C: as a system disk. However, you should never have to do this, as the normal DOS installation procedure will do it for you. Let's assume the following:

- We have just replaced our first fixed disk with a new one. We did this because we already had two drives and needed more room. Since the system will only hold two drives, we had to get a bigger one. We have decided to replace the first one, drive C:.

- We have backed up all of the files on both drive C: and D:.

- We have already used FDISK to set up a partition.

- We are executing FORMAT from the A: diskette drive.

```
C:\>FORMAT C: /S /V:DRIVE-C

WARNING, ALL DATA ON NON-REMOVABLE DISK
DRIVE C: WILL BE LOST!
Proceed with Format (Y/N)?Y

 Format complete
 System transferred

   xxxxxxxx bytes total disk space
   xxxxxxxx bytes used by system
   xxxxxxxx bytes available on disk

   xxxxxxxx bytes in each allocation unit
   xxxxxxxx allocation units available on disk

 Volume Serial number is 0B2F-19E5

C:\>_
```

When you first start the FORMAT command, you should see a message that says "1 percent of disk formatted." The percentage complete should continue to increase until the entire disk is formatted. At that time, the message "Format complete" is written over the "100 percent of disk formatted."

During the formatting of a fixed disk, it may occasionally appear that FORMAT has stalled. In these situations, FORMAT has found a part of the disk that is not working correctly. This is normal. At these times, FORMAT is simply looking at the problem area of the disk a little closer. The percentage complete message will start to increase again shortly.

Everything should have gone well in formatting drive C:. If the new drive has not been formatted before, you should not be prompted to enter the volume label of the drive you wanted to format.

Now, let's try to format drive D: as a data drive. Because the new C: drive is much larger, we have already restored all of the files that were on drive D: to drive C:. Everything is working fine, and we are now executing on our new drive C:. We are expecting DOS to perform a "sanity check" and ask us for the volume name of the drive that we are trying to format.

```
C:\>FORMAT C:
Enter the Volume Label for drive C:DRIVE-D
Invalid Volume ID
Format terminated

C:\>_
```

What happened? We entered the volume name of our drive D:. Whoops! We typed in the FORMAT command incorrectly. This is why DOS makes this check. We almost wiped out our new drive C:. Let's try again.

```
C:\>FORMAT D:
Enter the Volume Label for drive C:DRIVE-D

WARNING, ALL DATA ON NON-REMOVABLE DISK
DRIVE C: WILL BE LOST!
Proceed with Format (Y/N)?Y

 Format complete
 Volume label (11 characters, ENTER for none)?DRIVE-D

   xxxxxxxx bytes total disk space
   xxxxxxxx bytes used by system
   xxxxxxxx bytes available on disk

   xxxxxxxx bytes in each allocation unit
   xxxxxxxx allocation units available on disk

 Volume Serial number is 0B2F-19E5

C:\>_
```

Things worked better this time. Also, notice that when we did not enter the /V switch on the FORMAT command line, we were asked to enter a new volume label for the drive.

Whenever you use the FDISK command to create a new disk partition or change the size of an existing disk partition, you must reformat that partition.

PUTTING DOS ON YOUR DISKS

You use the SYS command to copy the two hidden DOS files IBMBIO.COM and IBMDOS.COM from one disk or diskette to another. You cannot use the COPY command to copy these two files because COPY cannot copy hidden files. Also, these files must be in a special place on the disk, and COPY does not make sure this is true. The SYS utility will not copy any files other than IBMBIO.COM and IBMDOS.COM.

The major usage of SYS is to upgrade your existing diskettes from one DOS release to another. With DOS 1.0 through DOS 3.3, this sometimes did not work. Starting with DOS 4.0, this should no longer be a problem. SYS can also be used to add DOS to diskettes after other files have been created.

This used to work only if the first two root directory entries were empty. Again, starting with DOS 4.0, these restrictions no longer apply.

In early releases of DOS, IBMBIO.COM and IBMDOS.COM had to be the first two entries of the root directory for DOS to boot. Additionally, IBMBIO.COM was required to start in the first allocation unit. It also had to be written all in one place. In normal DOS file handling terms, this is very restrictive. DOS will put files anywhere in the directory that it chooses. It will write the contents of the file in as many parts as it takes.

Three changes introduced with DOS 4.0 removed these restrictions:

1. Only the first 1024 bytes of IBMBIO.COM have to be in one part at the start of the disk. The rest can be broken up as much as necessary and scattered all over.

2. When occupied, SYS will move the first two directory entries to another part of the root directory. This will allow SYS to put IBMBIO.COM and IBMDOS.COM in the first two directory entries.

3. When the first two sectors are occupied, SYS will move the data that is in them to another location on the disk.

Now, if there is enough free room on a diskette to contain DOS, and at least two unused root directory entries exist, SYS can transfer DOS to the target drive. When necessary, SYS will move directory entries and data but it will transfer DOS whenever possible.

> **Warning:** Because SYS can make these major changes to your disk, if you SYS a fixed disk we recommend that you make a backup of it first.

The SYS command is very easy to use; just enter SYS and the drive that you want to transfer DOS to.

```
C:\>SYS B:
System transferred

C:\>_
```

Even with the improvements in SYS, some things can still prevent the system files from being transferred. SYS will not allow you to transfer to an imaginary drive that has been created with ASSIGN, with SUBST, or on a remote network server. If there is not enough room on the target drive, then SYS will not be able to transfer DOS. If you try to transfer to a drive that does not exist, or if the disk or diskette is no longer usable, the system will not be transferred. In all of these cases, SYS will issue a message to tell you what the problem is.

After you have used SYS to copy the two hidden DOS files, you must then use the COPY command to copy COMMAND.COM to the new fixed disk or diskette. Many people set up a batch file to do this:

@ECHO OFF

SYS %1

COPY \DOS\COMMAND.COM %1

You could call this batch file SYSC.BAT. SYS for the SYS command and C for the COPY command. If you did this, you could transfer DOS to another fixed disk or diskette with just one command.

```
C:\>SYSC B:
System transferred
    1 file(s) copied

C:\>_
```

This batch file shows COMMAND.COM being copied from the DOS subdirectory. You may not have installed DOS in a subdirectory named DOS. If not, you will need to change the batch file to use the correct subdirectory for your installation. The "System transferred" message indicates that SYS successfully transferred IBMBIO.COM and IBMDOS.COM. The "1 file(s) copied" message indicates that COMMAND.COM was successfully copied.

Another SYS feature was introduced with DOS 4.0 — the ability to tell SYS where to get IBMBIO.COM and IBMDOS.COM from. Many of you will never need this feature. It is mostly used in large network installations.

You use this feature just as you would the source and target file specifications in the COPY command. You enter "SYS source drive target drive." If the DOS files are not in the root of the source drive, you can enter an optional path as well. Here is an example:

```
C:\>SYS C:\ B:
System transferred

C:\>_
```

This example transfers IBMBIO.COM and IBMDOS.COM from the root directory of drive C: to drive B:. This could also have been done with just a regular SYS B: command.

COPYING ENTIRE DISKETTES

The DISKCOPY command allows you to quickly copy the contents of one diskette to another diskette. It does this by copying each sector of the original diskette to the same sector of the new diskette (see "What the Diskette Looks Like" for more information on disk sectors). Also, because DISKCOPY copies each sector, the original diskette and the new diskette must be the exact same type (see "Diskette Compatibility" for more information on diskette compatibility).

> **Warning:** Do not use diskettes that have bad areas on them as the new diskettes for DISKCOPY. If the target diskette has bad areas, the data that was in these areas on the original diskette will not be accessible.

If DISKCOPY indicates that there are bad areas on the new diskette, throw it away and make another copy. If DISKCOPY indicates that there are bad areas on the original diskette, try using the XCOPY command. If you are lucky, the bad area will be in an unused spot on the diskette and XCOPY will never even see the bad spot.

In early releases of DOS, DISKCOPY was the only way to quickly copy diskettes. Since the XCOPY command has been added to DOS, it has become the preferred method of copying all of one diskette to another. XCOPY has the advantage of being able to copy across diskette types and even between fixed disks and diskettes.

Because DISKCOPY works on a sector by sector basis, it does not know (or care) about the directories and files on the original diskette. DISKCOPY will read as many sectors into your computer's memory as will fit and then write them to the new diskette. If you are using the same diskette drive for both the original diskette and the new diskette (e.g., DISKCOPY A: A:), then DISKCOPY will tell you when to change diskettes in the diskette drive.

> **Warning:** Do not get the original diskette and the new diskette confused. If you incorrectly switch them in the middle of the DISKCOPY, the contents of your original diskette will be lost.

Also, because DISKCOPY works on a sector by sector basis, you cannot use DISKCOPY for drives that have been created by the NET USE or SUBST commands. The DISKCOPY command will ignore any ASSIGNs or JOINs that are in effect. DISKCOPY cannot be used to copy from or to a virtual drive.

One good thing about DISKCOPY is that the new diskette does not have to be formatted before you can use it. The DISKCOPY command will format the new diskette as it goes along. If you are using XCOPY, you must use the FORMAT command before you can copy to a new diskette.

There is one useful switch for DISKCOPY, the /V switch. This switch tells DISKCOPY to verify that the data is correctly copied to the target diskette. Using this switch will make DISKCOPY take longer. This switch was not available before DOS 5.0.

There is one additional switch for DISKCOPY, the /1 switch. This tells DISKCOPY to only copy one side of the original diskette. Never use this switch. It was useful back in the days when single-sided diskette drives were popular, but it can only cause you trouble now.

You may be using a computer that does not have a fixed disk. In this case, DOS may display the message "Insert diskette with \COMMAND.COM in drive A: and press any key when ready." This is because the DISKCOPY command has overwritten the transient portion of the command processor and it must be reloaded before you can continue. Put your DOS diskette back in drive A: and press Enter (↵).

DISKCOPY Error Levels

DOS 5.0 users can check the success of the DISKCOPY utility through the error level that it returns. DISKCOPY returns the following error levels:

0   No errors occurred, the disk copy was successful.

1   A disk read or disk write error occurred, and the operation was successfully retried. The disk copy was successful, but one or both of the disks may not last much longer.

2   The disk copy procedure was aborted due to user intervention, either Ctl+C or Ctl+Break.

3   A disk read or disk write error occurred and persisted during retries. The disk copy was not successful, and at least one of your disks is no longer usable.

4   An error occurred during the utilities initialization, and the disk copy procedure was aborted.

COMPARING ENTIRE DISKETTES

The DISKCOMP command works much as the DISKCOPY command does, except that it allows you to compare diskettes rather than copy their contents. It does so by comparing each sector of one diskette to the same sector of another diskette (see "What the Diskette Looks Like" for more information on disk sectors). Because DISKCOMP compares each sector, the two diskettes must be the exact same type (see "Diskette Compatibility" for more information on diskette compatibility).

If DISKCOMP indicates that there are bad areas on either diskette, then you cannot be sure if the diskettes are the same or not. If you are lucky, the bad area will be in a unused spot on the diskette. If not, you can try using the XCOPY and RECOVER commands to get all of your data off of the diskette.

The DISKCOMP command is still the only way to quickly compare two full diskettes. There is no "XCOMP" command in DOS. Unfortunately, almost the only good use of DISKCOMP is to be sure that DISKCOPY created an exact copy of the original diskette.

Because DISKCOMP works on a sector by sector basis, it does not know (or care) about the directories and files on the original diskette. DISKCOPY will read as many sectors into your computer's memory as will fit and then will compare them to the other diskette. If you are using the same diskette drive for both the original diskette and the new diskette (e.g., DISKCOMP A: A:), then XCOPY will tell you when to change diskettes in the diskette drive. Because of the way that DOS handles disk space allocation to files, even if all of the files are the same, DISKCOMP will often say that the diskettes are different. This is because the files may be stored in different sectors on the two different diskettes.

Also because DISKCOMP works on a sector by sector basis, you cannot use DISKCOMP for drives that have been created by the NET USE or SUBST commands. The DISKCOMP command will ignore any ASSIGNs or JOINs that are in effect. DISKCOMP cannot be used to compare from or to a virtual drive.

There are two switches for DISKCOMP — /1 and /8. These switches tell DISKCOMP to compare only one side of the diskettes and to compare only 8 sectors per track. Never use these switches. They were useful back in the days when single-sided diskette drives were popular, but they can only cause you trouble now.

Some of you will be using a computer that does not have a fixed disk. In this case, DOS may display the message "Insert diskette with \COMMAND.COM in drive A: and press any key when ready." This is because the DISKCOMP command has overwritten the transient portion of the command processor and it must be reloaded before you can continue. Put your DOS diskette back in drive A: and press Enter (↵).

DISKCOMP Error Levels

DOS 5.0 users can check the success of the DISKCOMP utility through the error level that it returns. DISKCOMP returns the following error levels:

0   No errors occurred, the disk compare was successful.

1   A disk read or disk write error occurred, and the operation was successfully retried. The disk compare was successful, but one or both of the disks may not last much longer.

2   The disk compare procedure was aborted due to user intervention, either Ctl+C or Ctl+Break.

3   A disk read or disk write error occurred and persisted during retries. The disk compare was not successful, and at least one of your disks is no longer usable.

4   An error occurred during the utilities initialization, and the disk compare procedure was aborted.

LABELING YOUR DISKS

The LABEL utility provides you with the ability to display and change the volume label of your disks. The volume label is the "name" of the disk. You use the FORMAT utility to create a disk, and then you can give it a volume label. You can change the volume label whenever you like.

The volume label can be up to 11 characters long and can consist of any of the characters allowed in filenames plus the blank character. With this capacity, you can give your disks a first and last name. You should try to give each fixed disk and diskette a unique volume label. This will help you keep them straight in the future.

There are actually four different operations you can do with LABEL:

ADD   To add a volume label to a disk, enter LABEL and the drive that you want to work with. When the message "Volume label (11 characters, ENTER for none)?" is displayed, enter the new volume label. You can also put the new volume label on the command line, immediately after the drive you want to work with.

CHANGE   To change the volume label of a disk, enter LABEL and the drive that you want to work with. When the message "Volume label (11 characters, ENTER for none)?" is displayed, enter the new volume label. You can also put the new volume label on the command line, immediately after the drive you want to work with.

DELETE   To delete the volume label of a disk, enter LABEL and the drive that holds the disk you want to work with. When the message "Volume label (11 characters, ENTER for none)?" is displayed, just press Enter (↵). When the message "Delete current volume label (Y/N)?" is displayed, press the Y key.

DISPLAY   To display the volume label of a disk, simply enter LABEL and the drive that holds the disk you want to know about. When the message "Volume label (11 characters, ENTER for none)?" is displayed, just press Enter (↵). When the message "Delete current volume label (Y/N)?" is displayed, press the N key. It is easier to use the VOL command to perform this function. You do not have to answer any of the questions.

```
C:\>LABEL B:
Volume in drive B has no label
Volume Serial number is 353E-0FED
Volume label (11 characters, ENTER for none)?ONENAME

C:\>LABEL B:
Volume in drive B is ONENAME
Volume Serial number is 353E-0FED
Volume label (11 characters, ENTER for none)?

Delete current volume label (Y/N)? N

C:\>LABEL B:TWO NAMES

C:\>LABEL B:
Volume in drive B is TWO NAMES
Volume Serial number is 353E-0FED
Volume label (11 characters, ENTER for none)?

Delete current volume label (Y/N)? Y

C:\>_
```

The first LABEL command was used to add the label ONENAME to the disk in drive B:. The second LABEL command was used to display the label without deleting it. The third LABEL command was used to change the label to "TWO NAMES." The fourth LABEL command was used to delete the label from the disk in drive B:.

In this example, we were working with drive B:. If you do not enter a drive, the LABEL utility will work with the current drive. DOS will not allow you to use the LABEL utility on imaginary drives.

The volume label is your way of knowing which disk is which. DOS will display the volume label as part of the output of several commands and utilities:

- DIR

- LABEL

- VOL

- CHKDSK

When you are using the FORMAT utility, DOS will ask you to enter the volume label of the fixed disk you are formatting. This is just a sanity check, to make sure that the fixed disk you asked DOS to format is the fixed disk you wanted formatted.

WHAT ARE THE LABELS ON MY DISKS?

The VOL command provides only the display features of the LABEL command we just discussed. If you wish to know what the volume name and serial number (DOS 4.0 and later only) of a disk or diskette are, simply type VOL and (optionally) the desired drive.

The volume serial number concept was introduced in DOS 4.0. Disks with volume serial numbers are usable by DOS 3.3, but DOS 3.3 will not look at, use, or display them.

DIRECTORY FUNCTIONS

We will cover the following utilities in this section:

BACKUP   Saves files from your fixed disk to one or more diskettes (or another fixed disk). If your files are backed up and for any reason you lose the files on your fixed disk, you can get them back from these diskettes.

REPLACE   Replaces files from some other disk. You would use this most often when you upgrade to a new version of an application program.

RESTORE   Puts back files saved by BACKUP.

XCOPY   Copies files the way the COPY command does, but it can also copy files in subdirectories. It makes copying files on disks with a complicated directory structure much easier.

These utilities work on all of the files in a directory or set of directories. They can be restricted to working in just one subdirectory. They can be told to work on a whole fixed disk or diskette as well, just like the fixed disk and diskette functions utilities. The difference is that even when these utilities are processing an entire disk, they are doing it one file at a time. Also, these utilities can be used on imaginary drives. The utilities we discussed in the previous sections could not process imaginary drives.

MAKING BACKUPS OF YOUR FILES

The BACKUP command provides you with the ability to quickly and efficiently make backup copies of the files on your fixed disks. The importance of keeping backup copies of your files cannot be overemphasized. If you do not keep regularly updated backups, you will be in real trouble if you accidentally erase all of the files on your fixed disk. While some programs are available that help you to overcome this type of situation, they cannot recover from all possible disasters. A good example of this is if your fixed disk breaks. After you replace your fixed disk with a new one, the data recovery programs will not be able to get the data from your old fixed disk. You can suddenly be faced with a complete loss of your programs and data.

Your loss can be significantly reduced if you frequently make backup copies of your files. If you manage to struggle through a data loss experience, you will start backing up your files. Guaranteed! You would be better off, however, to start making regular backups before your first experience of this nature.

The BACKUP command does not simply copy files from your fixed disk to your diskettes. If it did, then you would not be able to back up a very large file. You would only be able to back up a file no larger than a single backup diskette. Also, each backup file would take a minimum of 512 bytes. Since many files are less than 512 bytes, this would waste a large amount of space on your backup diskettes.

The BACKUP command will create two files on each of your diskettes, a control file and a data file. The control file contains a description of each file that is backed up (path, filename, filename extension, size, and so on). The data file contains the actual data that was in all of the original files.

The BACKUP command does not limit you to backing up files only on your fixed disks. You can also use it to back up the files on your diskettes. Likewise, you can back up your files to a fixed disk, or even to a remote network drive. These are not the normal uses of BACKUP; we mention them here only for completeness.

Because the BACKUP procedure usually takes several diskettes, you should have them available before starting your backup procedure. They do not have to be formatted; if the diskettes are not formatted, BACKUP will automatically run the FORMAT command for you. If they are formatted, all of the files will be erased! Do not back up to diskettes that have good files on them. Prior to DOS 5.0, BACKUP will only format diskettes to their largest capacity; for example, DOS 4.0 BACKUP will not format a 1.44MB diskette to just 720KB. However, with DOS 5.0, you can control the formatted size of the BACKUP diskettes with the /F: switch. The values for this switch are the same as for FORMAT (see Figure 10-4).

Each time a diskette becomes full, you will be asked to insert a new diskette. You should carefully record the backup sequence number on each backup diskette. Later, if you need to restore a file from the backup diskettes, you will have to put the diskettes back into the drive in the same order in which they were backed up.

There are two main ways that the BACKUP command is used:

Complete Backup   This process makes a backup copy of every file on your fixed disk. You should do this the first time you run the BACKUP command. You may also want to do this occasionally throughout the year. A good rule of thumb is to make a complete backup whenever the number of backup diskettes has doubled. In other words, if your first backup takes five diskettes, then you should do another complete backup when you have added five more backup diskettes through the incremental backup procedure described next.

Incremental Backup   This process makes a backup copy of only the files that have been changed since the last complete backup. This greatly reduces the number of diskettes and time a backup takes. The frequency of this type of backup depends on how much data you are processing and how much you can afford to lose. Once a week seems to be a widely accepted standard.

Performing a Complete Backup

The following example shows how you would start a complete backup:

```
C:\>BACKUP C:\*.* A: /S

Insert backup diskette 01 in drive A:

WARNING! Files in the target drive
A:\ root directory will be erased
Press any key to continue . . .

C:\>_
```

In this example, all of the files on drive C: will be backed up to diskettes you put into drive A:. The parameter C:*.* tells BACKUP that you want all files backed up from the root directory of drive C:. The switch /S tells BACKUP that you want BACKUP to look in all of the directories below the root also. Without the /S switch, BACKUP would only look in the root directory of drive C:.

As each file is backed up, its name will be displayed. When the first diskette is filled, BACKUP will ask you to insert the next diskette:

```
\FILE.072
\FILE.073
\FILE.074

Insert backup diskette 01 in drive A:
Press any key to continue . . .

C:\>_
```

After you put the second diskette in and press a key, BACKUP will continue. Each time a diskette is filled, you will be asked to insert another diskette.

Note that when you enter the BACKUP command, you must tell BACKUP which files are to be backed up. The *.* indicates that all files should be backed up. If you wanted to, you could limit the backup process to just certain files. For example, BACKUP C:*.TMP A: /S: would back up only files with a filename extension of .TMP.

Performing an Incremental Backup

The following example shows how you would start an incremental backup:

```
C:\>BACKUP C:\*.* A: /A /M /S

Insert last backup diskette in drive A:
Press any key to continue . . .

C:\>_
```

In this example, all of the files on drive C: that have been modified since the last backup will be backed up to diskettes you put into drive A:. The parameter C:*.* tells BACKUP that you want all files checked to see if they have been modified. The /A switch tells BACKUP that you want to add to the existing set of backup diskettes. The /M switch tells BACKUP to back up only those files that have been modified since the last backup. As with the complete backup, the /S switch tells BACKUP that you want BACKUP to look in all of the directories below the root also.

When BACKUP asks you for the last backup diskette, it is asking for the diskette with the highest sequence number from the last backup you performed. The /A switch tells BACKUP to start backing up to that diskette rather than starting with a new diskette. This saves you some diskette space. From this point on, the backup appears to work the same as a complete backup. When a diskette is filled, you will be asked for a new one.

Other BACKUP Controls

There are three other switches you can use to control the backup process:

/D:mm-dd-yy   Tells BACKUP to back up only those files that have a last modified date that is equal to or newer than the date you enter.

/T:hh:mm:ss   Tells BACKUP to back up only those files that have a last modified time that is equal to or newer than the time you enter. If you have not entered a /D: switch and date, then BACKUP will back up all files that have been modified after the /T: time on any date. This switch is somewhat useless unless used with the /D: switch.

/L:filename   The switch creates a backup log file. The backup log file simply contains a listing of what the BACKUP command did. By creating a log file, you can always see what BACKUP did while you were not looking. You can tell BACKUP to put the log data in any file in any directory on any drive in your system. If you do not enter a filename, BACKUP will put the log data in the file BACKUP.LOG in the root directory of the drive that you are backing up. If the log file already exists, BACKUP will add the new data to the end of the file.

The backup log file only contains simple ASCII text. You can use the TYPE command to see its contents. You can also print the file and store it with your backup diskettes.

BACKUP Error Levels

Since DOS 3.3, you have been able to check the success of the BACKUP utility through the error level that it returns. BACKUP returns the following error levels:

0   No errors occurred, the backup was successful.

1   There were no files found to be backed up.

2   Because of file sharing errors, one or more files were not backed up. The backup log file will indicate which files had a problem.

3   The backup procedure was aborted due to user intervention, either Ctl+C or Ctl+Break.

4   BACKUP encountered an error that it could not get past, and the backup procedure was aborted.

REPLACING FILES ON YOUR DISKS

The REPLACE command is primarily used to install software on your fixed disks. Due to restrictions in earlier versions of DOS and some versions of application programs, the same file often existed in several directories at one time. When a new release of DOS or an application is issued, each copy of these files must be updated during the installation process.

You can also use REPLACE for the same purpose. If you have one or more files that exist in several directories, you can use REPLACE to update all copies of the files at one time.

To tell REPLACE what to do, you have to enter two parameters:

1. The first parameter is a file specification. Like other copy commands, it can contain the * and ? filename matching characters. This parameter tells REPLACE which files will be copied to the path specified by the second parameter. This parameter tells REPLACE what the source of the copying will be.

2. The second parameter is a path specification. Like other copy commands, it can be a drive or drive and directory combination. Unlike other copy commands, though, it cannot contain a filename or filename extension. This parameter tells REPLACE what the target of the copying will be.

For example, REPLACE A:\ONEFILE C:\ONEDIR will copy the file A:\ONEFILE to C:\ONEDIR\ONEFILE. This seems almost like the actual COPY command. However, it is not really the same. There are two functions that REPLACE provides, and REPLACE will only perform one of these functions at a time:

File Replacing   This function will copy files that already exist on your fixed disk. If the file does not exist in the target directory, the file will not be copied. This is the normal function of the REPLACE command. It is the function that will be performed if the /A switch is not part of the command line.

Using the earlier example, REPLACE A:\ONEFILE C:\ONEDIR, the file ONEFILE will be copied only if it already exists in C:\ONEDIR.

File Adding   This function will add files that do not already exist on your fixed disk. If the file does exist in the target directory, it will not be copied. This function is enabled by the /A switch.

If we change the previous example slightly, REPLACE A:\ONEFILE C:\ONEDIR /A, the file ONEFILE will only be copied if it does not exist in C:\ONEDIR.

There are five other switches you can use to control the replacement process:

/P   This switch tells REPLACE that it should check with the operator before each file that it is going to replace. If the operator responds Yes, the file will be replaced. If the operator responds No, the file will not be replaced.

/R   This switch tells REPLACE that it can go ahead and overwrite files on the target disk that have the ReadOnly attribute set on.

/S   This switch is only valid for the File Replace functions. It cannot be entered together with the /A switch. This switch tells REPLACE to search all subdirectories of the target and perform the File Replace function in those subdirectories also.

/U   This switch is only valid for the File Replace functions. It cannot be entered together with the /A switch. It tells REPLACE to replace only those files that are newer on the source disk than on the target disk.

/W   This switch tells REPLACE to wait so that you can change the source or target diskettes before the replacement process actually begins. This is useful only for single-diskette-drive computers with no fixed disk.

Since DOS 3.3, you have been able to check the success of the REPLACE utility through the error level that it returns. REPLACE returns the following error levels:

0   No errors occurred, files were successfully replaced.

2   No files were found that matched the source file specification. No files were replaced.

3   The drive or path specified in the source file specification could not be found. No files were replaced.

5   An Access Denied error occurred while trying to write to the destination files. This is usually caused by the files being marked with the ReadOnly attribute, or by trying to replace to a network drive that you only have read access to. One or more files may have been replaced, but not all files were.

8   The REPLACE command could not allocate enough memory to perform the request. No files were replaced.

11   There was an error in the parameters you entered on the command line. This could be caused by an unrecognized switch character. No files were replaced.

15   The destination drive you entered was not valid. No files were replaced.

RESTORING FILES FROM YOUR BACKUPS

The RESTORE command provides you with the ability to recover files from the backup copies that you made earlier.

Again, the importance of keeping backup copies of your files cannot be overemphasized. You should read the earlier section on BACKUP for a better understanding of how frequent backups can make your life easier.

Since the BACKUP command does not simply copy files from your fixed disk to your diskettes, you cannot simply copy them back to your fixed disks. The RESTORE command understands the control and data files that BACKUP created and can get back just the files that you need.

As RESTORE finishes processing each diskette, you will be asked to insert the next diskette in sequence. Fortunately, because you very carefully recorded the backup sequence number on each backup diskette, this will not be difficult.

There are two main ways in which the RESTORE command is used:

Complete Restore   This process completely copies all of the backed up files from your diskettes to your fixed disk. It is used most often when you are switching releases of the operating system or changing your fixed disk. If you have just changed your fixed disk, it is most likely that you are upgrading to a larger fixed disk. As we said earlier, many people do not perform regular backups. When their fixed disk breaks, they do not have backup copies of their files and they are faced with a complete loss of their programs and data.

Partial Restore   This process only copies the requested files from your backup diskettes to your fixed disks. This procedure is most often used when your fixed disk has "grown" a bad spot in the middle of an important file. It is also used when you accidentally erase files that you cannot live without.

Performing a Complete Restore

The following example shows how you would start a complete restore:

```
C:\>RESTORE A: C:\ /S

Insert backup diskette 01 in drive A:
Press any key to continue . . .

C:\>_
```

In this example, you will be putting the backup diskettes into drive A:. The files that were previously backed up will be copied onto drive C:, starting in the root directory. The /S switch tells RESTORE to restore all of the files in all of the subdirectories also.

RESTORE will start processing the first backup diskette as soon as you press a key. The date when you performed the backup operation will be displayed. As each file is restored, its name will also be displayed.

When RESTORE has finished with the first diskette, you will be asked to insert the second diskette. After you put the second diskette in and press a key, RESTORE will continue. Each time RESTORE finishes with a diskette, you will be asked to insert the next diskette in sequence.

If you are working with a set of backup diskettes that was created from a combination of a complete backup and one or more incremental backups, just keep inserting diskettes as you are asked for them. Some files may be restored many times because they were backed up many times. This is what should happen, so do not get worried if you see the same file being restored more than once.

Performing a Partial Restore

The following example shows how you would start a partial restore:

```
C:\>RESTORE A: C:\SOMEPATH\*.*

Insert backup diskette 01 in drive A:
Press any key to continue . . .

C:\>_
```

In this example, you will be putting the backup diskettes into drive A:. The files that were previously backed up will be copied onto drive C:, but only in the C:\SOMEPATH directory.

Keep putting diskettes into drive A: when RESTORE asks for them. Some diskettes may not restore any files; others may restore several files. This is OK, because the files are being restored from the diskettes that BACKUP put them on.

As with a complete restore, if you are working with a set of backup diskettes that was created from a combination of a complete backup and one or more incremental backups, just keep inserting diskettes as you are asked for them. Some files may be restored many times. This is because they were backed up many times. This is what should happen, so do not get worried if you see the same file being restored more than once.

Other RESTORE Controls

There are seven other switches you can use to control the restore process:

/A:mm-dd-yy This switch tells RESTORE to restore files only if they were modified after the date you enter.

/B:mm-dd-yy This switch tells RESTORE to restore files only if they were modified before the date you enter.

/E:hh:mm:ss This switch tells RESTORE to restore files only if they were modified earlier than the time you enter.

/L:hh:mm:ss This switch tells RESTORE to restore files only if they were modified later than the time you enter.

/M This switch tells RESTORE to restore files only if (1) the file no longer exists on the disk being restored to, or (2) the file already exists on the disk being restored to and has been modified since the backup you are working with.

/N The switch tells RESTORE to restore files only if they no longer exist on the disk being restored to.

/P This switch tells RESTORE to ask you before each file that it is going to restore if (1) the file already exists on the disk being restored to and the file is marked read only, or (2) the file already exists on the disk being restored to and has been modified since the backup you are working with.

Remember that the two time switches, /E: and /L:, should only be used together with the corresponding date switches, /B: and /A:. Otherwise, RESTORE will process files that meet the time restriction, regardless of the modification date.

Since DOS 3.3, you have been able to check the success of the RESTORE utility through the error level that it returns. RESTORE returns the following error levels:

0   No errors occurred, the restore was successful.

1   There were no files found to be restored.

3   The restore procedure was aborted due to user intervention, either Ctl+C or Ctl+Break.

4   RESTORE encountered an error that it could not get past, and the restore procedure was aborted.

COPYING DIRECTORY STRUCTURES

The XCOPY command is just an extension to the COPY command. Its main use is to copy selected files from more than one directory to another location. This is very different from the COPY command, whereby only selected files from one directory can be copied.

There are several switches that you can use to control how XCOPY works, and they will be explained later. The main use of XCOPY relates to how it copies files and how it searches for files to copy.

Basic Uses of XCOPY

The XCOPY command is often much simpler to use than the COPY command, even when you are only copying files from a single directory. This is because XCOPY will fill all of your computer's memory with data that it reads from the original files before it starts writing data to the new files. The COPY command will only read in one original file at a time.

Look at it this way. If you enter COPY A:*.* B:\, this will copy all of the files in the root directory of drive A: to the root directory of drive B:. If you are using a computer that has only one diskette drive, then that drive is being used for both the original files on the A: diskette and the new files on the B: diskette. Since COPY will only read one original file at a time, you will have to switch the diskettes twice for every file that is copied. You will have to switch from diskette A: to diskette B: after each original file has been read. Then you will have to switch from diskette B: back to diskette A: after each new file is written. This means two switches for each file copied. Figure 10-6 shows what would happen if this command caused four files to be copied.

However, if you enter the command XCOPY A:*.* B:\, you will have to switch the diskettes only when your computer's memory fills up. Figure 10-7 shows what might happen if this command were used to copy the same four files as the previous COPY command. Using XCOPY can often divide the number of diskette swaps by ten or even more.

There is another good reason to use XCOPY. After you tell it how to select the files to copy, you can also tell it to search additional directories.

```
Read A:\File.1
  1. Switch to diskette B:
Write B:\File.1
  2. Switch to diskette A:
Read A:\File.2
  3. Switch to diskette B:
Write B:\File.1
  4. Switch to diskette A:
Read A:\File.3
  5. Switch to diskette B:
Write B:\File.1
  6. Switch to diskette A:
Read A:\File.4
  7. Switch to diskette B:
Write B:\File.1
  8. Switch to diskette A:
Total diskette swaps = 8.
```

Figure 10-6
Diskette Swaps Using
COPY

By using the /S switch, you can tell XCOPY to copy all of the matching files from the starting directory, plus all of the matching files from all of the sub-directories of the starting directory. For example, Figure 10-8 is a listing of the directory structure of a diskette. You can see that there are two directories in the root directory of drive A:, SUBDIR.ONE and SUBDIR.TWO, and one file, FILE.00. Each of the two directories contain more files and more directories. With a single XCOPY command, all of the files can be

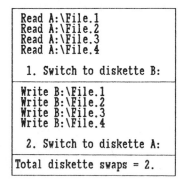

```
Read A:\File.1
Read A:\File.2
Read A:\File.3
Read A:\File.4
  1. Switch to diskette B:
Write B:\File.1
Write B:\File.2
Write B:\File.3
Write B:\File.4
  2. Switch to diskette A:
Total diskette swaps = 2.
```

Figure 10-7
Diskette Swaps Using
XCOPY

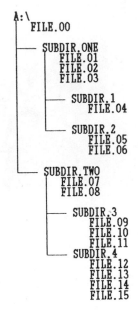

Figure 10-8
XCOPY Starting Directory Layout

copied. Additionally, if the disk that the files are being copied to does not have the same directories, they will be created automatically.

All you need to do is enter the command XCOPY A:*.* B:\ /S. The parameter A:*.* tells XCOPY to select all files, starting in the root directory of drive A:. The /S switch tells XCOPY to also process the subdirectories of the root. XCOPY will keep going down the directory structure until there are no deeper directory levels.

If you had only wanted to copy the files in the SUBDIR.ONE branch of the tree, you could have used the command XCOPY A:\SUBDIR.ONE*.* B:\ /S. This would have copied files FILE.01, FILE.02, and FILE.03 to the root directory of drive B:. It would have also copied FILE.04 to B:\SUBDIR.1 and FILE.05 and FILE.06 to B:\SUBDIR.2. Figure 10-9 shows what the

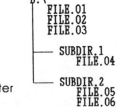

Figure 10-9
Directory Layout After XCOPY

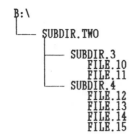

```
B:\
  └── SUBDIR.TWO

        ┌── SUBDIR.3
        │       FILE.10
        │       FILE.11
        └── SUBDIR.4
                FILE.12
                FILE.13
                FILE.14
                FILE.15
```

Figure 10-10
Another Diskette Lay-
out After XCOPY

directory structure would look like on drive B: after this XCOPY command
was executed.

You do not have to always use *.* to select the original files. For example, the command XCOPY A:\FILE.1? B:\ /S would create the directory
structure shown in Figure 10-10.

Notice how XCOPY created two levels of directories in Figure 10-10.
This matches the original directory structure. Also note that SUBDIR.TWO
does not have any files because FILE.07 and FILE.08 do not match FILE.1?.

There are several points you should remember when using XCOPY:

- You should enter the original file selection just as you would for the COPY
  command. This includes all of the assumptions that XCOPY will make
  about current drive and current directory. It also means that if you enter just
  a directory name, the entire directory will be processed.

- You should enter the new file selection just as you would for the COPY
  command. This includes the ability to create new filenames and filename
  extensions that do not match the original filenames and filename extensions.

- The new files do not have to be created at the same level in the directory structure as the original files. The command XCOPY C:\DOS*.* C:\
  DEEPER.AND\DEEPER.AND\DEEPER.DOS is perfectly acceptable.

- Like COPY, the XCOPY command cannot find files that have the Hidden or
  System attributes set. It cannot copy to a file that already exists if that file
  has the ReadOnly attribute set.

- XCOPY does not support file concatenation (file1+file2). You must use the
  COPY command to do this.

Advanced Uses of XCOPY

The following switches are available for you to use in controlling how XCOPY selects files for copying and how XCOPY treats the new directories created by the XCOPY command:

/A

This switch restricts the original file selection process. A file must match the original file specification, and the file's Archive attribute must be set. The Archive attribute means that the file has been modified since the last BACKUP was done. The Archive attribute will not be reset as a result of using this switch.

/D:mm-dd-yy

This switch restricts the original file selection process. A file must match the original file specification, and the last modification date of the file must be the same or later than the date you enter with the /D: switch. The format of the date that you enter is the same as it is for the DATE command. Just like the DATE command, XCOPY changes the way it looks at dates depending on the country you are working in.

/E

This switch tells XCOPY to create all of the original directories in the target of the copy, even if they will not contain any files or directories.

/M

This switch restricts the original file selection process. A file must match the original file specification and the file's Archive attribute must be set. The Archive attribute means that the file has been modified since the last BACKUP was done. The Archive attribute will be reset as a result of using this switch.

Warning: You should not use the /M switch if you are using the BACKUP command to create backups of your files. Because the /M switch causes the Archive attribute to be reset, the next BACKUP command that is run will not be able to tell that the XCOPYed files have been modified.

/P   This switch tells XCOPY to ask you before it copies each
            file. If you respond with Y, then XCOPY will copy the file.
            If you respond with N, then XCOPY looks for the next file
            to copy.

/S   As described earlier, the /S switch tells XCOPY to search
            subdirectories for more files to copy.

/V   The /V switch is the same as the /V switch for the COPY
            command. It tells XCOPY to turn on VERIFY while it is
            writing the new files and directories. This will slow down
            the performance of XCOPY.

/W   This switch tells XCOPY to wait for you before copying
            files. This allows you to put the diskette that has the files
            you want to copy into a diskette drive before XCOPY starts
            working.

XCOPY Error Levels

Starting with DOS 5.0, you can check the success of the XCOPY utility
through the error level that it returns. XCOPY returns the following error
levels:

0   No errors occurred, the files were successfully copied.

1   No files were found that matched the source file specification. No files
        were copied.

2   The extended copy procedure was aborted due to user intervention,
        either Ctl+C or Ctl+Break.

3   An error occurred during the utilities initialization, and the extended
        copy procedure was aborted. This may have been caused by a lack of
        memory, a lack of disk space, or an incorrectly entered parameter or
        switch.

4   A disk read or disk write error occurred; retries were not successful.
        The extended copy was not successful, and at least one of your disks is
        no longer usable.

DRIVE LETTER MAPPING FUNCTIONS

We will cover the following utilities in this section:

ASSIGN   The ASSIGN utility maps all requests for one drive letter to another drive letter. This mapping can involve both real and imaginary drive letters. This utility lets you make one drive look like another.

JOIN   The JOIN utility allows you to map the entire contents of one drive letter into a subdirectory of another drive. This mapping can involve both real and imaginary drive letters, but there are restrictions. This command lets you make two or more drives look like one large drive.

SUBST   The SUBST utility lets you map an imaginary drive letter to a physical drive and path. This command enables you to create a shorter way of addressing a file.

TRUENAME   The TRUENAME command allows you to see the real, or true, name of a file. It unravels the active ASSIGNs, JOINs, and SUBSTs so that the name displayed is the actual name of the file as it exists on your disks. The TRUENAME command was introduced in DOS 4.0; earlier versions of DOS did not provide a mechanism to enable you to determine the true name of the files you were working with.

These utilities are used to create and control imaginary drives for DOS to work with.

Warning: The following commands should not be used in combination with imaginary drives. While DOS will function correctly, it may not do what you are expecting. In any case, it just isn't worth it.

- BACKUP
- CHKDSK

- DISKCOMP
- DISKCOPY
- FDISK
- FORMAT
- LABEL
- MIRROR
- RECOVER
- RESTORE
- SYS
- UNDELETE
- UNFORMAT

In addition, CHKDSK will process across JOIN boundaries.

ASSIGNING ONE DRIVE TO ANOTHER

The ASSIGN command allows you to "assign" one drive letter to another. When you do this, part of the ASSIGN program stays in your computer's memory and will redirect the requests for one drive to another drive.

To use the ASSIGN command, simply enter ASSIGN and then a series of drive assignments:

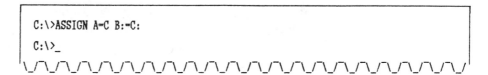

```
C:\>ASSIGN A=C B:=C:
C:\>_
```

This example assigns all accesses to both drives A: and B: to drive C:. Many people use this ASSIGN command so that all diskette accesses are redirected to the fixed disk. Notice that the use of the colon (:) is optional. You do not have to assign both drives at once; this example just shows you how to make multiple assignments. If you only wanted to assign drive A: to drive C:, you would have left off the B:=C: parameter.

This type of control is very useful for applications that will only run on a specific drive. Such applications do not allow you to tell them where the data that you want to work with is. Fortunately, most developers have learned that coding their applications to always use the same drive is not a very good idea, and this type of application seems to be disappearing from the marketplace. If you find that one of your applications always requires you to put your files on drive A: or drive B:, you can use the ASSIGN command to change this.

This is different from applications that require you to install from a specific drive. This often means that the application is copy protected. Because of the complexities involved with copy protection, it is not reasonable to expect them to be as flexible as normal operating procedures.

Each time you use the ASSIGN command, all previous assignments are lost. If you want to just change one, you must reenter all of them. If you want to cancel just one assignment, just reenter all but that one. Likewise, if you want to cancel all assignments, just enter ASSIGN with no parameters.

```
C:\>ASSIGN A=C B=C
C:\>ASSIGN A=C
C:\>ASSIGN
C:\>_
```

After the first ASSIGN command in this example, both drives A: and B: are assigned to drive C:. After the second ASSIGN command, only drive A: is assigned to drive C:; drive B: is no longer assigned to drive C:. After the third ASSIGN command, no drives are assigned.

Once you have made an assignment, DOS is no longer working in the "real world." In this example, all of the drives still exist. In fact, the drives you enter on both sides of the = character must exist. They are all real drives. But DOS cannot access the real drive A:. If you try to get to drive A:, DOS will actually go to drive C:. In this respect, DOS is working in an "imaginary" world. This is OK, as long as you remember this, too. For instance, what would happen if you tried to FORMAT a new diskette in drive A:? DOS would reassign FORMAT's accesses away from drive A: to drive C:, so you would actually end up formatting your fixed disk! Because formatting causes all files to be lost, you would have just accidentally deleted all of your files.

The ASSIGN command is not used to create an imaginary drive. It is used to change how DOS processes an existing drive. See the "SUBST," "JOIN," or "VDISK" sections for information on creating imaginary drives.

Actually, if you tried to FORMAT drive A:, DOS would not let you do this. Instead, the message "Cannot format an ASSIGNed or SUBSTed drive" would be displayed. Many of the DOS commands and utilities will not allow themselves to be run with assigned drives. The reason for these restrictions is to prevent someone from making mistakes like this one, especially when the results are as catastrophic as in this example.

Of course, you are not restricted just because an ASSIGN is in place. The restriction is there only if you are working with an ASSIGNed drive. For example, if drive A: is assigned to drive C: and drive B: is not assigned to anything. You will not be able to format drive A: but you will be able to format drive B:.

Two DOS utilities, DISKCOPY and DISKCOMP, are not affected by drive assignments. This is because they do not work at the same level as normal applications do. They use special interfaces that go around DOS directly to ROM BIOS. Because the drive assignment takes place in DOS, it has no chance to work.

In releases prior to DOS 4.0, it was not possible to determine the active assignments. Starting with DOS 4.0, the /STATUS switch has been added. You simply enter ASSIGN /STATUS to see the active assignments.

JOINING TWO DRIVES TOGETHER

You use the JOIN utility to create an imaginary situation where DOS will look at two or more drives like they were one. In essence, you are making one drive disappear and, at the same time, making the files and directories on that drive reappear in a directory of another drive.

It is easy enough to enter a JOIN command; you just enter JOIN, the drive that you want to disappear and the path where you want it to reappear.

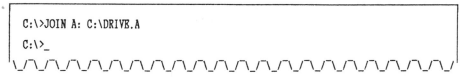

```
C:\>JOIN A: C:\DRIVE.A
C:\>_
```

In this example, drive A: will disappear. The files and directories on drive A: will now be visible under the C:\DRIVE.A directory. Before the

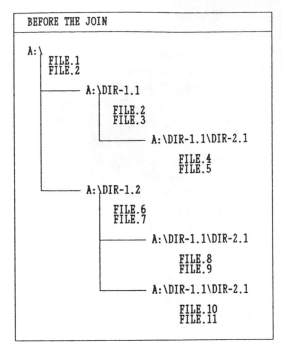

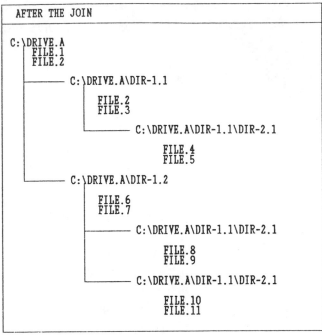

Figure 10-11
Disk Structure Before
and After JOIN

JOIN command can be executed, the directory C:\DRIVE.A has to exist and it has to be empty. This means that a DIR of C:\DRIVE.A shows only the DOT and DOTDOT directory entries. Also, you cannot join into the root directory of a drive. You are not allowed to use network drives in a JOIN command.

Let's look a little closer. Figure 10-11 shows how the files and directories would look before and after the JOIN command was run.

After the JOIN command has been run, you can no longer get to drive A:. If you try, DOS will display the message "Invalid drive specification."

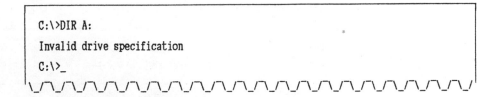

```
C:\>DIR A:
Invalid drive specification
C:\>_
```

If you want to know what drives are currently JOINed, just enter the JOIN command with no additional parameters:

```
C:\>JOIN
 A: -> C:\DRIVE.A
 C:\>_
```

Unlike the ASSIGN command, you do not have to specify all of the JOINs on one command. One JOIN command does not undo previous JOIN commands (unless you ask for them to be undone). If more than one JOIN is in effect, then DOS will display one assignment for each.

If you want to go back to looking at drive A: as a drive, you must delete the JOIN. This is done with the /D switch. Since there can be multiple JOINs at the same time, you must enter the drive that you want to un-JOIN.

```
C:\>JOIN A: /D
 C:\>_
```

SUBSTITUTING A DRIVE FOR A PATH

You use the SUBST utility to create an imaginary situation where DOS will look at one drive as two or more drives. This is almost exactly the opposite of the JOIN utility. In essence, you are making a new drive that does not span the entire disk but only one part of the directory structure.

Some applications do not support paths. All of the data and code that they use must be in the root directory of whatever drive they are working on. The SUBST command was created to enable you to move the data and code for these applications out of the true root directory of your drives into whatever subdirectory you choose. By creating a substitution, you can then make the application run in an imaginary situation where it believes that it is running in the root of a drive. It is actually running in the root of the substituted drive, which is not the real root of the real drive.

It is very easy to enter a SUBST command: You just enter SUBST, the drive that you want to create, and the path you want the drive to refer to.

```
C:\>SUBST T: C:\DUMB.APP
 C:\>_
```

With SUBST, unlike JOIN, drive T: does not disappear. Rather, it suddenly appears. The files and directories that are part of C:\DUMB.APP will now also be visible on drive T:. Also, unlike JOIN, with SUBST you can substitute to the root directory of a drive. You are not allowed to use network drives in a SUBST command.

The created drive does not have to exist before the SUBST command is run. If the drive does exist, then you will not be able to get to the real drive until SUBST is canceled.

The created drive letter must be less than or equal to the LASTDRIVE for your system. If you do not have a LASTDRIVE statement in your CONFIG.SYS, then LASTDRIVE = E:. If you do have one, then LASTDRIVE can be set up to Z:. You can add a LASTDRIVE (or increase the value it is set to) without giving up too much memory. Each drive letter takes about 95 bytes of your computer's memory.

Let's look at SUBST a little closer. Figure 10-12 shows how the files and directories would look before and after running the SUBST command.

Unlike the case with JOIN, you can now access the files on both drive C: and drive T:. The file specifications C:\DUMB.APP\DIR-1.1\DIR-2.1\FILE.10 and T:\DIR-1.1\DIR-2.1\FILE.10 both refer to the same file.

Figure 10-12
Disk Structure Before and After SUBST

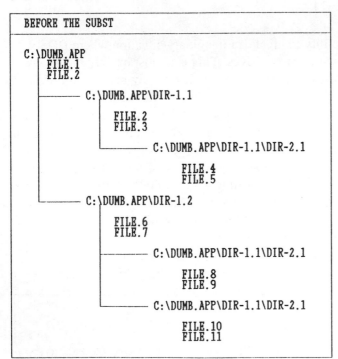

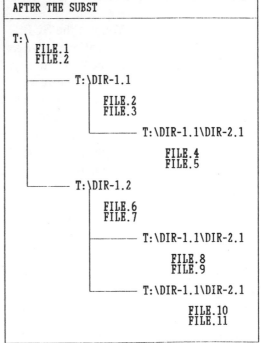

If you want to know what substitutions are currently in effect, just enter the SUBST command with no parameters:

```
C:\>SUBST
 T: => C:\DUMB.APP
C:\>_
```

As with the JOIN command, you do not have to specify all of the substitutions on one command. One SUBST command does not undo previous SUBST commands, unless you are changing the substitution for a substituted drive. If there is more than one substitution in effect, DOS will display one assignment for each substitution.

If you want to change a drive's substitution, you do not have to delete the substitution first. Just tell DOS how you want it substituted.

If you want to cancel a substitution, you use the /D switch. Like JOIN, there can be multiple substitutions at the same time, so you must enter the substituted drive that you want to cancel.

```
C:\>SUBST T: /D
C:\>_
```

DISPLAYING THE TRUE NAME OF A FILE

Once you start using the imaginary drive utilities (ASSIGN, JOIN, or SUBST), you are no longer working with real filenames. The filenames you enter and the filenames that DOS and your applications display are all based on the imaginary situation that you have built. However, you sometimes want to know the real name of a file that you are working with. To accomplish this, the TRUENAME command was added to DOS 4.0.

To find out the true name of a file, simply enter the TRUENAME command and the filename you are interested in:

```
C:\>TRUENAME S:\MAIN.C
C:\IBMC\SOURCE\MAIN.C
C:\>_
```

In this example, drive S: is substituted to the path C:\IBMC\SOURCE. When asked for the true name of file S:\MAIN.C, DOS responded with the name C:\IBMC\SOURCE\MAIN.C.

SYSTEM FUNCTIONS

We cover the following commands, utilities, and concepts in this section:

COMMAND.COM   The DOS Command Processor.

VER   Displays the DOS Version number

The DOS Environment   An area where DOS can hold values to be used by Batch Files and your applications. Examples of values in the DOS Environment are the DOS PATH, the DOS APPEND PATH and the DOS Command Prompt string.

SET	Displays or sets an Environment value.
PATH	Displays or sets the DOS PATH.
PROMPT	Sets the DOS Command Prompt.
APPEND	Displays or sets the DOS APPEND PATH.
COMSPEC	Defines the disk filename, including a directory path, of the DOS Command Processor.
DIRCMD	Defines the default parameters to use for DIR commands.

THE COMMAND PROCESSOR

The command processor is the part of DOS that contains the support for the internal commands, like DIR and COPY. Your primary interface to DOS is either through the DOSSHELL or COMMAND.COM. In fact, the DOSSHELL is actually just an external command to COMMAND. If you used SELECT to install DOS 4.0 or SETUP to install DOS 5.0, then the DOSSHELL is run as the last step in your AUTOEXEC.BAT.

The last step in the DOS startup procedure is to run whatever the

SHELL= statement in CONFIG.SYS says to run. If there is no SHELL= statement in CONFIG.SYS, then \COMMAND.COM on the boot drive will be run. If you want to change the parameters to the primary command processor, you will have to change (or add) the SHELL= statement in CONFIG.SYS. These changes will not take effect until the next time you restart your computer.

If COMMAND.COM is installed on drive C:, in the directory DOS50, then you could use the following statement in CONFIG.SYS to tell DOS 5.0 to load COMMAND.COM:

SHELL=C:\DOS50\COMMAND.COM C:\DOS50 /P

The parameters for COMMAND.COM are the same whether you are editing CONFIG.SYS or starting a secondary command processor (see "Starting a Secondary Command Processor" for more information on starting a secondary command processor). The parameters for command are:

search dir   This optional parameter is used to tell DOS where to find COMMAND.COM. It will also be used to set the value of COMSPEC in the environment (see "Displaying and Changing Where COMMAND Finds Itself").

console   This optional parameter is used as the command processor's console device. This is the device that COMMAND will read from and write to. The default for this value is CON (your keyboard and screen).

/C command line   Using the /C switch tells COMMAND that you want it to execute the command line that you enter. After the command line is executed, COMMAND will automatically terminate.

/E:size   The /E: switch allows you to specify the minimum size of the environment. If you do not specify the /E: switch, the minimum size of the environment will be 160 bytes. You can specify a value from 160 to 32,768. We recommend that you use a value of 256 or more.

/P   This switch tells COMMAND to ignore the EXIT command. Without the /P switch, COMMAND would terminate when you entered the EXIT command. If you are adding a SHELL= statement to your CONFIG.SYS, be sure to use the /P switch. If you use both the /P and /C switches, the /P switch will be ignored.

/MSG   This switch tells COMMAND (for DOS 4.0 and DOS 5.0 only) to keep a copy of the Extended and Parse errors in memory. If you do not use this switch, then the messages will be read from the disk whenever they occur. You do not need this switch for fixed-disk systems. It is recommended, however, that you use this switch if you are working on a diskette-only system. These messages are used not just by the command processor, but by all of the DOS programs to display errors. If DOS cannot find the Extended and Parse errors (they are not loaded into memory, and DOS cannot access the disk file), then an abbreviated message only will be displayed. When specified, the /MSG switch must be used together with the /P switch.

The command processor is broken up into two parts, resident and transient. The resident portion stays in memory all the time. The transient is put at the high end of memory. It is not kept in an allocated portion of memory. This allows the DOS utilities and your applications to use this memory. When the resident portion of COMMAND gets control back, it checks to see if the transient has been changed. If not, it uses the code there as needed.

If the transient has been modified, then COMMAND must reload the transient. To do this, COMMAND looks at the value of COMSPEC in your environment. It will use the string that COMSPEC is set to in order to find and read the transient. For more information on COMSPEC, see "Displaying and Changing Where COMMAND Finds Itself." After the transient is reloaded, COMMAND will continue processing with the next command you enter.

Starting a Secondary Command Processor

You can have more than one copy of the command processor loaded at one time. There are numerous reasons to do this, but probably the only one that you will be interested in is to redirect the output of an entire batch file to somewhere other than your display. If you want to run a batch filename DUMMY.BAT and have the output go to your printer, you do this:

```
C:\>COMMAND /C DUMMY.BAT > PRN
C:\>_
```

After the batch file is finished, the output will be on the printer. You can do the same thing to get the output into a file; just change PRN to the name of the file in which you want to put the output.

You do not need to use the /MSG switch when starting a secondary command processor. Once the messages are in your computer's memory, they are available to the DOS programs.

Exiting a Secondary Command Processor

If you have started a secondary command processor, you can terminate it by using the EXIT command. There are no parameters, and you will be returned to the previous level of command processor.

```
C:\>COMMAND

IBM DOS Version 5.00
         (C) Copyright International Business Machines Corp 1981-1991
C:\>_EXIT

C:\>_
```

You cannot exit from the primary command interpreter. If you use the EXIT command while you are in the primary command interpreter, it will be ignored.

DISPLAYING THE DOS VERSION

The VER command is used to show the version number of the DOS product that you are using. There are no parameters. Each release displays a different version number. The IBM version of DOS will use the name "IBM DOS"; others may use a different name, such as "MS-DOS."

WORKING WITH THE DOS ENVIRONMENT

When programs are run by DOS, they are provided an "environment" area that contains information that they may want to use. DOS provides this area for every utility and application that you run. Even the command processor, COMMAND.COM, has an environment that it runs with.

When you enter a command that is the name of a utility or application, that program "inherits" a copy of COMMAND.COM's environment. The new program can modify its own copy of the environment as much as it wants. When the new program is finished and COMMAND.COM starts running again, the original environment is unchanged. The technique allows COMMAND.COM to save information without the chance of another program interfering with it.

If you have just entered the command BACKUP C: A:, the command processor will have to run the BACKUP.COM utility. In this situation, COMMAND.COM is called the *parent program*. The BACKUP.COM utility is called the *child program*. A child program can in turn run another program. In this case, BACKUP.COM may have to run the FORMAT.COM utility to format a diskette before it can be used. BACKUP.COM would then be a parent of FORMAT.COM; FORMAT.COM would be a child of BACKUP.COM. COMMAND would be FORMAT's grandparent.

Each of these programs — COMMAND, BACKUP, and FORMAT — has its own environment. If FORMAT modifies its environment, this will not affect BACKUP or COMMAND. If BACKUP modifies its environment, COMMAND will not be affected.

Displaying and Changing Environment Strings

You can control the environment by using the SET command. You can use SET to see the environment or to change it. To see the current contents of your environment, simply enter SET and press Enter (↵).

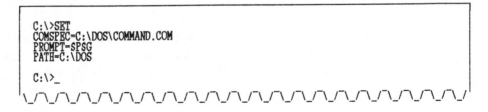

```
C:\>SET
COMSPEC=C:\DOS\COMMAND.COM
PROMPT=$P$G
PATH=C:\DOS

C:\>_
```

Your environment may be different. This shows what the minimum information in the environment should be. There can always be more. DOS will always put the following items into the environment when your computer is started:

APPEND   This value is what APPEND uses to tell DOS where to look for your data files. This value is not always present in the environment, and was not used prior to DOS 4.0.

COMSPEC This value tells DOS how to find the transient portion of COMMAND.COM. It is changed through the SET COMSPEC= command.

DIRCMD This value tells DIR what you want the standard parameters for directory listings to be. This value was not used prior to DOS 5.0 and is not always present in the environment. It is changed through the SET DIRCMD= command.

PROMPT This value tells DOS how you want the DOS prompt displayed.

PATH This value tells DOS where to look for utilities and applications that you ask to be run.

To change what is in the environment, you would use the SET command again. This time you would add a symbolic name and the string you want it to be set to.

```
C:\>SET MyName=WhoEver
C:\>_
```

This example has set the symbolic name MYNAME to the string Who-Ever. The symbolic name will be capitalized; the string it is set to will not be. This is not a very exciting symbolic name to set; there is nothing that uses it. Let's create a batch file that will use it.

```
C:\>COPY CON HELLO.BAT
@ECHO OFF
ECHO Hello %MYNAME%, I hope that you are feeling well.
^Z

C:\>_
```

Now, when you say hello to your computer, it will respond.

```
C:\>HELLO
Hello WhoEver, I hope that you are feeling well.
C:\>_
```

At this point, you might want to change the value that MYNAME is set to. Try setting MYNAME equal to your name. This time, when you say hello to your computer, it will address you by your own name.

If you want to get rid of a symbol, simply set the symbolic name to nothing.

```
C:\>SET MyName=

C:\>HELLO
Hello , I hope that you are feeling well.
C:\>_
```

Because a batch file is not a program, it runs with the current environment. This means that you can have SET commands in the batch file and the values that they set will not be lost.

Since each child program that is started gets its own environment, you do not want them to be too large. The size of the environment can usually grow, but there are several things that can prevent its growth. One of the things that affects the ability to increase the size of the environment is the /E: switch on COMMAND.COM. The /E: switch is entered on the SHELL= statement in CONFIG.SYS. If you change the /E: value, you will have to restart your computer for it to take effect. If you are trying to add to your environment, and DOS is displaying the "Out of environment space" message, you may have to increase the /E: value.

For DOS 5.0 users, you may want to use the SET command to provide a default setting for your DIR command parameters. This is done by setting the environment variable DIRCMD equal to the parameters you want DIR to normally use.

```
C:\>SET DIRCMD=/o:ned

C:\>_
```

In this example, we have set the DIRCMD environment variable to tell the DIR command to sort the directory listing first by name, then by extension, then by date and time. For more information on the parameters for DIR, see "Which Files Are Here?"

Displaying and Changing Your Search Path

The PATH command is a special form of the SET command. It displays and sets the symbolic name PATH in the environment. That is the only symbolic name that it can display or set. The string value of PATH is a set of directories that you want searched to find the utilities and applications you are working with.

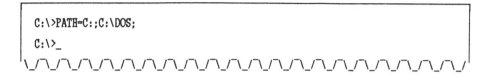

```
C:\>PATH=C:;C:\DOS;
C:\>_
```

The individual paths that are to be searched are separated by the semi-colon (;) character. In the preceding example, the first path entered is the root directory of drive C:. The second path is the \DOS subdirectory of drive C:.

When you enter a command name that the command processor does not recognize, it will look for a file with that filename. It will only allow you to run files with three filename extensions: .COM, .EXE, and .BAT. If you have two or more files with the same filename and different filename extensions, one from the first path where at least one exists will be started. If more than one exist in the same directory,

- The .COM file will be started before the .EXE or .BAT files.

- The .EXE file will be started before the .BAT file.

- The .BAT file will be started only if there is no .COM or .EXE file.

In DOS 4.0 and DOS 5.0, if you happen to know exactly which file it is you want to run, you can add the filename extension to the command that you enter. For example, if you have created a batch file named SYS.BAT you could enter the following:

```
C:\>SYS.BAT A:
This is the SYS.BAT batch file, not the SYS.COM program
C:\>_
```

When you enter a command name that the command processor does not recognize as one of its own, it will search the current directory on the current drive for the command you requested. If the command is not found, the search continues in the first path specified in the PATH string value. This continues until the file is found or the end of the PATH string is reached. If the name is never found, the message "Bad command or filename" is displayed.

If you specify a drive in front of the command name, the command processor will start the search with the current directory of that drive. It then continues with the PATH string paths. However, if you specify a path (or drive and path) in front of the command name, the command processor will search only the specified path.

PROGRAM	DOS will search the current directory of the current drive first. If the PROGRAM is not found, DOS will start searching the paths in the PATH string.
A:PROGRAM	DOS will search the current directory of drive A: first. If the PROGRAM is not found, DOS will start searching the paths in the PATH string.
\PROGRAM	DOS will search the root directory of the current drive. If the PROGRAM is not found, an error message will be displayed.
A:\PROGRAM	DOS will search the root directory of drive A:. If the PROGRAM is not found, an error message will be displayed.

When DOS installs itself, it puts a PATH statement in your AUTO-EXEC.BAT file. If you wish to change the search path, this is where you should change it.

You can set the PATH string to whatever you want. Nothing will happen until the command processor tries to search using the PATH string. If you have a drive that does not exist in your PATH string, you may get the message "Invalid drive in search path." Even if this occurs, the searching continues with the next path in the string.

You can enter fully or partially qualified paths in the string. This is what will happen in each case:

SUBDIR	The command processor will look for a subdirectory named SUBDIR in the current directory of the current drive.

\SUBDIR	The command processor will look for a subdirectory named SUBDIR in the root of the current drive.
A:SUBDIR	The command processor will look for a subdirectory named SUBDIR in the current directory of drive A:.
A:\SUBDIR	The command processor will look for a subdirectory named SUBDIR in the root directory of drive A:.

We highly recommend that you always enter fully qualified paths. This eliminates any problems you will have if you change drives or directories.

You can also change the PATH string by using the SET command. The PATH command is just a short way to enter SET PATH=.

Displaying and Changing Your DOS Prompt String

Like PATH, the PROMPT command is a special form of the SET command. It sets the symbolic name PROMPT in the environment, and PROMPT is the only symbolic name that it can display or set.

Each time the command processor is ready for you to enter a command, it will display the DOS Prompt. You can customize the DOS Prompt to be almost anything you would like. The PROMPT string value simply contains the characters that you want displayed in the DOS prompt.

```
C:\>PROMPT What would you like to do?
What would you like to do?_
```

The command processor simply displays the string you enter whenever it is ready for you to enter a command. In the preceding example, the new prompt is "What would you like to do?"

The command processor looks at all command lines before running them. When it does this, it sees certain characters and interprets them as file redirection and piping requests. Because of this, the >, <, and ¦ characters cannot be put directly into a prompt string (see "File Redirection" for more information on file redirection and piping).

Because you might want to have these characters in your prompt, DOS has provided a way to get them there. The command processor will treat the $ character in prompt strings in a special way. When the $ character is found, the command processor looks at the next character in the prompt string to see what should be displayed. If you want a > character, you would use the characters $G in your prompt string.

```
What would you like to do?PROMPT What would you like to do? $g
What would you like to do? >_
```

There are also some things you might like in your prompt that change as you use DOS. A good example of this is the current directory. It would be nice to always know what directory you are in, but you would not want to change your prompt each time you changed directories. The $P characters are used to put the current directory into your prompt.

```
What would you like to do?PROMPT ($P) What would you like to do?
(C:\) What would you like to do?_
```

Here is a list of all of the special character pairs that the command processor supports:

$$ The $ character.

$_   This causes the command processor to start a new line.

$B   The ¦ character.

$D   The current date.

$E   The escape character. This is used to generate ANSI.SYS control sequences in your prompt.

$G   The > character.

$H   This will cause the prompt to backspace, erasing the previously displayed character.

$L   The < character.

$N   The current drive character. This does not include the colon (:) character. You would have to add that yourself. This is not necessary if you are using the $P sequence.

$P   This current drive and current directory.

$Q   The = character.

$T   The current time.

$V   The DOS version string. This is the same as what the VER command displays. This automatically goes to the next line; you do not need $_.

One of the most used command prompts is the PG sequence. This will always display the current drive and directory, which makes it hard to forget where you are. This is the value set by SELECT for DOS 4.0 users.

If there is no PROMPT string in the environment, the command processor will use NG, which is better than nothing, but not great. If you want to get rid of the PROMPT string, just enter PROMPT with no parameters.

If you are using the $P characters in your PROMPT string, your current drive is read before the prompt is displayed. If for any reason your drive cannot be accessed, DOS will display a critical-error message. This will usually only happen with diskette or network drives. You must respond with the F character to tell DOS to fail the disk or diskette operation. The command processor will substitute the string "current drive is no longer valid" into your DOS prompt. You should get to an accessible current drive as quickly as possible!

If you have the ANSI.SYS device driver loaded, you can do some really interesting things with your prompt. This is especially true if you have a color monitor on your computer. We show here just two examples. You will have to understand the PROMPT string and the ANSI.SYS controls if you want to change these very much. You can try these prompts to get an idea of what they can do.

To display the prompt (PG) in high-intensity blue, then display what you enter in high-intensity white, with both on a black background, enter the following:

PROMPT $E[1;40;34m$PGE[1;40;37m

To display the time, date, and DOS version on the top of your screen, and also display the current drive, current directory, and > character on the line you are being prompted on, see the PROMPT in Figure 10-13. A brief explanation of each step in this prompt is provided. The prompt is processed from left to right, and the explanation is sequenced from top to bottom.

You can also change the PROMPT string by using the SET command. The PROMPT command is just a short way to enter SET PROMPT=.

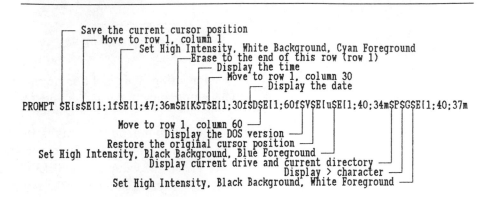

Figure 10-13
Example PROMPT
with Explanation

Displaying and Changing Your Appended Directories

The APPEND command is used to tell DOS where to look for files that are not found where they were expected to be. It is very similar to the PATH command, except that PATH only covers files with filename extensions of .BAT, .COM, and .EXE. Also, the PATH string is only used to find programs and batch files to be executed. The APPEND command allows DOS to look around for any file that is not found where requested.

Getting APPEND Loaded   Not everyone will want to use APPEND. It was originally designed to allow programs that expected all of their files in a single directory to use data that was in other directories. This is especially important in a network, where several computers may share a single directory.

Because not everyone wants to use APPEND, it is not always loaded into your computer's memory. If you want to use APPEND, you need to load it into your computer's memory. Once APPEND is in memory, DOS will not have to go look for it on your disks again.

Before you can load APPEND, you need to decide if you want APPEND to look in the DOS Environment for the list of appended directories. The alternative is that APPEND will keep the list of appended directories inside itself. We recommend that you keep the appended directory list in the DOS Environment.

To tell APPEND to keep the appended directory list in the DOS Environment, add the /E switch the first time you enter the APPEND command. You cannot provide a list of appended directories on an APPEND command that contains the /E switch.

Note: The original APPEND command was part of the IBM PC Network Program. That version was named APPEND.COM. The APPEND command that ships with DOS is named APPEND.EXE. The APPEND.COM program did not have the ability to look in the DOS Environment to get the appended directory list. For compatibility, APPEND.EXE allows the same functionality.

If you first enter APPEND without the /E switch, APPEND will keep the list of appended directories inside itself. Once APPEND has been loaded the first time, you cannot change where the appended directory list is kept without restarting your computer.

If you are going to use APPEND, we recommend that you put the APPEND /E command in your AUTOEXEC.BAT file. This will get APPEND loaded into your computer's memory and ready for you to set the list of appended directories.

Controlling the Appended Directory List   The list of appended directories is a simple string of paths separated by the semicolon (;) character. This is just like the PATH command described earlier. You can only replace the entire list of appended directories. You cannot add, remove, or replace a single directory. If you have told APPEND to keep the appended directory list in the DOS Environment, there are two ways to change the list:

1. **Use SET APPEND=pathlist.** This will change the APPEND string in the environment and change where APPEND looks for files. This method only works for computers that are keeping the appended directory list in the DOS Environment.

2. **Use APPEND pathlist.** This will change the appended directory list wherever it is being kept. Because this method will work for both the DOS Environment and internal storage of the appended directory list, it is the preferred method of controlling the APPEND list.

As with the first APPEND command to get APPEND into your computer's memory, we recommend that you set up the appended directory list in your AUTOEXEC.BAT file. You can always change it as needed. This way, you are starting out with the same set of appended directories every time you start your computer.

Other APPEND Controls   There are a few other switches that control how APPEND works:

/X or /X:ON   The /X and /X:ON switches tell APPEND that it should search for files that DOS is trying to run. If the command processor cannot find a file that you are trying to run, this allows APPEND to look for it in the list of appended directories. DOS 3.3 only allows the /X versions of this switch.

/X:OFF   The /X:OFF switch tells APPEND not to search for files that DOS is trying to run. This is how APPEND will work until you use the /X or /X:ON switches. This switch is not supported prior to DOS 4.0.

/PATH:ON   The /PATH:ON switch tells APPEND that it can try to find any file that is not where a program has looked for it. This is how APPEND will work until you use the /PATH:OFF switch. This switch is not supported prior to DOS 4.0.

/PATH:OFF   The /PATH:OFF switch tells APPEND that it cannot look for files that were not found if (1) the program included the drive letter telling DOS where to look for the file, or (2) the program included a directory telling DOS where to look for the file. This switch is not supported prior to DOS 4.0.

You can use the /X and /PATH switches anytime you wish to change the way that APPEND is working.

APPEND Examples   The following example shows how to load APPEND and use the DOS Environment to keep the appended directory list.

```
C:\>APPEND /E

C:\>APPEND C:\FILES.DIR;C:\STUFF.DIR
C:\>SET
COMSPEC=C:\DOS
PROMPT=$p$g
PATH=C:\;C:\DOS
APPEND=FILES.DIR;STUFF.DIR

C:\>APPEND
APPEND=FILES.DIR;STUFF.DIR

C:\>_
```

The first APPEND command in this example is used to load APPEND into your computer's memory and tell APPEND to keep the appended directory list in the DOS Environment. The second APPEND command tells APPEND to look in the C:\FILES.DIR directory first, then to look in the C:\STUFF.DIR. The SET command shows that APPEND has stored the appended directory list in the DOS Environment. The third APPEND command shows how you can use the APPEND command to look at the appended directory list.

Displaying and Changing Where COMMAND Finds Itself

The command processor (COMMAND.COM) uses the value that COMSPEC is set to in the environment. This value is used whenever the transient portion of the command processor has been wiped out by an external command (see "The Command Processor" for more information on how this works).

When the memory image of the transient portion is altered, the command processor must reload it from one of your disks. The command processor looks into the current environment for the value of COMSPEC. Whatever COMSPEC is set to is the name that will be given to DOS to reload the transient from.

This is not normally a problem; however, sometimes it is. When DOS sets the original COMSPEC value, it is set without specifying a drive. This is for diskette-only systems. On these systems, you want to be able to take your DOS diskette out of the diskette drive and put in an application diskette. Later, when the transient needs to be reloaded, you want to be able to put the DOS diskette into whatever the current drive is. This makes things a little simpler.

But this sometimes causes problems, especially if you always want to load the transient from the same drive. This is usually the case for fixed-disk users. In this case, you can put a SET COMSPEC= command in your AUTOEXEC.BAT file. You should fully specify the value, starting with the drive that COMMAND.COM is on. Two typical versions of this are:

SET COMSPEC=C:\COMMAND.COM   This will cause the transient to be loaded from the file COMMAND.COM in the root of drive C:.

SET COMSPEC=C:\DOS\COMMAND.COM   This will cause the transient to be loaded from the file COMMAND.COM in the DOS directory of drive C:.

Of course, you can set the value of COMSPEC from the keyboard, but to do this, you would have to enter the command every time you started DOS.

You can improve the performance of the transient reload if you are using RAMDRIVE or VDISK to create a virtual disk. First, copy COMMAND.COM to the virtual disk. Then set COMSPEC to point at where you copied it on the virtual disk, including the virtual disk drive. Now, when the transient is reloaded, it will be much quicker. This will be most effective on diskette-based computers.

DOS Support for Advanced Computer Features

In this chapter, we explore the advanced DOS features that are provided to support the advanced features of your computer.

CONFIG.SYS STATEMENTS

In this section, we discuss four of the statements you can use to load the advanced computer features with DOS:

REM   Used to put comments into your CONFIG.SYS file. REM is not supported in DOS 3.3.

DEVICE   Used to load device drivers to support your computer's advanced devices.

DEVICEHIGH   Like DEVICE, this statement is used to load device drivers to support your computer's advanced devices. However, the DEVICEHIGH statement tries to load the device driver into high memory first.

INSTALL   Used to load DOS Installable Extensions to support your computer's advanced devices.

If you add or change statements in your CONFIG.SYS file, these changes will not take effect until the next time you restart your computer.

COMMENTS IN CONFIG.SYS

Before we get started describing the various configuration statements that you can use to enable advanced DOS and computer features, we should tell you how to put comments or remarks into your CONFIG.SYS file. It is really very simple; just start a line with REM and then follow it with the comment you want to put in. Each line that contains a comment must start with REM. REM is not supported in DOS 3.3.

To add comments indicating that the CONFIG.SYS file was changed on January 10, 1991 at 8:30 P.M., and who it was that changed the file, you could use the statements

REM CONFIG.SYS changes on January 10, 1991 at 8:30pm

REM Modifications made by ...

THE DEVICE= CONFIGURATION STATEMENT

The mechanism used to define additional device support to DOS is the DEVICE= statement in your CONFIG.SYS file. This statement identifies a device driver that defines the device to DOS and your applications. It is called a device driver because it contains all of the code necessary to drive the device; the driver provides a standard interface for DOS to call, and it handles all of the details of making the device work.

The use of the DEVICE= statement is fairly simple; you put a statement in your CONFIG.SYS file that contains DEVICE= and the name of the device driver that you want DOS to load. If required, device driver-specific parameters can also be supplied.

The syntax of the DEVICE= statement is:

DEVICE={d:}{path}{ddname} {ddparms}

where

ddname   is the filename that contains the device driver. If the file is not in the root directory of the drive that DOS is booting from, the drive and path must also be specified.

ddparms   are the parameters for the device driver that you are requesting DOS to load. These parameters have no meaning to DOS
and are ignored until the device driver starts running.

As an example,

DEVICE=C:\DOS\ANSI.SYS

would load the device driver ANSI.SYS from the DOS subdirectory of drive C:.

THE DEVICEHIGH= CONFIGURATION STATEMENT

The DEVICEHIGH= statement was introduced in DOS 5.0. It is very similar to the DEVICE= statement. Its fundamental reason for being used is to
define an additional device to DOS. However, there is one significant difference: DEVICEHIGH= will try to load the device driver into the Upper
Memory Blocks (see "Extended Memory Support") rather than into your
lower memory. This will allow more room for your applications to run in
your conventional memory.

The syntax of the DEVICEHIGH= statement is almost the same as the
DEVICE= statement.

DEVICEHIGH={d:}{path}ddname {ddparms}

or

DEVICEHIGH SIZE=size {d:}{path}ddname {ddparms}

The additional parameter, **SIZE=size,** specifies the maximum size of the
device driver (in hexadecimal). If the size is omitted, then the device driver's
file size is used.

You must have an extended memory manager loaded prior to using the
DEVICEHIGH= statement. This can be accomplished by adding the following lines to your CONFIG.SYS file before the DEVICEHIGH= statement

DEVICE=C:\DOS\HIMEM.SYS

DOS=UMB

You may gain UMB space from being able to specify the SIZE=size
parameter. Most device drivers contain code that is used to initialize the
device driver and the actual device. Good device drivers will free the memory used for this initialization code once the device and driver are initialized.
This makes the device driver smaller in memory.

To determine the SIZE= value that you should use, you can first consult your device driver documentation. If there is no indication there, you can use the following method:

1. Edit your CONFIG.SYS to contain the DEVICEHIGH= statement without the SIZE=size parameter.

2. Restart your computer. You cannot continue with this procedure until you are sure that the device is working correctly. If it is, continue. If not, the device driver may not be compatible with the DEVICEHIGH= statement, and you will have to go back to using the normal DEVICE= statement.

3. Run a MEM /DEBUG report (see "Who's Using My Memory?" for instructions on how to do this). Look up how much memory is being used by your device driver. This value should be in the Size column of the report.

4. Edit your CONFIG.SYS file again, this time adding the SIZE= parameter to the DEVICEHIGH statement.

5. Restart your computer.

THE INSTALL= CONFIGURATION STATEMENT

The mechanism used to load DOS Installable Extensions during DOS's configuration phase is the INSTALL= statement in CONFIG.SYS. This statement identifies the installable extension that you want to load.

The use of the INSTALL= statement is fairly simple; you put a statement in your CONFIG.SYS file that contains INSTALL= and the name of the installable extension that you want DOS to load. If required, extension specific parameters can also be supplied.

The syntax of the INSTALL= statement is:

INSTALL={d:}{path}{progname} {parms}

The parameters are:

progname   Indicates the program that you want to install at this point.

parms   Controls the program that you are installing at this time. These parameters have no meaning to DOS and are ignored until the program looks at them.

As an example,

INSTALL=C:\DOS\NLSFUNC C:\DOS\COUNTRY.SYS

would load the code page switching code that DOS needs to coordinate the switching of code pages in your computer's devices.

ADDITIONAL DISKETTE DRIVE SUPPORT

When DOS starts on your computer, it asks ROM BIOS several questions. One of the most important is "How many diskette drives are there?" There are times when ROM BIOS will tell DOS there are fewer diskette drives than you would like there to be.

The configuration statement DRIVPARM and the device driver DRIVER. SYS are used to tell DOS that a diskette drive exists that ROM BIOS did not tell DOS about, or that the parameters about the drive are different than DOS has been led to believe. You would use DRIVER.SYS for two reasons:

- You want to create logical drives for the diskette drives that ROM BIOS does know about.

- You have an optional diskette drive attached to an older computer that does not know how to tell if it is there.

You would use DRIVPARM for a slightly different reason. DRIVPARM is used to change the characteristics of a drive already known to DOS.

OVERRIDING DRIVE PARAMETERS

You can override what ROM BIOS tells DOS about devices by using the DRIVPARM statement.

An example of this would be when you add a 3.5-inch diskette drive to a computer that was produced before the 3.5-inch diskette drives existed. If you put the drive into one of the internal diskette bays, the ROM BIOS of the machine may tell DOS that the diskette drive is a 5.25-inch diskette drive.

In this situation, the diskette would not be used properly. So, you would have to use the DRIVPARM statement in CONFIG.SYS to override the values that are in DOS's internal tables.

The DRIVPARM statement was not available prior to DOS 4.0. To use DRIVPARM, simply add a statement that says

DRIVPARM=...

Add the required parameters from the following list. Do not worry about determining what the correct parameters are, you should be able to find them in the documentation that comes with your computer device.

/D: Tells DOS what the ROM BIOS drive number of the physical drive will be. If you are adding an optional drive, this must be the drive that your documentation tells you to use. If you are creating a logical drive, you can use the values shown in Figure 11-3.

/C Tells DOS if the diskette drive knows when the diskette has been changed.

/F: Tells DOS what the form factor of the diskette drive is. It is somewhat like telling DOS if the drive is 3.5-inch or 5.25-inch, but there are more than just two form factors.

/H: Tells DOS how many heads there are in the diskette drive.

/I Tells DOS that the diskette drive is compatible with diskette drives available before 3.5-inch were introduced. Use /I to support 3.5-inch diskette drives on computers that have built-in support only for 5.25-inch diskette drives.

/N Tells DOS that the device does not support removable media (in other words, the medium is not removable, similar to a fixed disk).

/S: Tells DOS the maximum number of sectors per track on the diskette.

/T: Tells DOS the maximum number of tracks on the diskette.

See Figure 11-2 for information on the values to use for these switch settings. Figure 11-1 lists the values and meanings for the /F: form factor switch.

/F: Value	Form Factor Description
0	5.25-inch 160KB/180KB/320KB/360KB diskettes
1	5.25-inch 1.2MB diskettes
2	3.5-inch 720KB diskettes
5	Media is not removable
6	Tapes
7	3.5-inch 1.44MB diskettes
8	Read/Write Optical Media
9	3.5-inch 2.88MB diskettes

Figure 11-1
Form Factor Values
and Meanings

LOGICAL DRIVE SUPPORT

Support for logical drives has been part of DOS since the very early releases. Logical drives occur whenever you have two or more drive letters that reference the same physical diskette drive. This is not the same as an imaginary drive. The physical drive exists.

In a system where both A: and B: refer to the only diskette drive, we can see what happens. As programs are executing, DOS keeps track of what logical drive is assigned to each physical drive in the system. If a program tries to access a logical drive that is currently not assigned to its physical drive, DOS will ask you to put the correct diskette in the drive. Let's watch it work. In this example, the diskette for drive A: is already in the drive.

```
C:\>VOL A:

  Volume in drive B has DISKETTE-A
  Volume Serial number is 353E-OFED

C:\>VOL B:

  Insert diskette for drive B: and press any key when ready

  Volume in drive B has DISKETTE-B
  Volume Serial number is OFED-353E

C:\>_
```

At this point, DOS will not ask you to put the diskette for drive A: back in until it needs to be accessed again.

The ability to use logical drives can be very helpful. If you have only one diskette drive, using a logical drive is the only way to copy a file from one diskette to another one. The same is true if you have two diskette drives that are of different types. If you have no fixed disk, but do have a 1.2MB diskette drive and a 360KB drive, how would you copy a file from one 1.2MB diskette to another? You might try to copy the file from the 1.2MB diskette to the 360KB diskette, then from the 360KB diskette to the other 1.2MB diskette. But this will not always work. If the file on the 1.2MB diskette is larger than can be put on a 360KB drive (400KB for instance), you could not use the 360KB diskette as a temporary holding place.

However, you could create an additional logical drive for the 1.2MB drive. If the logical drive was created as drive C:, you could copy the file from A: to C:. While the copy is taking place, closely follow the directions that DOS gives you.

Drive Type	/T: Value	/S: Value	/H: Value	Use /C	/F: Value
180KB	40	9	1	No	0
360KB	40	9	2	No	0
720KB	80	9	2	Yes	2
1.2MB	80	15	2	Yes	1
1.44MB	80	18	2	Yes	7
2.88MB	80	36	2	Yes	9

Figure 11-2
DRIVER.SYS Parameter Table

Number of Internal Diskette Drives	Number of External Diskette Drives	Number of Disk Drives See Note 1	ROM BIOS Diskette Drive Number	DOS Drive Letter
1	0	0	00	A,B
		1	00	A,B
		2	00	A,B
	1	0	00	A,B
			02	C
		1	00	A,B
			02	D
		2	00	A,B
			02	E
2	0	0	00	A
			01	B
		1	00	A
			01	B
		2	00	A
			01	B
	1	0	00	A
			01	B
			02	C
		1	00	A
			01	B
			02	D
		2	00	A
			01	B
			02	E

Figure 11-3
Logical Drive Mapping Table

Many people use logical drives every day. DOS automatically creates one additional logical drive for systems that only have one diskette drive. If you have only one diskette drive, it will be used for both drive A: and drive B:.

Starting in DOS version 3.20, you also had the ability to create logical drives when you wanted to. You do this with the DRIVER.SYS device driver.

UNRECOGNIZED DISKETTE DRIVES

There are diskette drive options that exist today for machines that were sold in the past (before these newer drives were designed). If you add one of the new drives to one of the older machines, the ROM BIOS in that machine might not be able to tell that it is there. This is OK, because you can use DRIVER.SYS to tell DOS that your diskette option is there.

If you look in the documentation that comes with your diskette drive option, it should tell you if you need to use DRIVER.SYS. It should also tell you what parameters to use.

DEFINING A DRIVE WITH DRIVER.SYS

Defining a drive to DOS is very simple. You need to add a DEVICE=DRIVER.SYS statement to your CONFIG.SYS file. You also have to supply other parameters:

/D: This parameter tells DOS what the ROM BIOS drive number of the physical drive will be. If you are adding an optional drive, this must be the drive that your documentation tells you to use. If you are creating a logical drive, you can use the values shown in Figure 11-3.

/C   This parameter tells DOS if the diskette drive knows when the diskette has been changed.

/F: This parameter tells DOS what the form factor of the diskette drive is. It is somewhat like telling DOS if the drive is 3.5-inch or 5.25-inch, but there are more than just two form factors. See Figure 11-1 for a listing of the form factors available.

/H: This parameter tells DOS how many heads there are in the diskette drive.

/S: This parameter tells DOS the maximum number of sectors per track on the diskette.

/T: This parameter tells DOS the maximum number of tracks on the diskette.

When defining additional drives with DRIVER.SYS, you should use the parameter values that your drive documentation tells you to use. If you cannot find this information, or if you are creating logical drives, Figure 11-2 lists the values to use for several drive types.

Figure 11-3 shows the ROM BIOS drive numbers and their mapping to DOS drive letters. The mappings in this figure are for systems that do not have any DEVICE= statements before the DEVICE=DRIVER.SYS statement. The DOS drive letters for the external drives (ROM BIOS drive number 2) might be different if any block devices were in CONFIG.SYS prior to the DEVICE=DRIVER.SYS.

ENHANCED KEYBOARD SUPPORT

Over the life of DOS, there have been several different keyboards with different numbers of keys and different layouts. The ROM BIOS of the various machines provided a layer of isolation to DOS until the introduction of the keyboards with 101 keys. These keyboards are generically referred to as the *101-key keyboards*.

When the 101-key keyboards were being developed, we discovered that the new scan codes that they returned for the new keys would cause some applications problems. To overcome this situation, the ROM BIOS interface was extended. The old ROM BIOS interfaces do not return the scan codes for the new keys. The new ROM BIOS interface will return both the old and the new scan codes.

To enable DOS to work properly in this environment, the SWITCHES statement was introduced in DOS 4.0. This statement allows you to tell DOS not to use the new ROM BIOS interfaces in reading from the keyboard, thereby preventing DOS from returning keys that applications do not understand.

To tell DOS not to use the advance ROM BIOS keyboard interfaces, use the following statement in your CONFIG.SYS file:

SWITCHES=/K

The /K switch on the DEVICE=ANSI.SYS causes the same restriction to be applied to the CON device driver that is built into ANSI.SYS.

EXTENDED DISPLAY AND KEYBOARD SUPPORT

The ANSI.SYS device driver is a replacement CON device driver that extends the capabilities that the base CON device driver provides. The CON device driver supports both your keyboard and display.

In this section, we have broken the description of ANSI.SYS into two separate parts:

1. Installing ANSI.SYS. In this section you will see what the installation parameters are that control what parts of ANSI.SYS that stay in your computer's memory.

2. Using ANSI.SYS. In this section, you will see how to use ANSI.SYS to take advantage of the extended features it provides.

INSTALLING ANSI.SYS

You install ANSI.SYS by putting a DEVICE= statement into your CONFIG.SYS file. This tells DOS to load the ANSI.SYS device driver the next time you start your computer. The DEVICE= statement should tell DOS exactly where you have the ANSI.SYS file. If you have installed the DOS files in a directory named \DOS on drive C:, then the statement would look like this:

DEVICE=C:\DOS\ANSI.SYS

If you are using DOS 4.0 or DOS 5.0, there are three switches that you can also add to the DEVICE= statement. In DOS 3.3, these switches are ignored.

/L   This switch tells ANSI.SYS to try to keep the number of rows that you set with the MODE command. If you use this switch, ANSI.SYS will try to force applications to use the number of rows you have set with

MODE. Without this switch, ANSI.SYS will not try to force your wishes on your applications.

> **Warning:** Using this switch can cause problems for some applications. If your application's screens become "trashed," remove the /L switch from your DEVICE= statement.

/K   This switch tells ANSI.SYS to use only the old interfaces when asking ROM BIOS for keystrokes from the keyboard. This switch provides compatibility for old applications that do not understand the new keystrokes generated by the new keyboards. This switch has the same effect on ANSI.SYS that the SWITCHES /K statement in CONFIG.SYS has on the base CON device driver.

/X   This switch tells ANSI.SYS to allow redefinition of the extended keys that are available on the newer keyboards. These keys are all identified by the fact that they start with the hexadecimal value E0 (decimal value 240). For example, without this switch, the PgUp key on the numeric keypad (under number 9) would be treated exactly the same as the Page Up key between the normal keys and the numeric keypad.

USING ANSI.SYS

In order for you to use the functions that ANSI.SYS provides, you must learn how to tell ANSI.SYS what it is you want done. In essence, you need to learn how to program ANSI.SYS to do what you want. The way to do this is to send characters to ANSI.SYS. The CON device driver that is inside ANSI.SYS sees every keystroke that you input and every character that is displayed through the CON device driver. This is how you will communicate with ANSI.SYS to tell it what you want.

Most of the ANSI.SYS functions are used by the programs that you run. The writing of programs and applications is outside the scope of this book, but if you are interested in writing programs that use the ANSI.SYS functions, they are covered in our companion book, *Developing Applications Using DOS*. There are only two cases where ANSI.SYS functions are used directly by the computer's operators:

1. You can use the ANSI.SYS Display controls to create and customize a DOS prompt that is uniquely yours. Customizing your prompt is described in "Displaying and Changing Your DOS Prompt String."

2. You can use the ANSI.SYS Keyboard Redefinition controls to reduce the number of keys you have to use when telling DOS what you want done. We describe how ANSI is used to redefine your keyboard here.

Normally, ANSI.SYS just watches the characters going by on their way to the display. It doesn't react until it sees the Escape character (<ESC>), which has decimal value 27 (hexadecimal value 1B). When ANSI.SYS sees this character, it starts collecting the characters as they come in. ANSI.SYS keeps watching and collecting characters, and as soon as it recognizes a string of characters that is one of its function control strings, it performs the function. Also, as soon as it determines that the string of characters is not one of its function control strings, it sends them on to the display.

All of the ANSI.SYS functions start with the two characters Escape (<ESC>) and Left Bracket ([). Following the [character are numbers and characters that tell ANSI.SYS exactly what it is suppose to do. Like the DOS command parameters, these numbers and characters control how the functions are performed.

Figure 11-4 shows a summary of the various functions that ANSI.SYS provides. You can see that each control string starts with <ESC>[.

If you want to customize your DOS prompt, see "Displaying and Changing Your DOS Prompt String" for information on how to use the ANSI.SYS functions in defining a new prompt string.

We will go into some detail here on how you can redefine your keys to reduce the effort it takes for you to work with DOS. This is something many people want to do.

The first step is to decide what commands you enter over and over again. One example of this might be "DIR" followed by Enter (↵). The second step is to determine what keystroke or keystroke combination you want to redefine. For this example, you could redefine your keyboard so that pressing the Ctrl and D keys together would automatically tell DOS to execute a DIR command. To do this, you would use the Redefine-A-Key function of ANSI.SYS.

You identify the key that you want to redefine by its ROM BIOS interface values or by enclosing its symbol in quotes (e.g., "E" for Shift+E). There are values for all of the keys and for many of the keystroke combinations (a keystroke combination is generated when you press and hold down one or more of the shift keys, Ctrl, Alt, or Shift and then press another key). In this case, we want to identify the Ctrl+D keystroke combination. The only good place to find the decimal values for the keystroke and keystroke combinations is in your computer's technical reference manual. In the keyboard

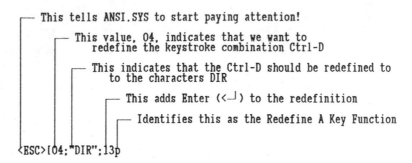

Figure 11-4
ANSI.SYS ESC
Sequence Example

section there should be a chart that identifies the values that ROM BIOS will generate. The value that ROM BIOS generates for Ctrl+D is 04. At this point, we know that the string we want to send to ANSI.SYS is as in Figure 11-4.

Now, you only have to overcome one more problem. How do we get this string sent to the CON device driver? There are two ways of accomplishing this:

1. You can change your prompt so that the string will be displayed. This is effective but not very elegant. To do this, you would enter the command

    PROMPT $e[04;"DIR";13p

As soon as the new prompt is displayed, the Ctrl+D keystroke combination will be redefined and we can go back to a reasonable prompt.

If you are going to use this method, you should create a batch file that will reset your prompt to what you want to run with normally. This way, you can just run the prompt-setting batch file after you have redefined your keys. This is much better than having to enter it all over again each time.

2. Another method is to use the BASIC interpreter (see "The BASIC Interpreter" for information on how to start BASIC). After BASIC has started, it will display the message "OK." This is the BASIC prompt. It is like the DOS prompt, and it means that BASIC is ready for you to enter something at the keyboard. Enter the following lines:

    10 OPEN "filename" FOR OUTPUT AS #1

    20 PRINT #1,CHR$(27)+"[04;"+CHR$(")+"DIR"+CHR$(")+";13p"

    30 CLOSE #1

    RUN

    SYSTEM

ANSI Function	Control Sequence
Set Cursor Position or	`<ESC>[r;cH` `<ESC>[r;cf`
Move Cursor Up	`<ESC>[rsA`
Move Cursor Down	`<ESC>[rsB`
Move Cursor Right	`<ESC>[csC`
Move Cursor Left	`<ESC>[csD`
Device Status Request	`<ESC>[6n`
Cursor Position Report[1]	`<ESC>[r;cR`
Save Cursor Position	`<ESC>[s`
Restore Cursor Position	`<ESC>[u`
Erase The Whole Display	`<ESC>[2J`
Erase To End Of Row	`<ESC>[K`
Set Display Attributes	`<ESC>[a`
Set Display Mode	`<ESC>[=mh`
Reset Display Mode	`<ESC>[=ml`
Enable Extended Key Redefinitions[2]	`<ESC>[0q`
Disable Extended Key Redefinitions[2]	`<ESC>[1q`
Redefine A Key	`<ESC>[ki;kd;...p`

Figure 11-5
ANSI.SYS Display
Functions

[1] The cursor position report is sent to your program in response to the device status request being sent from your program. This string is read from the standard input device.
[2] These two functions are not available prior to DOS 4.0.

After each line, BASIC will prompt you with the "OK" message. This means it is ready for you to enter the next line. You can substitute any file specification you want for filename, but it must be enclosed in quotes. The CHR$(27) string tells BASIC that you want to output an escape character. The CHR$(34) strings tell BASIC that you want to output the quote character.

You cannot use BASIC to output the string directly to ANSI.SYS; the BASIC interpreter does not go through DOS when it writes to your display, so you have to have BASIC create a file. Once that is done, you can use the TYPE or COPY commands to send the file to ANSI.SYS. If you use TYPE, just enter TYPE filename. To copy the file to ANSI.SYS, enter COPY filename CON:. Once either of these is done, the Ctrl+D keystroke combination is redefined.

One reason for using the BASIC method, is that once you have the file, you can type or copy it to the display every time you restart DOS. If you have several keystrokes or keystroke combinations that you want to redefine, you can create a file for each of them.

Following are definitions for the values shown in Figure 11-5.

r   A row number. If absent, zero will be used (topmost line on your screen).

rs   A count of rows to move.

c   A column number. If absent, zero will be used (topmost line on your screen).

cs   A count of columns to move.

a   A display attribute indicator. There are three classes of display attributes, which interact with each other, but do not redefine each other.

    1. Character Attributes

       0   All character attributes turned off.

       1   Display characters in bold.

       4   Underline displayed characters (text-mode monochrome displays only).

       5   Blink the displayed characters.

       7   Swap the foreground and background colors.

       8   Make the displayed characters invisible.

    2. Foreground Colors

       30   Black

       31   Red

       32   Green

       33   Yellow

       34   Blue

       35   Magenta

       36   Cyan

       37   White

3. Background Colors

40	Black
41	Red
42	Green
43	Yellow
44	Blue
45	Magenta
46	Cyan
47	White

m   A screen mode from the following list:

0	40 x 25 text, monochrome
1	40 x 25 text, color
2	80 x 25 text, monochrome
3	80 x 25 text, color
4	320 x 200 graphics, 4 colors
5	320 x 200 graphics, monochrome
6	640 x 200 graphics, monochrome
7	Turn on line wrapping
13	320 x 200 graphics, color
14	640 x 200 graphics, color
15	640 x 350 graphics, monochrome
16	640 x 350 graphics, color
17	640 x 480 graphics, monochrome
18	640 x 480 graphics, color
19	320 x 200 graphics, color

Not all of these modes are available for all computers, displays, or versions of DOS.

ki   A key identifier. Each key in each shift state on your computer's keyboard can be identified by a specific identifier. Keys and shift states can also be identified by a single ASCII character between quotes. For example, to redefine the caret character (^), which is the character displayed by the combination of the normal (not numeric keypad) 6 and the shift key (Shift+6), you can use either of the following sequences:

<esc>["^";"DIR"p

or

<esc>[94;"DIR"p

To reset a key's definition, just define it back to itself. Continuing the example of SHIFT+6, to reset this back to a caret character, you would use

<esc>[94;94p

kd   A key definition. This can be a single decimal numeric value that identifies a single ASCII character (65 = A), or it can be an ASCII string enclosed in quotes ("DIR").

ENABLING GRAPHICS CHARACTERS ON YOUR DISPLAY

You need the GRAFTABL extension to DOS if you are using an IBM Color Graphics Adapter (or compatible adapter) and you are using character values above 127 (such as the double-line box characters) while your display is in graphics (not text) mode.

The IBM CGA and compatible adapters can generate 256 different characters in both text and graphics modes; however, in graphics mode, only the first 128 characters are defined. The GRAFTABL extension provides the definition of the remaining 128 characters.

To define the characters (or to load the graphics table), you would use the GRAFTABL command and specify the code page you want to use. Like this:

GRAFTABL 437

In this example, the upper 128 characters for code page 437 (the code page used in the United State) would be loaded. You can also find out what code page character definitions are currently loaded by using either a question mark (for DOS 4.0) or the /STATUS switch (for DOS 5.0).

GRAFTABL /STATUS

DOS 5.0 users can check the success of the GRAFTABL utility through the error level that it returns. GRAFTABL returns the following error levels:

0   Specified table successfully loaded. No prior table was loaded.

1   Specified table successfully loaded. A prior table was replaced.

2   A disk error occurred. The specified table was not loaded.

3   Unrecognized code page specified. The specified table was not loaded.

4   Incorrect DOS version.

PRINTING GRAPHICS DISPLAYS

Many computer screens can be put into two types of display modes, text and graphics. DOS usually runs in text mode. In this mode, your screen can display only text characters and some predefined graphical characters. When you press the PrtSc (Print Screen) key, your computer will copy the contents of the screen to your printer. This is a simple and useful way get a paper copy of what is on your screen.

Unfortunately, your computer will not do this correctly if the screen is in any of the graphics modes. In these modes, your applications can build their own graphics and pictures. If you press the PrtSc key in these modes, only garbage will be printed. Your computer does not know how to process the complex information on your screen to get it to your printer.

The GRAPHICS.COM extension to DOS solves this problem. If GRAPHICS.COM has been loaded, it will get control whenever you press the PrtSc key. This utility knows how to convert what is on your computer's screen and get it printed correctly on your printer.

If you wish to load the GRAPHICS.COM extension, it is relatively easy. If you used SELECT to install DOS 4.0, it might already be loaded for you. If not, simply enter GRAPHICS and the type of printer you are using. There

Printer Class	Supported Printers
COLOR1	IBM 5182 Color Printer, Black ribbon
COLOR4	IBM 5182 Color Printer, Red-Green-Blue-Black (RGB) ribbon
COLOR8	IBM 5182 Color Printer, Yellow-Magenta-Cyan-Black (YMC) ribbon
DESKJET	Hewlett-Packard DeskJet Printer
GRAPHICS	IBM 5152 Graphics Printer Model 2 IBM 3812 PagePrinter IBM 4201 Proprinter IBM 4201 Proprinter II IBM 4202 Proprinter XL, 8½" wide paper IBM 4207 Proprinter X24 IBM 4202 Proprinter XL24, 8½" wide paper IBM 5201 Quietwriter II IBM 5202 Quietwriter III
GRAPHICSWIDE	IBM 4202 Proprinter XL, 13½" wide paper IBM 4202 Proprinter XL24, 13½" wide paper IBM 5202 Quietwriter II, 13½" wide paper
HPDEFAULT	Any Hewlett-Packard PCL Printer
LASERJET	Hewlett-Packard LaserJet Printer
LASERJETII	Hewlett-Packard LaserJet II Printer
PAINTJET	Hewlett-Packard PaintJet Printer
QUIETJET	Hewlett-Packard QuietJet Printer
QUIETJETPLUS	Hewlett-Packard QuietJet Plus Printer
RUGGEDWRITER	Hewlett-Packard RuggedWriter Printer
RUGGEDWRITERWIDE	Hewlett-Packard RuggedWriterWide Printer
THERMAL	IBM 5140 PC Convertible Printer
THINKJET	Hewlett-Packard ThinkJet Printer

Figure 11-6
GRAPHICS Parameter
and Printers

are other optional parameters, and they will be explained later. Figure 11-6 shows the parameters to use for the supported printers. The majority of the printers fall under the type GRAPHICS, and this is the type that is used if you do not specify any printer type.

The following example installs the GRAPHICS extension to support any of the printers that fall under the GRAPHICSWIDE type in Figure 11-6. If you want to install another type, simply replace GRAPHICSWIDE with the type you need.

```
C:\>GRAPHICS GRAPHICSWIDE
C:\>_
```

> **Note:** It may take several minutes to print a high-resolution graphics screen on your printer.

There are also several optional parameters to the GRAPHICS extension:

Profile Name   This parameter was added in DOS 4.0. It is the name of the file that contains the profiles that GRAPHICS needs to understand how to print the screen on the printer. The name of the file supplied with DOS is GRAPHICS.PRO. This file should be found wherever the rest of your DOS files are. If you need to use another file, you simply enter the profile's filename after the type of printer you are using.

/R   This switch indicates that GRAPHICS should reverse its normal mapping of black and white. Your computer's screen usually displays white characters on a black background. Your printer usually displays black characters on a white background. If you use the /R switch, GRAPHICS will reverse its printing on your printer. It will print the black background of your screen, leaving the white characters showing.

/B   This switch causes GRAPHICS to print the background colors on your color printer.

/LCD   This switch is provided for compatibility with previous releases of DOS. This performs the same function as /PB:LCD.

/PB: or   This parameter was also added in DOS 4.0. Because of the
/PRINTBOX: extreme difference between the usual Cathode Ray Tube (CRT) screen and the Liquid Crystal Display (LCD) screen, there must be two ways of printing out these screens.

   The standard method is identified by /PB:STD or /PRINTBOX:STD. This is the method that you would use for CRT-type screens. If you do not specify /LCD, /PB:LCD, or /PRINTBOX:LCD, this is the method that will be used. If you are using a computer with an LCD display,

and the graphics displayed on the screen looks like someone sat on the top of it (sort of squished down), you want to
use the standard mode.

The LCD method is identified by the /LCD, /PB:LCD,
or /PRINTBOX:LCD switch. You probably do not want to
use this mode unless you are using a computer with an LCD
display. Even if you are using this type of equipment, you
do not want to use this method unless your graphics screen
looks normal. If this is the case, then the LCD method will
produce printed output that looks correct. You should
remember that in this mode, the printed version of the
screen is approximately 3.5 inches tall by 10.5 inches wide.

The GRAPHICS command can also be loaded by the INSTALL= statement in CONFIG.SYS. The parameters are the same as discussed here.

Once GRAPHICS has been installed, you cannot remove it from memory without restarting your computer.

GRAPHICS COMMAND PROFILES

In releases of DOS prior to 4.0, the GRAPHICS extension had to be recoded
each time we added a new display or printer. Starting with DOS 4.0, the
product does not have this restriction. The new GRAPHICS extension uses a
profile file that describes the different display adapters, monitors, and printers that can be attached to your computer. The profile file,
GRAPHICS.PRO, did not exist on releases prior to DOS 4.0. These descriptions allow the GRAPHICS code to figure out how to print a graphics screen
as it goes.

If you are using a supported printer, it should already be described in the
GRAPHICS.PRO file that is supplied with DOS. If you are using a printer
that became available after your release of DOS was shipped, you should
look in your printer documentation to find out how to install the GRAPH-
ICS extension. Contact your printer's manufacturer for information on how
to define your printer.

In some cases, there may not be a description in the GRAPHICS.PRO
file that will allow your printer to work. You should contact your printer's
manufacturer to find out how to add a description of your printer so that you
can use the GRAPHICS extension to DOS.

REDIRECTING THE DOS CONSOLE

You can use the CTTY command to redirect the DOS Console away from the CON device to some other device name. The CON device driver supports both the local keyboard and local screen. You would use the CTTY command to redirect the console to a remote terminal attached by a communication line.

```
C:\>MODE COM1:1200

COM1: 1200,e,7,1,-

C:\>CTTY COM1
```

This example uses the MODE command to set communications speed for COM1 to 1200 baud. The CTTY command is then used to redirect the DOS console to the COM1 device driver. You see that here, unlike in the other examples, there is no other prompt after the CTTY command. This is because it was sent to the COM1 device, not the CON device.

When a program is executed by the command processor, it inherits several open files. The CTTY command changes the device that COMMAND.COM opens for two of those files, standard input (file handle 1) and standard output (file handle 2). Rather than using the CON device, COMMAND.COM will use whatever device you specify.

Not all programs use the inherited files to get input from the keyboard and write to the screen. The BASIC interpreter is one example of this. The BASIC interpreter does not use the standard DOS interfaces to access the keyboard and screen; it accesses your computer's hardware directly. Most programs that display graphics also circumvent DOS. If you are executing these types of programs, your remote terminal will not see the output. Also, you may not be able to enter data from the remote terminal.

The local keyboard is not totally disabled. Even when CTTY is in effect, DOS will be affected by certain keystroke combinations:

- Ctrl+Alt+Del
- Ctrl+Break
- Ctrl+C

- Ctrl+NumLock

- Pause

- Shift+PrtSc

If you are using CTTY, be careful not to use these keystroke combinations.

CHANGING CODE PAGES

Most users of DOS in the United States will never need to change code pages. In fact, most users will never even care if they know what a code page is.

Your computer's display and printers treat each byte of data as a single character. Since each byte can contain only 256 different values, this means a byte can handle only 256 different characters. Unfortunately, there are many more than 256 different characters in the world. To help this situation, code pages were created.

A code page is a mapping of byte values to characters or symbols. Each code page is identified by a number. The code page that most computers in the United States support is code page 437. In other countries, additional code pages are needed. Figure 11-7 shows the code pages that DOS supports.

Code Page	Country or Language
437	United States
850	Multilingual
860	Portugal
862	Hebrew[1]
863	Canadian-French
864	Arabic[1]
865	Norway
932	Japanese[2]
934	Korean[2]
936	Simplified Chinese[2]
938	Traditional Chinese[2]

[1] The standard DOS package does not support this code page. You must purchase a separate language enabling package to use the Arabic and Hebrew code pages.

[2] The standard DOS package and normal computer hardware do not support Asian characters. You must purchase a special Asian version of DOS and hardware to use these code pages.

Figure 11-7
Code Page Definitions

Some countries actually need more than one code page to support all of the characters and symbols that they use. For these countries, you must be able to switch back and forth between code pages. This is what code page switching is all about.

For a full discussion of code page switching, you should refer to the books included with your copy of DOS. The following is a list of the commands and device drivers that are used to control code page switching.

CHCP	Changes the active code page of DOS and all devices. Also displays the active DOS code page.
COUNTRY=	This CONFIG.SYS statement indicates the country that DOS is being used in.
DISPLAY.SYS	Enables code page switching for displays.
KEYB	Tells the keyboard handler what code page to use.
MODE	Prepares, selects, activates, and refreshes code pages. Also displays the active code pages.
NLSFUNC	Contains some DOS code associated with code page switching.
PRINTER.SYS	Enables code page switching for printers.

CONTROLLING DEVICE MODES

The MODE command is used to control the mode in which your devices and computer process information. The devices that MODE controls are:

Communications   Allows you to change the characteristics of how your asynchronous communications adapters work. Your communications adapters are usually used to attach serial printers or modems that communicate over telephone lines. The DOS communications device names are COM1 (AUX), COM2, COM3, and COM4.

Displays   Allows you to change your display mode between text (only characters) and graphics (text plus pictures) modes. It also allows you to set the number of characters per line and the number of lines on your screen. The DOS display device name is CON.

Keyboards   Allows you to change the Type-a-matic characteristics of your keyboard. The DOS keyboard device name is CON.

Printers   Allows you to control the number of characters on a single line and the number of lines per inch of paper printed. You can also redirect your printer to a communications adapter. The DOS printer device names are LPT1 (PRN), LPT2, and LPT3.

The DOS names COM1 and AUX refer to the same communications device. Also, the DOS names LPT1 and PRN refer to the same printer device.

The MODE command also allows you to control the way that your computer and devices interpret and display characters and symbols. This function is called *code page switching* and is covered in "Changing Code Pages."

WHAT MODE IS IT IN NOW?

You can use the MODE command to determine what the current mode is for your display and printers. For your display, MODE will report the number of columns, the number of lines (rows), and the code page switching status. For your printers, MODE will report the redirection status, the retry status, and the code page switching status. Here is a typical example:

```
C:\>MODE

Status for device LPT1:
-----------------------
LPT1: not rerouted
RETRY=NONE
Code page operation not supported on this device

Status for device LPT2:
-----------------------
LPT2: not rerouted
RETRY=NONE
Code page operation not supported on this device

Status for device LPT3:
-----------------------
LPT3: not rerouted

Status for device CON:
----------------------
COLUMNS=80
LINES=25
Code page operation not supported on this device

C:\>_
```

You can get a shorter report by telling MODE what device you are interested in. However, if you are requesting a status report for a printer, you must use the /STATUS or /STA switch. If you do not use one of these two switches, MODE will cancel the printer redirection for the named printer.

You can get a report of the communications status, but MODE will only tell you the retry status of the device that you request. The status of a communications device is not normally reported; you must ask for it explicitly. DOS 3.3 cannot display the status of your devices.

CONTROLLING COMMUNICATIONS

You can also use the MODE command to change the characteristics of your communications support. You can set the following parameters:

BAUD=   This tells MODE how fast you want to communicate. The number you set is the maximum number of bits that will be sent or received each second. The values allowed are 110, 150, 300, 600, 1200, 2400, 4800, 9600, and 19,200. Not all values are available on all computers.

A bit is a very small piece of information. A bit can represent two values, zero and one. It takes eight bits to make a byte (or character).

The MODE command will accept just the first two digits of each of the BAUD values. For example, BAUD=11 actually means BAUD=110. This is not really useful and leads towards confusion. This shorthand way of entering the BAUD rate is supported only for compatibility with previous releases and should be avoided where possible.

DATA=   This tells MODE how many data bits to transmit. The valid values are 5, 6, 7, and 8. The default is 7 data bits.

STOP=   This tells MODE how many stop bits to transmit. The valid values are 1, 1.5, and 2. Except for BAUD=110, the default is 1 stop bit. For BAUD=110, the default is 2 stop bits.

PARITY=   This tells MODE what type of parity that you want to use. The valid parity options are NONE, ODD, EVEN, MARK, and SPACE.

The MODE command will accept just the first letter of

each of the PARITY values. For example, PARITY=N actually means PARITY=NONE. This is not as bad as the BAUD shorthand, but there is still no real reason to use this type of shortcut. It is supported for compatibility with previous releases and should be avoided where possible.

RETRY= Before your computer can send a character across the communications line, it has to first see if the line is busy, or if it is ready to be sent a character. If the line is ready, the character will be sent. If the line is busy, then your computer cannot send the character. Using the MODE command with the RETRY= parameter is how you tell DOS and your computer what you want done when the device is busy.

Unless told otherwise, we recommend that following settings:

RETRY=B Use this setting if you have been told to use the "P" parameter on previous versions of DOS.

RETRY=E Use this setting if you are communicating with a printer or plotter that is shared through the IBM PC Local Area Network Program.

RETRY=R Use this setting when you are redirecting your local printer to serial adapter.

RETRY=N This is the normal setting and should be used unless one of the previous situations applies. This allows your communications package to handle the line status.

We have provided these explanations so that you will have some idea of what you are asking MODE to do. You should follow the directions provided with your modem, printer, or plotter. If you do what they tell you, it will probably work. If you do not, it is highly likely that things will not work correctly.

CONTROLLING DISPLAYS

In this section, we show you how to use the MODE command to control the following aspects of your displays:

- Choosing the display mode
- Shifting displayed information
- Setting columns per line
- Setting lines on the screen

Not all of these functions will be available on all display adapters and displays. Since many of these functions can be combined into a single MODE command, we show additional examples at the end of this section.

Choosing the Display Mode

Many of the display adapters and displays that you can attach to your computer support more than one mode of operation. By using the MODE command, you can control which mode your display will operate in. If you have both a monochrome and color display adapter in your computer, you can chose which one DOS will use.

The following list defines the keywords that are used to control the display mode. To select one of these modes, enter the MODE command followed by one of the mode selection keywords, like this:

MODE MONO

This would select the MONOchrome display mode and screen. The mode selection keywords are listed here:

MONO   This is the only valid mode for the old monochrome monitors. These displays usually used green characters on a black background. The newer monochrome displays now use white characters on a black background. Many of the newer models can also use gray shading to simulate colors. This means that they do not just support black and white, but display shades of gray.

BW80   This mode is valid for all color displays. The number of characters on each line is set to 80. The display mode is changed to black (background) and white (foreground). This means that you will get white characters on a black background. If you are using ANSI.SYS or any program that sets the display mode to color, this will override the MODE command's settings and the colors will change.

BW40   This mode is identical to BW80, except that the number of characters on each line is set to 40.

CO80   This mode is valid for all color displays. The number of characters on each line is set to 80. The display mode is changed to color, with the background color set to black and the foreground color set to white. This means that you will get white characters on a black background. If you are using ANSI.SYS or any program that changes the foreground and background color, CO80 will override the MODE command's settings, and the colors will change.

CO40   This mode is identical to CO80, except that the number of characters on each line is set to 40.

80   This mode is valid for all color displays. The number of characters on each line is set to 80. The display mode is not changed.

40   This mode is valid for all color displays. The number of characters on each line is set to 40. The display mode is not changed.

Shifting Displayed Information

The way that the ROM BIOS treats a display does not always work for every display that can be attached for your computer. For example, for some displays, the characters that are displayed on the left or right screen edges may not be as readable as the rest of the screen. The MODE command allows you to adjust this by shifting the displayed characters left or right.

The screen shifting ability only works with the Color Graphics Adapter and the Color Graphics Display. To shift the screen, you must tell MODE what display mode to put the display in and then tell it which direction to shift the displayed characters, like this:

MODE CO80,R

This command tells MODE to put the console into Color80 mode and shift the display right one character position. The following command would shift the screen back one character to the left:

MODE CO80,L

When you are using a 40-column display mode, you can shift the display one character left or right. If you are using an 80-column display mode, you can shift the display two characters left or right.

By adding an additional parameter, T (for Test), you can get MODE to display a test pattern on the display. You will be asked if the display looks good. If you answer Y, MODE will return to DOS. If you answer N, MODE will shift the display once more in the same direction. MODE will then ask if the display looks OK again.

Setting the Number of Columns on the Display

You can set the number of columns on the screen in two ways. You can select one of the display modes that changes the number of columns. An example of this would be BW40.

Starting with DOS 4.0, you can also use the parameter COLUMNS= or COLS=. Use the MODE CON: COLS=40 or MODE CON: COLS=80 command. If you are in the MONO mode, you can only use COLS=80.

Setting the Number of Lines on the Display

Not all display adapters will allow you to set the number of lines that you can display. Also, if you want to use this function of MODE, you must have the device driver ANSI.SYS loaded (see "Extended Display and Keyboard Support"). If you have ANSI.SYS loaded, you can try to set the number of lines on your display. The MODE command will display the message "Function not supported on this computer" if you are not allowed to change the number of display lines.

Use the MODE CON: LINES= command. The number of lines you can use depends on your computer. All computers allow 25 files. Most VGA-equipped computers also allow 43 or 50 lines. XGA-equipped computers also allow 60 lines. (See Figure 11-8 for some examples of the MODE command.)

DOS 3.3 MODE does not allow you to set the number of lines.

Figure 11-8
MODE CON Device Examples

MODE CO80,R,T	color, 80 columns, shift right and test
MODE BW40	black and white, 40 columns
MODE CON: BW40	illegal, cannot use display mode with CON:
MODE COLS=80 LINES=43	illegal, cannot use COLS= or LINES= without CON: on the MODE command line
MODE CON: COLS=40 LINES=43	40 columns, 43 lines

CONTROLLING PRINTERS

The MODE utility allows you to control two aspects of printer operation:

1. The way information is printed. This includes the number of characters on a print line, the number of lines printed per inch of paper and whether or not to reprint a failed character.

2. Where the printer is attached. This is how you tell DOS that your printer is attached to a communications adapter rather than to a parallel adapter.

These two aspects of printer control cannot be mixed on a single MODE command line. You use MODE to do both, but you can only control one aspect at a time.

You can control both aspects of printer operation for all of your printers. To control print operations, you tell MODE which of the printer device drivers you want to work with—LPT1, LPT2, or LPT3.

Note: You can control the setting of characters per print line, print lines per inch, and printer retries with a single MODE command for each printer.

Warning: If you have already redirected printing to a communications adapter, changing the number of characters on a print line or the number of print lines per inch will cancel the redirection. If this happens, you will have to reestablish the redirection with another MODE command.

Setting Characters per Print Line

Since DOS 4.0, you can change the characters per print line by using the COLUMNS= or COLS= parameters. You are allowed to choose either 80 or 132 characters per print line. If you have more than one printer attached to your computer, the printers do not have to be set the same way. The MODE command lets you change the characteristics of each printer individually.

```
C:\>MODE LPT1 COLUMNS=132
LPT1: not rerouted
LPT1: set for 132
No retry on parallel printer time-out
C:\>_
```

In this example, LPT1 is set to print 132 characters on each print line. We see from what DOS displayed that LPT1 has not been redirected to a communications adapter and that the printer retry has been set to none.

When most printers are first turned on, they are usually set for 80 characters per print line. This is not true of all printers, so check the publication that was provided with your printer when you purchased it. Also, some printers support only one setting of characters per print line. Others require additional options such as print wheels or character-definition cartridges.

You can use the MODE command to change the number of characters per print line, but if your printer is turned off and on again, it will revert to its own default value. Also, your application programs may change the number of characters per print line and not restore your original setting when done. In either of these cases, you can use the MODE command again to tell the printer how you want to print.

With DOS 3.3, you could still set the number of characters per print line; it just required a different command syntax.

MODE LPT1:132

This example would set the number of characters per print line to 132.

Setting Print Lines per Inch

To change the number of print lines per inch, use the LINES= parameters. You are allowed to choose either six or eight print lines per inch. Again, if you have more than one printer attached to your computer, the printers do not have to be set the same way. The MODE command lets you change the characteristics of each printer individually.

```
C:\>MODE LPT2 LINES=8
LPT2: not rerouted
Printer lines per inch set
No retry on parallel printer time-out
C:\>_
```

In this example, LPT2 is set to print eight print lines per inch. We see from what DOS displayed that LPT2 has not been redirected to a communications adapter and that the printer retry has been set to none.

When they are first turned on, most printers are set for six print lines per inch. This is not true of all printers, so check the publication that was provided with your printer when you purchased it. Also, some printers support only one setting of print lines per inch.

You can use the MODE command to change the print lines per inch, but if your printer is turned off and on again, it will revert to its own default value. Also, your application programs may change the print lines per inch and not restore your original setting when done. In either of these cases, you can use the MODE command again to tell the printer how you want to print.

With DOS 3.3, you could still set the number of print lines per inch; it just required a different command syntax.

MODE LPT1: 132,8

This example would set the number of characters per print line to 132 and the number of print lines per inch to 8.

Controlling Printer Retries

Before your computer can send a character to your printer, it has to ask if the printer is busy, or if it is ready to receive a character. If the printer is ready, the character will be sent. If the printer is busy, your computer cannot send the character. Using the MODE command with the RETRY= parameter is how you tell DOS and your computer what you want done when the printer is busy.

Unless told otherwise, we recommend the following settings:

RETRY=B   Use this setting if you have been told to use the P parameter on previous versions of DOS.

RETRY=E   Use this setting if you are sharing your printer on a network.

RETRY=N   This is the normal setting and should be used unless one of the previous situations applies. When your printer has a problem, DOS will tell you.

```
C:\>MODE LPT3 RETRY=E
LPT3: not rerouted
Infinite retry on parallel printer time-out
C:\>_
```

In this example, printer retries have been set to E for LPT3. We see from what DOS displayed that LPT3 has not been redirected to a communications adapter and that the printer retries have been set.

As was mentioned in earlier sections, you can control the setting of characters per print line, print lines per inch, and printer retries with a single MODE command for each printer. This is demonstrated in the following example.

```
C:\>MODE LPT1 COLUMNS=132 LINES=8 RETRY=N
LPT1: not rerouted
LPT1: set for 132
Printer lines per inch set
No retry on parallel printer time-out
C:\>_
```

Redirecting Printer Output

DOS normally talks to a printer through the parallel adapter. Because many printers attach to the serial adapter, DOS supports this as well. It does so by loading special code that redirects data from the parallel adapter to the serial adapter. This redirection is very similar to a road detour.

If your printer is attached to the serial adapter, you will have to use the MODE command to redirect the printer data to the serial adapter that it is attached to. DOS supports three printers (LPT1, LPT2, and LPT3), and you can redirect any or all of them to any of the serial adapters (COM1, COM2, COM3, or COM4). You are not allowed to use the alternate printer and communications names, PRN and AUX.

To redirect a printer name, you simply tell MODE to set a printer name equal to a communications name. For example,

```
C:\>MODE LPT1=COM1
LPT1: rerouted to COM1:
C:\>_
```

You are only allowed to redirect one printer with each MODE command. However, you can enter several MODE commands to redirect as many printers as you need. If you want to cancel the redirection, just tell MODE to set the printer name equal to nothing:

```
C:\>MODE LPT1=
LPT1: not rerouted
No retry on parallel printer timeout
C:\>_
```

Before you can redirect a printer to a communications adapter, you must first initialize the communications adapter. This was explained earlier in "Controlling Communications." If you are going to use printer redirection, you should also tell the communications adapter to perform retries.

When you use the MODE command to redirect printer output, a small part of its code remains in your computer's memory. See Figure 12-2 for more information on the amount of memory that MODE uses for this support.

CONTROLLING KEYBOARDS

Starting with DOS 4.0, you can use the MODE command to change the Type-a-matic characteristics of some keyboards (not all computers will allow this). In other words, MODE allows you to control how the keys on your computer will act when you hold them down rather than just pressing them. The Type-a-matic characteristics are defined as follows:

RATE=   RATE allows you to control how fast the keys will automatically repeat themselves when held down. You do not need to know the exact keys-per-second rate; just realize that the larger the number you enter here, the faster the keys will repeat. You may choose a rate between 1 and 32.

DELAY=   The DELAY you enter tells your computer how long to wait before starting to repeat a key. This is different from the RATE specified above. When you first press down a key, your computer will wait a short time before it starts repeating the keys. Once it starts repeating the keys, it will repeat them at the rate you requested with the RATE= value. The DELAY value you enter is the number of quarter seconds that will be delayed. You may choose a rate between 1 and 4.

The DOS Console Device Driver talks to the keyboard. Therefore, to set the keyboard characteristics, you must direct MODE to talk to the CON device driver. You must always enter both the DELAY and RATE values. If you do not enter them both, DOS will tell you to enter them both.

The following example shows you how to set the keyboard so that when you press and hold a key,

1. The key will be entered once.

2. If you hold down the key longer than a half second, it will start repeating.

3. Once the key starts repeating, it will repeat ten times a second until you release the key.

```
C:\>MODE CON DELAY=2 RATE=20

C:\>_
```

If you try this command and DOS responds with the message "Function not supported on this computer," then your computer does not allow DOS to change these characteristics.

CONTROLLING THE DOS VERSION

The SETVER device driver gives DOS 5.0 the ability to make various applications and device drivers believe that they are running on a different release of DOS. To use SETVER, you must put the following statement in your CONFIG.SYS file:

DEVICE=d:path\SETVER.EXE

Later, to control the content of the version table, you would use the commands

SETVER d:path\filename ver

or

SETVER d:path\filename /DELETE /QUIET

where

d:path\SETVER.EXE   Indicates where you want the version table modified. SETVER.EXE keeps the version table inside of itself. If you use multiple diskettes or drives to start DOS, you may want to have multiple version tables. In this case, you can have the SETVER program loaded from one drive modify the SETVER program and version table on another drive.

d:path\filename   Indicates the name of the application that you want DOS to show a different version number to. You should include the filename extension as well.

ver   Is the DOS version number that you want the applications to see. It can be from 2.11 through 9.99.

/DELETE   Tells SETVER to delete or remove the application name from the version table. After this, the application will see the true version number of DOS. This switch can be abbreviated as /D.

/QUIET   Tells SETVER not to display any messages when deleting applications from the version table. This switch is only valid in combination with the /DELETE switch.

SETVER is available only in DOS 5.0. Most applications check to see what release of DOS that they are running on. This is usually due to the historical buildup of functions that DOS has provided; for example, you could not run an application that needed to use the DOS internal interface that creates a file with a unique name (INT 21H, AH=5AH, Create Unique File) prior to DOS 3.1. If you tried, the application would fail to work properly. So, most applications check to see that the release of DOS that they are running on is at least up to the level that they require.

Unfortunately, many applications do not make open-ended version checks. They check for one and only one release of DOS, and refuse to run on all other releases, even newer ones. The SETVER device driver and utility were provided to allow you to trick the application into believing that it is running on a different version of DOS.

When loading the device driver, you use no additional parameters. The parameters are used later to manage the SETVER version table.

If you enter SETVER with no parameters, the version table will be displayed. The version table is only loaded into memory when you start DOS. If you use the SETVER command to change the version table, the changes will not take effect until the next time you start DOS. The version table that SETVER displays is the one that is recorded inside itself on the disk, not the one that is in memory; therefore, it is not necessarily the one that is in effect (e.g., it will not be the current version table loaded if you have modified the version table since you started DOS).

> **Warning:** Be very careful when using SETVER. Through its use, you can allow an application to run that has not been tested on your version of DOS. This could cause disastrous results, including such things as loss of data and unreported damage to your data and program files. Only use SETVER when you have been told to do so.

You can check the success of the SETVER utility through the error level that it returns. SETVER returns the following error levels:

0 No errors occurred. The version table was successfully updated.

1 Invalid switch on the SETVER command. The version table was not updated.

2 Invalid filename on the SETVER command. The version table was not updated.

3 There was not enough memory for SETVER to work in. The version table was not updated.

4 The version number entered on the SETVER command was not acceptable. The version table was not updated.

5 SETVER could not find the filename you specified in the version table to delete it. The version table was not updated.

6 SETVER could not find the system files it needed to work with. The version table was not updated.

7 The drive or path you entered on the SETVER command was not valid. The version table was not updated.

8 You entered too many parameters on the SETVER command. The version table was not updated.

9 You did not enter enough parameters on the SETVER command. The version table was not updated.

10 SETVER could not read the system files it needed to work with. The version table was not updated.

11 The version table in SETVER.EXE has been damaged and can no longer be used. The version table was not updated.

12 SETVER could not find the version table in the system files it needed to work with. The version table was not updated.

13 The version table is full; you cannot add more programs to it. The version table was not updated.

14 SETVER could not write the system files it needed to work with. The version table was not updated.

To enable the SETVER function, you would add the following line to your CONFIG.SYS file

device=c:\dos\setver.exe

To tell SETVER that you want PROGRAM.EXE to always see the version number 7.14, you would enter

setver program.exe 7.14

To tell SETVER that you want to delete PROGRAM.EXE from the version table, you would enter

setver program.exe /d

To display the version table, you would enter

setver

ADVANCED MEMORY SUPPORT

In the computers that DOS supports today, there are several types of memory. In order to understand what is happening inside your computer, you need to have a fundamental understanding of the types of memory and what the differences are.

A LITTLE HISTORY

When the IBM Personal Computer was first introduced, the heart of the computer was Intel's 8088 Central Processor Unit (CPU). The CPU is the processor that does the actual computation in a computer. The rest of the processors and electronics are there to get data from you to the CPU to be processed and to get the results out of the CPU so that you can see them.

Because of how the Intel 8088 CPU works, a computer that uses this processor can normally only have up to 1 megabyte of memory (remember, 1 megabyte = 1024 kilobytes, and 1 kilobyte = 1024 bytes). In other words, the 8088 processor has the ability to tell the rest of the computer that it wants to read or write one of up to 1,048,576 different bytes of memory. You can compare this to an old television set, which had only 12 channels that you could look at (channels 2 through channel 13). The television could only display one channel at a time, but it could select up to 12 different channels. Similarly, the 8088-based computer could only look at one byte of memory at a time, but it could select from up to one million bytes. If you look at it this way, the address of a byte of memory is just like the channel number in a television set.

Your computer's memory is used for many different purposes. DOS takes some of the memory, your applications take some of your memory, ROM BIOS takes some of the memory, and even some of the computer adapter cards take some of your memory (the display adapters are a good example of this). When the IBM Personal Computer was first introduced, a standard was established: ROM BIOS and the adapters would use the memory whose addresses were greater than 655,360, and DOS, and the applications would use the memory whose addresses were less than 655,360. This is actually not an unfair split, because 62.5 percent of the computer's memory is available for DOS and applications. With this standard, DOS and the applications and ROM BIOS and other hardware were kept from getting in each other's way. The number 655,360 just happens to be 640 kilobytes (or 640K), which is the source of the now famous 640KB memory limitation in DOS. (See Figure 11-9.)

Later, when Intel introduced the 80286 processor, IBM built the IBM Personal Computer AT. While the 8088 processor only worked one way, the new 80286 processor had two modes of operation:

Real Mode   In this mode, the 80286 processor acted almost like the 8088 processor, only faster. In this mode, the 80286 could access up to 1MB of memory. Most programs that were written to run on an 8088-based computer could be run on an 80286-based computer running in real mode.

Protect Mode   This new mode allowed the 80286 processor to access up to 16MB of memory. Most programs that were written to run on an 8088-based computer could *not* be run on an 80286-based computer running in protect mode.

The new 80286 processor could access 16 times more memory than the older 8088 processor. Unfortunately, you would need all new programs to do this. Now what? At this point in time, there were already thousands of programs that were available on the 8088-based computers. A real-mode 80286-based computer was faster than an 8088-based computer, and it could run the existing programs. So, ROM BIOS and DOS stayed with running the

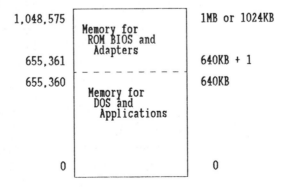

Figure 11-9
DOS Conventional
Memory Address
Division

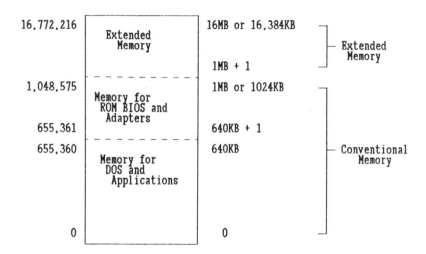

Figure 11-10
DOS Extended Memory Address Division

80286-based computers in real mode. This meant that the 1MB and 640KB memory limitations were carried into the 80286-based computers.

What could be done with the extra memory capability? Other operating systems like XENIX and Operating System/2 took advantage of it. They did not have the problem of compatibility with the 8088-based programs like DOS did. The extra memory became known as *extended memory* (see Figure 11-10).

Now there are computers that use the Intel 80386 processor. Like the 80286 processor, the 80386 processor has more than one mode. In fact, it has three modes:

Real Mode   In this mode, the 80386 processor acts almost like the 8088 processor, only faster. In this mode, the 80386 can access up to 1MB of memory. Most programs that are written to run on an 8088-based computer can be run on an 80386-based computer running in real mode.

Protect Mode   This mode provides the same support as the 80286 protect mode did, allowing the 80386 processor to access up to 16MB of memory. Most programs that are written to run on an 8088-based computer still cannot be run on an 80386-based computer running in protect mode.

Native Mode   This is the new mode of the 80386 and 80486 processors. It allows addressing of up to 4 GigaBytes (4 x 1024 megabytes) of memory. Of course, programs that were written for 8088- and 80286-based computers cannot be run in native mode.

For a long time, the only DOS support for extended memory was the VDISK device driver. By using a VDISK, you could substantially improve your computer's performance. Later, with the announcement of the IBM Personal System/2 Models 50 and 60, the IBMCACHE device driver could also use extended memory. With DOS 5.0, RAMDRIVE and SMARTDRV device drivers can also use extended memory.

EXTENDED MEMORY SUPPORT

Extended memory is any memory located at address 1MB or above. Any computer with more than 640KB of memory has some extended memory. For example, a computer with 1MB of memory has 1024 KB (or 1MB) − 640 KB = 384 KB of extended memory.

Extended memory was introduced with the IBM PC-AT computer. Until recently it had only limited use for functions such as RAM disks. Due to this infrequent use, there was not a universally accepted way to access extended memory. When the Microsoft Corporation introduced the Windows™ 2.0 product, it provided a new way to control access to extended memory. This new way, called the Extended Memory Specification (XMS), quickly became an industry standard. XMS was provided by a device driver named HIMEM.SYS. DOS 5.0 is the first version of DOS to provide HIMEM.SYS. HIMEM.SYS, as provided in Windows 2.X or 3.0, can be used with DOS 3.3 and DOS 4.0.

HIMEM provides access to three different areas of memory (see Figure 11-11).

1. Upper Memory Blocks (UMBs). UMBs are small areas of otherwise unused memory in the area reserved for ROM BIOS and adapters. This reserved area is located between 640 KB and 1MB. UMBs may be as small as sixteen bytes or as large as the biggest free area in the reserved area.

2. The High Memory Area (HMA). The HMA is a special area of memory just under 64 KB in size that starts at the 1MB (or 1024 KB) address. It is special because it can be addressed by an 80286, 80386, or 80486 when the processor is running in real mode. Thus it is accessible to DOS and your applications. The HMA is the first part of your computer's extended memory.

3. Extended Memory Blocks (EMBs). EMBs are areas in extended memory

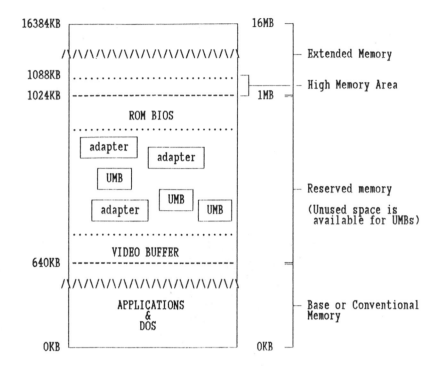

Figure 11-11
Extended Memory
Specification Sup-
ported Memory
Areas

outside of the HMA. They may be as small as 1KB or as large as all of extended memory.

> **Note:** UMBs, the HMA, and EMBs are not always provided by HIMEM. The areas provided depend on the amount of extended memory in your computer and the parameters you provide when loading HIMEM.

INSTALLING THE HIMEM DEVICE DRIVER

To install HIMEM, you must add a DEVICE=HIMEM.SYS statement to your computer's CONFIG.SYS file. If the HIMEM.SYS file is not in the root directory, you must include the full path to it (e.g., DEVICE= C:\DOS\HIMEM.SYS). You must include a DEVICE=HIMEM.SYS statement before any other device driver that uses extended memory, or DOS will display an error message.

All HIMEM.SYS parameters are optional. The HIMEM.SYS statement has the following form:

DEVICE=HIMEM.SYS /HMAMIN=size

/NUMHANDLES=count

/INT15=size

/MACHINE:id

where

/HMAMIN=size   Sets the minimum amount of HMA space (in KB) a program must use before it is allowed access to the HMA. Because there is only one HMA and more than one program may want to use it, HMAMIN allows you insure that only programs that use at least this much of the HMA will get access to it. Valid values are zero to 63. If you do not provide a HMAMIN value, the first program to request the HMA will get access to it.

/NUMHANDLES=count   Sets the number of EMB handles that HIMEM will provide. Valid values are 1 to 128. The normal value is 32. See your application documentation for more information on setting the NUMHANDLES value.

/INT15=size   Sets the amount of extended memory (in KB) to reserve for applications that use the older INT 15H method of requesting extended memory. Valid values are 0 to all of extended memory. The normal value is 0. See your application documentation for more information on setting the INT15 value.

MACHINE:id   Identifies the type of computer you have. Normally, HIMEM is able to determine the type of computer you have. If it cannot, it may not work correctly, and you will need to tell it what type of computer you have. See your DOS 5.0 Reference for more information on the supported computer types.

HIMEM has some additional parameters that are infrequently used. For more information on these parameters, see your DOS 5.0 Reference book.

To set the minimum size to use the HMA to 32 KB and reserve 128 KB of extended memory for older INT 15H applications, you would add the following line to your CONFIG.SYS file.

DEVICE=C:\DOS\HIMEM.SYS /HMAMIN=32 /INT15=128

DOS USE OF EXTENDED MEMORY

DOS 5.0 can make use of extended memory to hold parts of itself. These parts would normally be located in the base area (0 to 640 KB). By moving parts of DOS to extended memory, DOS 5.0 can allow larger applications to run. By using extended memory, DOS 5.0 can use as little as 16 KB of base memory. This is in contrast to DOS 3.3, which used at least 48 KB of base memory, and DOS 4.0, which used at least 64 KB of base memory.

Because of this improvement in available memory, we highly recommend you place DOS in the HMA. If you use the DOS 5.0 SETUP or INSTALL programs, your computer will be set up to put DOS in the HMA. It is possible, although unlikely, that some of your applications may not work correctly if DOS is in the HMA. If you find this to be true, you should remove the DOS=HIGH statement from your CONFIG.SYS file.

To place DOS in extended memory, you must add both the HIMEM.SYS device driver and the DOS statement to your CONFIG.SYS file. We discussed HIMEM.SYS in the previous section. The DOS statement instructs DOS to load itself into the HMA. DOS can also put programs into UMBs. To do this you must instruct DOS to let this happen. The DOS statement has the following forms:

DOS=HIGH

DOS=UMB

DOS=HIGH,UMB

The DOS=HIGH statement instructs DOS to load itself into the HMA. The DOS=UMB statement instructs DOS to make any UMBs available for use by itself and your applications. The DOS=HIGH,UMB statement combines these functions.

To create UMBs so that DOS can make them available, you must have the following statements in your CONFIG.SYS files:

DOS=UMB

DEVICE=HIMEM.SYS ...

DEVICE=EMM386.EXE ... RAM ...

INSTALLING DEVICE DRIVERS INTO UMBS

If your computer has available UMBs, you may load DOS device drivers into them. To do this, you use the DEVICEHIGH statement in the CONFIG.SYS file. The DEVICEHIGH statement has the following forms:

DEVICEHIGH=d:path\device parameters

or

DEVICEHIGH SIZE=size d:path\device parameters

where

d:path\device   Specifies the name and location of the device driver.

parameters   Specifies any device-driver-dependent parameters.

SIZE=size   Specifies the minimum size (in bytes, in hexadecimal notation) of the UMB that is used to hold the device driver. If no UMB at least as large as "size" can be found, the device driver is loaded into base memory. If SIZE=size is not provided, then the size of the device driver is used to set the minimum size. If DOS cannot load the device driver into a UMB (because the driver is too large or no UMBs are available), then the program is loaded into base memory. See your device driver documentation for more information on setting the SIZE value.

INSTALLING PROGRAMS INTO UMBS

If your computer has available UMBs, you may load small programs into them. To do this you use the LOADHIGH statement in the AUTOEXEC.BAT file or from the DOS Command Prompt. Typically you would use LOADHIGH to install a terminate-and-stay-resident program. The LOADHIGH statement has the following form:

LOADHIGH program parameters

where

program   Specifies the name and location of the program.

parameters   Specifies any program-dependent parameters.

If DOS cannot load the program into a UMB (because the program is too large or no UMBs are available), then the program is loaded into base memory.

EXPANDED MEMORY SUPPORT

As DOS and application programs grew in size, the amount of memory that your computer needed grew also. Eventually, many applications could not execute in a computer with only 640KB of memory. This situation was eventually solved by something called *expanded memory support* (EMS).

We go back to our previous television example to illustrate EMS. Old televisions are not "cable ready," which means that they cannot receive all of the over 100 channels of television that a cable can bring into your home. So, a cable converter was created. By using a cable converter, you can select from over 100 channels and receive them all on channel 3 of your television. In this way, you can take a television that could only receive 12 channels, add in a cable converter, and be able to receive over 100 channels. (See Figure 11-12.)

The expanded memory support works the same way. There can be several megabytes of expanded memory, but your computer can see only a small part (16 KB) of it at one time. In the television example, you select the expanded channels through the cable converter. In your computer, a program selects the expanded memory it wants to use through the EMS software and/or hardware.

Many television cable converters provide the ability to map the incoming channels to either channel 2 or channel 3. The EMS support in DOS has the same capability. You can tell it where to map the EMS memory in the 1MB conventional address range. The EMS memory is mapped in 16KB pieces called *pages*. When grouped together, four contiguous EMS pages are called a *frame*. There are two ways to map the memory: with the page control settings and with frame control settings. A page control selects a 16KB address range that will be used for the specified page. A frame control selects a 64KB address range that will hold the four pages P0, P1, P2, and

Figure 11-12
Television Cable Converter and EMS Address Converter

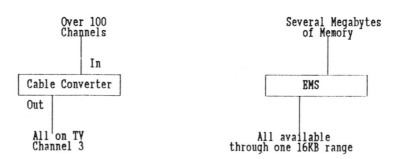

Valid Page Values	Valid Frame Values
C000 C400 C800 CC00	C000
D000 D400 D800 DC00	D000
E000 E400 E800 EC00	E000

Figure 11-13
Valid Page and
Frame Values

P3. Figure 11-13 shows the valid page and frame address values and illustrates their relationship.

DOS 4.0 and DOS 5.0 support Lotus/Intel/Microsoft Expanded Memory Specification version 4.0. This means that applications that use the LIM 4.0 interfaces can run on DOS 4.0 or DOS 5.0, using the EMS device drivers that are supplied with DOS.

While both DOS 4.0 and DOS 5.0 support EMS, the implementations and installations are somewhat different. The next two sections describe how to install EMS for both DOS 4.0 and DOS 5.0.

EXPANDED MEMORY SUPPORT IN DOS 4.0

The DOS 4.0 support for EMS is provided through two device drivers, XMA2EMS.SYS and XMAEM.SYS. The following sections will tell you how they are installed.

Installing the XMA2EMS Device Driver

The XMA2EMS.SYS device driver provides LIM 4.0 support for computers that have the following types of adapters:

- Computers with the IBM 2MB Expanded Memory Adapter option installed.

- Computers with the IBM Personal System/2 80286 Expanded Memory Adapter/A option installed.

● Computers with the IBM Personal System/2 80286 Memory Expansion Option installed.

● Computers that use the Intel 80386 processor, provided that the XMAEM.SYS device driver has previously been loaded.

To install XMA2EMS, you must add a DEVICE=XMA2EMS.SYS statement to your computer's CONFIG.SYS file. If the XMA2EMS.SYS file is not in the root directory, you must include the full path to it (e.g., DEVICE=C:\DOS\XMA2EMS.SYS). Normally, you should start with

DEVICE=C:\DOS\XMA2EMS.SYS FRAME=D000 P254=C000 P255=C400

Installing the XMAEM Device Driver

The XMAEM.SYS device driver is used only on 80386-based computers. This device driver makes your computer believe that it has an IBM Personal System/2 80286 Expanded Memory Adapter/A when it really does not. It does this by using the extended memory (the memory in your computer whose addresses are greater than 1MB) and the 80386 Memory Mapping Registers. In your 80386-based computer, all of the expanded memory can be used as EMS memory, not just the expanded memory that is provided by adapter cards that support EMS.

To install XMAEM, you must add a DEVICE=XMAEM.SYS statement to your computer's CONFIG.SYS file. If the XMAEM.SYS file is not in the root directory, you must include the full path to it (e.g., DEVICE=C:\DOS\XMAEM.SYS). The DEVICE= statement for XMAEM must precede the DEVICE= statement for XMA2EMS in your CONFIG.SYS file.

If you do not provide any additional parameters, then all of your expanded memory will be used as EMS memory. You can limit the amount of expanded memory that will be used as EMS memory by adding a count of 16KB pages that should be used for EMS. For example, DEVICE=C:\XMAEM.SYS 64 will reserve 64 pages for EMS support and leave the rest of extended memory available as extended memory. We used 64 pages here because that is the minimum amount of memory that XMAEM will allow for EMS usage.

EXPANDED MEMORY SUPPORT IN DOS 5.0

DOS 5.0 provides a different way to use EMS memory. In DOS 4.0, you use a combination of the XMA2EMS.SYS and the XMAEM.SYS device drivers. In DOS 5.0 you use the EMM386.EXE device driver.

EMM386 is a more efficient implementation of EMS, but it can be used only on 80386- or 80486-based computers. It takes extended memory (provided by the HIMEM.SYS device driver) and converts it to expanded memory. It uses a feature of the 80386 processor called *page tables* to do this. It has better performance and uses less of your computer's memory. To your application programs there is very little difference between the DOS 4.0 and DOS 5.0 methods.

Installing the EMM386 Device Driver

To install EMM386, you must add a DEVICE=EMM386.EXE statement to your computer's CONFIG.SYS file. If the EMM386.EXE file is not in the root directory, you must include the full path to it (e.g., DEVICE=C :\DOS\EMM386.EXE). You must include a DEVICE=HIMEM.SYS statement before the DEVICE=EMM386.EXE statement, or DOS will display an error message and EMM386 will not start.

All EMM386.EXE parameters are optional. If you do not provide any additional parameters, then EMM386 will convert 256KB of your extended memory to expanded memory. If you do not provide a value for FRAME or P0-P3 values, EMM386 will attempt to find an address for the page frame. You can control the areas EMM386 uses by the I and X parameters. The EMM386.EXE statement has the following form:

DEVICE=EMM386.EXE memory L=size

        FRAME=address Pn=address

        I=start-end X=start-end

        W=ON

        H=count

        RAM

where

memory   Sets the amount of extended memory (in KB) that EMM386 will convert to expanded memory. The smallest value is 16 and the largest is 32767. The size you select cannot be larger than the amount of available extended memory provided by HIMEM.SYS.

L=size   Sets the amount of extended memory to leave after EMM386 is loaded. The smallest amount is zero. You should use this parameter to leave memory available for other uses such as RAMDRIVE.SYS or SMARTDRV.SYS.

FRAME=address   Sets the segment location of the EMS 3.2 page frame (equivalent to P0 through P3). This segment address must not be used by any other program or device adapter. Some computer manufacturers provide a method to find unused memory segments. The SETUP program provided by IBM can provide this information. Valid values are hexadecimal addresses C000 through E000 in steps of 0400.

Pn=address   Sets the segment location of an EMS 4.0 page. A page is a 16 KB area or EMS memory. The n of Pn specifies the page number (0 through 255), and the address follows the same rules described for FRAME=address.

I=start-end   Sets a range of addresses that are valid to use to locate the page frame. Start is the start of the range and End is the end of the range. Start and end follow the same rules described for FRAME=address. Valid values are hexadecimal addresses 8000 through E000 in steps of 0400.

X=start-end   Sets a range of addresses that are not to be used to locate the page frame. The X parameter is the opposite of the I parameter. If the ranges for I and X overlap, the overlapping range is excluded from consideration.

W=ON   Includes support for the Weitek math coprocessor. If you do not have a Weitek coprocessor installed in your computer, do not provide this parameter.

H=count   Sets the number of EMS handles provided to EMS applications. The normal value is 64. Valid values are 2 to 255. See your application documentation for more information on setting the H value.

RAM   Causes EMM386 to provide additional memory, called *upper memory blocks* (UMBs), that can be used by some applications. See your application documentation for more information on using UMBs.

EMM386 has some additional parameters that are infrequently used. For more information on these parameters, see the documentation provided with your copy of DOS 5.0.

To provide 2 MB of EMS memory with a EMS page frame at segment address D000 and supporting UMBs, you would add the following lines to your CONFIG.SYS file.

```
DEVICE=C:\DOS\HIMEM.SYS

DEVICE=C:\DOS\EMM386.EXE 2048 FRAME=D000 RAM
```

BALANCING EXPANDED MEMORY USAGE

Once you have installed EMS, you will need to decide how to use it. DOS can use EMS for the following:

BUFFERS　　The DOS sector buffers can be put into EMS memory.

FASTOPEN　　The FASTOPEN program and data areas can be put into EMS memory.

RAMDRIVE　　You can put a RAMDRIVE into EMS memory.

SMARTDRV　　You can put the SMARTDRV disk cache into EMS memory.

VDISK　　You can put a VDISK into EMS memory.

For DOS 4.0, you will get the biggest performance improvement from putting your DOS sector buffers into EMS memory. When the buffers are in EMS memory, you are not limited to a maximum of BUFFERS=99. By using the /X switch, you can set your buffer count up to 10,000 (or the amount of available EMS memory). An example of this would be BUFFERS=1000 /X.

For DOS 5.0, you can get outstanding performance improvements through the use of SMARTDRV in EMS.

FASTOPEN, VDISK, and RAMDRIVE will not run any faster if they are put into EMS memory. By doing this, however, you can save the conventional memory that they would have taken. (Remember, RAMDRIVE, SMARTDRV, and VDISK can all use either EMS or XMS memory.)

The major reason for installing EMS is so that your applications can take advantage of it. Not all applications have added EMS support. If you have applications that use EMS, you will not want to tell DOS to use all of the EMS memory. Save as much for your applications as they can use.

For instance, if you have a spreadsheet program that will use EMS memory when available, you do not want to give so much EMS memory to DOS and its device drivers that you cannot load your largest spreadsheets. At the same time, you do want to use as much of your memory as possible. Many programs provide a method to start a DOS prompt without having to exit the program. If you can do this with your programs, you can start a DOS prompt and run a MEM /DEBUG report, thereby getting a good picture of which programs are using your computer's memory.

Consider again a spreadsheet program. With your largest spreadsheet (or largest document in a word processor) loaded, start a DOS prompt and run the MEM /DEBUG report. If the combination of your programs and DOS is not using almost all of your computer's memory, then you can allow DOS to use more memory. The first priority would be to create or to increase the size of your SMARTDRV cache. Next, you might want to add a few more DOS buffers or increase the size of your FASTOPEN buffer.

There are no simple rules on balancing the use of your system's memory. You can follow the guidelines here and in Chapter 12, but remember that these are just guidelines. You will have to experiment with your system to determine what the best balance for your situation is.

Tuning DOS Storage Use and Performance

In this chapter, we are going to describe many of the "tuning knobs" that affect how quickly you will be able to get your work done. The various DOS extensions, utilities, and parameters described here have all been provided to enable you to control your computer and how DOS works with it.

With the exception of the VERIFY setting, all of the controls presented in this chapter can only be modified by restarting your computer. Once the DOS extensions have been loaded, they cannot be removed without restarting. Once DOS has set the size of its control blocks, their size can only be increased or decreased by restarting your computer.

When you install DOS 4.0, the SELECT program tries to set the various performance tuning factors based on the specific computer and adapters you have, as well as your answers to the questions it asks. To change these performance tuning factors, you do not have to reinstall DOS; you can simply edit the AUTOEXEC.BAT and CONFIG.SYS files that contain these controls. For DOS 3.3 and DOS 5.0, you will have to perform the initial performance tuning yourself; SELECT and SETUP do not assist in this area.

STORAGE VERSUS PERFORMANCE

There is a common saying, "There is no such thing as a free lunch." Nowhere is this more true than in tuning your computer's performance. All of the DOS tuning knobs are provided because making your computer run faster will require you to give something up, usually storage (or memory). In order for DOS to work more efficiently, it needs more room — more room for smarter code and more room to hold data so DOS will not have to read it from the disk.

The storage that DOS and your applications can use is limited. Even if your computer has extended or expanded memory, most of the applications and many parts of DOS can only use the conventional memory in your system. There are many cases where DOS is restricted to using conventional memory, which is one reason why IBM has provided Operating System/2.

The bottom line is that the more memory you allow DOS to use to improve performance, the faster it will run. You can compare this to a child moving toys with a wagon. He has two wagons, a large one and a small one. Using the large wagon, he will be able to move a lot of toys with each trip. Using the small wagon will take more trips, but it will be easier to pull. The child has to make a trade-off, fewer trips versus easy wagon pulling.

When you tune DOS performance, you must also make trade-offs. As we said earlier, the more memory you give to DOS, the faster it can run. The trade-off is that there is less memory for your applications to use. If you give DOS too much memory, then some of your applications may not be able to run.

In the rest of this chapter, we discuss how you control the amount of storage that is used by DOS. We tell you what DOS uses the memory for and what the performance paybacks will be, and provide some guidelines for making the storage versus performance trade-offs.

When you first installed DOS, the installation program may have asked you questions and then made some of the trade-offs based on your answers. Now, you will be making the trade-offs based on what you want to do with your computer. You can experiment with the controls that are described here until you are satisfied that you have arrived at the best usage of your computer's resources.

STORAGE AND PERFORMANCE CONTROLS

There are three ways in which you can affect the amount of memory that DOS will use:

1. You can change the configuration statements in your CONFIG.SYS file. Figure 12-1 lists the different configuration statements that affect the amount of your computer's memory that DOS will use. The figure also shows the amount of memory that is needed as you increase the values for each of the parameters.

2. You can change the DOS extensions that you have loaded. Figure 12-2 lists the different DOS extensions that affect the amount of your computer's memory that DOS will use. The figure also shows the amount of memory that is needed as you increase the values for each of the parameters.

3. You can change the optional DOS device drivers that you have loaded. Figure 12-3 lists the different device driver statements that affect the amount of

Configuration Statement	3.3 Size	4.0 Size	5.0 Size	Comments
BREAK	0	0	0	
BUFFERS	528 -	528 512	532 512	Each ReadWrite Buffer Each LookAhead Buffer
COUNTRY	0	0	0	
DEVICE	0	0	0	Plus the size of the device driver
DEVICEHIGH	0	0	0	Plus the size of the device driver
DRIVPARM	0	0	0	
FCBS	48	48	48	Each File Control Block
FILES	48	64	64	Each File
INSTALL	-	0	0	Plus the size of the program installed
LASTDRIVE	80	80	96	Each Drive
REM	-	0	0	
SHELL	0	0	0	Plus the size of the shell program
STACKS	2,128	1,984	704	Plus the size of the stacks
SWITCHES	-	0	0	

Figure 12-1
DOS Configuration Statement Memory Usage

Extension Name	3.3 Size	4.0 Size	5.0 Size	Comments
APPEND	4,512	7,712	8,864	
ASSIGN	1,408	1,568	1,568	
DOSKEY	-	-	4,144	Plus Buffer Size
FASTOPEN	2,496	8,496	-	C:=(20,20)
	-	4,336	4,160	C:=(20,)
	-	5,920	-	C:=(,20)
	32	48	48	Each additional (1,)
	-	16	-	Each additional (,1)
GRAFTABL	1,456	1,184	1,184	
GRAPHICS	2,256	5,280	5,824	
KEYB	5,568	6,128	7,040	
MIRROR	-	-	6,528	For deletion tracking
MODE	496	480	464	All resident MODE functions
NLSFUNC	2,576	2,752	2,688	
PRINT	5,520	5,808	5,744	Default = /B:512 /Q:10
	64	64	64	Each additional /Q:1
SHARE	5,008	5,344	5,232	Default = /F:2048 /L:20
	16	16	16	Each additional /L:1

Figure 12-2
DOS Extension Memory Usage

Device Driver	3.3 Size	4.0 Size	5.0 Size	Comments
ANSI	1,584	4,496	4,208	
DISPLAY	18,000	18,176	18,032	CON=(EGA,437,1) Size is display type dependent
DRIVER	192	224	224	
EMM386	-	-	9,216	
HIMEM	-	-	1,136	
PRINTER	14,640	15,168	14,912	LPT1=(4201,437,1) Size is printer type dependent
RAMDRIVE	-	-	1,184	Plus size of the ram disk
SETVER	-	-	416	
SMARTDRV	-	-	20,688	Plus size of the cache
VDISK	768	1,248	-	Plus size of the virtual disk
XMA2EMS	-	19,312	-	
XMAEM	-	320	-	

Figure 12-3
DOS Extension Memory Usage

your computer's memory that DOS will use. (*Note:* The sizes presented in Figures 12-1 through 12-3 are approximate and may vary slightly between releases and versions.)

DOS only reads the CONFIG.SYS file when it first starts. If you make changes in CONFIG.SYS, you will have to restart your computer before the changes will take effect.

Once you have loaded a DOS extension, it stays in your computer's memory until the next time you restart your computer. The parameters you provide cannot be changed without restarting your computer.

WHO'S USING MY MEMORY?

When you are trying to make the trade-offs between storage and performance, one of the most valuable tools will be the MEM command. With this command, you will be able to see how much memory is being used by each of the DOS extensions, device drivers, and configuration statements.

> **Note:** The MEM command was introduced in DOS 4.0. For DOS 3.3 users, there is no way to get the detailed memory usage information that MEM provides.

```
 1->| Address    Name       Size       Type
 2->| -------    --------    ------     ------
 3->| 000000                 000400     Interrupt Vector
 4->| 000400                 000100     ROM Communication Area
 5->| 000500                 000200     DOS Communication Area
 6->|
 7->| 000700     IBMBIO      000AE0     System Data
 8->|            CON                    System Device Driver
 9->|            AUX                    System Device Driver
10->|            PRN                    System Device Driver
11->|            CLOCK$                 System Device Driver
12->|            A: - D:                System Device Driver
13->|            COM1                   System Device Driver
14->|            LPT1                   System Device Driver
15->|            LPT2                   System Device Driver
16->|            LPT3                   System Device Driver
17->|            COM2                   System Device Driver
18->|            COM3                   System Device Driver
19->|            COM4                   System Device Driver
20->|
21->| 0011E0     IBMDOS      0013F0     System Data
22->|
```

Figure 12-4
MEM /DEBUG Report

Continued

```
23->| 0025D0      IBMBIO      00A9D0      System Data
24->|             HIMEM       000470      DEVICE=
25->|              XMSXXXX0               Installed Device Driver
26->|             EMM386      002400      DEVICE=
27->|              EMMXXXX0               Installed Device Driver
28->|             SMARTDRV    0050D0      DEVICE=
29->|              SMARTAAR               Installed Device Driver
30->|             RAMDRIVE    0004D0      DEVICE=
31->|              E:                     Installed Device Driver
32->|                         000380      FILES=
33->|                         000100      FCBS=
34->|                         001200      BUFFERS=
35->|                         0008F0      LASTDRIVE=
36->|                         000BC0      STACKS=
37->| 00CFB0      IBMDOS      000040      System Program
38->|
39->| 00D000      COMMAND     000D50      Program
40->| 00DD60      MSDOS       000040      -- Free --
41->| 00DDB0      COMMAND     000100      Environment
42->| 00DEC0      MEM         000050      Environment
43->| 00DF20      MEM         0176F0      Program
44->| 025620      MSDOS       07A9C0      -- Free --
45->| 09FFF0      SYSTEM      020010      System Program
46->|
47->| 0C0010      IBMBIO      001080      System Data
48->|             ANSI        001070      DEVICE=
49->|              CON                    Installed Device Driver
50->| 0C10A0      MSDOS       000050      -- Free --
51->| 0C1100      DOSKEY      001030      Program
52->| 0C2140      MSDOS       003E90      -- Free --
53->| 0C5FE0      SYSTEM      002020      System Program
54->|
55->| 0C8010      MSDOS       001FC0      -- Free --
56->| 0C9FE0      SYSTEM      001020      System Program
57->|
58->| 0CB010      MSDOS       000FC0      -- Free --
59->| 0CBFE0      SYSTEM      002020      System Program
60->|
61->| 0CE010      MSDOS       001FE0      -- Free --
62->|
63->|
64->|    655360 bytes total conventional memory
65->|    655360 bytes available to IBM DOS
66->|    598208 largest executable program size
67->|
68->| Handle       EMS Name       Size
69->| ------       --------       ------
70->|      0                      060000
71->|      1                      010000
72->|
73->|   4587520 bytes total EMS memory
74->|   4128768 bytes free EMS memory
75->|
76->|   7733248 bytes total contiguous extended memory
77->|         0 bytes available contiguous extended memory
78->|   3194880 bytes available XMS memory
79->|           IBM DOS resident in High Memory Area
```

Figure 12-4
Continued

When you are trying to tune your system, you will be using the /DEBUG switch with the MEM command. This tells MEM to produce the most detailed report that you can get. DOS 5.0 allows you to abbreviate /DEBUG as just /D. Figure 12-4 shows a typical DOS 5.0 MEM /DEBUG report.

The columns of the report refer to the following items:

Address   This is the starting memory address (or location) to which this line of the report refers. By adding the Address and Size values, you can get the next address in the list. These numbers are displayed in hexadecimal because this report is primarily used by program developers when they are debugging their programs.

Name   This column identifies the name of the item that the line is describing. This is also considered the owner of the described memory. When there are nested names (names that do not have a starting address), the nested name is a separate part of the larger memory piece. For example, HIMEM (on report line 24) is considered to be part of IBMBIO. It is a part of the IBMBIO block of memory that contains system data.

Size   This column shows the size of the memory block that belongs to the name shown in the Name column. This size is the number of bytes or characters that the program or code owns. Like the address, this column is displayed in hexadecimal.

Type   This column describes what the memory is being used for. These descriptions are somewhat technical; here is what they mean:

Interrupt Vector   This area is reserved for the computer's interrupt vector. It is always in the same place. It is always the same size.

ROM Communication Area   This area is used by ROM BIOS for storing data. This area is needed because the memory that ROM BIOS is loaded in cannot be written to. It is like writing in ink; once written, it cannot be changed. ROM BIOS needs this memory to be able to keep track of what it is doing for your programs. This area is always in the same location and is always the same length.

DOS Communication Area   This area is used by DOS to store special data that some programs need to look at. It is always in the same place and the same size.

System Program   This description refers to the two programs IBMBIO.COM and IBMDOS.COM, and to the address space taken up by your computer's adapter cards. These two programs make up the base DOS operating system (the Kernel).

The adapter card address space can easily be identified because the Name column will always say SYSTEM for adapter cards (your computer SYSTEM owns the address space).

System Device Driver   These are the device drivers that are built into DOS. If they are there, you cannot get rid of them. Their size is not shown, because there is nothing that you can do to change it. They are included in the size of the IBMBIO memory block.

System Data   This is memory that IBMBIO and IBMDOS has allocated for their own use. IBMBIO is considered the owner of these pieces of memory. This is where the configuration tables and optional device drivers are loaded.

— Free —   This indicates that the memory block is not being used. These parts of memory belong to IBMDOS. When a program asks for memory, IBMDOS will give the program part of one of the free blocks of memory.

Program   This is where a program is loaded in memory. This could be a DOS extension, a utility, or one of your application programs.

Environment   This is the part of memory that holds the DOS environment for the named program.

Data   This is a part of memory that the named program has asked for. Any block of memory that DOS has not loaded a program or environment into is considered a data block.

The remainder of the types (BUFFERS=, FCBS=, etc.) are configuration statements from your CONFIG.SYS file.

For your convenience, we have numbered the lines of the report. Each line refers to a part of memory that is separate from the rest of memory. Let's take a closer look:

Lines 3–21   These lines show you the fixed memory in your computer. There is nothing that you can do to control the amount of memory these items will take. The report does show you what controls each memory area, and it also lists the built-in device drivers that you have available. Both the Address and the Size columns are displaying hexadecimal numbers.

Lines 24–31 These lines show device drivers that were loaded with a DEVICE= statement in your CONFIG.SYS file. The HIMEM.SYS device driver is reported to be 470 bytes long. Since the size values are hexadecimal, we will have to convert this to a decimal size. It turns out that HIMEM.SYS is taking 1136 decimal bytes of the computer's memory. Likewise, the RAMDRIVE.SYS device driver is taking 1232 bytes of the computer's conventional memory, and SMARTDRV.SYS is taking 20,688 bytes of conventional memory.

Lines 32–36 These lines show how much memory is being used for the various tables that you can control with configuration statements. Based on the guidelines in the rest of this chapter, you want to minimize the memory that these tables take up. Of course, you do not want to make them too small, as this may restrict your ability to get work done.

Lines 40 & 44 These lines show where there are pieces of unused conventional memory. These parts of unused memory are owned by IBMDOS.

Lines 41 & 42 These lines show the DOS Environments that are in your computer's memory. The owner of the first DOS Environment (line 41) is COMMAND. This is the command processor, and this environment must always exist. The owner of the second DOS Environment (line 42) is the MEM command. In order to produce this report, the MEM command had to be in memory. Since it was running, it had an environment. When the MEM command finishes, its DOS Environment will become free.

There may be occasions when you will find other environments. Not all terminate-and-stay-resident programs (TSRs) are well behaved enough to release the memory used by their environment before returning to DOS. A terminate-and-stay-resident (TSR) program is one that, once run, always stays in memory. A TSR does not have to keep its environment, as this report shows. The DOSKEY TSR that is found on line 51 had released its DOS environment.

Lines 39, 43, & 51 These lines show programs that are loaded into your computer's memory. One of these lines is a DOS Extension (line 52).

Lines 45, 53, 56, & 59 These lines show places in the conventional memory address space that are taken up by your computer's adapter cards. When DOS is supporting upper memory blocks (UMBs), it will wrap these adapters in appropriate memory-control-block-chain envelopes so that your programs and your memory cards do not try to compete for the same memory.

Line 47   This line shows that a portion of the device drivers that were loaded in this computer's CONFIG.SYS file were loaded by using the DEVICEHIGH statement. This causes the device driver to be loaded into an UMB if there is UMB space available. In this case there was, and the ANSI.SYS device driver (shown on lines 48 and 49) was loaded in the UMB space. All of the device drivers that are loaded into the UMB space through the DEVICEHIGH statement will be a part of the IBMBIO System Data block in the UMB.

Line 51   This line shows that a DOS extension was loaded into the UMB space. This was accomplished by the LOADHIGH command. The DOSKEY.COM program was loaded into the UMB space. This is very similar to the DEVICEHIGH statement just described.

Line 79   This line shows that the DOS Kernel has been loaded into the High Memory Area (the 64K memory region at the 1M memory address).

As you proceed with tuning the performance of your computer, you will become more familiar with this report and what each of the entries mean. You can run as many MEM reports as you like.

If you want to see for yourself how each of the DOS extensions, configuration statements, and device drivers affects your computer's memory, go ahead and experiment with them. Increase or decrease configuration statements (or device driver parameters, or DOS extension parameters) by just one and restart your computer. Look at how the MEM /DEBUG reports before and after the change differ. This is how you can learn what effect each of the statements has on your computer.

CONFIGURATION STATEMENTS

In this section, we discuss how each of the configuration statements shown in Figure 12-1 affects your computer's performance.

CONTROL+BREAK CHECKING

DOS will occasionally check to see if you are trying to interrupt what is running in your computer. You tell DOS that you want to interrupt by using the

Control (Ctrl) key together with either the C or Break keys. Throughout this book, the Control and C combination is indicated by Ctrl+C, and the Control and Break combination is indicated by Ctrl+Break.

You can tell DOS to check for Ctrl+C and Ctrl+Break more frequently by using the BREAK command. This command is valid both from the keyboard and in your CONFIG.SYS file. To tell DOS to check more frequently, you would use:

BREAK=ON

or

BREAK ON

To tell DOS to check less frequently, you would use:

BREAK=OFF

or

BREAK OFF

The performance impact is not that serious; however, if you want the fastest possible system, turn BREAK off.

READ/WRITE BUFFERS

The single control that most affects performance is the BUFFERS= statement in CONFIG.SYS. This is how you control the number of disk buffers that DOS will keep in your computer's memory. This is also how you control the DOS look-ahead buffer.

A disk buffer contains a copy of the information that is recorded in a single sector on your disks. A single disk sector is the smallest amount of data that can be read from or written to your disks. For more information on disk sectors, see "What the Diskette Looks Like."

As DOS reads and writes your disks, it keeps copies of the sectors in the disk buffers. Later, if your applications need data from a sector that is already copied in memory, DOS does not have to go back to the disk to read the information. Because your computer's memory is hundreds of times faster than your disks, this really improves the performance of your system.

You might wonder why you do not always set the BUFFERS= to the maximum value. Primarily, this is because each buffer takes 532 bytes of your computer's memory. If we always set the BUFFERS= to the maximum value, you would lose a large portion of your computer's memory for this one item. The memory that DOS is using for disk buffers cannot be used by your applications. You have to balance the number of disk buffers against the amount of memory that your applications need to run in.

There is another reason why we do not set the BUFFERS= to the maximum value. It is not always true that the more disk buffers there are, the faster the system will run. The effect of a single new disk buffer gets smaller and smaller as you add more and more disk buffers. Too many buffers can even slow down your computer's performance.

The best value of BUFFERS= depends on many things:

- The speed of your computer system. A 33mHz 80386-based computer system can handle more buffers than a 6mHz 8086-based computer system can. This is because the faster computer can search the disk buffers faster than the slower one; not as much time is lost trying to find out if the requested sector is in memory, or if it needs to be read from the disk.

- The speed of your disks. Buffers help diskettes more than fixed disks. This is because diskettes are slower and the gain of finding a diskette sector in memory is greater than the gain of finding a fixed-disk sector in memory.

- How you and your applications are using the disks.

If you do not have a BUFFERS statement in the CONFIG.SYS file, DOS sets the number of disk buffers based on the amount of memory your computer has. Figure 12-5 shows the rules for the DOS default disk buffers settings.

You can change the values that DOS selects for you. To do this, you need to edit your CONFIG.SYS file. If there is already a BUFFERS= state-

Figure 12-5
DOS Default
BUFFERS= Values

BUFFERS=	Reason
2	All diskette drives less than 360KB, memory size less than or equal to 128KB
3	One or more diskette drives greater than 360KB, memory size less than or equal to 128KB
5	Memory size greater than 128KB, less than or equal to 256KB
10	Memory size greater than 256KB, less than or equal to 512KB
15	Memory size greater than 512KB

ment, simply change the number that BUFFERS= is set to. If not, add a line and set BUFFERS= to the value you would like to use. Save the new CONFIG.SYS file, and restart your computer. This is an important step. DOS looks at the BUFFERS= statement only when it first starts. Normally, you can set the number of disk buffers to be from 1 to 99.

For DOS 4.0 users, if you are using Expanded Memory Support (EMS), then you may want DOS to put the disk buffers in expanded memory. This will make the conventional memory that DOS would have used for disk buffers available for your applications to use. To tell DOS to use expanded memory, add the /X switch to the end of the BUFFERS= statement. If your computer does not have expanded memory and you have used the /X switch on your BUFFERS= statement, DOS will display an error message when you restart your system. If this happens, either you do not have any expanded memory or you do not have the EMS support correctly installed. See "Expanded Memory Support" for more information on installing and using EMS.

If you are going to use expanded memory, you can set the number of disk buffers up to 10,000, provided you have enough expanded memory to support 10,000 disk buffers. Of course, just like the conventional memory buffers, the expanded memory that DOS uses for disk buffers cannot be used by your applications.

For DOS 5.0 users, if DOS is loaded in the HMA, the buffers will be located there as well. This will provide more room in conventional memory for your programs.

You can easily experiment with the number of disk buffers. Just change the number on the BUFFERS= statement in CONFIG.SYS and restart your computer. As long as the computer seems to keep getting faster, keep increasing the number of buffers. If you reach a point where your applications cannot fit in memory, reduce the number. If your computer does not get any faster (or if it seems to slow down), then go back to the last number that was better. We recommend that you start by increasing the number of disk buffers by five or ten each time.

LOOK-AHEAD BUFFER

The DOS look-ahead buffer was introduced in DOS 4.0 and is still available in DOS 5.0. It is used when DOS reads from your disks. (See Figure 12-6 for examples of look-ahead buffers.)

As DOS is reading from your disks, it keeps track of what and where it is reading. If DOS notices that your application is reading several sectors in

Statement	Description
BUFFERS=20,1	Use 20 disk buffers and look ahead 1 sector
BUFFERS=10,4	Use 10 disk buffers and look ahead 4 sectors
BUFFERS=1000,8 /X	Use 1000 disk buffers in Expanded Memory and look ahead 8 sectors

Figure 12-6
Look-Ahead Buffer
Examples

the same place, then DOS will read them before being requested to. It does this by reading more than what the application actually asks for.

For instance, if your application has requested the data from sector 100, then sector 101, then sector 102, DOS will anticipate that the application will next want the data in sector 103. When DOS reads sector 102, it will also read sector 103. The data from sector 102 will be returned to your application and DOS will hold the data from sector 103 in the look-ahead buffer. Later, when the application asks for the data in sector 103, DOS will already have it in memory.

The DOS look-ahead buffer helps mostly when your applications are going to be reading or writing files from the beginning to the end. This is called *sequential I/O*. It is not very helpful for applications that read or write a little here and then a little there. This is called *random I/O*. Most editors and language processors (compilers and assemblers) perform sequential I/O. Even many of the spreadsheet applications perform mostly sequential I/O. On the other hand, most large database applications perform mostly random I/O.

To turn the DOS look-ahead buffer on, you add a second number to the BUFFERS= statement in CONFIG.SYS. Doing this will cause DOS to create one look-ahead buffer. It will be large enough to hold the number of sectors that you tell DOS to look ahead into. You can tell DOS to look ahead from one to eight sectors. This takes from 512 to 4096 bytes of your computer's memory (512 bytes per look-ahead sector).

THE DEVICEHIGH= CONFIGURATION STATEMENT

The DEVICEHIGH= statement provides an outstanding opportunity for you to increase the amount of memory that is available to your applications. If you are loading optional device drivers, you can free up the memory that they normally would have used below the 640KB boundary by loading them into the UMB memory space. Although they are still taking conventional memory space, this will allow DOS to keep a larger contiguous memory area below the 640KB boundary.

See "The DEVICEHIGH= Configuration Statement" for instructions on how to use DEVICEHIGH. Remember, you must have an extended memory manager (DEVICE=HIMEM.SYS) and upper memory blocks enabled (DOS=UMB) before DEVICEHIGH can load a device driver into the UMB space.

The HIMEM.SYS and EMM386.EXE device drivers cannot be loaded into UMBs, but the rest of the DOS-supplied device drivers can be.

THE DOS= CONFIGURATION STATEMENT

The DOS= statement provides another outstanding opportunity for you to increase the amount of memory that is available to your applications. If you are using a computer that supports upper memory blocks (see "Extended Memory Support" for information on what types of computers are supported), you can enable this additional address space and, optionally, tell DOS to load itself into the High Memory Area (HMA). Each of these options helps with memory availability below the 640KB boundary.

By enabling the UMB support in DOS, you can allow device drivers to be loaded into the UMB memory ranges with DEVICEHIGH statements, thereby freeing up the lower memory they would have normally used. You can also load the DOS extensions into the UMB memory ranges by using the LOADHIGH command.

By telling DOS to load in the HMA, you free up the lower memory that it would have normally used.

You should use the DEVICEHIGH and LOADHIGH to load as many of the DOS device drivers and extensions as you require into the UMB address space. Do not load any device drivers or extensions that you do not need, but do load the ones you require into UMBs.

FCBS

The only real effect that the FCBS configuration statement has on performance is the amount of memory that DOS uses to keep the table that the FCBS statement controls (see Figure 12-1). Normally, you will be able to run with the DOS default values (see Figure 12-7). If any of your applica-

Figure 12-7
FCBS= Default Values

	DOS 3.3	DOS 4.0	DOS 5.0
FCBS=	4.0	4.0	4

tions require you to increase the number of FCBs, then follow the application guidelines. Also, if DOS displays the message "FCB Unavailable" while running your applications, you should try increasing the number of FCBs. The maximum number of FCBs allowed is 255.

If your programs open more files through FCBs than you have specified with the FCBS= statement, DOS will close as many of the older files as it needs to allow the new files to be opened. If your programs then try to read or write the closed files, they will get errors. In DOS 3.3 and DOS 4.0, the second parameter of FCBS= allowed you to specify how many FCBs DOS was not allowed to automatically close. This parameter was removed in DOS 5.0. There no longer is a control for how many FCBs to keep open. DOS 5.0 should ignore the second parameter; however, if DOS 5.0 is showing you an error on the FCBS= statement, you may want to remove the second parameter.

FILES

Like FCBS, the only real effect that the FILES configuration statement has on performance is the amount of memory that DOS uses to hold the table that the FILES statement controls (see Figure 12-1). Normally, you will be able to run with the DOS default values. If any of your applications require you to increase the number of FILES, then follow the application guidelines. Also, if DOS or your applications display the messages "Too many open files" or "No handles left" (or any similar message), you should try increasing the number of FILES.

LASTDRIVE

Like FCBS and FILES, the only real effect that the LASTDRIVE configuration statement has on performance is the amount of memory that DOS uses to hold the table that the LASTDRIVE statement controls (see Figure 12-1). Normally, you will be able to run with the DOS default values. DOS will default the setting of LASTDRIVE to the larger of E: or one letter more than the number of disk drives in your computer. If any of your applications require you to increase the LASTDRIVE letter, then follow the application guidelines.

If you are using SUBST to create imaginary drives, you will want to increase the LASTDRIVE letter to the highest drive letter you want to create.

Also, if you are connected to a network, you may want to increase the LASTDRIVE letter so that you will be able to make remote drive connections.

STACKS

Like FCBS, FILES, and LASTDRIVE, the only real effect that the STACKS configuration statement has on performance is the amount of memory that DOS uses to hold the table that the STACKS statement controls. Normally, you will be able to run with the DOS default values. If any of your applications require you to increase the number or size of STACKS, then follow the application guidelines.

Also, if DOS ever displays the message

Internal stack overflow

System halted

this means that a new stack was needed, but there were none available. You should try increasing the number of STACKS. If you continue to get the stack error message, try increasing the size of the stacks. If increasing the size and number of stacks does not solve the problem, you will have to contact the publisher of your application for help.

The DOS stack management support is not active on all machines. To determine if the stack support is there, DOS 4.0 and DOS 5.0 users can use the MEM /DEBUG command and look for the STACKS= line in the report.

The statement STACKS=0,0 will disable the DOS stack management support.

DOS EXTENSIONS

In this section, we will discuss how each of the DOS Extensions shown in Figure 12-2 affects your computer's performance.

There are three ways you can load most of these extensions into your computer:

1. You can type them in at the keyboard. This will cause them to be loaded immediately into your computer's conventional memory. DOS 5.0 users can also use the LOADHIGH command to try to immediately load them into high memory. If high memory is not available, they will be immediately loaded into conventional memory.

2. You can start them in your AUTOEXEC.BAT file. This way, each time you start your computer, they will automatically be started and waiting for your use. This helps to keep the way your computer runs more consistent.

   As with the keyboard, you can also use the LOADHIGH command in your AUTOEXEC.BAT file.

3. You can start them with the INSTALL= statement in your CONFIG.SYS file (DOS 4.0 and DOS 5.0 users only). This will get the extension loaded and running even before your AUTOEXEC.BAT file is processed.

LOADHIGH

DOS 5.0 users may be able to use the LOADHIGH command to load the DOS extensions into high memory if it is available.

By using LOADHIGH, you will be able to load some of the DOS extensions without taking so much of your computer's conventional memory. This will leave more conventional memory for your applications to use.

To use LOADHIGH, simply enter the LOADHIGH command, followed by the name of the extension you want to load and any parameters the extension requires.

The LOADHIGH command is used to load a terminate-and-stay-resident (TSR) program into an upper memory block (UMB) (see "Extended Memory Support") if one that is large enough can be found. Otherwise, LOADHIGH will load the program into base or conventional memory. Using an UMB for your TSR programs will leave more memory available for your application programs to use. To use LOADHIGH you must also have the DOS=UMB statement and an UMB provider (such as EMM386.EXE and HIMEM.SYS) in your CONFIG.SYS file.

Normally you would place all of your LOADHIGH commands in the

AUTOEXEC.BAT file. By doing this, you will cause DOS to load your TSR programs each time DOS is restarted.

For example, to load the DOS extension APPEND into an UMB (if one is available), you would enter:

loadhigh c:\dos\append.exe /e

APPEND

The order of paths in the DOS APPEND PATH can greatly affect the performance of finding files. Because DOS searches each appended path in order, the files that are in the last path will take the longest to find. These should not be the files you use most often!

Changing the order of paths searched will not affect the performance of reading and writing a file once it has been opened. It can, however, have a great effect on how quickly the file is opened. This is especially true if DOS has to search diskettes or network drives. The amount of time taken to find a file in the first directory searched can be over 30 seconds less than the time needed to find a file in the last directory.

The search order is very simple to change; just change the APPEND (or SET APPEND=) statement in your AUTOEXEC.BAT file. The first path entered should be the path that contains most of the files that will be found by searching the appended directories. After that, keep listing paths in order of decreasing use.

Remember, the appended paths are not searched until after DOS has been unable to find the file where it first looked. If you are going to spend most of your time in a single subdirectory, it does not need to be the first path on the APPEND statement.

If you are using APPEND to find additional programs to run, the order of the APPEND paths can also affect the performance of starting programs. In these cases, you may want to balance the ordering of the appended paths between searching for programs to run and searching for files to open. You may be better off using the DOS PATH to find programs.

If you are using PATH to find additional programs to run, the order of the PATH paths can also affect the performance of starting programs. In these cases, you may want to investigate the ordering of the DOS PATH (see "PATH").

FASTOPEN

The FASTOPEN extension gives DOS the ability to remember the location of your files on the fixed disks. It does not support diskette drives. There are two different ways that FASTOPEN remembers file locations:

1. It remembers the first cluster of a file. This makes opening a file much quicker.

2. For DOS 4.0 users, it remembers where each cluster of the file is. This makes moving around in a file much quicker.

A cluster is the smallest part of your fixed disk that DOS can allocate to a file. It is one or more sectors. The number of sectors in a cluster depends on the total fixed-disk size.

Opening Files More Quickly

When your application opens a file, DOS must go out and look at the disk to find the file. For instance, let's look at what happens if your application tries to open the file C:\MASTER\PAYROLL\EMPLOYEE\ID-05276.

1. DOS will search the root directory of drive C: looking for the subdirectory named MASTER. Because the root directory is in a fixed location on the disk, DOS can do this in just a couple of disk reads of the root directory.

2. DOS will search the directory C:\MASTER looking for the directory named PAYROLL. Because the C:\MASTER directory is not in a fixed location on the disk, this could take two or more reads of the C:\MASTER directory plus one or more reads of the file allocation table (FAT) to find where the C:\MASTER directory is.

3. DOS will search the directory C:\MASTER\PAYROLL looking for the directory named EMPLOYEE. Like C:\MASTER, the C:\MASTER\PAY-ROLL directory is not in a fixed location of the disk. This could take two or more reads of the C:\MASTER\PAYROLL directory plus one or more reads of the FAT.

4. DOS will search the directory C:\MASTER\PAYROLL\EMPLOYEE, looking for the file named ID-05276. Again, like C:\MASTER and C:\MAS-TER\PAYROLL, the C:\MASTER\PAYROLL\EMPLOYEE directory is not

in a fixed location of the disk. This could take two or more reads of the C:\MASTER\PAYROLL\EMPLOYEE directory plus one or more reads of the FAT.

The FASTOPEN extension speeds up this entire process because it remembers the locations of directories and files that DOS has already worked with. This is like taking notes during a lecture so that you can remember what was said. When an application tries to open a file, DOS asks FASTOPEN if the file has been seen recently. Then FASTOPEN looks through its notes to see what it can remember. It will return to DOS a pointer that is as close as it can come to the location of the file. In the previous example, FASTOPEN could tell DOS:

- It cannot remember the file or any of the directories.

- It remembers that C:\MASTER starts at cluster 100.

- It remembers that C:\MASTER\PAYROLL starts at cluster 395.

- It remembers that C:\MASTER\PAYROLL\EMPLOYEE starts at cluster 440.

- It remembers that C:\MASTER\PAYROLL\EMPLOYEE\ID-05276 starts at cluster 510.

If FASTOPEN tells DOS where the file starts, DOS does not have to read the disk at all. Otherwise, DOS will continue the open process from the point that FASTOPEN remembers.

Without FASTOPEN, even if we assume that all of the FAT sectors are in the disk buffers, we still have to do six or more disk reads to open the file. If the FASTOPEN extension was in memory and we had already processed any file in the C:\MASTER\PAYROLL\EMPLOYEE directory, then the number of disk reads could be reduced to just two. This is a performance improvement of at least 67 percent! If we had already looked at the file C:\MASTER\PAYROLL\EMPLOYEE\ID-05276, we would not have to read the disk at all. This would be a performance improvement of almost 100 percent!

Moving Around in Files More Quickly

After your application has opened a file, FASTOPEN can also help DOS 4.0 to find the data that is in the file. The contents of a file are not all stored in the same part of the disk but are scattered all over. To locate the data that is in a file, DOS has to follow the file chains that are in the FAT.

FASTOPEN helps find data in a file quickly by remembering the locations of each of the clusters that contain data for the file. When your application calls DOS to read or write to a specific location in the file, DOS will ask FASTOPEN if it knows where that file location is. FASTOPEN will search through its notes and tell DOS the closest point it remembers. Just as before, DOS will then do whatever is necessary to finish locating the file data.

Starting FASTOPEN

There are three ways that you can get FASTOPEN started:

1. Enter the FASTOPEN command at the DOS prompt. If you do this, you will have to reenter the command each time you start DOS.

2. Add the FASTOPEN command to your AUTOEXEC.BAT file. If you do this, each time you restart your computer, FASTOPEN will automatically be started. DOS 5.0 users can use the LOADHIGH command in AUTOEXEC.BAT to cause the FASTOPEN extension to be loaded into high memory (if enabled). See "Installing Programs into UMBs" for more information on LOADHIGH.

3. DOS 4.0 and DOS 5.0 users can add an INSTALL= statement to your CONFIG.SYS file. Like AUTOEXEC.BAT, this will automatically start FASTOPEN each time you restart your computer. It will also give you faster performance for your AUTOEXEC.BAT and any other batch files that run each time you restart your computer. If you use the INSTALL= statement, you must tell DOS the drive, path, filename, and filename extension to identify FASTOPEN. For example,

INSTALL=C:\DOS\FASTOPEN.EXE

You can only start FASTOPEN once each time you restart your computer. Once FASTOPEN is started, you cannot change any of its parameters without restarting your computer.

Regardless of where you use the FASTOPEN command, the parameters are the same. For each drive that you want FASTOPEN to take notes on, you tell DOS how many names and DOS 4.0 users can also specify how many file pieces you want remembered. In general, the parameters should look something like this:

DOS 3.3 and DOS 5.0 Users

drive1:=names drive2:=names

DOS 4.0 Users

drive1:=(names,pieces) drive2:=(names,pieces)

Here is an example of entering FASTOPEN at the DOS prompt:

```
C:\>FASTOPEN C:=(100,400) D:=50
C:\>_
```

In this example, FASTOPEN will remember 100 names and 400 file pieces for drive C:. It will also remember 50 names for drive D:. The ratio of four pieces for each name is a good one to start with.

Figure 12-1 shows the amount of memory that FASTOPEN uses; it also shows the amount of memory each remembered filename and file piece requires. The minimum number of names for any drive is 10 and the maximum number of names for all drives together is 999. The minimum number of file pieces for each drive is 1 and the maximum number of file pieces for all drives is 999.

> **Note:** FASTOPEN will work only on fixed disks. If you ask FASTOPEN to keep notes on a diskette drive, it will display an error and it will not be started.

In general, the number of names you want FASTOPEN to remember should be the total number of filenames and pathnames that you (and your applications) will look at in an hour. If you are editing memos or using a spreadsheet, you can probably use a small number like 50. If you are using many of the DOS utilities, or if you are processing a large number of files, you may want to use a larger number, such as 100 to 200.

The number of file pieces you want FASTOPEN to remember is the total number of file pieces in all of the files you will look at in one hour. This number could get very large, but four to seven times the number of filenames is usually sufficient. If you make the number of file pieces too small, it could cause a performance degradation. If you follow the "four to seven times" guideline, this will not be a problem.

For DOS 4.0 users, you should know that if you do not specify any file-names, or if you do not specify any file pieces, then the part of FASTOPEN that takes those notes will not stay in your computer's memory. Because the memory used for either of these parts of FASTOPEN is not large enough to worry about, you probably will not want to do this. If you do want to, here is how:

FASTOPEN C:=(,600)   This will only load the code to take notes on the location of the file pieces. This command tells FASTOPEN to keep track of up to 600 file pieces.

FASTOPEN C:=(50,) D:=(50,)   This will only load the code to take notes on the filenames. This command tells FASTOPEN to keep track of up to 50 files on both drive C: and drive D:.

FASTOPEN C:=(50) D:=(50)   This example is not the same as the previous one. Without the comma, FASTOPEN will keep track of 34 file pieces for each drive.

For DOS 4.0 users, if you are using expanded memory support (EMS), then you may want DOS to put the FASTOPEN notes in expanded memory. This will make the conventional memory that DOS would have used for the FASTOPEN notes available for your applications to use. To tell DOS to use expanded memory, add the /X switch to the end of the FASTOPEN command (or INSTALL= statement). DOS will use EMS page 254 to access the disk buffers. If your computer does not have expanded memory and you have used the /X switch on your FASTOPEN command, DOS will display an error message when you try to start FASTOPEN. If this happens, either you do not have any expanded memory, or you do not have the EMS support correctly installed. See "Expanded Memory Support" for more information on installing and using EMS.

If you are using expanded memory for the FASTOPEN notes, all of the notes for all of the drives you enter must fit in one EMS page. If you enter numbers that are too large, FASTOPEN will display the message "FASTOPEN EMS entry count exceeded. Use fewer entries." You should reduce the numbers until you no longer get this message.

MODE

The MODE extension can have three effects on your computer's performance:

1. It changes the speed of your keyboard. See "Controlling Keyboards" for information on how to change your keyboard's speed. This does not affect the overall performance of your computer, but it does affect your satisfaction with how you interact with the computer. If your computer supports changing the keyboard speed, experiment with it until you get the feel that you like the best.

You may find that you like different keyboard speeds for different applications. If this is true, you can put MODE commands in batch files to change the keyboard speed and then start your applications. If you do this, don't forget to set the speed back to what you normally like at the end of the batch file.

2. It changes the speed of your communications. See "Controlling Communications" for information on how to change your communication speed. This can also affect the speed of some of your computer's external devices, such as serial printers, serial plotters, and serial scanners. Whenever you can, you want to set the speed as high as possible to get the best performance. However, you can only set the communication speed to what your devices will support. For instance, if you are using a 1200-baud modem, you cannot set the communication speed to 9600 baud.

3. It affects the amount of memory that MODE takes when it has to stay resident in your computer. There are two good things about the memory that MODE uses:

a. MODE does not take much when it stays in your computer's memory (see Figure 12-2).

b. There are only three reasons for MODE to stay in your computer's memory: changing printer retries, changing serial retries, and redirecting parallel printers to serial adapters.

PRINT

The PRINT extension provides DOS with the ability to print files on your printers while DOS is doing something else. Because printers tend to take a long time to print big files, this can be a great improvement in the productivity of your computer.

There are several switches that you can use with the PRINT command. Some of them control how much of your computer's memory PRINT will use. Others control how frequently PRINT will try to print your data. They are described here:

/B:size   The size of the memory buffer that PRINT should use. PRINT will read data that you are printing from the disk and then send it to the printer later. If you do not enter the /B: switch, DOS will set the buffer size to 512 bytes (you will not be prompted for a value). You can set the buffer size to anywhere from 512 bytes to 16KB.

Increasing the size of the buffer will not always improve the performance of printing your files. If you want to increase the size of the buffer, you should keep it in multiples of the size of your disk's allocation units. For example, if your disk allocation unit size is 2048 bytes, then good values for /B: are 2048 (2048 x 1), 4096 (2048 x 2), 6144 (2048 x 3), and so on. You should not set the /B: value to 1500 or 3000. You can use the CHKDSK command to determine the size of your disk's allocation units (see "Using CHKDSK").

/M:count   The count of timer intervals that PRINT can borrow from your computer at one time. Each timer interval is approximately 1/18th of a second. You can enter a count from 1 to 255. If you do not enter a count, DOS will use 2.

Every now and then (actually after every /S: timer ticks), DOS will give PRINT control over your computer. When this happens, PRINT will give control of the computer back after a maximum of /M: timer ticks have gone by. It may give control of the computer back sooner, especially if the printer is not ready to accept any new characters. Increasing this value can improve the performance of printing. It can also make the fact that PRINT has control over your computer more noticeable. For instance, if you are typing at the keyboard, you may notice that occasionally it take a short time before the characters appear on your display. This is caused by PRINT taking over control of your computer for a short time.

A good indication of when you should increase the /M: value is when your printer seems to pause in the middle of printing. This is caused by the printer starving for characters to print. The only way to solve this is to give PRINT more time to send characters to your printer. One way to do this is to give PRINT more time every chance it gets. Another way is to give it a chance more often. See the /S: switch for information on how to do this.

/Q:count   The count of files that you have waiting to be printed at one time. This is the number of files that PRINT will keep in its queue of work to do. You can enter a count from 4 to 32. If you do not enter a count, DOS will use 10. Changing this value does not really affect your computer's performance. It does allow you to have more files waiting to be printed. It also will increase the amount of your computer's memory that PRINT uses (see Figure 12-2).

/S:count   The count of timer intervals between opportunities for PRINT to borrow the computer. Each timer interval is approximately 1/18th of a second. You can enter a count of from 1 to 255. If you do not enter a count, DOS will use 8.

The /S: value controls how much time you get to use your computer before PRINT gets a chance to use it again. A value of 8 gives you about half a second before PRINT gets a chance. You may want to lower this value if your printer frequently pauses while printing your documents (see "/M: count"). You may also want to increase this value if your printer does not print as fast as it can. This value is too large when your printer starts to pause (or when you notice that the printer seems to be printing more slowly).

/U:count   The count of timer intervals that PRINT will keep the computer, even if the printer is busy. Each timer interval is approximately 1/18th of a second. You can enter a count from 1 to 255. If you do not enter a count, DOS will use 1.

Do not increase the /U: value unless someone you trust tells you to. As long as the printer is busy, there is nothing PRINT can do except check to see if the printer is still busy. You could be using the computer to do something useful.

The default values of /M:2 and /S:8 give PRINT up to 20% of your computer's ability to do work. For most computer/printer combinations, this is more than adequate. If you have a very fast printer, like the HP LaserJet printer, you may have to give more time to PRINT. Many printers that require you to change the PRINT switch values tell you how to set the switches in their installation procedures.

Note: These PRINT switches can only be entered the first time the PRINT command is used. When you installed DOS, a PRINT command may have been added to your AUTOEXEC.BAT file (directly with the PRINT command, or indirectly through the LOADHIGH PRINT command), or PRINT may have been installed with an INSTALL= statement in your CONFIG.SYS file. If so, this is where these switches must be used to control how PRINT works.

SHARE

You do not need the SHARE extension unless your applications require it, or if you are a DOS 4.0 user and you have one or more partitions that are greater than 32MB.

If one or more of your applications require SHARE, follow their guidelines for what parameter values to use when loading SHARE. For DOS 4.0 and DOS 5.0 users, if you have one or more partitions that are larger than 32MB, simply use SHARE with no parameters.

In either case, if DOS displays the message "Sharing buffer overflow" or the message "DOS Error 24," you should increase the /F: parameter value. If this does not solve the problem, try increasing the /L: parameter value. If increasing both of the values does not solve the problem, you will have to contact the publisher of your application for assistance.

If you are using DOS 4.0 and you are getting these messages, you may have to use the INSTALL statement to change the SHARE parameters. This is because DOS 4.0 will automatically load SHARE if it finds a partition greater than 32MB. If this is the case, you simply put this statement in your CONFIG.SYS file, prior to any statement that references the disk partition that is larger than 32MB.

INSTALL=C:\DOS\SHARE.EXE /F:size /L:locks

In this example, you would replace "size" and "locks" with the values you want to use.

OTHERS

There are a few other DOS extensions that provide function without significantly affecting your computer's performance. Their only drawback is that they use memory that your applications may want or need. We recommend that you do not use these extensions unless you require the function they provide:

GRAFTABL

GRAPHICS

KEYB

NLSFUNC

DEVICE DRIVERS

In this section, we will discuss how each of the device drivers shown in Figure 12-3 affects your computer's performance.

ANSI

The ANSI device driver affects the performance of your computer in two ways:

1. It very slightly slows down the performance of your computer's display. This slowdown is not noticeable, so do not worry about it. The additional function supplied through ANSI is more than worth the performance hit.

2. It takes up memory that could be used for your applications or other DOS functions.

If you have applications that require ANSI, use it. If you would like to take advantage of it yourself, use it (see "Using ANSI.SYS"). If you are not going to use its functions, do not load the ANSI device driver.

DISPLAY

DOS provides support for code page switching through the DISPLAY and PRINTER device drivers and the KEYB extension (see "Changing Code Pages" for more information on Code Page Switching). If you need to use code page switching, use DISPLAY. Otherwise, there is no reason to load the DISPLAY device driver.

DRIVER

The DRIVER device driver has only one effect on performance—it takes up memory that could be used for your applications or other DOS functions. If you have an optional diskette drive that requires you to use DRIVER, use it. It does not take up much memory and it has no bad performance effects.

If you would like to make use of logical drives (see "Logical Drive Support" for more information on logical drives), use the DRIVER device driver to provide this capability.

If you do not need DRIVER for an optional diskette drive and you are not defining any logical drives, then do not load the DRIVER device driver.

EMM386

The EMM386 device driver has only one function, which is to provide expanded memory support on your computer. On a computer with an 80386 or 80486 processor, EMM386 takes extended memory and converts it to expanded memory. It does this so that applications that use the EMS interfaces can make use of this additional memory. DOS can also use EMS memory. If you are going to tell DOS to make use of EMS, or if you have applications that can use EMS, then you should use EMM386. If you are not going to take advantage of EMS, then do not load the EMM386 device driver.

EMM386 is available only in DOS 5.0. If you are using DOS 4.0, see the XMA2EMS and XMAEM device drivers. If you are using DOS 3.3, then you must provide your own EMS device driver. DOS 3.3 does not include one.

For more information on Expanded Memory Support, see "Expanded Memory Support."

PRINTER

DOS provides support for code page switching through the DISPLAY and PRINTER device drivers and the KEYB extension (see "Changing Code Pages" for more information on code page switching). If you need to use code page switching, use PRINTER. Otherwise, there is no reason to load the PRINTER device driver.

RAMDRIVE

The RAMDRIVE device driver provides you with the ability to create temporary or virtual disk drives that are actually stored in regions of your computer's memory. From a performance viewpoint, this can be very helpful. Your computer's memory is hundreds of times faster than your fixed disks or diskettes.

The name RAMDRIVE is very descriptive of what actually happens. The RAMDRIVE device driver uses a portion of your computer's RAM (memory) and makes it look like a disk drive to DOS. Because the RAM-DRIVE is so much faster than a regular disk, DOS can work much faster on a RAMDRIVE than on a regular disk. The RAMDRIVE device driver is similar to the VDISK device driver (see "VDISK").

Because the RAMDRIVE disk is in your computer's memory, all of the files and directories in your RAM disk are lost every time your computer is turned off or restarted (Ctrl+Alt+Del). This is different from regular disks, which are not affected by turning off the power.

> **Note:** This is true only to a certain point. You should not turn off the power while your computer is accessing your disks. You know the computer is accessing your disks when the fixed-disk or diskette drive lights are on. This can cause severe damage to the data on your disks.

Creating a RAMDRIVE disk is very simple. You need to add a DEVICE=RAMDRIVE.SYS statement to your CONFIG.SYS file. You may want to supply other parameters as well.

Total RAMDRIVE Size   RAMDRIVE will use the first number it sees as the total size of the RAM disk that is created. The number you enter is actually the number of kilobytes, which means that it will be multiplied by 1024 and the result will be used as the number of bytes in the RAM disk. The number you enter should be between 1 and 4096 (1KB to 4MB). If you do not enter any numbers, RAMDRIVE will create a 64KB RAM disk.

The total size of the RAM disk does not include the size of the RAMDRIVE.SYS code. However, it does include all of the normal disk overhead: the boot record, the FAT, and the root directory. The total size of all of the files on your RAM disk will always be less than the total RAM disk size.

Sector Size   RAMDRIVE will use the second number it sees as the size of each of the RAM disk sectors (see "What the Diskette Looks Like" for more information on sector size). You can select from three values: 128, 256, and 512. This number is the actual number of bytes that will be in each sector. If you do not supply a second number, RAMDRIVE will use 512 bytes as the sector size.

There is a trade-off to be made here. If you are putting mostly small files on your RAM disk, then you should use a smaller sector size. For instance, if most of the files on your RAM disk are less than 128 bytes, use 128 for the sector size. If most of the files are between 128 and 256 bytes, use 256 for the sector size. If most of the files are larger than 256 bytes, use 512 for the sector size. The larger the sector size, the faster you can read from and write to your RAM disk.

You cannot control the sector size or root directory entry count without entering a total RAMDRIVE size.

Root Directory Entry Count   The third number that RAMDRIVE sees will be used as the number of entries that will be allowed in the root directory. If you do not enter a third number, RAMDRIVE will allow 64 root directory entries. If you do enter a third number, it should be between 2 and 1024.

The trade-off here is simple: the more root directory entries, the less space there is for files. Make this value only a little larger than the number of root directory entries you will need on your RAM disk. It should be somewhat larger so that you can use an additional entry or two that you had not planned on.

You will need a root directory entry for each file that you put into the root directory. You will also need a root directory for each directory that you create in the root.

You cannot control the root directory entry count without entering both a total RAMDRIVE size and a sector size.

/E   If RAMDRIVE sees the /E switch, it will put your RAM disk in your computer's extended memory. Not all computers have extended memory. If yours does, a RAM disk is an excellent way to make use of the extended memory.

Before RAMDRIVE can use extended memory, you must install an extended memory manager such as HIMEM.SYS (which comes with DOS 5.0). The DEVICE=RAMDRIVE.SYS statement must be preceded by a DEVICE=HIMEM.SYS statement in CONFIG.SYS.

/A   If RAMDRIVE sees the /A switch, it will put your RAM disk in your computer's expanded memory. Not all computers have expanded memory. If you have expanded memory, you can use it for a RAM disk. You have to decide if it is more important to use the expanded memory for your applications.

If you do not enter a /E or /A switch, RAMDRIVE will put your RAM disk in your computer's conventional memory. See "Expanded Memory Support" for more information on the different types of memory. See "VDISK" for information on deciding on where to put your RAM disk and how you can use it.

VDISK

The VDISK device driver provides you with the ability to create imaginary disk drives that are actually stored in regions of your computer's memory. From a performance viewpoint, this can be very helpful. Your computer's memory is hundreds of times faster than your fixed disks or diskettes are.

The name VDISK stands for Virtual**DISK.** It is called a *virtual* or *imaginary, disk* because it is not actually a disk at all. The VDISK device driver takes part of your computer's memory and makes it look like a disk to DOS. Because the VDISK is so much faster than a regular disk, DOS can work much faster on a VDISK than it can on a regular disk.

Because the virtual disk is in your computer's memory, all of the files and directories in your virtual disk are lost every time your computer is turned off or restarted (Ctrl+Alt+Del). This is different from regular disks, which are not affected by turning off the power.

> **Note:** This is only true to a certain point. You should not turn off the power while your computer is accessing your disks. You know the computer is accessing your disks when the fixed-disk or diskette drive lights are on. This can cause severe damage to the data on your disks.

Creating a virtual disk drive is very simple. You need to add a DEVICE=VDISK.SYS statement to your CONFIG.SYS file. You may want to supply other parameters as well.

Total VDISK Size   VDISK will use the first number it sees as the total size of the virtual disk that is created. The number you enter is actually the number of kilobytes, which means that it will be multiplied by 1024 and the result will be used as the number of bytes in the virtual disk. The number you enter should be between 1 and 4096 (1KB to 4MB). If you do not enter any numbers, VDISK will create a 64KB virtual disk.

The total size of the virtual disk does not include the size of the VDISK.SYS code. However, it does include all of the normal disk overhead: the boot record, the FAT, and the root directory. The total size of all of the files on your virtual disk will always be less than the total virtual disk size.

Sector Size   VDISK will use the second number it sees as the size of each of the virtual disk sectors (see "What the Diskette Looks Like" for more information on sector size). You can select from three values: 128, 256, and 512. This number is the actual number of bytes that will be in each sector. If you do not supply a second number, VDISK will use 128 bytes as the sector size.

There is a trade-off to be made here. If you are putting mostly small files on your virtual disk, then you should use a smaller sector size. For instance, if most of the files on your virtual disk are less than 128 bytes, use 128 for the sector size. If most of the files are between 128 and 256 bytes, use 256 for the sector size. If most of the files are larger than 256 bytes, use 512 for the sector size. The larger the sector size, the faster you can read from and write to your virtual disk.

You cannot control the sector size or root directory entry count without entering a total VDISK size.

Root Directory Entry Count   The third number that VDISK sees will be used as the number of entries that will be allowed in the root directory.

If you do not enter a third number, VDISK will allow 64 root directory entries. If you do enter a third number, it should be between 2 and 512.

The trade-off here is simple: The more root directory entries, the less space there is for files. Make this value only a little larger than the number of root directory entries you will need on your virtual disk. It should be somewhat larger so that you can use an additional entry or two that you had not planned on.

You will need a root directory entry for each file that you put into the root directory. You will also need a root directory for each directory that you create in the root.

You cannot control the root directory entry count without entering both a total VDISK size and a sector size.

/E:Transfer Size   If VDISK sees the /E switch, it will put your virtual disk in your computer's extended memory. Not all computers have extended memory. If yours does, a virtual disk is an excellent way to make use of the extended memory.

You can also enter a transfer size value. This number can range from 1 to 8. If you do not specify a number, VDISK will use 8. This number will be used as the maximum number of sectors that VDISK will transfer (read or write) at one time. If you are not using any communications packages, you do not need to worry about this value. Even if you are using communications, you only need to worry about this value if you are having problems.

While VDISK is transferring data to or from a virtual disk that is in extended memory, it has to turn off your computer's interrupts. Because the interrupts are turned off, your computer may miss an important communications interrupt. You usually see this as an error message from your communications package—"Data Overrun Error," for example. If this starts to happen, you will have to reduce the amount of data that VDISK transfers at a time.

The amount of data that VDISK transfers at one time is the sector size multiplied by the transfer size. Start by lowering the transfer size and keep lowering it until the problem goes away. If the problem still occurs with /E:1, then you can try lowering the sector size as well. If the problem still occurs with a sector size of 128 and /E:1, then you cannot use a virtual disk when you are using communications. Remove the DEVICE=VDISK.SYS statement from your CONFIG.SYS file.

If the problem still occurs after you have removed the DEVICE= statement, then the problem was not caused by your virtual disk and you can go back to using the virtual disk. You will also have to contact the publisher of your communications package for assistance.

/X:Transfer Size   If VDISK sees the /X switch, it will put your virtual disk in your computer's expanded memory. Not all computers have expanded memory. If you have expanded memory, you can use it for a virtual disk. This feature was added in DOS 4.0. You have to decide if it is more important to use the expanded memory for your applications.

The /X:Transfer Size value is identical to /E:Transfer Size (described earlier).

The parameter handling in VDISK is somewhat different from the rest of DOS. The VDISK code looks at the parameters and ignores everything except the numbers and switches. This means that you can put comments in between the numbers that you supply, as shown here:

DEVICE=C:\DOS\VDISK.SYS Total Size 100 Sector Size 512 Root Entries 50

DEVICE=C:\DOS\VDISK.SYS 100 512 50

These two device statements will cause the same VDISK to be created.

Note: We do not recommend using the first format.

If you do not enter a /E or /X switch, VDISK will put your virtual disk in your computer's conventional memory. See "Expanded Memory Support" for more information on the different types of memory.

When deciding on a virtual disk, you have to trade off the memory that it will use against the improved performance it will give you. There are three types of memory that can be used and the trade-offs are different for each:

1. The VDISK device driver will always use some conventional memory. Even if you have entered the /E or /X switches, the VDISK device driver code will stay in your conventional memory. Only the virtual disk space will go into the extended or expanded memory. The size of the VDISK code is rather small (see Figure 12-3); however, your conventional memory may be your most scarce resource.

2. If you use the /E switch, VDISK will use extended memory to store the actual virtual disk data. About the only other good use of extended memory is SMARTDRV.SYS or IBMCACHE.SYS. If neither of these will run on your computer, you can use all of your extended memory for a virtual disk. If either will run on your computer, you should use as much extended memory as necessary for a disk cache (see "Disk Caching" for disk cache size guidelines). Then use what's left for a virtual disk.

3. If you use the /X switch, VDISK will use expanded memory to store the actual virtual disk data. There are various ways in which DOS can use expanded memory and many applications can also use it. The trade-offs here are more difficult. See "Balancing Expanded Memory Usage" for guidelines on how to balance the use of expanded memory.

If you create a virtual disk, you should give careful thought to what files you put on it. It is a good place for compiler, linker, and word processor temporary files. It is not a good place to keep spreadsheet files or documents. This is because your updates will be lost if the power suddenly goes off.

In general, your virtual disks are good places to put DOS and application programs that you use frequently. This way, your computer can respond to your commands much more quickly. It is also OK to put data that is rarely updated on your virtual disks. An example of this would be a text editor profile. When you do update your profile, update it on your real disk and then copy the updated profile to your virtual disk.

Once you have decided what you want on your virtual disk, you can create a batch file that will copy the desired files to your virtual disks. If you want to create directories on your virtual disks, this batch file can do this also. By creating this batch file, you can call it from your AUTOEXEC.BAT file. This way, your virtual disk will be loaded automatically every time you start your computer.

For example, suppose your batch file was named V-LOAD.BAT and that it was in the directory C:\BATCH. You could add this statement to your AUTOEXEC.BAT file:

CALL C:\BATCH\V-LOAD.BAT

Now, every time you turn your computer on, the files will automatically be copied to your virtual disk.

XMA2EMS

The XMA2EMS device driver has only one function, which is to help provide expanded memory support on your computer. It takes memory that could be used by your applications or other DOS extensions. However, if your computer will support it, EMS can provide additional memory for your applications and DOS to use.

If your computer can support EMS, you may want to use XMA2EMS. If you are going to tell DOS to make use of EMS, or if you have applications that can use EMS, then use XMA2EMS. If you are not going to use EMS, then do not load the XMA2EMS device driver.

For more information on expanded memory support, see "Expanded Memory Support."

XMAEM

The XMAEM device driver has only one function, which is to help provide expanded memory support on 80386-based computers. This device driver is only used with DOS 4.0. It does take some of your computer's conventional memory, but not much. If you do not have a 80386-based computer, do not load the XMAEM device driver.

If you do have an 80386-based computer, you may want to use XMAEM. If you are going to tell DOS to make use of EMS, or if you have applications that can use EMS, then use XMAEM. If you are not going to use EMS, then do not load the XMAEM device driver.

For more information on Expanded Memory Support, see "Expanded Memory Support."

OTHER PERFORMANCE FACTORS

In this section, we will discuss how each of the following additional factors affect performance:

- Disk Caching
  - SMARTDRV
  - IBMCACHE
- PATH
- VERIFY

DISK CACHING

The concept of disk caching is fairly simple: If you keep copies of data that is on the disk in your computer's memory, your programs can get to the data more quickly. As with the DOS disk buffers, this is because your computer's memory is so much faster than your computer's disks, even the fixed disks.

There is a difference between disk caching and disk buffers. The primary use of the DOS disk buffers is to provide a work area where DOS can build up the data that your programs write to the disk until there is a complete sector's worth of data to be written (see "What the Diskette Looks Like" for more information on how this works). The DOS disk buffers are also used to read a sector's worth of data into memory, even though your program may only need a few bytes. These operations are frequently referred to as *blocking* and *deblocking*. You may hear the DOS disk buffers referred to as *blocking/deblocking buffers*.

The DOS disk buffers serve a limited caching function as well. Because DOS will look into the disk buffers before trying to read or write the disk, they are acting somewhat like a disk cache. But because there are so few of the DOS disk buffers, they cannot serve this function very well.

So, as a mechanism to improve the performance of your computer, you may want to dedicate some of your computer's memory to a disk cache. There are many different disk caches available to support DOS. For example, the IBM Personal System/2 series of computers provides a device driver called IBMCACHE.SYS, and DOS 5.0 provides a device driver called SMARTDRV.SYS. There are others as well.

In the following subsections we describe SMARTDRV.SYS and IBM-CACHE.SYS.

SMARTDRV

The SMARTDRV device driver improves your disk performance in a manner similar to the DOS buffers. SMARTDRV is a "disk cache." SMART-DRV can use extended memory or expanded memory to hold parts of your disk contents in memory. Generally, if you have any expanded or extended memory, you have a lot of it. Thus, SMARTDRV can hold a lot more of your disk's contents than the DOS buffers can, so SMARTDRV can give you even better performance than the DOS buffers will. If you have a fixed disk and either extended or expanded memory, we recommend that you use SMARTDRV.

SMARTDRV is available only in DOS 5.0. If you are using DOS 3.3 or DOS 4.0, then you should check to see if your computer manufacturer has provided a disk cache program. For example, IBM provides the IBM-CACHE disk cache with most IBM Personal System/2 models. See the next section for more information on IBMCACHE.

Installing the SMARTDRV Device Driver To install SMARTDRV, you must add a DEVICE=SMARTDRV.SYS statement to your computer's CONFIG.SYS file. If the SMARTDRV.SYS file is not in the root directory, you must include the full path to it (e.g., DEVICE=C:\DOS\ SMARTDRV.SYS). You must include a DEVICE=HIMEM.SYS statement before the DEVICE=SMARTDRV.SYS statement, or DOS will display an error message and SMARTDRV will not start.

All SMARTDRV.SYS parameters are optional. If you do not provide any additional parameters, then SMARTDRV will use up to 256 KB of your extended memory as a disk cache. The SMARTDRV.SYS statement has the following form:

DEVICE=SMARTDRV.SYS maxsize minsize /A

where

maxsize   Sets the maximum amount of memory (in KB) SMARTDRV will use to hold disk information. The smallest value is 128 and the largest is 8192. The size you select cannot be larger than the amount of available extended memory provided by HIMEM.SYS or the amount of available expanded memory provided by EMM386.EXE. If less than maxsize memory is available, SMARTDRV uses the available size.

minsize   Sets the minimum amount of memory (in KB) SMARTDRV will use to hold disk information. The smallest value is 0 and the largest is maxsize. SMARTDRV uses a large amount of your extended or expanded memory. At times other applications may need to use some of this memory. These applications can ask SMARTDRV to give up some of its memory. Minsize sets the smallest disk cache size SMARTDRV will retain after giving up memory to your applications.

/A   Instructs SMARTDRV to use expanded memory. Normally it uses extended memory.

To provide a disk cache up to 2MB in size in extended memory, you would add the following lines to your CONFIG.SYS file.

DEVICE=C:\DOS\HIMEM.SYS

DEVICE=C:\DOS\SMARTDRV.SYS 2048

To provide the same disk cache in expanded memory, you would add the following lines to your CONFIG.SYS file.

DEVICE=C:\DOS\HIMEM.SYS

DEVICE=C:\DOS\EMM386.EXE 2048

DEVICE=C:\DOS\SMARTDRV.SYS 2048 /A

IBMCACHE

IBMCACHE does not come with DOS. It comes with several IBM Personal System/2 models. IBMCACHE improves your disk performance in a manner similar to the DOS Buffers. IBMCACHE can use the extended memory of an IBM Personal System/2 computer, whereas DOS buffers can only use conventional memory or expanded memory. For more information about IBMCACHE, see your hardware documentation.

If you have the device driver SMARTDRV.SYS, you should use it rather than IBMCACHE, as your performance will be better with SMARTDRV. See "SMARTDRV" for information on SMARTDRV.

PATH

Your computer's performance in finding the utility and application names you enter can be affected by the order of drives and subdirectories that DOS searches. If it seems to take a long time to start the programs you want to run, you may want to change the order in which DOS searches your drives and directories.

Changing the order of paths searched will not greatly affect the performance of a program after it has started running. It can have a great effect on how quickly the application starts. This is especially true if DOS has to search diskettes or network drives. The amount of time it takes to find a program in the first directory searched can be over 30 seconds less than the time it takes to find a program in the last directory.

The search order is very simple to change; just change the PATH statement in your AUTOEXEC.BAT file. The first path entered should be the path that contains most of the commands that you enter. Very often, this will be the path that contains the DOS files. After that, keep listing paths in order of decreasing use.

Remember, the paths listed on the PATH command are not searched until after the current directory of the current drive is searched. If you are going to spend most of your time in a single subdirectory, it does not need to be the first path on the PATH statement.

If you are using APPEND to find additional programs to run, the order of the APPEND paths can also affect the performance of starting programs. In these cases, you may want to investigate the ordering of the appended paths (see "APPEND").

VERIFY

Changing the VERIFY state of your computer is one of the few options in DOS that does not trade storage for performance; however, it does force you to trade data integrity for performance. To more fully understand the benefits of turning VERIFY on, see "Using VERIFY."

Fortunately, most of today's computers are so reliable that VERIFY is not usually needed, and we recommend you normally run with VERIFY off.

Data Integrity

When your computer reads and writes data on your fixed disks and diskettes, it is essential that everything work correctly. It is especially important that if something does go wrong, your computer realizes this and lets you know. In this chapter, we discuss data integrity as it applies to your computer recording and playing back data correctly or at least notifying you when there are problems.

We will also discuss several additional data integrity features of DOS. These features allow you to restore files or disks that you accidentally erase. In addition, we discuss ways to restore data that is lost due to wear and tear that can damage your disks.

First, let's discuss the concept of disk file data integrity. In general, you expect your computer always to work correctly. But when compared to displaying data on your screen or even sending data to a printer, the process of recording and playing it back with magnetic media provides many more opportunities for problems to occur. We are not saying that it is not important to send the correct data to your printer; it would be a problem to print a check for $1,000.00 when it should only have been for $100.00. Similarly, you would not want to record on your disk that $1,000.00 was deposited in your account when the amount was actually $100.00. If nothing else, when data is recorded on paper, you can read it; when it is recorded on a disk or diskette, only your computer can read it — you cannot.

Fixed-disk and diskette data integrity are important to you and your computer at two different times:

1. When the data is recorded (written), you want to be sure that it is written correctly.

2. When the data is played back (read), you want to be sure that what was read was correct, or that you know it was not correct.

Another time that you care about diskette data integrity is between the recording and playback of the data. There is not much that DOS can do about this situation, but you can do a lot to be sure that the data stays put by treating your disk properly rather than poorly.

Typically, the worst problem is considered to be when your computer reads back incorrect data that it believes to be correct.

In this chapter, you can learn how your computer and DOS work to ensure that the data your applications put onto your fixed disks and diskettes is recorded correctly, how they work to be sure that the data is correct when it is read back, how DOS notifies you when something is not right, and certain specific actions you can take when you experience problems.

If you are interested only in the specifics of how to use these commands, you can skip directly to the sections that deal with them. However, if you would like to develop a basic understanding of how your computer deals with your computer's disks and diskettes, and how this affects data integrity, you can read through the rest of this section.

HOW DOS USES THE DISK

Before continuing, we need to discuss briefly how DOS works with your computer and how your computer knows when the data on your disk is correct.

The programs, commands, and utilities that make up DOS never actually access the disk or diskette directly; they always request the computer's built-in program, ROM BIOS, to perform the desired functions. It is somewhat similar to a lazy person who always asks the librarian to get a book rather than getting the book himself. However, in the case of DOS, it is not because DOS is lazy, but because each of the different computers that DOS runs on works differently. The ROM BIOS that is built into the computer provides DOS with a consistent way of working with the system. For example, all of the systems provide DOS with a single way to read data from a disk and a single way to write data to the disk. If it were not for the system's ROM BIOS, DOS would have to have separate built-in programs for each system, which would make DOS take much more of your computer's memory.

DOS makes three different requests that interest us in this chapter:

- The WRITE DATA request. DOS makes this request to put data on the disk from your computer's memory. ROM BIOS will copy the data from your computer's memory onto your disk; it also writes some additional data that is used later to be sure data read from the disk is correct.

- The READ DATA request. DOS makes this request to get data off the disk and into your computer's memory. ROM BIOS will copy the data from your disk into your computer's memory. ROM BIOS also checks to be sure that the extra data that the WRITE DATA request wrote matches the data that was transferred into the computer's memory.

● The VERIFY DATA request. DOS will optionally make this request to ensure that the data just written was written to the disk correctly. ROM BIOS checks to be sure that the extra data that the WRITE DATA request wrote matches the real data that was also written.

WHAT THE DISKETTE LOOKS LIKE

Data on the diskettes is not processed one character at a time. Instead, it is processed in groups called *sectors,* with each sector containing 512 characters. The sectors are further grouped into *tracks* (Figure 13-1). Tracks are similar to the scoring rings on an archery target or dart board. All of the sectors for a single track are arranged within one ring (track) around the diskette. The diskette provides each sector with a unique address that is used to identify which group of characters is being processed. This address is similar to the room numbers in any hotel building.

For example, take a 40-story hotel building with just nine rooms on each floor. The floors are numbered from 01 to 40 and the rooms are numbered from 01 to 09 on each floor. Each door is labeled with the floor number and room number (i.e., 0101 to 0109 on the ground floor, 4001 to 4009 on the top floor). This is similar to a diskette with forty tracks and nine sectors on each track. The track numbers are like floor numbers, and the sector numbers are like room numbers.

Most diskettes go one step further and have data recorded on both the top and bottom surfaces. Diskette drives that support diskettes with data recorded on both sides have two different heads, one on the top and one on the bottom. The diskette head is almost identical to the heads in a tape recorder. They are used to record data onto the diskette (write) and to play back data from the diskette (read). For these diskettes, the two sides are referenced by their head numbers.

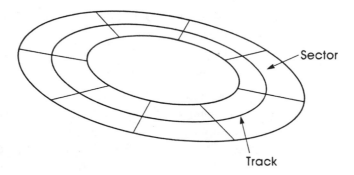

Figure 13-1
Diskette Layout

Blank diskettes from the factory frequently do not have the sector and track identifiers recorded on them. This is one of the details that the FORMAT command takes care of and is one reason why you must format your diskettes before you can use them.

DOS supports a variety of diskette layouts. The diskettes that are supported range from 40 tracks with 8 sectors in each track (all 40 tracks are recorded on one side of the diskette), up to 160 tracks with 36 sectors in each track (80 tracks are recorded on each side of the diskette).

WHAT THE FIXED DISK LOOKS LIKE

For the most part, the fixed disk looks like a stack of diskettes without their protective covers. Of course, the diskettes are made of plastic and the fixed disk is made of metal, but it still looks like a stack of diskettes. The fixed disks also rotate at a much higher speed than the diskettes do. Data, however, is still grouped in terms of sectors, tracks, and heads (see Figure 13-2). On disks, there is a further grouping, called a *cylinder,* which is a vertical stack of tracks on each of the disk surfaces.

As with diskettes, DOS supports a variety of disk layouts.

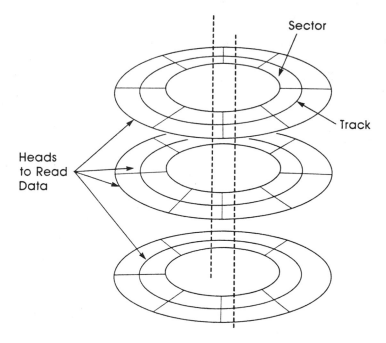

Figure 13-2
Fixed-Disk Layout

HOW YOUR COMPUTER KNOWS THERE IS A DATA PROBLEM

Your computer records a sector's address in front of every sector; it also records some information behind every sector. The trailing information is used as a double check to determine if the data in the sector is correctly read.

Most fixed-disk and diskette adapters today use what is called a *cyclic redundancy check* (CRC) to make this determination. This is a fancy name for a very complex mathematical formula to which all of the sector data is subjected. When the data is written to the sector, the CRC for that data is calculated and recorded just behind the sector.

To demonstrate how this works, let's replace the complicated CRC formula with simple addition. This formula, simple addition, is often called a *check-sum*. Check-sums are used as double checks for other types of computer data, but the CRC formula provides much better protection. In our examples, we will use a sector size of five characters.

The term *check-sum* is used because that is what actually happens; the values are summed up and checked against a total. An example of a check-sum for a good sector is given in Figure 13-3.

If the computer were to write the five listed values (10, 22, 15, 29, 23) to the disk sector, it would also write the character total (99) immediately after the sector. From then on, whenever the computer reads the data back from the disk, it will add the character values up and compare the calculated total and the recorded total. As long as the calculated total and the recorded total match, the computer believes the data is correct.

An example of a check-sum for a bad sector is given in Figure 13-4.

Now, here is a case where something has gone wrong. The computer reads back the character values (10, 21, 15, 29, 23) and the recorded total of 99. When it calculates the total, the computer only gets 98. Because 98 and 99 do not match, it knows that there is a problem. When ROM BIOS finds

Character 1	10
Character 2	22
Character 3	15
Character 4	29
Character 5	23
Check-sum	99

Figure 13-3
Good Sector

Character 1	10	
Character 2	21	(should be 22)
Character 3	15	
Character 4	29	
Character 5	23	
Check-sum	99	

Figure 13-4
Bad Sector #1

Character 1	10	
Character 2	22	
Character 3	15	
Character 4	29	
Character 5	23	
Check-sum	98	(should be 99)

Figure 13-5
Bad Sector #2

this situation, it will tell DOS, and DOS will notify the user through a critical error.

Because of the simple check-sum formula that we have used in this example, the computer has no idea where the problem is. Figures 13-5 and 13-6 are two more examples of bad sectors that show why your computer does not use a simple check-sum technique for disk data.

In the example in Figure 13-5, the computer will read in the sector data (10, 21, 15, 29, 24) and calculate the check-sum value (99). Because the calculated value of 99 will not match the recorded value of 98, the computer will think that the sector data is incorrect when it actually is correct. In this situation, a critical error would make you believe your data was bad when it wasn't. While the thought of this might be worrisome, this is still not the worst data integrity situation.

Finally, in the example in Figure 13-6, the computer will read in the sec-

Character 1	10	
Character 2	21	(should be 22)
Character 3	15	
Character 4	29	
Character 5	24	(should be 23)
Check-sum	99	

Figure 13-6
Bad Sector #3

tor data (10, 21, 15, 29, 24) and calculate the check-sum value (99). Because the calculated value of 99 will match the recorded value of 99, the computer will think that the sector data is correct when it is not. No critical error will occur to alert you to a problem; this is where we write the check for $1,000.00 rather than $100.00!

These examples show why the more complex CRC formula is used. In all three of the bad sector cases, the computer using CRC techniques will be able to determine what the problem is. An additional benefit of the CRC technique is that in many situations, the computer will be able to repair the data that has been read from the disk.

This is what happens with CRC during the three primary requests that DOS makes to ROM BIOS when handling your disks:

READ DATA	The CRC value is calculated against the incoming sector data and compared with the recorded CRC value on the disk. If they match, ROM BIOS tells DOS everything is OK. If they do not match, but the data can be fixed, ROM BIOS tells DOS everything has been repaired and that it is now OK. In previous releases of DOS, this would cause a critical error to occur. Now, DOS simply treats the data as if ROM BIOS had returned the message that everything is OK. If the data cannot be fixed up, ROM BIOS returns a data incorrect error, and this causes a critical error to occur.
WRITE DATA	As the sector data is being written to the disk, the CRC value is calculated. It is written immediately behind each sector of data.
VERIFY DATA	Similar to the READ DATA request, except that no data is transferred into memory. The CRC value is calculated and checked against the recorded CRC value on the disk. Mismatches are treated just like they are in the READ DATA request.

See "Critical Errors" for more information on critical errors.

USING VERIFY

There are three things that you can do with the VERIFY command:

1. Find out what the current VERIFY setting is.

2. Set VERIFY off.

3. Set VERIFY on.

The purpose of the VERIFY command in DOS is to try to ensure that data written to the disk has actually gotten there correctly. When VERIFY is off, DOS simply calls ROM BIOS to write the data to the disk and then believes ROM BIOS when it says the data was written correctly. When VERIFY is on, DOS always follows the ROM BIOS write data calls with a call asking ROM BIOS to verify the data.

The VERIFY setting applies to all fixed-disk and diskette drives attached locally to your computer, but it has no effect on the processing of remote network drives. To check or control the VERIFY processing of a network drive, the VERIFY command must be used on the network server machine that is sharing the drive.

When your computer is first turned on, VERIFY is off. It will stay off until you or one of your applications turns it on. Once turned on, it will stay on until turned off again. Although your applications can modify the VERIFY setting, if you want to always run with VERIFY on, you can put a VERIFY ON command in the AUTOEXEC.BAT or a VERIFY=ON statement in the CONFIG.SYS files; most applications will leave the VERIFY setting alone.

When VERIFY is on, DOS will make additional calls to ROM BIOS; therefore, your computer will not perform as quickly as when VERIFY is off. For more information on this, see "VERIFY."

IS VERIFY ON OR OFF?

At the DOS prompt, simply type VERIFY and press Enter (↵). A message will be displayed indicating if VERIFY is on or off.

```
C:\>VERIFY
VERIFY is off

C:\>_
```

This indicates that VERIFY is currently turned off.

TURNING VERIFY ON

At the DOS prompt, simply type VERIFY ON and press Enter (↵).

```
C:\>VERIFY ON

C:\>_
```

This will turn VERIFY on. Alternatively, you can use VERIFY=ON.

TURNING VERIFY OFF

At the DOS prompt, simply type VERIFY OFF and press Enter (↵).

USING CHKDSK

The CHKDSK utility is provided as a way to check the system control structures on your disks. The file allocation table (FAT) will be read and verified against all of the directories on the disk. If discrepancies are noted, CHKDSK will display appropriate messages. CHKDSK also produces a memory status report of the conventional memory. Starting with DOS 4.0, this function has been replaced by the MEM utility.

When you run CHKDSK, it will always perform the verification of the FAT and directories. There are additional functions that CHKDSK can perform that are controlled by the following parameters:

/F   This switch allows CHKDSK to "fix" some of the problems it may encounter on your disk. Without the /F switch, CHKDSK will report the problems it finds, but it will not repair them.

/V   This switch tells CHKDSK to display the drive, path, filename, and filename extension of each file it looks at in the directories it processes. Unlike the DIR and ATTRIB commands, CHKDSK will display the Hidden and System entries also.

File Specification   If you specify a file specification, CHKDSK will report the number of separate pieces (often called *extents*) that the file or files are recorded in. You can use the * and ? characters in the filename and filename extension parts of the file specification. CHKDSK will only report on the files in one directory at a time.

You should run CHKDSK frequently to ensure that there are no problems on your disks. If your computer has a fixed disk, we suggest placing a CHKDSK command for each fixed-disk partition (C:, D:, etc.) in your AUTOEXEC.BAT file. You do not need to add any other parameters unless CHKDSK finds problems. If this happens, you may want to add parameters to help determine the cause of the problem or to allow CHKDSK to fix it.

The following examples show how to use CHKDSK and explain what it displays.

```
C:\>CHKDSK C:

Volume FEIGENBAUM  created 07-19-1988 10:00
Volume Serial number is 1856-1828

    1 lost allocation units found in 1 chains.
      2048 bytes disk space would be freed

21317632 bytes total disk space
   71680 bytes in 3 hidden files
  137216 bytes in 46 directories
19376128 bytes in 1679 user files
 1732608 bytes available on disk

    2048 bytes in each allocation unit
   10409 total allocation units on disk
     846 available allocation units on disk

  655360 total bytes memory
  260000 bytes free
C:\>_
```

This example shows the normal operation of CHKDSK for fixed disks. Following is an explanation of the report from CHKDSK:

Volume ? created ?   This line shows the volume label and the date that the volume label was created or changed. This is not the date that the disk was created. If there is no volume label, this line is not displayed.

Volume Serial number ? This line shows the volume serial number. If there is no volume serial number, this line is not displayed. DOS 3.3 will not look at, use, or display volume serial numbers.

? lost allocation units found in ? chains This line shows the number of allocation units that are not associated with any file. This line is not shown if there are no lost allocation units. You should rerun CHKDSK and provide the /F switch to correct this problem.

An allocation unit is also called a *cluster*. The name *cluster* comes from the allocation being a cluster of sectors. An allocation unit can be one or more disk sectors.

? bytes disk space would be freed This line shows the amount of space that would be reclaimed by using CHKDSK /F.

? bytes total disk space This line shows you how many bytes of data can be recorded on your entire disk. This line should be equal to the sum of the next five lines.

? bytes in ? hidden files This line shows you how many hidden files are on your disk. It also tells you how many bytes are allocated to those files. A hidden file is a file that you cannot see with the DIR command. Applications may create hidden files. Typically, DOS creates three files:

1. **IBMBIO.COM or IO.SYS.** This file contains the base DOS device drivers.

2. **IBMDOS.COM or MSDOS.SYS.** This file contains the DOS function call handlers.

3. **Volume Label.** This is a directory entry in the root of your disk. No disk space is allocated to the volume label.

? bytes in ? directories This line shows you how many directories are on your disk. It also shows you how many bytes are allocated to those directories. Each directory entry is 32 bytes long. Like files, directories are expanded one allocation unit at a time.

? bytes in ? user files This line shows you how many normal files are on your disk. It also shows you how many bytes are allocated to those files.

? bytes in bad sectors This line shows you how many bytes of your disk are unusable due to bad sectors. Because the disk is managed in terms of allocation units, each bad sector will disable an entire allocation unit. That is, if any sector in an allocation unit is bad, the whole allocation unit is marked as bad. Prior to DOS 4.0, if any sector on a disk track was bad, all of the clusters on the track were marked bad. Beginning with DOS 4.0, only the clusters that contain bad sectors will be marked as bad. This means that there is more space on your disk that you can use.

? bytes available on disk   This line shows you how many bytes are available to be allocated to files and directories on your disks.

? bytes in each allocation unit   This line shows you how many bytes of data will fit into each allocation unit on the disk. An allocation unit is the smallest amount of disk space that can be given (allocated) to a file at one time. Even if the file is only one or two bytes long, it take this much disk space. As the file grows, when one allocation unit becomes full, another allocation unit is given to the file. Again, even if the file is only one byte bigger than an allocation unit, it will take two full allocation units of disk space. In the earlier lines, the "number of bytes" showed how many bytes were allocated to the files and directories. This is not the same as how many bytes are actually being used by those files. The number of bytes being used in the file is always less than the number of bytes allocated to the file. This line is not shown in DOS 3.3.

? total allocation units on disk   This line shows you how many allocation units there are on your disk. The difference between this line and the next line is the number of allocation units that are have already been allocated to files and directories. This line is not shown in DOS 3.3.

? available allocation units on disk   This line shows you how many allocation units on your disk are not currently allocated to files and directories on your disks. This is how many you have left to use. This line is not shown in DOS 3.3.

? total bytes memory   This line shows you how many bytes of memory are in your computer.

? bytes free   This line shows you how many bytes of memory are not being used in your computer.

Warning: You should not redirect the output of CHKDSK to a file on the disk that CHKDSK is processing (for example, CHKDSK A: >A:CHKDSK.OUT). This will cause problems when CHKDSK verifies the FAT against the directory that contains the entry for the redirected output file. Don't do it!

Use CHKDSK /F to recover lost allocation units. After CHKDSK finds lost allocation units, it asks if you want to recover them. If you answer Y it will. The recovered allocation units are attached to files that are built in the root directory. The files are named FILExxxx.CHK. The xxxx will be replaced with 0000 for the first file, 0001 for the second file, and so on. You can find the files by using the DIR command like this:

```
C:\>DIR \*.CHK

 Volume in drive C is FEIGENBAUM
 Volume Serial number is 1856-1828
 Directory of  C:\

FILE0000 CHK       2048 06-08-88    3:53p
FILE0001 CHK       2048 06-08-88    3:53p
FILE0002 CHK       2048 08-06-88    3:56p
FILE0003 CHK       2048 08-06-88    3:56p
FILE0004 CHK       2048 08-06-88    3:56p
FILE0005 CHK       2048 08-06-88    3:56p
FILE0006 CHK       2048 08-06-88    3:56p
FILE0007 CHK       2048 08-06-88    3:56p
FILE0008 CHK       2048 08-06-88    3:56p
FILE0009 CHK       4096 08-06-88    3:56p
        10 File(s)   1728512 bytes free
C:\>_
```

At this point, you can look at the contents of the files. If you do not need the files, just erase them. If you do need them, you may need to do a significant amount of work to put them back together again.

Use CHKDSK *.* to show the contiguity of files. A contiguous file is one that has all of its allocation units allocated together and in order. If a file uses allocation units 100, 101, 102, 103, 104, they are all contiguous. But if a file uses allocation units 200, 201, 170, 171, 172, 190, they are not all contiguous. There are three separate contiguous pieces: 200, 201; 170, 171, 172; and 190.

Earlier we examined lost clusters. Now we are going to address the situation that causes CHKDSK to display the message "filename is cross linked on allocation unit x." This happens when two or more files have their FAT chains pointing to the same cluster. For example, FILE.1 has the FAT chain 100, 101, 140, 141, and FILE.2 has the FAT chain 120, 123, 140, 141. In this situation, FILE.1 and FILE.2 are cross linked at cluster 140. That is, they both share clusters 140 and 141. This is bad news.

To recover from this situation, you should copy all of the files that are cross linked to another location on the disk. This should be done with separate COPY commands for each of the cross-linked files, as shown here:

```
C:\>MD TEMP

C:\>COPY FILE.1 TEMP\FILE.1
   1 file(s) copied

C:\>COPY FILE.2 TEMP\FILE.2
   1 file(s) copied

C:\>_
```

Preferably, you should copy the files to other disks (diskettes). This prevents any further problems from occurring on the disk you are trying to fix. After all of the cross-linked files are copied, erase them all. Now you can copy them all back.

```
C:\>ERASE FILE.1

C:\>ERASE FILE.2

C:\>COPY TEMP\FILE.1 FILE.1
   1 file(s) copied

C:\>COPY TEMP\FILE.2 FILE.2
   1 file(s) copied

C:\>ERASE TEMP\FILE.1
   1 file(s) copied

C:\>ERASE TEMP\FILE.2
   1 file(s) copied

C:\>RD TEMP

C:\>_
```

Now, for the hard part. The two files, FILE.1 and FILE.2, will contain data that is different and data that is the same. You have to go look at the files, typically with an editor like EDLIN or EDIT, try to figure out what data belongs in each file, and repair the files manually.

USING SHARE

The SHARE extension provides DOS with the following capabilities:

File Sharing   This support is the DOS code that handles situations where more than one program wants to open the same file at the same time.

Diskette Change   This support is an improvement to the base diskette change protection. It works on the diskette drives that have the ability to notify DOS when the drive door has been opened. When DOS is told that a drive door has been opened, it needs to be sure that the correct diskette is still in the drive. If SHARE is loaded, DOS asks SHARE to make this check. SHARE uses the volume label and (for DOS 4.0 and later releases) volume serial number to determine if the correct diskette is in the diskette drive. If it is the correct diskette, then everything continues normally. If it is not, DOS displays the critical error "Invalid disk change," and you need to put the correct diskette back into the drive.

Large Fixed Disks   For DOS 4.0 only, this support is required if you have a fixed-disk partition that is greater than 32MB. The ability to have a fixed-disk partition larger than 32MB was added in DOS 4.0. For large fixed disks, SHARE is used to keep track of the location of files that are opened by the file control block (FCB) interfaces. SHARE is used because the fields in the FCB are not large enough to point to a file that is not within the first 32MB of a partition. SHARE fixes that problem by keeping track of the files for the application programs that use FCB interfaces. Under DOS 5.0, SHARE is not required to process fixed disks larger than 32MB.

There are three ways that you can get SHARE started:

1. You can enter the SHARE command at the DOS prompt. If you do this, you will have to reenter the command each time you start DOS.

2. You can add the SHARE command to your AUTOEXEC.BAT file. If you do this, each time you restart your computer, SHARE will automatically be started.

3. For DOS 4.0 and later releases, you can add an INSTALL= statement to your CONFIG.SYS file. Like AUTOEXEC.BAT, this will automatically start SHARE each time you restart your computer. When DOS is starting, after it has completely processed the CONFIG.SYS file, it checks to see if you have a fixed-disk partition greater than 32MB. With DOS 4.0 only, if you do and if you have not used INSTALL= to load SHARE, SHARE will automatically be loaded for you. If you do not want the default parameters, then you must use INSTALL= to override them. If you use the INSTALL=

statement, you must tell DOS the drive, path, filename, and filename extension for SHARE (e.g., INSTALL=C:\DOS\SHARE.EXE).

You can only start SHARE once each time you restart your computer. Once SHARE is started, you cannot change any of its parameters without restarting your computer.

Regardless of where you use the SHARE command, the parameters are the same. SHARE needs memory for two types of information:

Filename Space   For each file that is open in your system, SHARE keeps a copy of its full name, including the drive, path, filename, and filename extension. The full filename can take up to 64 bytes. SHARE also keeps an additional 11 bytes of control data. The total for each file can be up to 75 bytes. By keeping this information, SHARE can prevent illegal access to files that are being processed by other programs. The amount of memory that SHARE uses for this information is controlled by the /F: switch. If you do not enter a /F: switch and value, 2,048 bytes will be used. This is more than enough room for the normal 20 files that DOS will allow you to open. If DOS ever displays the critical error "System resource exhausted," then you need to increase the size of the /F: value.

Lock Range Space   As with the open filenames, SHARE keeps track of each lock range in your files. By doing this, SHARE can prevent other programs from accessing those ranges. The amount of memory that SHARE uses for this information is controlled by the /L: switch. If you do not enter a /L: switch and value, there will be room for 20 lock ranges. If DOS ever displays the critical error "System resource exhausted," then you need to increase the size of the /L: value.

The following example loads SHARE from the DOS prompt. There will be 3,000 bytes for the filename space and room for 200 lock ranges.

```
C:\>SHARE /F:3000 /L:200
C:\>_
```

USING RECOVER

You do not want to ever have to use the RECOVER command. You only need to use RECOVER when something really bad has happened to one of your disks. Preferably, you will have a backup copy rather than having to use RECOVER.

You will need to use RECOVER when one of your disks develops a bad sector. You will know that you have a bad sector when DOS displays the critical error "Data error" or "Sector not found." This means that DOS could not read the disk because of a bad sector. The bad sector can be either in a file (which is easy to recover from) or in a directory (which is very difficult to recover from).

RECOVERING A FILE

It is actually not too difficult to recover a file — you simply enter RECOVER and the name of the file with the problem. The RECOVER utility will read through the file from the beginning to the end. When RECOVER encounters a part of the file that cannot be read, the following occurs:

- The unreadable portion of the disk is marked as bad in the FAT. This keeps any other data from being written in the unusable areas of the disk.

- Another part of the disk is allocated to the file that is being recovered. As much of the data as possible from the bad area is transferred. Usually, at least 512 bytes will not be able to be recovered.

RECOVER then continues through the rest of the file. If more bad spots are encountered, the same actions will be taken.

When RECOVER is finished, it displays the message "x of y bytes recovered." The "y" number is the file size that is recorded in the directory entry for the file. The "x" number is the number of bytes that were successfully read from the disk. The difference ("y – x = z") is the number of bytes that were not readable from the disk. Here is an example of recovering an AUTOEXEC.BAT file:

```
C:\>RECOVER C:\AUTOEXEC.BAT
 143 of 655 bytes recovered
C:\>_
```

In this example, only 143 bytes were recovered. Most of the file, 512 bytes, was lost. You would now have to use your editor to replace the data that was lost.

You can now begin to see problems with using RECOVER. There are "z" bytes of data that are unrecoverable in the file. If you are lucky, this was a plain text file and you can just edit the missing text back into the file. If you are not so lucky, this was some other type of file and you have no idea how to repair the lost data. This type of situation illustrates why you want to keep up-to-date backups on your files. Things do not go wrong very often. You can easily get lazy and not make the backups. Unfortunately, when something does go wrong, not much can be done about it.

At this point, you can see that the main advantage to recovering a file is that no other data will be written to these bad spots on the disk. You may not have been able to get all of your data back, but you will not lose any more data to the bad spots that caused you these problems.

RECOVERING A WHOLE DISK

When a sector in a directory has gone bad, you will need to use this recovery procedure, which is somewhat different from recovering one file. The good thing about this procedure is that you should be able to recover all of the data in all of the files. The bad thing is that it takes a good deal of work.

The first step is to get all of the files you can off the disk. You can use COPY, XCOPY, or BACKUP to do this. If you are having problems with using XCOPY or BACKUP to process whole directories, use them to process the files one at a time. Once you have a copy of the files on another disk (usually a diskette), ERASE them from the disk. By doing this, you are making the rest of the recovery procedure much easier.

Once you have gotten all of the files you can off of the disk, you enter RECOVER and the drive you want to recover on. Because you are having problems with the directory, RECOVER will ignore that. It searches through the FAT, creating one new file for each chain that it finds. The files will be created in the ROOT directory of the disk and they will be named

FILExxxx.REC. The xxxx will be replaced with 0001 for the first file, 0002 for the second file, and so on. When the root directory is full, RECOVER will stop with the message "WARNING - directory full." At this point, you need to copy the files off the disk and erase them. Enter RECOVER and the drive again, and more files can be recovered. You keep doing this until there are no files left to recover.

> **Warning:** Every time you restart RECOVER, the filenames start over with FILE0001.REC. If you copy these files to the diskette to which you copied the first set of recovered files, they will overwrite the first set of files. This is because their names are the same! You will want to use a different diskette for each group of recovered files. If you are recovering a fixed disk, you may need several diskettes for each RECOVER cycle.

Because RECOVER does not have the directory to work with, you have lost all of the information that was in the directory. Mainly this is the following:

Filename   You will have to look at the contents of each recovered file to determine what its real name should be.

Filename Extension   As with the filename, you will have to look at the contents of each recovered file to determine what its real name should be. We can offer one hint, though, if the first two characters are MZ, it is likely to be an .EXE filename extension.

File Size   This is the worst problem. Even if you can figure out what the filename and filename extension should be, you no longer know how many bytes were in the file. After this procedure, all recovered file sizes will be a multiple of the cluster size of the disk. Again, we can only offer one hint here. If the file is a text file, the last byte of the file is often the character →. The decimal value of this character is 26, the hexadecimal value is 1A. Many editors will automatically stop reading in a file when this character is encountered. If this happens, you do not need to do anything else. If not, you may see gibberish after the → character. If there is gibberish, delete it and save the file.

File Date and Time   This is almost no problem at all. The recovered file will have the date and time of its recovery, because that is the last time the file was modified.

File Attributes The only attributes that you are concerned with here are the Archive and ReadOnly attributes. The Archive bit should be set by the recovery procedure. And, like the file date and time, this is valid since the FILExxx.REC file has not ever been backed up. You will have to decide on the ReadOnly attribute yourself. There are actually very few ReadOnly files around. If you believe that the file should be ReadOnly, use the ATTRIB command to set the ReadOnly attribute on.

As you can see, even when things go well, recovering files is not easy to do. If you work in a large organization or company, you may be able to find a "systems programmer" or other computer expert to help. You may be able to find a friend that can help. Some people can literally work miracles in recovering data from diskettes and fixed disks that have gone bad. But beware, this is a tedious and laborious procedure. You will most likely be forever in debt to whomever helps you!

USING MIRROR, UNDELETE, AND UNFORMAT

In Chapter 10 we discussed the BACKUP and RESTORE utilities. These utilities are used to save and restore copies of your important files in case these file are lost or deleted. Accidental deletion is a common way in which you can lose your important files. DOS 5.0 provides a set of utilities that, together, allow you to restore accidentally deleted files or formatted disks. You can restore files that were deleted by use of the ERASE or DELETE commands. You can also recover files that were deleted by reformatting a disk with FORMAT.

You restore deleted files with the UNDELETE utility and you restore formatted disks with the UNFORMAT utility. Both of these utilities depend on special information saved by the MIRROR utility, so we will discuss that before we discuss UNDELETE and UNFORMAT.

WHAT MIRROR DOES FOR YOU

The MIRROR utility is a terminate-and-stay-resident extension to DOS. It is loaded into memory and then monitors all ERASE and DELETE commands you or your applications do. Thus, with MIRROR, DOS is able to restore any deleted files when requested. MIRROR also provides information to help the UNFORMAT command restore a formatted disk.

MIRROR works by saving information about a disk's file allocation table and directories in a hidden file on the disk. UNDELETE and UNFOR-MAT use the information in this file to do their jobs. MIRROR can also keep a log of all files as they are deleted. This makes it easy to restore these deleted files. MIRROR saves the disk information only when you use the MIRROR command. Thus, if you make major changes to your disk contents (e.g., delete a lot of files), you should rerun MIRROR to update this saved information. We suggest you also place the MIRROR command in your AUTOEXEC.BAT file. Thus, it will be run each time you restart your computer.

The MIRROR command has the following forms:

MIRROR d: /Td-n /1

MIRROR /U

MIRROR /PARTN

which can be explained as follows:

d: Selects the drive to save information for. This drive must be local to your computer (e.g., not a network drive) and not defined by any ASSIGN or SUBST commands. We recommend that you repeat d: for each fixed-disk drive letter you have.

/Td-n   Specifies that you want MIRROR to track deleted files for drive D:. More than one drive can be tracked. You can also specify the number of deleted files, up to 999, that MIRROR will track for that drive by supplying -n (for example, /tc-100 says that up to 100 deleted files for drive C: are to be tracked). If more files are deleted, the oldest deleted files beyond the limit are forgotten, and you may not be able to UNDELETE them. If no limit is provided, MIRROR will select a limit based on the size of the disk. MIRROR uses approximately 200 bytes for each file it saves, which means 999 entries would use nearly 200KB of disk space. Thus, you should set a limit based on the number of files you might reasonably delete at one time. We recommend that you repeat /Td-n for each fixed-disk drive letter you have.

/1	Causes MIRROR to save only one copy of the disk information. Normally, MIRROR saves the previous disk information in a backup file. You would use /1 if you already have a backup file from a previous use of MIRROR that you want to retain.
/U	Using /Td-n causes the MIRROR command to remain in memory. /U is used to remove (unload) it. MIRROR can only be removed from memory if it is the most recently started terminate-and-stay-resident DOS extension.
/PARTN	Requests MIRROR to save information about a fixed disk's partitions. This allows the partitions to be restored if they are accidentally lost (for example, by a misuse of the FDISK utility). This information must be saved on a different drive than the drive being saved. MIRROR will ask you which drive to save this information on.

The following example shows how to save control information and a deleted file log on fixed-disk drives C: and D:.

```
C:\>mirror c: d: /tc-100 /td-200
MIRROR, UNDELETE, and UNFORMAT (C) 1987-1991 Central Point Software Inc.

Creates an image of the SYSTEM area.

Drive C being processed.

Drive D being processed.

MIRROR successful.

Resident Delete Tracker.

The following drives are supported:
Drive C - 100  Drive D - 200
Installation complete.
C:\>
```

Here MIRROR is indicating that it has saved control information for drives C: and D:. It also indicates that it has loaded the deleted file tracking program.

The following example shows how to save partition information for all of your fixed disks.

```
C:\>mirror /partn
MIRROR, UNDELETE, and UNFORMAT (C) 1987-1991 Central Point Software Inc.

Disk Partition Table saver.

The partition information from your hard drive(s) has been read.

Next, the file PARTNSAV.FIL will be written to a floppy disk.  Please
insert a formatted diskette and enter the name of the diskette drive.
What drive? A

Successful.
C:\>
```

Here MIRROR saves the information to diskette drive A:.

If you have used the MIRROR utility to save control information about a disk, you can restore the files on that disk after you have formatted the disk. This allows you to undo a mistaken format. Any new files placed on the formatted diskette will be lost when you unformat the disk.

RECOVERING FORMATTED DISKS

You unformat disks with the UNFORMAT utility. UNFORMAT uses the information saved by the MIRROR utility. UNFORMAT can restore a disk without a MIRROR save file. This restoration may be incomplete, so it should only be used as a last resort. We highly recommend you use the MIRROR command so that UNFORMAT can make a complete disk recovery.

The UNFORMAT command has the following forms:

UNFORMAT d: /P /J /TEST /U /L

or

UNFORMAT /PARTN /P /L

which can be explained as follows:

d: Selects the drive to unformat. This drive must be local to your computer (e.g., not a network drive) and not defined by any ASSIGN or SUBST commands.

/P   Sends any messages to the PRN (or LPT1) printer.

/J   Specifies that you want UNFORMAT to verify that the current disk information matches the information saved by a prior MIRROR command. No actual unformat is performed.

/**TEST**   Specifies that you want UNFORMAT to show you how your disk would be recovered without a MIRROR save file. This allows you to decide if you want it to go ahead or leave your disk as it is. No actual unformat is performed. /J should not be used in combination with /TEST.

/**U**   Instructs UNFORMAT to recover the disk without using the MIRROR save information file, even if that file is available.

/**PARTN**   Uses the information saved by MIRROR /PARTN to restore your fixed-disk partitions.

/**L**   When used with d:, displays all the files and directories as they are unformatted. If /L is omitted, only files for which UNFORMAT requires assistance from you are displayed. When used with /PARTN, displays the partition information for the current drive or the information saved by a prior MIRROR /PARTN command.

While UNFORMAT is running, it displays a lot of information and frequently asks for assistance or if you wish to proceed. Refer to the books included with your copy of DOS for more information before proceeding. We hope you will have little occasion to use this utility. If you do, you want to make sure you understand what you need to do.

Since UNFORMAT makes major changes to your disk's contents, you should only use it when you have no other choice for restoring your files. Even if you use the MIRROR utility, we still recommend you take frequent BACKUPs of your disks. Thus, if UNFORMAT is unable to recover your disk completely, you can use the backed-up copy to restore your files.

RECOVERING DELETED FILES

It is unlikely that you will frequently format your disks by mistake. This is not as true for deleting files. You can accidentally delete the wrong files in many different ways, such as by using a wildcard name that matches files you did not expect it to, or by using the DELETE command in the wrong directory or on the wrong diskette. You can use the UNDELETE utility to recover accidentally deleted files.

When you delete a file, DOS releases the space the file takes up on the disk to be used again. You can only undelete a file if this space has not been reused. Space is reused when you create new files. Thus, it is very important that you UNDELETE files as soon as possible after they are DELETEd to insure that they can be recovered.

The UNDELETE command has the following form:

UNDELETE path /LIST /DT /DOS /ALL

which can be explained as follows:

path	Selects the file or files to be undeleted. If this is omitted, all deleted files in the current directory are undeleted. You may use wildcards in the path.
/LIST	Requests a list of files available to recover. If this is omitted, the files are recovered.
/DT	Specifies that you want UNDELETE to use the MIRROR tracking file to recover deleted files. You are prompted before each file is recovered.
/DOS	Specifies that you want UNDELETE to use the DOS disk directory to recover deleted files. You are prompted before each file is recovered.
/ALL	Specifies that you want UNDELETE to recover all deleted files without any prompting. UNDELETE attempts to recover all files by using the MIRROR tracking file, if one is available; otherwise, it uses the DOS directory.

The following example lists all deleted files in the current directory using the MIRROR tracking file.

```
C:\>undelete *.* /list
Directory: C:\
File Specs: *.*

    Searching Delete Tracking file....

    Delete Tracking file contains    1 deleted files.
    Of those,   1 files have all clusters available,
                0 files have some clusters available,
                0 files have no clusters available.
    MS-DOS Directory contains   16 deleted files.
    Of those,    1 files may be recovered.
Using the Delete Tracking file.

    Searching Delete Tracking file....

    FILE     3        23 2-12-91 10:41a ...A Deleted: 2-12-91 10:41a
C:\>
```

Here UNDELETE shows that the MIRROR tracking file has one deleted file recorded in it. This file can be fully recovered. You can fully recover only files that have all their clusters available. Files that have partial clusters available will only be partially recovered. Some of the data in those files will be lost. Files with no clusters available cannot be recovered.

The following example lists all deleted files in the current directory using the DOS directory.

```
C:\>undelete *.* /dos /list
Directory: C:\
File Specs: *.*

    Searching Delete Tracking file....

    Delete Tracking file contains    1 deleted files.
    Of those,     1 files have all clusters available,
                  0 files have some clusters available,
                  0 files have no clusters available.
    MS-DOS Directory contains    7 deleted files.
    Of those,     1 files may be recovered.
Using the MS-DOS Directory.
    **  ?ILE    1       330  1-20-91 11:39p  ...A
    **  ?ILE    2        89  1-12-91 15:40p  ...A
        ?ILE    3      7663  1-21-91 11:18p  ...A
    **  ?ILE    4      4555  1-21-91 11:06p  ...A
    **  ?ILE    5      1028  1-20-91 13:48p  ...A
    **  ?ILE    6       168  1-20-91 13:49p  ...A
    **  ?ILE    7      4470  1-20-91 13:53p  ...A

    "**" indicates the first cluster of the file
        is unavailable and cannot be recovered
        with UNDELETE.
C:\>
```

Here UNDELETE shows the deleted files recorded in the DOS disk directory. The first character of the filename is lost when you delete files. You must provide that character again when you undelete the file. UNDELETE will prompt you for it. You can only recover files that are not marked by **. Thus, in this example, you can recover only the FILE.3 file.

Index